Fighter Command
Air Combat Claims
1939-45

Volume Three

July 1943 - May 1945

*This book is dedicated to the fighter aircrew of
Fighter Command, Second Tactical Air Force
and the intruder crews of
No.100 (Bomber Support) Group
and particularly...
to my wife Pam, who has put up with so much!*

Fighter Command
Air Combat Claims
1939-45
by
John Foreman

July 1943 - May 1945

Red Kite

First published 2012 by
Red Kite
PO Box 223, Walton-on-Thames,
Surrey, KT12 3YQ
England

Typeset in Great Britain by
A.C.E.Services,
Radlett, Herts, WD7 8LU

Printed by
Dimograf, Sp. Z.o.o. Poland

ISBN 978-1-906592-07-3

CONTENTS

The Legend of the Fighter Pilot

"At first, pilots of the opposing nations would pass each other in the air and wave at each other. Then someone took a pistol with them, and ruined a perfectly good thing".

- General Charles 'Chuck' Yeager

Throughout recorded history, civilisation has required its military heroes. The concept of 'hand-to-hand' and 'face-to-face' individual combat has held a perhaps over-romanticised fascination for many. This scenario has been manifested in the Gladiators of ancient Rome, the Arthurian knights, the gunfighters of the old West and, in more recent times, the fighter pilots. All of these manifestions of single combat have, to a large degree, been over-dramaticised and 'over-chivalrised' by novels and films until the truth has been totally swamped by the legend. However, in the beginnings of combat aviation there does seem to have been a degree of chivalry – but this did not last long.

The early military aircraft of the First World War were too fragile to carry weapons and the air war over France was a gentlemanly affair. *"We were there to lend a little tone to what would otherwise have been a vulgar brawl"*, as one pilot put it. By 1916 however the aircraft were faster, more powerful and well armed and the 'gentlemanly affair' had evolved into bloody carnage, with sixty or more fighter aircraft, known then as 'scouts' wheeling and turning in deadly meleés over the trenches, the machine-guns turning the highly flammable aircraft into potential torches. From this was born the legend of the fighter pilot and the concept of the 'ace' was born. A pilot who had downed five opponents was admitted to that fairly exclusive circle, but precisely when and how the term originated is unclear. What is certain is that the standing of a pilot was marked by his combat successes and this was carried forward into the Second World War.

Although I confess to having been fascinated by the subject and have been privileged to have met many British, German and American fighter pilots, I also feel strongly that that the highly successful deeds of the few have overshadowed the tireless courage of the many, who were not fortunate enough to have the opportunity to engage the enemy so often; it is worth considering why this was.

The real 'shooting war' started in 1940 and culminated in the huge struggle over southern England that has gone down in history as the Battle of Britain. Rightly described as our 'Finest Hour' by Winston Churchill, the campaign has thrown up an interesting fact; roughly one-third of all RAF aces achieved most, if not all, of their combat successes during this period and the reason for this is clear. Outnumbered, and fighting over their own soil, they faced a determined and skilful enemy coming at them in large numbers and thus there was no shortage of targets – assuming that the ground control organisation was effective, and it usually was. In 1941, all this changed. The German invasion of Russia stripped the Germans of their forces in the west as the RAF went on the offensive. Now it was the *Luftwaffe* that was outnumbered, but with a significant advantage. The range of the British daylight bomber formations was necessarily tied to that of their short-range escorts, covering a fairly limited area over western France. Within that area there was little of strategic importance that required air defence at all costs, unlike the situation in 1940 where the RAF were forced to defend strategic targets. The Germans could pick their fights and did so carefully, only engaging the RAF under the most favourable tactical conditions and in relatively small formations. Therefore the opportunities for combat were, for the RAF, vastly reduced. Certainly, squadron, flight and section commanders, leading their pilots into battle, had opportunities, but those following could often only watch as their opponents power-dived to safety. There was also the question of temperament and sheer natural ability. As Lynn Garrison, ex-403 Squadron, once remarked, *"In every squadron there were perhaps four or five pilots who exuded confidence. They knew that they were going out to shoot. The rest knew sub-consciously that they would make up the numbers, mill about, and get shot at"*. Perhaps over-stated, it does bear at least an element of truth. Any scrutiny of squadron claims will reveal that the same names appear, time after time. These men were truly the hunters. There have been many books written about the great pilots such as Johnnie Johnson, Douglas Bader, Ginger Lacey and Bob Tuck. It is to all of the others, the 'ordinary Joes' who never became aces, milled about, got shot at and, above all, those who were frightened but still went, that this book is respectfully dedicated.

John Foreman

Notes

This book is about fighter claims, not combat victories, or actual 'shoot downs', for the two are very different; to confuse claims with victories would be a mistake. The business of air fighting was and is fast and deadly and the pilot could seldom be certain of what he saw. Claims are what pilots thought they saw, but were not necessarily what actually happened and are explained by the term 'over-claiming'. This happened all the time, even with the use of cine cameras as supporting evidence. The 'norm' as researched by my friend Chris Shores, was an average of three claims to two actual 'shoot downs' and this ratio held for all air forces in World War II. The over-claim rate was higher in 1940 – 41 around 5:1, but reduced later, evening up the average.

The principal sources at Public Record Office were:-

Fighter Command Combats and Casualties

2nd Tactical Air Force Combats and Casualties

Squadron Operation Record Books

Personal Combat Reports.

Format of the Tables

The format is simple, runs in chronological order, subdivided into theatres of operation (France, Norway etc.) and contains the following details:-

1)   **Date**

2)   **Squadron**, arranged in ascending order. Where a unit appears more than once on a particular day it indicates that combats occurred on different sorties.

3)   **Aircraft Type**
abbreviated as:

Spit	Spitfire
Hurr	Hurricane
Beau	Beaufighter
Whir	Whirlwind
Mosq	Mosquito
Must	Mustang
Temp	Tempest

4)   **Organisation** e.g. FC (Fighter Command), 1TAF / 2TAF (1st or 2nd Tactical Air Force), BC (100 Group)

5)   **Pilot's Name**

6)   **Claim**: There were three classifications:

     a)   Destroyed. Where an aircraft was seen to crash, to be on fire, or where the pilot/ crew was seen to parachute from the aircraft.

     b)   Destroyed unconfirmed. Where the aircraft was not seen to crash but was so badly damaged that, in the opinion of the claiming pilot, it could not have reached safety.

     c)   Damaged – self explanatory.

7)   **Location**: taken from either the Combat Report or the General area noted in Fighter Command Combats and Casualties. One anomaly has come to light regarding 'shared' claims. In some cases, pilots' combat reports claim an aircraft destroyed, probably destroyed or damaged, but make no mention of other pilots present. Indeed, in one instance, three pilots from the same unit, in the same formation and attacking a lone German aircraft, all make the same claim for the aircraft, none mentioning the presence of the others. Where this has occurred I have tried to rectify this in the listings.

8)   **Time**. Where possible, times have taken from Combat Reports. However. For many reasons, the author was unable to do this. One reason is that so many of these vital documents were stolen from Public Record Office by an alleged historian to, 'protect them from the morons who were supposed to be looking after them'. Since so many of the documents were never recovered - indeed, the author has even seen original Combat Reports being offered for sale – this rings a little hollow. The convicted thief not only brought shame on himself, but has done irreparable harm to the efforts of the many honest researchers and to our military history in general. In many other cases, the time stated is noted thus: 10.30~, indicating that it is an approximate time taken from the take-off and landing times given in

FCC & C. Even in the Combat Reports, times are often approximate i.e. 15.40 – 15.55 and again an approximate time has been inserted. These 'guesstimates' are necessarily my own.

Some claims have come from sources other then the above and do not appear on official listings. They could be spurious, or could be claims that were submitted but disallowed. Some claims are actually 'shares' but are not so indicated in the official documentation. Any mistakes are necessarily my own, but I would say that this work is intended as a basis for research and should be viewed as such.

Published works that were especially helpful were:

Aces High by Chris Shores and Clive Williams

Those Other Eagles, by Chris Shores and Clive Williams

RAF Victory Listings by Frank Olynyk

The Typhoon and Tempest Story by Chris Shores and Chris Thomas

2nd Tactical Air Force by Chris Shores and Chris Thomas

Acknowledgements

I owe grateful thanks to Simon Parry, my publisher, for his was the idea behind this work and he also supplied many photographs. Also to Chris Goss, Mark Postlethwaite, Serge Bonge, Alan Hillman, Dan Johnson, Steve Brew, Chris Shores, Terry Spencer DFC, Peter Cowell DFC, Knut Larsen, Bjorn Bjornstad, Cato Guhnfeldt and Frank Olynyk for photographs and information. And finally, but by no means least, to my wife Pam, who has never understood my obsession with fighter aviation but, like marvellous wives everywhere, still puts up with it.

Chapter One

The Turning of the Tide

In Volumes I and II we have seen how the *Luftwaffe,* in northwest Europe, was halted at the shores of the United Kingdom by a relative handful of fighter squadrons and pilots during 1940 - 41. We have seen how the defensive stance of the Royal Air Force altered dramatically in mid-1941, when the British commenced all-out offensive operations over France, Belgium, Holland and, by night, over Germany itself. We have seen also how the introduction of the remarkable Focke Wulf FW190 into the front-line *Staffeln* of *JG 2* and *JG 26* had virtually halted RAF daylight operations at the French coast. The British fighters were simply not sufficient to the task. The Hurricane was by this time practically useless as a front-line fighter. The Spitfire VB, although a match for the Messerschmitt Bf109F, had been outclassed by the FW190, and the Hawker Typhoon, although fast and heavily armed, was not able to dogfight either of the German fighters with any chance of success unless in the hands of an exceptional pilot. However, by the summer of 1943 things had changed dramatically. The new Spitfire IXB was beginning to reach the squadrons in increasing numbers. This aircraft, with the Merlin 61 engine and two-stage supercharger, was a match for anything the *Luftwaffe* could put against it. It had the additional advantage of appearing, at any distance, to be a Spitfire VB. Thus the *Luftwaffe* pilots could never be sure whether they were in for an 'easy kill' or the fight of their lives.

Numerically, Fighter Command had expanded beyond recognition, although the term 'Fighter Command' had, on 1st June 1943, now been officially replaced by Air Defence of Great Britain (ADGB) and Second Tactical Air Force (2TAF). There were now 105 UK-based fighter squadrons. Of these, ten were equipped with the Spitfire IXB, one each with the Spitfire VI and VII, both with extended wintips for extremely high altitude interceptions, 33 had the Spitfire V, two flew the new Spitfire XII, 18 flew the Typhoon, one retained Whirlwinds, but would soon convert to Hurricane IVs, which equipped three units. In addition, a detached flight, No.1449, still flew Hurricane IIs from the Scilly Isles. There were also 16 squadrons of Mustang Is, for use as low-level tactical reconnaissance.

The RAF was well equipped with nightfighters also, with ten Mosquito squadrons and nine equipped with Beaufighters, one of the latter being the Fighter Interception Unit. Several of these units operated mainly as night intruders, notably No.141 Squadron, led by the almost legendary Wing Commander J.R.D. "Bob" Braham. This Beaufighter unit was the first to be equipped with *Serrate,* designed to home onto the *Lichtenstein SN-2* radar carried by the German night fighters. Beginning in June, it would be the start of what was to become known as 'The Mosquito Scourge' by *Luftwaffe* crews.

The Allied line-up was completed by four American Fighter groups from the 8th Army Air Force. The 4th, 56th, 78th and 353rd Fighter Groups were equipped with the big Republic P-47 Thunderbolt and had begun operations in June. The American pilots, initially possessed of more confidence than experience, began to learn quickly that their German opponents were a force to be reckoned with.

Against this force, the *Luftwaffe* could put four full day fighter *Geschwadern*, *JG 1, JG 2, JG 11* and *JG 26*, plus *I./JG 27*, *II./JG 3* and *III./JG 54*, these units based in the occupied territories in the west or in western and north Germany. With American forces now pouring into the United Kingdom, the scene was set for battles of epic proportions.

Sven Heglund of 331 Squadron (left) made his tenth claim on 1st July. He later converted to Mosquito intruders, claiming three Bf110s to bring his score to fourteen confirmed. On the same day Hugh Godefroy, (centre) leading 403 Squadron, claimed his sixth confirmed kill, of a total of seven. Both men survived the war. Walter Conrad (right) claimed his fifth and last confirmed victory on 6th July also flying with 403 (RCAF) Squadron. Like Godefroy, he would survive the war with the rank of Wing Commander.

1st July 1943

3 Sqn	Typh	FC	F/O J.L.Foster	FW190 damaged	Off The Hook	1200±
			F/L R.W.A.McKichan	FW190 damaged	Off The Hook	1200±
331 Sqn	Spit	FC	Sgt R.Dogger	FW190 damaged	Near Ypres	1530
			Capt S.Heglund	FW190 prob.dest	Near Ypres	1530
			Maj H.O.Mehre	FW190 damaged	Merville area	1530
			2/Lt R.H.Olsen	FW190 destroyed	Near Ypres	1530
403 Sqn	Spit	FC	F/O N.R.Fowlow	Bf109 destroyed	Hesdin-St Pol	1534
			S/L H.C.Godefroy	Bf109 destroyed	Hesdin-St Pol	1534
			F/S G.M.Shouldice	Bf109 destroyed	Hesdin-St Pol	1534

2/3rd July 1943

FIU	Beau	FC	W/C R.A.Chisholm	Ju88 destroyed	50m S Ford	0200±

3/4th July 1943

418 Sqn	Mosq	FC	F/L N.H.Spencer	E/A destroyed	Melun A/D	0119

4th July 1943

122 Sqn	Spit	FC	Capt T.Johnsen	Bf109 damaged	Amiens	1740
222 Sqn	Spit	FC	F/L A.Tofield Hornchurch Wing	FW190 prob.dest - shared -	15m NW Etretat	1330

(left) A Bf109 shot down by George Shouldice of 403 Squadron on 1st July. (right) Luftwaffe pilots from an unidentified Geschwader climb aboard their FW190As for what seems to be an Alarmstart. By mid-1943 the Spitfire IXBs were becoming more plentiful and the Luftwaffe pilots could not be certain whether or not they were facing them or the earlier VBs until it was too late.

222 Sqn Spit	FC	F/L A.Tofield	Bf109 destroyed	ESE Abbeville	1735±
		F/L P.V.K.Tripe	FW190 destroyed	ESE Abbeville	1735±
316 Sqn Spit	FC	F/O L.Ciastula	FW190 destroyed	N Argentan	1315
411 Sqn Spit	FC	F/O D.R.Matheson	Bf109F damaged	10-15m S Abbeville	1726
Hch Wg Spit	FC	W/C J.R.Ratten 222 Squadron	FW190 prob.dest - shared -	15m NW Etretat	1330
		W/C J.R.Ratten	FW190 destroyed	10m ESE Abbeville	1734
Nth Wg Spit	FC	W/C A.K.Gabszewicz	FW190 destroyed	Argentan	1310

5th July 1943

611 Sqn Spit	FC	S/L E.F.J.Charles	FW190 damaged	N Egmond	1735±
		F/L F.Colloredo -Mansfeld	FW190 damaged	N Egmond	1735±

6th July 1943

303 Sqn Spit	FC	F/O M.Szelestowski	FW190 damaged	Off Berck	1040
		Sgt A.Kwasniewski	Bf109 destroyed	SE Amiens	1045
		F/O T.Kolecki	FW190 destroyed	Off Berck	1050
		F/O S.Socha	FW190 damaged	Off Berck	1050
316 Sqn Spit	FC	F/S P.Gallus	Bf109F destroyed	SE Amiens	1045
403 Sqn Spit	FC	F/L H.D.MacDonald	Bf109 destroyed	S Abbeville	1031
403 Sqn Spit	FC	F/L W.A.G.Conrad	FW190 destroyed	20m S Abbeville	1945
421 Sqn Spit	FC	S/L R.W.McNair	Bf109 damaged	N Amiens	1037
		F/L A.H.Sager	Bf109 damaged	Near Amiens	1037
Nth Wg Spit	FC	W/C A K.Gabszewicz	Bf109F destroyed	SE Amiens	1045

8th July 1943

4 Sqn	Must	AC	F/O E.W.Skirrow	Do24 destroyed	Texel		2055
400 Sqn	Must	AC	F/O F.E.W.Hanton	Fi156 destroyed	5m E Cambourg		1435
			F/O J.M.Robb	- shared -			

9th July 1943

316 Sqn	Spit	FC	Sgt A.Murkowski	FW190 destroyed	Montreuil	0825
			Sgt A.Murkowski	FW190 prob.dest	Montreuil	0825
			F/O J.Sobolewski	FW190 damaged	Montreuil	0825
421 Sqn	Spit	FC	S/L R.W.McNair	Bf109 damaged	Near Thielt	1225

9/10th July 1943

85 Sqn	Mosq	FC	F/L J.P.M.Lintott	Do217 destroyed	Detling	1730

10th July 1943

421 Sqn	Spit	FC	F/O H.P.M.Zary	Bf109 damaged	Near Elboeuf	0809
			S/L R.W.McNair	Bf109 destroyed	Near Bernay	0813
			F/L A.H.Sager	Bf109 damaged	Near Elboeuf	0815

11/12th July 1943

410 Sqn	Mosq	FC	S/L A.G.Lawrence	Do217 destroyed	10m E Humber mouth	0052

12th July 1943

400 Sqn	Must	AC	F/L D.M.Grant	Do217 destroyed	12m NE Chartes	1710

12/13th July 1943

68 Sqn	Beau	FC	S/L F.Sykora	Ju88 damaged	E Lowestoft	2330±
141 Sqn	Beau	FC	F/S W.F.Frost	Bf110 damaged	E Schouwen	0150
605 Sqn	Mosq	FC	S/L R.E.X.Mack	Do217 damaged	Eindhoven	0238
			F/O R.R.Smart	Do217 destroyed	Eindhoven	0254

13/14th July 1943

85 Sqn	Mosq	FC	F/L E.N.Bunting	Me410 destroyed	5m off Felixstowe	0010
604 Sqn	Beau	FC	S/L W. Hoy	Do217 damaged	Off Grimsby	0144
			W/O D.W.Ray	Do217 destroyed	E Scarborough	0123

14th July 1943

129 Sqn	Spit	FC	F/L E.O.Watson	FW190 destroyed	10m E Evreux	0750
317 Sqn	Spit	FC	P/O Z.Makowski	FW190 destroyed	Bernay-Lisieux	0900
			F/O M.Wedzik	FW190 damaged	Bernay-Lisieux	0902
			F/S W.Karasinski	FW190 prob.dest	Bernay-Lisieux	0903
402 Sqn	Spit	FC	P/O M.Quinnie	Bf109 damaged	E Bernay	0900

Flight Lieutenant J.P.M.Lintott of 85 Squadron destroyed his second enemy aircraft, a Do217, on the night of 9th July, but his Mosquito crashed nearby and he and his RO were killed. Alan Deere (centre) led the Biggin Hill Wing from March until September 1943. On 14th July he claimed an FW190 probably destroyed. It would be his final claim of the war and he ended with seventeen confirmed victories. (ww2images.com). Squadron Leader A.G.Lawrence (far right) of 410 Squadron claimed a Do217 destroyed on the night of 11th July. It was his fifth and last claim.

485 Sqn Spit	FC	S/L J.M.Checketts	FW190 damaged	Bernay	0845
BH Wg Spit	FC	W/C A.C.Deere	FW190 prob.dest	Bernay	0845
Dig Wg Spit	FC	W/C L.V.Chadburn	FW190 prob.dest	S Bernay	0900

15th July 1943

222 Sqn Spit	FC	F/L G.A.Mason	FW190 damaged	Crecy	1700±
		F/O O.Smik	FW190 destroyed	Crecy	1700±
403 Sqn Spit	FC	P/O H.S.Dowding	Bf109 destroyed	Oisemont	1652
		F/L H.D.MacDonald	- shared -		
411 Sqn Spit	FC	S/L G.C.Semple	FW190 damaged	NW Poix	1641
485 Sqn Spit	FC	S/L J.M.Checketts	FW190 destroyed	Foret de Crecy-Berck	1705
		F/O J.D.Rae	FW190 destroyed	Foret de Crecy-Berck	1705
		F/O J.D.Rae	FW190 prob.dest	Foret de Crecy-Berck	1705
		P/O H.S.Tucker	FW190 prob.dest	Foret de Crecy-Berck	1705
486 Sqn Typh	FC	F/L R.H.Fitzgibbon	FW190 destroyed	40-50m SE Selsey Bill	1325
		S/L D.J.Scott	- shared -		
		P/O F.Murphy	FW190 prob.dest	40-50m SE Selsey Bill	1325
		P/O A.N.Sames	FW190 destroyed	40-50m SE Selsey Bill	1325
		F/L A.E.Umbers	FW190 prob.dest	40-50m SE Selsey Bill	1325
602 Sqn Spit	FC	F/L W.W.J.Loud	FW190 destroyed	Cayeux	1645
		F/O A.Robson	FW190 destroyed	Cayeux	1645
Ken Wg Spit	FC	W/C J.E.Johnson	Bf109 destroyed	Blangny-Senarpont	1650

Fighter Leaders at Biggin Hill Summer 1943 (l to r) Squadron Leader Jack Charles 611 Sqn, Commandant Rene Mouchotte, 341 Sqn, Group Captain Adolph 'Sailor' Malan (Station Commander) Wing Commander Al Deere.

15/16th July 1943

85 Sqn	Mosq	FC	F/O B.J.Thwaites	Me410 destroyed	Off Dunkirk	0100±
141 Sqn	Beau	FC	F/O H.E.White	Bf110 destroyed	8m SE Rheine	0200

16th July 1943

91 Sqn	Spit	FC	S/L R.H.Harries	FW190 destroyed	Poix	2000±
129 Sqn	Spit	FC	F/O D.F.Ruchwaldy	Bf109 damaged	NE Blangy	1959
331 Sqn	Spit	FC	Maj R.A.Berg 2/Lt F.S.Fearnley	FW190 prob.dest - shared -	Abbeville	2010
			Lt N.K.Jorstad	FW190 damaged	Abbeville	2010
332 Sqn	Spit	FC	2/Lt K.Bolstad	FW190 destroyed	Abbeville	2010
			Maj H.O.Mehre	FW190 damaged	Abbeville	2010
341 Sqn	Spit	FC	Capt M.Boudier	FW190 damaged	Abbeville	2008
			Capt M.Boudier	FW190 damaged	Abbeville	2008
			Sgt/Ch F.Guinamard	FW190 damaged	Abbeville	2008

17/18th July 1943

256 Sqn	Mosq	FC	F/O C.V.Bennett	FW190 destroyed	S Isle of Wight	2359

18th July 1943

91 Sqn	Spit	FC	S/L R.H.Harries	Bf109 destroyed	Near Poix	1840
			S/L R.H.Harries	Bf109 destroyed	Near Poix	1840
			S/L R.H.Harries	Bf109 damaged	Near Poix	1840
118 Sqn	Spit	FC	P/O R J.Flight F/L J.B.Shepherd	Bf109 destroyed - shared -	Den Helder	2100
			F/L R.A.Newbery	Bf109 destroyed	Den Helder	2100
			F/L J.B.Shepherd	Bf109 destroyed	Den Helder	2100

The Master. Wing Commander J.E.Johnson with his Spitfire XIB 'JE-J' while leading the Canadian Kenley Wing in the summer of 1943. On 25th July 1943 during Ramrod 154 to Holland he claimed his eighteenth confimed kill in addition to many more victories shared with other pilots.

416 Sqn Spit	FC	F/L J.A.Rae Digby Wing	Bf109 destroyed - shared -	Den Helder	2100
613 Sqn Must	AC	F/O S.T.Sitwell	Bf109 damaged	10m off NL S Ijmuiden	0710
		F/O J.B.Dalgleish	Bf109 damaged	4m W Ijmuiden	0715
		F/L W.T.Hawkins	Bf109 destroyed	4m W Ijmuiden	0715
613 Sqn Must	AC	F/O C.H.Pigg	Bf109 destroyed	3m W Egmond	1100
Dig Wg Spit	FC	W/C L.V.Chadburn 416 Squadron	Bf109 destroyed - shared -	Den Helder	2100

19th July 1943

401 Sqn Spit	FC	F/O R.K.Hayward F/L I.C.Ormston Sgt D.M.Wilson Sgt K.B.Woodhouse	FW190 prob.dest - shared - - shared - - shared -	5m S Dunkirk	1650
412 Sqn Spit	FC	F/S H.W.Bowker	Bf109 prob.dest	8-10m SE Bourbourgville	1653
		P/O J.Lush	FW190 damaged	8-10m SE Bourbourgville	1653

23rd July 1943

198 Sqn Typh	FC	F/O A.R.F.Jonas	Bf109 prob.dest	12m SE Dunkirk	1528
		F/O A.R.F.Jonas	Bf109 damaged	12m SE Dunkirk	1528

24/25th July 1943

25 Sqn Mosq	FC	F/L E.R.F.Cooke	Ju88 destroyed	Sylt	2335
605 Sqn Mosq	FC	F/L C.E.Knowles	Do217 destroyed	Soesterburg	0240±

25th July 1943

118 Sqn Spit	FC	F/L J.B.Shepherd	Bf109 damaged	Near Schipol	2010
122 Sqn Spit	FC	P/O W.W.Gent	Bf109 destroyed	3m S San Ven Ghent	1610
		P/O J.L.Lush	FW190 damaged	Ghent	1610
		P/O J.L.Peet	Bf109 damaged	Ghent	1610
		S/L P.R.W.Wickham	FW190 damaged	Ghent	1610
		S/L P.R.W.Wickham	FW190 damaged	Ghent	1610
453 Sqn Spit	FC	F/L J.H.Ferguson	FW190 damaged	Near Ghent	1500
		F/O R.H.S.Ewins	FW190 damaged	Near Ghent	1503
504 Sqn Spit	FC	F/S J.D.Gerrard-Gough	Bf109 prob.dest	Amsterdam	1500
		F/S C.B.Wright	Bf109 damaged	Amsterdam	1500
611 Sqn Spit	FC	F/O R.H.B.Hicking	Bf109 damaged	NE Amsterdam	1510
		F/O C.C.S.Hodgkinson	Bf109 damaged	NE Amsterdam	1520
		P/O H.E.Walmsley	Bf109 destroyed	8m W Amsterdam	1520
		S/L E.F.J.Charles	FW190 destroyed	Amsterdam	1529
		S/L E.F.J.Charles	Bf109 damaged	Amsterdam	1529
Ken Wg Spit	FC	W/C J.E.Johnson	Bf109 destroyed	E Schipol	1957

25/26th July 1943

157 Sqn Mosq	FC	P/O G.Deakin	E/A destroyed	Twente	0205
410 Sqn Mosq	FC	F/L E.A.Murray	E/A damaged	Twente	0310±
		F/L E.A.Murray	Do217 destroyed	Twente	0310±
604 Sqn Beau	FC	S/L W.Hoy	Do217 destroyed	Bridlington Bay	0100±
604 Sqn Beau	FC	W/C M.H.Constable -Maxwell	Do217 damaged	Off Yorks coast	0145±
604 Sqn Beau	FC	F/O B.R.Keele	Do217 destroyed	Off Yorks coast	0200±
		F/O B.R.Keele	Do217 destroyed	Off Yorks coast	0200±
605 Sqn Mosq	FC	F/L C.E.Knowles	Do217 destroyed	Soesterburg	0230
605 Sqn Mosq	FC	S/L R.E.X.Mack	Do217 damaged	Eindhoven	0230

26th July 1943

129 Sqn Spit	FC	Squadron	Bf109 destroyed	Courtrai	1135±
222 Sqn Spit	FC	Squadron	E/A destroyed	Courtrai	1130±
317 Sqn Spit	FC	F/L J.Radomski	FW190 damaged	Lille-Tournai	1130
		F/L Z.Wroblewski	FW190 destroyed	Lille-Tournai	1130
504 Sqn Spit	FC	P/O W.J.Warwick	Bf109 damaged	Lille-Tournai	1130
		F/S C.B.Wright	FW190 destroyed	Lille-Tournai	1130
Ex Wg Spit	FC	W/C W.Zak	Bf109 damaged	Lille-Tournai	1130

Squadron Leader E.F.J.Charles of 611 Squadron (left) claimed his thirteenth confirmed victory on 25th July. He would finish the war as a Wing Commander with fifteen kills to his credit. Pilot Officer J.D.Mitchner of 402 (RCAF) Squadron (right) claimed his first confirmed victory on the 27th and would survive the war with a total of ten.

26/27th July 1943

85 Sqn	Mosq	FC	S/L W.P.Green	Ju88 destroyed	25m E Ramsgate	0045
604 Sqn	Beau	FC	S/L W.Hoy	Ju88 destroyed	120m NE Sunderland	0646

27th July 1943

118 Sqn	Spit	FC	F/O C.Tallalla P/O R.J.Flight	Bf109 prob.dest - shared -	Schipol-Ijmuiden-south	2020
			2/Lt S.J.Liby	Bf109 destroyed	Schipol-Ijmuiden-south	2020
332 Sqn	Spit	FC	Capt W.Christie	Bf109 destroyed	3m S Haarlem	2025
341 Sqn	Spit	FC	Sgt R.B.Bruno	FW190 destroyed	S Trouville	1840
			Sgt P.H.Clostermann	FW190 destroyed	S Trouville	1840
			Sgt P.H.Clostermann	FW190 destroyed	S Trouville	1840
			Capt L.C.Martel	FW190 destroyed	S Trouville	1840
			Capt L.C.Martel	FW190 destroyed	S Trouville	1840
402 Sqn	Spit	FC	P/O J.D.Mitchner	Bf109 destroyed	Schipol	2015
			P/O J.D.Mitchner	Bf109 damaged	Schipol	2015
416 Sqn	Spit	FC	Sgt G.F.Burden	Bf109 damaged	Schipol	2015
			Sgt G.F.Burden	Bf109 damaged	Schipol	2015
			S/L F.E.Grant	Bf109 prob.dest	Schipol	2015
			F/L R.H.Walker	Bf109 damaged	Schipol	2015

Werner Christie of 332 Squadron (right) claimed his second victory on 27th July and scored again on 31st. He woukld end the war as leader of the Hunsdon Wing Mustangs with the rank of Lieutenant Colonel and nine confirmed kills. John Checketts (far right) leading 485 Squadron claimed four kills in July to bring his score to six confirmed. He too would survive the war, leading 142 Wing and with a total of fourteen victories.

485 Sqn Spit	FC	S/L J.M.Checketts	FW190 destroyed	Trouville area	1840
		S/L J.M.Checketts	Bf109 destroyed	Trouville area	1840
		S/L J.M.Checketts	FW190 damaged	Tricqueville area	1840
		F/O J.D.Rae P/O H.S.Tucker	FW190 destroyed - shared -	Trouville area	1840
		F/S W.T.H.Strahan	FW190 destroyed	Trouville area	1840
501 Sqn Spit	FC	F/O A.J.Grottick	Bf109 destroyed	Somme estuary	2145
611 Sqn Spit	FC	F/L F.F.Colloredo -Mansfeld	Bf109 destroyed	Haarlem-coast	2015
		F/L F.F.Colloredo -Mansfeld	Bf109 damaged	Haarlem-coast	2015
		Lt K.L.L'Abbe-Lund	Bf109 damaged	Haarlem	2020

28th July 1943

485 Sqn Spit	FC	S/L J.M.Checketts	Bf109 damaged	E Amsterdam	1015
		F/L B.E.Gibbs	Bf109 damaged	W Zandvoort	1030
Dig Wg Spit	FC	W/C L.V.Chadburn	Bf109 prob.dest	Schipol	2015
MSFU Hurr	FC	F/O J.A.Stewart	FW200 destroyed	Biscay, 43 03N, 16 06W	1945
MSFU Hurr	FC	P/O P.J.R.Flynn	FW200 destroyed	Biscay, W Bordeaux	2015±

29th July 1943

331 Sqn Spit	FC	Capt M.Y.Gran	Bf109 damaged	Near Lille	1900
		Capt S.Heglund	Bf109 destroyed	Near Lille	1900
		2/Lt R.H.Olsen	Bf109 destroyed	Near Lille	1900
421 Sqn Spit	FC	Sgt N.B.Dixon	Bf109 damaged	SW Amsterdam	1034
		F/L N.R.Fowlow	Bf109 destroyed	SW Amsterdam	1034

Pierre Clostermann of 341 Squadron claimed his first two kills on 27th July 1943. He has been the subject of a great deal of post-war controversy, due to many questionable claims made in his book 'The Big Show' and from other sources. However, a total of eleven confirmed kills, rather than the 33 he claimed, appears to be correct. The author deeply regrets the postwar suspicions, since 'The Big Show' was the single factor that fired his interest in fighter aviation - at the age of ten. By any standards, Pierre Clostermann was a courageous and skilful fighter pilot and should be remembered as such.

421 Sqn Spit	FC	P/O K.R.Linton	FW190 destroyed	SW Amsterdam	1034
		F/O J.W.E.Harten	Bf109 destroyed	N Leiden	1035
Ken Wg Spit	FC	W/C J.E.Johnson	Bf109 damaged	SW Amsterdam	1034

29/30th July 1943

256 Sqn Mosq	FC	W/C G.R.Park	Me410 destroyed	20m S Beachy Head	0145±
605 Sqn Mosq	FC	F/O A.G.Woods	Bf110 destroyed	Luneburg	0205
		F/O A.G.Woods	E/A damaged	Luneburg	0218

30th July 1943

165 Sqn Spit	FC	F/S T.A.Vance	FW190 destroyed	60m S Eddystone	1920
		F/O B.Warren	FW190 destroyed	60m S Eddystone	1920
403 Sqn Spit	FC	F/S G.M.Shouldice Kenley Wing	Bf109 destroyed - shared -	W Schipol	1057
		F/O J.F.Lambert	Bf109 destroyed	Near Schipol	1100
		F/L H.J.Southwood	Bf109 damaged	10m N Amsterdam	1105
609 Sqn Typh	FC	F/O R.Van Lierde	Bf109 destroyed	2-4m off Zandvoort	1110
		Capt E.Haabjoern	Bf109 destroyed	10-15m off Zandvoort	1115
616 Sqn Spit	FC	S/L L.W.H.Watts	FW190 damaged	Westerschelde	0710
Ken Wg Spit	FC	W/C J.E.Johnson 403 Squadron	Bf109 destroyed - shared -	W Schipol	1057

31st July 1943

65 Sqn Spit	FC	P/O P.J.Hearne	FW190 damaged	Trouville	1620
131 Sqn Spit	FC	P/O L.C.Luckhoff	FW190 damaged	Desvres-St Omer area	1135
		P/O L.C.Luckhoff	FW190 damaged	Desvres-St Omer area	1135
		F/L R.W.F.Sampson	FW190 damaged	Desvres-St Omer area	1140
132 Sqn Spit	FC	P/O J.J.Caulton	FW190 damaged	N Lisieux	1630±
		F/L D.Fopp	FW190 damaged	N Lisieux	1630±
332 Sqn Spit	FC	Capt W.Christie	FW190 destroyed	E Gravelines	1225
421 Sqn Spit	FC	P/O K.R.Linton	FW190 prob.dest	Bergues, N St Omer	1630±
485 Sqn Spit	FC	S/L J.M.Checketts	Bf109G destroyed	S Trouville	1645
		F/O B.E.Gibbs	FW190 damaged	Triqueville	1645

2nd August 1943

118 Sqn Spit	FC	F/L J.B.Shepherd	Bf109 prob.dest	Den Helder	1135
402 Sqn Spit	FC	S/L G.W.Northcott	Bf109 destroyed	8-10m off Texel	1135
		S/L G.W.Northcott	Bf109 destroyed	8-10m off Texel	1135
416 Sqn Spit	FC	P/O R.D.Booth P/O L.G.D.Pow Digby Wing	Bf109 destroyed - shared - - shared -	2-3m off Texel	1135
		F/L J.A.Rae	Bf109 destroyed	Near Texel	1150
Dig Wg Spit	FC	W/C L.V.Chadburn 416 Squadron	Bf109 destroyed - shared -	2-3m off Texel	1135

3rd August 1943

131 Sqn Spit	FC	P/O L.C.Luckhoff	FW190 damaged	Guipavas AD	2035
		P/O L.C.Luckhoff	FW190 damaged	Guipavas AD	2040
		F/S R.K.Parry	FW190 prob.dest	Guipavas AD	2040
		S/L R.W.F.Sampson	FW190 damaged	Guipavas AD	2040
		F/S A.F.Tate	FW190 damaged	Guipavas AD	2040
		F/S N.A.A.Turnbull	FW190 damaged	Guipavas AD	2040
302 Sqn Spit	FC	F/S W.Gretkierewicz	FW190 destroyed	5m NW Brest	2030
		F/S W.Gretkierewicz	FW190 prob.dest	5m NW Brest	2030

4th August 1943

485 Sqn Spit	FC	F/L M.G.Barnett	FW190 damaged	Near Fecamp	1940

Jack Rae of 416 (RCAF) Squadron (left) claimed his second and last confirmed kill on 2nd August. After the war he became a singer and entertainer. Squadron Leader L.W.H.Watts of 616 Squadron made his only claim - for an FW190 damaged - on 30th July. He would later become one of the first operational Meteor casualties when he collided with his wingman in cloud on 29th April 1945. Squadron Leader Geoff Northcott of 402 Squadron, another Canadian who would survive as Wing Leader. He claimed two Bf109s on 2nd August whilst fighting JG 54 pilots off Holland.

| 610 Sqn Spit | FC | F/OJ.G.A.Small | FW190 prob.dest | Ile de Vierge | 0745± |
| | | Unnamed pilot | FW190 damaged | Ile de Vierge | 0745± |

8/9th August 1943

| 141 Sqn Beau | FC | W/C J.R.D.Braham | Bf110 destroyed | 35m N Liege | 0115 |
| 418 Sqn Mosq | FC | P/O F.W.Hallwood | S/E A/C destroyed | Evreux A/D | 0116 |

9th August 1943

331 Sqn Spit	FC	Capt S.Heglund	FW190 destroyed	near Dunkirk	1930
400 Sqn Must	AC	F/L D.M.Grant	Ju88 prob.dest	Rambouillet	0950
485 Sqn Spit	FC	S/L J.M.Checketts	Bf109 destroyed	Lille-Merville	1920
		S/L J.M.Checketts	Bf109 destroyed	Lille-Merville	1920
		S/L J.M.Checketts	Bf109 destroyed	Lille-Merville	1920
		S/L J.M.Checketts	Bf109 prob.dest	Lille-Merville	1920
		F/O B.E.Gibbs	Bf109 destroyed	Lille-Merville	1920
		F/O J.D.Rae	Bf109 destroyed	Lille-Merville	1920
		P/O H.S.Tucker	Bf109 destroyed	Lille-Merville	1920

11th August 1943

| 501 Sqn Spit | FC | Capt S.Fuchs | FW 190 destroyed | Quendt | 1410± |
| 611 Sqn Spit | FC | F/O T.W.Berry | Bf109 damaged | Den Helder | 1525± |

23

1943 was a time of frustration for 29 Squadron. Just thirteen confirmed victories were claimed in the whole of year, none before July. Here, 'B' Flight poses for the camera.
(K.Lowes via F.E.Pringle)

11/12th August 1943

125 Sqn Beau	FC	Sgt W.H.Miller	Ju88 destroyed	8m S Bolt Head	0023

12th August 1943

403 Sqn Spit	FC	F/L W.A.G.Conrad 127 Wing	Bf109 destroyed - shared -	Axel area	1025
		F/L W.A.G.Conrad 127 Wing	Bf109 damaged - shared -	Axel area	1025
421 Sqn Spit	FC	F/L R.D.Phillip	Bf109 damaged	N Ghent	1005
		F/L R.D.Phillip	Bf109 damaged	W Flushing	1040
504 Sqn Spit	FC	F/L B.F.Darby	FW190 damaged	Guipavas	1515±
		F/O R.A.Milne	FW190 destroyed	Guipavas	1515±
610 Sqn Spit	FC	F/S H.Fallon	FW190 prob.dest	St Renan	1500±
127 Wg Spit	FC	W/C J.E.Johnson 403 Squadron	Bf109 damaged - shared -	Axel area	1025
		W/C J.E.Johnson 403 Squadron	Bf109 destroyed - shared -	Axel area	1025

12/13th August 1943

141 Sqn Beau	FC	S/L F.P.Davis	Ju88 destroyed	20-30m SW Paris	0020
263 Sqn Whir	FC	S/L E.R.Baker	Ju88 destroyed	Guernsey	2300±

On 15th August Typhoon pilots of 266 Squadron escorting Circus No.51 to Guipavas, engaged FW190s over the target. Flight Sergeant D.Erasmus claimed one destroyed and one damaged, the 'confirmed' kill shown by his camera gun film. (ww2images and C.Thomas)

15th August 1943

266 Sqn Typh	FC	F/S D.Erasmus	FW190 destroyed	Guipavas	1645±
		F/S D.Erasmus	FW190 damaged	Guipavas	1645±
		F/L J.D.Wright	FW190 damaged	Guipavas	1645±
		F/L J.D.Wright	FW190 damaged	Guipavas	1645±
331 Sqn Spit	FC	Capt S.Heglund	FW190 destroyed	10m N Vitry-en-Artois	1935
32 Sqn Spit	FC	Sgt A.Boge	FW190 destroyed	Arras-Douai	1935
		Capt W.Christie	FW190 destroyed	Arras-Douai	1935
400 Sqn Must	AC	F/O F.E.W.Hanton	Ju88 damaged	Rennes AD	0510
		F/O F.E.W.Hanton	Bf110 destroyed	Rennes AD	0524
421 Sqn Spit	AC	P/O P.G.Johnson	FW190 damaged	Flushing	1104
453 Sqn Spit	FC	F/L D.G.Andrews	FW190 destroyed	10m W Walcheren	1100

15/16th August 1943

256 Sqn Mosq FC	F/O C.B.Bryan	Me410 destroyed	5m off French coast	2335
256 Sqn Mosq FC	W/C G.R.Park	Do217 destroyed	40m S Ford	2340
256 Sqn Mosq FC	W/C G.R.Park	Do217 destroyed	40m S Ford	0001
256 Sqn Mosq FC	W/C G.R.Park	Do217 destroyed	40m S Ford	0355±
256 Sqn Mosq FC	F/S W.D.Brearley	Do217 damaged	nr Chichester	0005
256 Sqn Mosq FC	F/S W.D.Brearley	Do217 prob.dest	Just S Selsey	0023
400 Sqn Must AC	F/O J.A.Morton	Bf110 destroyed	St Andre AD	2245
410 Sqn Mosq FC	F/O R.D.Schultz	Do217 destroyed	17m S Beachy Head	2335

16th August 1943

124 Sqn Spit	FC	F/O B.Brooks	Bf109 destroyed	Isle of Wight	0900±
129 Sqn Spit	FC	F/L F.A.O.Gaze	FW190 damaged	10m NE Eecloo	1748
308 Sqn Spit	FC	F/S W.Stanski	FW190 damaged	Near Bernay A/D	1120
331 Sqn Spit	FC	Capt S.Heglund	FW190 destroyed	Poix	0920
		Sgt O.K.Roald	FW190 damaged	Poix	0920
611 Sqn Spit	FC	Capt A.Austeen	FW190 damaged	Bernay	1120±
		P/O C.C.S.Hodgkinson	FW190 destroyed	Bernay	1120±
Dig Wg Spit	FC	W/C L.V.Chadburn	FW190 damaged	Beaumont-le-Roger	1700

16/17th August 1943

141 Sqn Beau FC	F/O H.C.Kelsey	Ju88 destroyed	Chateaudun	2327
	F/O H.C.Kelsey	Bf110 prob.dest	Chateaudun	2330
	F/O H.C.Kelsey	Ju88 destroyed	Chateaudun	0330±

17th August 1943

129 Sqn Spit	FC	F/L F.A.O.Gaze	FW190 destroyed	Westerschelde	1350
222 Sqn Spit	FC	F/O R.B.Hesslyn	Bf109 destroyed	Westerschelde	1350±
		F/O R.B.Hesslyn	Bf109 destroyed	Westerschelde	1350±
		F/L P.V.K.Tripe	Bf109 destroyed	Westerschelde	1350±
		F/L P.V.K.Tripe	Bf109 destroyed	Westerschelde	1350±
		F/L P.V.K.Tripe	Bf109 damaged	Westerschelde	1350±
303 Sqn Spit	FC	F/L B.Arct	FW190 destroyed	S Antwerp	1400
		F/S A.Chudek	FW190 destroyed	S Antwerp	1400
		F/S A.Chudek	FW190 destroyed	S Antwerp	1400
		F/S A.Rutecki	FW190 prob.dest	S Antwerp	1400
331 Sqn Spit	FC	Maj K.Birksted	Bf110 destroyed	Eekloo	1650
		Capt M.Y.Gran	Bf110 destroyed	Near Belcele	1650
		Sgt C.Gran	- shared -		
332 Sqn Spit	FC	2/Lt K.Bakke	Bf110 destroyed	Near Eekloo	1700
341 Sqn Spit	FC	Lt M.Bouguen	FW190 prob.dest	25m E Le Touquet	1110
403 Sqn Spit	FC	F/L D.H.Dover	Bf110 destroyed	N Ghent	1652
		F/O L.Foster	- shared -		
		F/O J.Preston	- shared -		
		127 Wing	- shared -		
		F/L W.A.G.Conrad	FW190 destroyed	Bergues	1705
		Sgt G.M.Shouldice	- shared -		

Colin Hodgkinson of 611 Squadron (left) was the second British fighter pilot to fly with artificial legs. He claimed two FW190s, one on 16th August, but was captured on 24th November due to oxygen failure.(via Willy Horemans). Ray Hesselyn of 222 Squadron (right) claimed his 12th and 13th kills on 17th August against JG 3. He would claim a further four before being taken prisoner on 3rd October.

485 Sqn Spit	FC	F/O J.D.Rae	Bf109 destroyed	S Desvres	1110
		F/O J.D.Rae	Bf109 destroyed	S Desvres	1110
127 Wg Spit	FC	W/C J.E.Johnson	Bf110 destroyed	N Ghent	1652
		403 Squadron	- shared -		

17/18th August 1943

68 Sqn Beau	FC	W/O J.C.S.Adam	Do217 destroyed	Lincs coast	0045±
		W/O J.C.S.Adam	Do217 destroyed	Lincs coast	0050±
		F/L P.F.Allen	Do217 prob.dest	Wash	0015±
		F/S J.H.Peters	Do217 destroyed	Off Skegness	0030±
85 Sqn Mosq	FC	F/O E.N.Bunting	FW190 damaged	off Eastbourne	2355
141 Sqn Beau	FC	W/C J.R.D.Braham	Bf110 destroyed	Off Schiermonnikoog	2305
		W/C J.R.D.Braham	Bf110 destroyed	Ameland	2320
		F/O H.E.White	Ju88 destroyed	Groningen-Lingen	0100
		F/O H.E.White	Bf110 damaged	Groningen-Lingen	0200
400 Sqn Must	FC	F/O F.E.W.Hanton	Ju88 damaged	Beauvais	0015

James 'Jas' Storrar (above) fought during the 1940 campaigns with 145 Squadron before going to the Middle East with 73 Squadron. By the time he returned to the UK he had ten confirmed victories. Taking command of 65 Squadron, he claimed a Bf109 on 18th August and an FW190 on 18th September to bring his score to twelve. He survived the war. (ww2images.com)

On 19th August Jozef Jeka of 316 Squadron (right) claimed his eighth and last confirmed victory, plus a 'damaged'. He later flew with 308 Squadron and, on 21st May 1944, he was shot down, one of three squadron members to fall to Flak while 'train-busting'. He evaded capture and returned on 11th September 1944, after the invasion and the defeat of German forces in France. (ww2images.com)

604 Sqn Beau	FC	F/O J.Lomas	Do217 destroyed	24m SE Grimsby	2334
		F/O J.Lomas	Do217 prob.dest	8m E Mablethorpe	2343
		F/S J.Wilkinson	Do217 destroyed	20m NE Skegness	2343
		F/S J.Wilkinson	Do217 prob.dest	5-7m E Mablethorpe	0005
605 Sqn Mosq	FC	F/L D.H.Blomeley	Bf109 destroyed	E Schleswig	0110
		F/O A.G.Woods	E/A damaged	Parchim	0205

18th August 1943

65 Sqn Spit	FC	S/L J.E.Storrar	Bf109 destroyed	Cassel	1030

19th August 1943

65 Sqn Spit	FC	F/L J.R.Heap	FW190 destroyed	8m N Le Touquet	1720
		F/L J.R.Heap	FW190 damaged	8m N Le Touquet	1720
122 Sqn Spit	FC	F/S J.Crossland	Bf109	N Le Touquet	1720
		15 Wing- shared -			

Bf110s of NJG 1 (above) sustained two losses on the night of the 17th August. Bob Braham of 141 Squadron (right) had an eventful night, finding a Bf110 of 12./NJG 1 which he shot down into the North Sea near Schiermonniukoog and then, fifteen minutes later, destroyed a second near Ameland. One pilot, Feldwebel Georg Kraft, a 14-victory ace, was killed. The other was another ace Heinz Vinke of 11 Staffel. He was rescued from the sea, the sole survivor of the two crews. Vinke would fall to Typhoons in 1944 after claiming 50 RAF aircraft.

(ww2mages.com)

131 Sqn Spit	FC	S/L R.W.F.Sampson	FW190 damaged	Amiens	1100
182 Sqn Typh	FC	F/L G.F.Ball	Bf109 destroyed	Amiens (u/c)	1120±
222 Sqn Spit	FC	F/O R.B.Hesslyn	Bf109 destroyed	N Knocke	0800±
		F/L P.V.K.Tripe	- shared -		
234 Sqn Spit	FC	F/O R.J.Conroy	FW190 damaged	Amiens	1125
		F/L E.D.Glaser	FW190 damaged	Amiens	1125
316 Sqn Spit	FC	F/O C.Jaworowski	FW190 destroyed	N Amiens	1125
		F/L J.Jeka	FW190 destroyed	N Amiens	1125
		F/L J.Jeka	FW190 damaged	N Amiens	1125
		F/L B.Kaczmarek	FW190 destroyed	N Amiens	1125
		F/L B.Kaczmarek	FW190 destroyed	N Amiens	1125
		F/O L.Kurylowicz	FW190 destroyed	N Amiens	1125
		F/O F.Wiza	FW190 prob.dest	N Amiens	1125
		F/O F.Wiza	FW190 damaged	N Amiens	1125
331 Sqn Spit	FC	2/Lt K.Bache	Bf109 destroyed	Eekloo-Knocke	1755
		Sgt R.Dogger	Bf109 prob.dest	6m SSE Flushing	1800
		Capt M.Y.Gran	Bf109G destroyed	6m SSE Flushing	1800
		Lt N.K.Jorstad	Bf109G destroyed	6m SSE Flushing	1800
341 Sqn Spit	FC	Capt M.Boudier	Bf109 damaged	15m W Amiens	1110
		Capt M.Boudier	FW190 damaged	15m W Amiens	1110
		Cdt R.G.O.J.Mouchotte	FW190 prob.dest	Amiens	1150
403 Sqn Spit	FC	F/L A.C.Coles	Bf109 destroyed	E Abbeville	1330

403 Sqn Spit	FC	F/O T.A.Brannagan F/L H.J.Dowding	Bf109 destroyed - shared -	S Flushing	1810
		F/L D.H.Dover	Bf109 destroyed	S Flushing	1810
414 Sqn Must	AC	F/L C.H.Stover	Ju88 destroyed	Enghien AD	1710
421 Sqn Spit	FC	F/O A.E.Fleming	Bf109 damaged	E Abbeville	1330
485 Sqn Spit	FC	S/L J.M.Checketts	FW190 damaged	Abbeville	1110
		F/L M.R.D.Hume	Bf109 destroyed	NE Amiens	1110
		F/O M.G.Sutherland	FW190 damaged	W Abbeville	1110
		P/O H.S.Tucker	FW190 damaged	Abbeville	1110
602 Sqn Spit	FC	S/L M.L.ff.Beytagh	FW190 damaged	Amiens-Glisy	1125
15 Wg Spit	FC	G/C J.E.Rankin 122 Squadron	FW190 damaged - shared -	8m N Le Touquet	1720
Hch Wg Spit	FC	W/C W.V.Crawford -Compton	Bf109G destroyed	Near Sluis	1758
Ntht Wg Spit	FC	W/C A.K.Gabszewicz	FW190 destroyed	Near Amiens	1125
		W/C A.K.Gabszewicz	FW190 damaged	Near Amiens	1125

22nd August 1943

65 Sqn Spit	FC	F/L J.R.Heap	FW190 damaged	Frevent	1900
129 Sqn Spit	FC	P/O A.Bradshaw	FW190 damaged	3m NW Abbeville	1905
		F/L F.A.O.Gaze	FW190 damaged	3m NW Abbeville	1905
222 Sqn Spit	FC	F/O R.B.Hesslyn	FW190 prob.dest	NE Abbeville	0900±
303 Sqn Spit	FC	S/L J.P.Falkowski	FW190 destroyed	Near Sotteville	1910
		F/O S.Socha	FW190 damaged	Near Sotteville	1910

(opp left) Jan Falkowski of 303 Squadron claimed his eighth kill on 22nd August. After one more victory he was captured, escaped and evaded. (Opp right, right in photo) Bill Crawford Compton, the Hornchurch Wing Leader successful on 21st August, chats to 'Sailor' Malan at Hornchurch.
(ww2images.com)

(Right) Clive Kirkland of 29 Sqn (sitting) with Flying Officer R.Raspin. Kirkland claimed a Ju88 destroyed on the night of 22nd August. He would claim one further victory. (K Lowe via FE Pringle)

316 Sqn Spit	FC	F/O A.Cholajda	FW190 damaged	W Elboeuf	1900
		F/O F.Wiza	FW190 destroyed	W Elboeuf	1900
		F/O F.Wiza	FW190 damaged	W Elboeuf	1900
		F/O L.Kurylowicz	FW190 destroyed	Bernay-Beaumont	1920
341 Sqn Spit	FC	Capt M.Boudier	Bf109 destroyed	N Douai	1515
		Cdt R.J.O.J.Mouchotte	Bf109 damaged	Douai	1515
		Lt M.Bouguen	FW190 destroyed	10m E Le Havre	1845
		Asp A.De Saxce	FW190 destroyed	Quilleboeuf	1845
402 Sqn Spit	FC	S/L G.W.Northcott	FW190 destroyed	Beaumont-le-Roger	1905
		F/L H.A.Simpson	FW190 damaged	Beaumont-le-Roger	1905
485 Sqn Spit	FC	F/S L.S.McQ.White	FW190 destroyed	Feuville	1845

22/23rd August 1943

29 Sqn	Mosq	FC	F/L C.Kirkland	Ju88 destroyed	25m NE Foreness	0230
85 Sqn	Mosq	FC	S/L G.L.Howitt	Me410 destroyed	Chelmondeston	0202

23rd August 1943

403 Sqn Spit	FC	F/O R.G.Middlemiss	FW190 damaged	Gosnay	0825
604 Sqn Beau	FC	W/C M.H.Constable-Maxwell	Ju88 destroyed	130m NE Tees	0635
127 Wg Spit	FC	W/C J.E.Johnson	FW190 destroyed	Gosnay	0825

Both John Houlton of 485 Squadron (left) and Pat Lardner-Burke of 222 (centre) claimed Focke Wulfs destroyed on 27th August, for Houlton, it was his first confirmed of five and it was Lardner-Burke's sixth of seven. Both pilots survived the war. On that date Rene Mouchotte, CO of 341 (Free French) Squadron (right) was lost to an FW190 of 8./JG 26 flown by Unteroffizier Horst-Gunther Schöhl. He had claimed victories on 15th and 17th May plus two 'probables' in August and had been a greatly respected leader.

23/24th August 1943

29 Sqn	Mosq	FC	W/C R.E.X.Mack	Me410 destroyed	E Manston	2330±
			S/L P.W.Arbon	Me410 destroyed	10m N Knocke	0333
			F/L G.Goodman	Me410 destroyed	Near Dunkirk	0225±
85 Sqn	Mosq	FC	W/C J.Cunningham	FW190 destroyed	Dunkirk	0200±
			Lt J.Raad	Me410 destroyed	Off East Anglia	0240
418 Sqn	Mosq	FC	F/O D.O.Norcott	E/A damaged	Parchim A/D	2322
			F/S G.F.Labram	E/A damaged	Stendal A/D	0049

24th August 1943

91 Sqn	Spit	FC	F/L J.C.S.Doll	FW190 destroyed	Beaumont-le-Roger	1855
			S/L N.A.Kynaston	- shared -		
			F/L J.A.Maridor	- shared -		
604 Sqn	Beau	FC	W/O D.W.Ray	Ju88 damaged	200m E Middlesborough	1115
303 Sqn	Spit	FC	F/L L.Majewski	FW190 destroyed	Lisieux	1130
			F/S T.Szymkowiak	- shared -		

25th August 1943

421 Sqn	Spit	FC	F/O P.A.McLachlan	FW190 destroyed	S Caen	1945
			S/L R.W.McNair	FW190 damaged	Aeltre	1945

In the spring of 1943 I./JG 27, re-equipped with the new Bf109Gs, moved to the western front. They were to become fairly frequent opponents for their British and American counterparts. (ww2images.com)

26th August 1943

Sqn/Wg			Pilot	Claim	Location	Time
421 Sqn Spit	FC		P/O W.F.Cook	Bf109 destroyed	N Caen	1840
			F/O J.W.E.Harten	- shared -		
			F/O A.R.Mackenzie	- shared -		
			F/L R.D.Phillip	- shared -		
127 Wg Spit	FC		W/C J.E.Johnson	FW190 destroyed	SW Rouen	1830

27th August 1943

Sqn			Pilot	Claim	Location	Time
66 Sqn Spit	FC		F/L G.C.Elcombe	FW190 destroyed	4m N St Omer	1940
130 Sqn Spit	FC		S/L H.A.Wright	FW190 destroyed	Norville	0855
131 Sqn Spit	FC		F/S R.K.Parry	Bf109G damaged	NW Rouen	0837
222 Sqn Spit	FC		F/O R.B.Hesslyn	FW190 destroyed	St Omer	1850±
			F/L H.P.Lardner-Burke	FW190 destroyed	St Omer	1850±
			F/L H.P.Lardner-Burke	FW190 damaged	St Omer	1850±
			F/O O.Smik	FW190 destroyed	St Omer	1850±
312 Sqn Spit	FC		F/L K.Kasal	Ju88 destroyed	30m E Peterhead	1830
			F/O K.Posta	- shared -		
313 Sqn Spit	FC		S/L J.Himr	FW190 destroyed	7m SE SE Calais/Marck	1900
341 Sqn Spit	FC		Capt M.Boudier	FW190 destroyed	St Pol-Mardyck	1845
			Asp J.C.Buiron	FW190 damaged	St Pol-Mardyck	1845
			Sgt P.H.Clostermann	FW190 destroyed	St Pol-Mardyck	1845
			S/Lt P.L.Laurent	FW190 prob.dest	St Pol-Mardyck	1845
			S/Lt P.L.Laurent	FW190 damaged	St Pol-Mardyck	1845
485 Sqn Spit	FC		P/O J.A.Houlton	FW190 destroyed	St Pol-Mardyck	1845

The undoubted master of the Hawker Typhoon was Johnny Baldwin. He already had four kills to his credit when he and Squadron Leader Pat Thornton-Brown of 609 Squadron flew a Ranger to Evreux. They met FW190s and shot one down apiece, killing Leutnant Friedrich-Wilhelm Meyer and Unteroffizier Hermann Schmid, both of 10 Staffel JG 2. Baldwin woiuld go on to triple his score, making him the most sccessful Typhoon pilot of the war. Ironically, both men were to die as a result of 'friendly fire' incidents involving American fighters. (Chris Goss)

28th August 1943

609 Sqn Typh	FC	F/L J.R.Baldwin	FW190 destroyed	S Verneuil	1520
		S/L P.G.Thornton -Brown	FW190 destroyed	S Verneuil	1520

29th August 1943

400 Sqn Must	AC	F/O J.M.Robb	Bf109 destroyed	15m E Margny	1310

31st August 1943

65 Sqn Spit	FC	S/L J.E.Storrar	FW190 damaged	5m SW Dunkirk	0750
129 Sqn Spit	FC	P/O A.Bradshaw	FW190 destroyed	NE-SE Le Touquet	0725
		F/L G.A.Mason	FW190 destroyed	NE-SE Le Touquet	0725
		F/L G.A.Mason	FW190 damaged	NE-SE Le Touquet	0725
		P/O D.F.Ruchwaldy	FW190 destroyed	NE-SE Le Touquet	0725
		F/L E.O.Watson	FW190 damaged	NE-SE Le Touquet	0725
		P/O M.F.S.Young	FW190 damaged	NE-SE Le Touquet	0725
222 Sqn Spit	FC	F/L P.V.K.Tripe	FW190 prob.dest	S Lille	0730±
421 Sqn Spit	FC	S/L R.W.McNair	Bf109 destroyed	S Ghent	1750
		F/L R.D.Phillip	Bf109 destroyed	S Ghent	1750

31st August/1st September 1943

605 Sqn Mosq	FC	F/O K.F.Dacre	Bf110 damaged	Parchim	0030

2nd September 1943

91 Sqn Spit	FC	F/O G.W.Bond	FW190 destroyed	Le Touquet	1915±
		F/L I.G.S.Matthew	FW190 destroyed	Le Touquet	1915±
341 Sqn Spit	FC	Lt M.Bouguen	FW190 destroyed	St Pol	1900±

'Buck' McNair of 421 (left) was was successful on 3rd September and Mike Donnet of 64 (centre) and Clive 'Joe' Birbeck of 41 Sqn had similar success next day. (ww2images.com; Donnet; Dan Johnson-Brirbeck)

3rd September 1943

266 Sqn Typh	FC	F/S D.Erasmus	FW190 damaged	20m NW Guernsey	1830±
421 Sqn Spit	FC	F/O M.C.Love	Bf109 destroyed	N Evreux	1008
		S/L R.W.McNair	Bf109 destroyed	N Evreux	1008

4th September 1943

41 Sqn Spit	FC	F/O C.R.Birbeck	FW190 destroyed	Le Touquet	1835±
64 Sqn Spit	FC	S/L M.G.L.M.Donnet	FW190 destroyed	off Nieuport	1805
		F/O J.W.Harder	FW190 damaged	off Nieuport	1805
66 Sqn Spit	FC	F/O A.Deytrikh	FW190 damaged	Ault	0930±
		F/L F.A.O.Gaze	FW190 destroyed	Ault	0930±
91 Sqn Spit	FC	S/L N.A.Kynaston	FW190 destroyed	Le Touquet	1845±
		F/L G.Stenborg	FW190 destroyed	Le Touquet	1845±
122 Sqn Spit	FC	P/O J.L.Innes	FW190 damaged	Authie estuary	1850
129 Sqn Spit	FC	P/O M.F.S.Young P/O A.Bradshaw	FW190 destroyed - shared -	NE St Pol	1430
		F/O D.C.Byrne	FW190 damaged	NE St Pol	1430
		S/L H.A.C.Gonay	FW190 damaged	NE St Pol	1430
		F/O M.Twomey	FW190 damaged	Mardyck-Channel	1855
		Unnamed pilot	Bf109 prob.dest	Mardyck-Channel	1855
222 Sqn Spit	FC	F/O R.B.Hesslyn	Bf109 destroyed	Mardyck	1830±
		F/O O.Smik	Bf109 destroyed	Mardyck	1830±
		F/O O.Smik	Bf109 damaged	Mardyck	1830±
		F/L P.V.K.Tripe	Bf109 damaged	Mardyck	1830±
302 Sqn Spit	FC	F/O S.Brzeski Sgt R.Olender	FW190 destroyed - shared -	10m N Hazebrouck	1830
		Sgt R.Olender	FW190 damaged	10m N Hazebrouck	1830

Flight Sergeant T.Szymkowiak of 303 Squadron (left) claimed an FW190 destroyed on 4th September, as did Geoff Northcott, CO of 402 Squadron (centre). Mustang pilots, despite earlier heavy losses at low level to FW190s, were still being sent on fighter-reconnaissance missions and on 6th September two 168 Squadron pilots claimed Bf109s damaged, possibly from JG 2. Right, a Mustang 'poses' for the camera.

303 Sqn Spit	FC	F/S T.Szymkowiak	FW190 destroyed	Lille	1800±
316 Sqn Spit	FC	F/O T.Gora	FW190 prob.dest	Lille-Roubaix	1810
331 Sqn Spit	FC	Capt S.Heglund	Bf109 destroyed	Near Albert	0930
		Capt S.Heglund	Bf109 prob.dest	Near Albert	0930
402 Sqn Spit	FC	F/L J.D.Mitchner	Bf109 destroyed	St Pol-Le Touquet	1845
		P/O L.A.Moore	FW190 destroyed	St Pol-Le Touquet	1845
		S/L G.W.Northcott	FW190 destroyed	St Pol-Le Touquet	1845
		Sgt J.N.Thorne	FW190 destroyed	St Pol-Le Touquet	1845
403 Sqn Spit	FC	S/L F.E.Grant	FW190 destroyed	N Roubaix	1755
416 Sqn Spit	FC	F/L R.D.Booth F/L D.E.Noonan F/L A.H.Sager Digby Wing	Bf109 destroyed - shared - - shared - - shared -	St Pol-Le Touquet	1845
		F/L A.H.Sager Digby Wing	FW190 damaged - shared -	St Pol-Le Touquet	1845
602 Sqn Spit	FC	W/O F.S.Sorge	FW190 destroyed	W Nieuport	1830
127 Wg Spit	FC	W/C J.E.Johnson	FW190 destroyed	NE o/s Roubaix	1758
Dig Wg Spit	FC	W/C L.V.Chadburn	FW190 destroyed	St Pol-Le Touquet	1845
		W/C L.V.Chadburn 416 Squadron	FW190 damaged - shared -	St Pol-Le Touquet	1845
		W/C L.V.Chadburn 416 Squadron	Bf109 destroyed - shared -	St Pol-Le Touquet	1845

Faces of the enemy: On 4th September Feldwebel Gerhard Vogt of 6./JG 26 (left) claimed his 15th and 16th victories. He would be credited with 47 kills before his death in combat on 14th January 1945. Leutnat Karl-Heinz Willius of 2./JG 26 (centre) claimed his 35th kill on 4th. His total would reach 49 before he fell on 8th April 1944. Feldwebel Siegfried Lemke of 1./JG 2 (right) claimed his 5th victory on 6th September. He would survive the war with a confirmed tally of at least 54 victories.

5th September 1943

222 Sqn Spit	FC	S/L E.Cassidy F/L D.Thiriez	Bf109 destroyed - shared -	Nieuport	0834±
		F/L H.P.Lardner-Burke	FW190 destroyed	Nieuport	0834±
		F/O H.L.Stuart	FW190 prob.dest	Nieuport	0834±
421 Sqn Spit	FC	S/L R.W.McNair	Bf109 damaged	Deuze area	0834
127 Wg Spit	FC	W/C J.E.Johnson	Bf109 damaged	Deuze area	0834
Hch Wg Spit	FC	W/C W.V.Crawford -Compton	FW190 destroyed	Nieuport	0834±

5/6th September 1943

418 Sqn Mosq	FC	S/L R.J.Bennell	E/A destroyed	Biblis A/D	0020
		S/L R.J.Bennell	Do217 destroyed	Mainz A/D	0103

6th September 1943

129 Sqn Spit	FC	P/O A.Bradshaw	FW190 damaged	Grandvilliers	1208
		P/O I.G.Wood	FW190 damaged	Foucamont	1208
		F/O J.D.MacKay	FW190 destroyed	Amiens (by collision)	1754
168 Sqn Must	AC	F/L R.Cook	Bf109 damaged	Vitry-en-Artois	1000±
		F/O J.D.Stubbs	Bf109 damaged	Vitry-en-Artois	1000±
303 Sqn Spit	FC	F/L S.Wandzilak	FW190 destroyed	Amiens	1815±

On 6th September, Aleksander Chudek and Jan Falkowski of 303 Squadron (far left) each claimed their 9th confirmed kills. Stanislaw Wandzilak also from 303 Squadron, (centre) claimed an FW 190 destroyed for his 2nd kill. (right) A Spitfire IX of 303 Squadron at Northolt, summer 1943.

303 Sqn Spit	FC	Sgt J.Czezowski	FW190 destroyed	Amiens	1815±
		S/L J.P.Falkowski	FW190 destroyed	Amiens	1815±
		F/S A.Chudek	FW190 destroyed	Amiens	1815±
		P/O W.Sliwinski	FW190 destroyed	Amiens	1815±
317 Sqn Spit	FC	F/O J.Walawski	Bf109 destroyed	Amiens	1815±
403 Sqn Spit	FC	F/O H.J.Dowding	FW190 destroyed	Amiens	1815
		F/L H.J.Southwood	FW190 destroyed	Amiens	1815
		F/L H.J.Southwood	FW190 damaged	Amiens	1815
421 Sqn Spit	FC	S/L R.W.McNair	FW190 destroyed	SE Beaumont-le-Roger A/D	1215
		F/L R.D.Phillip	FW190 damaged	Amiens	1815
485 Sqn Spit	FC	S/L J.M.Checketts	FW190 destroyed	15m E Dieppe	1805
		F/L K.C.Lee	FW190 damaged	15m E Dieppe	1805

6/7th September 1943

85 Sqn Mosq	FC	F/L C.G.Houghton	FW190 destroyed	Bury St Edmunds	2045
		S/L G.L.Howitt	FW190 destroyed	off Clacton	2200
141 Sqn Beau		F/O H.E.White	Ju88 destroyed	Rheims	2210
605 Sqn Mosq	FC	F/O K.F.Dacre	Ju88 destroyed	Tirlemont	0152
		F/O K.F.Dacre	E/A prob.dest	Gossencourt	0159

8th September 1943

91 Sqn Spit	FC	F/S R.A.B.Blumer	FW190 destroyed	Vitry-en-Artois	1025±
222 Sqn Spit	FC	S/L G.J.Stonhill	FW190 damaged	Montdidier	1424
		F/L H.P.Lardner-Burke	Bf109 destroyed	N France	1759
		F/O O.Smik	- shared -		

On 8th September 'Mike' Gladych of 303 Squadron (right) claimed an FW190, his 8th with the RAF. He later transferred to the USAAF and was credited with 10 more.

John Cunningham, CO of 85 Squadron (far right) claimed an FW190 on the night of the 8th, one of three lost by I./SKG 10 this night, all to 85 Squadron Mosquito crews.

302 Sqn Spit	FC	F/L B.M.Gladych	Bf109 destroyed	Lille	0930±
		P/O J.Krajewski	FW190 destroyed	Lille	0930±
		F/S E.Loska	Bf109 destroyed	Lille	0930±
		W/O B.Malinowski	Bf109 destroyed	Lille	0930±
		W/O B.Malinowski	Bf109 destroyed	Lille	0930±
		P/O C.M.Sniec	Bf109 prob.dest	Lille	0930±
317 Sqn Spit	FC	F/L J.Radomski	Bf109 destroyed	Lille	0930±
		F/L J.Radomski	Bf109 damaged	Lille	0930±
		Sgt S.Rudowski	Bf109 destroyed	Lille	0930±
		F/O J.Zbrozek	Bf109 destroyed	Lille	0930±
331 Sqn Spit	FC	Maj K.Birksted	FW190 damaged	E Lille	1021
		Sgt C.Gran	FW190 damaged	E Lille	1021
		Capt M.Y.Gran	FW190 destroyed	E Lille	1021
		Sgt A.Hellan	FW190 damaged	E Lille	1021
332 Sqn Spit	FC	Sgt O.G.Aanjesen	Bf109 damaged	Near Bethune	1424
402 Sqn Spit	FC	P/O R.D.Mitchner	Bf109 prob.dest	33m N Arras	1020
403 Sqn Spit	FC	F/O H.J.Dowding	FW190 damaged	SE Douai	1020
132 Wg Spit	FC	Maj K.Birksted	Bf109G damaged	Near Bethune	1431

8/9th September 1943

85 Sqn Mosq	FC	F/O B.J.Thwaites	FW190 destroyed	Off North Foreland	2135
		F/O B.J.Thwaites	FW190 destroyed	Off North Foreland	2155
		W/C J.Cunningham	FW190 destroyed	Aldeburgh-Southwold	2140

Florian Martini of 317 Squadron (far left) claimed his second confirmed kill on 11th September and survived the war.

Aleksander Pietrzak of 302 Squadron made his first claim on 11th and would survive the war with a total of three, only to die in an accident on 2nd August 1945.

9th September 1943

65 Sqn Spit	FC	F/O P.J.Hearne	FW190 damaged	Bethune	1440
122 Sqn Spit	FC	Capt T.Jonnson	Bf109 prob.dest	N Somme estuary	1440
		Capt T.Jonnson	Bf109 prob.dest	N Somme estuary	1440
124 Sqn Spit	FC	F/O P.Phillips	Bf109 destroyed	15m S Isle of Wight	0720
129 Sqn Spit	FC	F/O R.D.Rosser	FW190 damaged	Near Merville	1500

10th September 1943

400 Sqn Must	AC	F/O A.T.Carlson	Ju52 destroyed	St Germaine-sur-Morin	1323

11th September 1943

129 Sqn Spit	FC	F/L G.A.Mason	Bf109 destroyed	Rouen area	1658
		F/L G.A.Mason	Bf109 damaged	Rouen area	1710
175 Sqn Typh	FC	F/0 N.C.R.Howe	FW190 damaged	Beauvais area	1735±
182 Sqn Typh	FC	F/O A.Leighton-Porter	FW190 damaged	10m SSW Poix	1735±
302 Sqn Spit	FC	Sgt A.Pietrzak	FW190 damaged	Near Rouen	1710
307 Sqn Mosq	FC	S/L J.Damsz	Bf110 prob.dest	380m W Brest	1412
		F/S Z.Dunin -Rzuchowski	Bf110 destroyed	380m W Brest	1412
		W/C J.Orzechowski	Bf110 prob.dest	380m W Brest	1412
		W/C J.Orzechowski	Bf110 damaged	380m W Brest	1412
		W/C J.Orzechowski	Bf110 damaged	380m W Brest	1412
		W/C J.Orzechowski	Bf110 damaged	380m W Brest	1412
		S/L M.Lewandowski	Ju88 destroyed	off Gironde	1627
		S/L M.Lewandowski	Ju88 destroyed	off Gironde	1627
		S/L M.Lewandowski	Ju88 damaged	off Gironde	1627

On 11th September 307 Squadron flew Instep patrols out over the Bay of Biscay and engaged both Bf110s and Ju88s. They had some success, although not as much as was believed. One of each type was actually shot down. (Left) Wing Commander J.Orzechowski - in centre - led one of the two formations. (Right) The Mosquito FB VI as used by 307 Squadron demonstrates its firepower.

307 Sqn Mosq	FC	W/O L.Szomplinski	Ju88 destroyed	off Gironde	1627
		W/O L.Szomplinski	Ju88 destroyed	off Gironde	1627
317 Sqn Spit	FC	F/L Z.Janicki F/L F.Martini	FW190 destroyed - shared -	Near Rouen	1710
		F/L Z.Janicki	FW190 damaged	Near Rouen	1710
		F/L Z.Janicki	FW190 damaged	Near Rouen	1710
		F/O S.Kurowicki	FW190 destroyed	Near Rouen	1710
		F/L F.Martini	FW190 destroyed	near Rouen	1710
		F/L F.Martini	FW190 damaged	near Rouen	1710
		F/O R.Wal	FW190 destroyed	Near Rouen	1710
331 Sqn Spit	FC	Capt S.Heglund	FW190 destroyed	Rouen	1703
		Sgt P.Thulin	FW190 destroyed	Rouen	1703
332 Sqn Spit	FC	Maj R.From	FW190 destroyed	Rouen	1703
403 Sqn Spit	FC	F/O H.J.Dowding	Bf109 destroyed	Near Barentin	1810
609 Sqn Typh	FC	P/O T.D.L.Leslie	Hs126 destroyed	Sissones	1400
16 Wg Typh	FC	G/C H.C.A.Woodhouse	FW190 damaged	SW Poix	1735±

14th September 1943

197 Sqn Typh	FC	P/O W.C.Ahrens F/S R.Shelton	Bf109 destroyed - shared -	40m S St Catherine's Pt	1850±
132 Sqn Spit	FC	Capt G.Fosse	Bf109G damaged	Dixmunde	1745
		Maj K.Birksted	Bf109 destroyed	Dixmunde	1745

15th September 1943

118 Sqn Spit	FC	F/O F.S.R.Everill	FW190 prob.dest	Merville	1745±
129 Sqn Spit	FC	P/O D.F.Ruchwaldy	Bf109 prob.dest	W Merville	1757

15/16th September 1943

29 Sqn Mosq	FC	F/O B.C.Jarvis	Me410 destroyed	Off Brighton	0300
85 Sqn Mosq	FC	F/O E.R.Hedgcoe	Ju88 destroyed	Tenterden	2200
		F/L E.N.Bunting	Ju88 destroyed	off Griz Nez	2205
488 Sqn Mosq	FC	F/L J.E.Gunn	He111 destroyed	4m N Foreness	2138
		P/O R.G.Watts	Do217 destroyed	30m SE North Foreland	2217
605 Sqn Mosq	FC	P/O K.F.Dacre	Do217 destroyed	Melun	2229

16th September 1943

91 Sqn Spit	FC	Lt J.Andrieux	Bf109 destroyed	Beaumont-le Roger	1745±
		F/S R.A.B.Blumer	FW190 destroyed	Beaumont-le Roger	1745±
		S/L N.A.Kynaston	FW190 destroyed	Beaumont-le Roger	1745±
		S/L N.A.Kynaston	FW190 damaged	Beaumont-le Roger	1745±
		F/L G.Stenborg	Bf109 destroyed	Beaumont-le Roger	1745±
421 Sqn Spit	FC	F/L R.A.Buckham	Bf109 destroyed	Bruay	1730
		F/O H.P.M.Zary	Bf109 damaged	Bruay	1730
485 Sqn Spit	FC	F/L B.E.Gibbs	Bf109 destroyed	25m S Beaumont -le Roger	1745
		P/O J.A.Houlton	FW190 damaged	25m S Beaumont -le Roger	1745
		P/O J.A.Houlton	Bf109 destroyed	25m S Beaumont -le Roger	1745
		W/O B.S.Wipiti	- shared -		
		F/O M.Metcalfe	FW190 destroyed	25m S Beaumont -le Roger	1745
611 Sqn Spit	FC	Capt A.Austeen	Bf109 destroyed	Texel	1815±

18th September 1943

65 Sqn Spit	FC	F/L R.C.Kitchen	FW190 damaged	12m N Rouen	1000
		S/L J.E.Storrar	FW190 destroyed	12m N Rouen	1000

On 16th September, Henry Zary of 421 Squadron (left) damaged a Bf109 over Bruary and on 19th claimed another damaged. He would go on to claim five 'confirmed' and survived the war as CO of 403 Squadron. On 21st, Martin Gran of 331 Squadron (centre) and Kaj Birksted of 332, each claimed an FW190 in a fight against JG 26. Both Norwegians would have distinguished careers and survive the war, Birksted with ten victories and Gran with eight.

19th September 1943

91 Sqn	Spit	FC	F/O J.C.S.Doll	FW190 destroyed	Lille-Nord	1150
			F/O J.C.S.Doll	FW190 damaged	Lille-Nord	1150
122 Sqn	Spit	FC	F/O A.F.Pavey	Bf109 damaged	Merville	1130
129 Sqn	Spit	FC	F/O R.D.Rosser	FW190 damaged	5-6m SW Merville	1745
302 Sqn	Spit	FC	F/O E.Wardzinski	FW190 destroyed	Near Bruay	1735
331 Sqn	Spit	FC	Capt S.Heglund	FW190 damaged	Bethune	1745
421 Sqn	Spit	FC	F/L R.A.Buckham	Bf109 destroyed	Bruay	1730
			F/O H.P.M.Zary	Bf109 damaged	Bruay	1730
WH Wg	Spit	FC	W/C R.H.Harries	FW190 destroyed	Lille-Nord	1150

21st September 1943

19 Sqn	Spit	FC	F/L P.Wigley	FW190 damaged	N Amiens	1000
			F/L P.Wigley	FW190 damaged	Location unknown	1200±
331 Sqn	Spit	FC	Capt M.Y.Gran	FW190 destroyed	Near Lens	0931
			Capt S.Heglund	FW190 prob.dest	Near Lens	0931
332 Sqn	Spit	FC	Maj K.Birksted	FW190 destroyed	Near Lens	0931
456 Sqn	Mosq	FC	P/O G.F.Gatenby	Ju88 prob.dest	Biscay	1708
			F/O J.W.Newell	Ju88 damaged	Biscay	1708
			F/L G.Panitz	Ju88 destroyed	Biscay	1708
			P/O C.S.Samson	- shared -		

605 Sqn Mosq	FC	F/L D.H.Blomeley	Ju88 destroyed	W entrance Skagerrak	1236
		F/L D.H.Blomeley	Ju88 destroyed	W entrance Skagerrak	1249

21/22nd September 1943

604 Sqn Mosq	FC	S/L I.K.S.Joll	Do217 destroyed	50m off Spurn Head	0113

22nd September 1943

41 Sqn Spit	FC	F/O C.R.Birbeck	FW190 destroyed	W Evreux	1615
		Sgt W.H.Vann	FW190 damaged	W Evreux	1615
		F/O B.B.Newman	FW190 prob.dest	Evreux	1620±
		F/L D.H.Smith	FW190 destroyed	W Evreux	1620
308 Sqn Spit	FC	F/L A.Glowacki	Bf109G damaged	Near Evreux	1620
341 Sqn Spit	FC	S/Lt R.Borne	FW190 damaged	10m S St Valery	1633
		S/Lt R.Borne	FW190 damaged	10m S St Valery	1633
		Lt M.Bouguen	FW190 destroyed	10m S St Valery	1633
416 Sqn Spit	FC	W/O E.A.Norris	Bf109 damaged	Near Evreux A/D	1610
453 Sqn Spit	FC	F/L D.H.Smith	FW190 destroyed	Brest/Guipavas artea	1615±
Dig Wg Spit	FC	W/C L.V.Chadburn	Bf109 damaged	Near Evreux A/D	1610
		W/C L.V.Chadburn	Bf109 damaged	Near Evreux A/D	1610
WH Wg Spit	FC	W/C R.H.Harries	FW190 destroyed	Evreux	1615±
		W/C R.H.Harries	FW190 prob.dest	Evreux	1615±

22/23rd September 1943

418 Sqn Mosq	FC	S/L C.C.Moran	E/A destroyed	Achmer/Hesepe A/D	0350±

23rd September 1943

91 Sqn Spit	FC	F/L I.G.S.Matthew	Bf109 damaged	20m S Dieppe	1545±
302 Sqn Spit	FC	F/O S.Brzeski	FW190 prob.dest	15-20m SE Le Treport	1620
		Sgt J.Durys	FW190 destroyed	15-20m SE Le Treport	1620
303 Sqn Spit	FC	F/S A.Chudek	FW190 destroyed	15-20m SE Le Treport	1620
		S/L J.P.Falkowski	FW190 prob.dest	15-20m SE Le Treport	1620
		F/S E.Martens	FW190 prob.dest	15-20m SE Le Treport	1620
		F/S A.Rokitnicki	FW190 prob.dest	15-20m SE Le Treport	1620
331 Sqn Spit	FC	Maj R.A.Berg	Bf109 damaged	Cambrai/Peronne	1545

On the night of 23rd September, Flight Lieutenant M.W.Beveridge of 418 Squadron (left) claimed his omly two confirmed kills whilst intruding over Germany. One was certainly a Bf110 of 10./NJG 1 that crashed in flames at Mainz-Finthen. Leutnant Hans Kräner and his crew were killed. Massy Beveridge died on 20th September 1944, when his Mosquito crashed near St Andre in bad weather. Next afternoon, the 24th, Squadron Leader Norman Kynaston of 91 Squadron (centre) claimed an FW190 and Flying Officer B.B.Newman (right) claimed a 'probable'. (via Dan Johnson).

341 Sqn Spit	FC	Capt M.Boudier	FW190 destroyed	Beauvais	1545
		Capt L.C.Martell	FW190 destroyed	Beauvais	1545
		Capt L.C.Martell	Bf109G destroyed	Beauvais	1545
416 Sqn Spit	FC	F/L R.D.Booth	FW190 damaged	Beauvais	1545
Hch Wg Spit	FC	W/C W.V.Crawford -Compton	FW190 destroyed	NW Beauvais	1545±

23/24th September 1943

418 Sqn Mosq	FC	F/L M.W.Beveridge	Bf110 destroyed	A/D SW Stuttgart	2307
		F/L M.W.Beveridge	Do217 destroyed	A/A SW Stuttgart	2333
418 Sqn Mosq	FC	P/O J.R.F.Johnson	FW190 destroyed	Near St Andre	0047
605 Sqn Mosq	FC	F/L C.E.Knowles	Do21y destroyed	Ober Olm	2308

24th September 1943

41 Sqn Spit	FC	F/L A.A.Glen	FW190 destroyed	N Beauvais	1600
		F/L A.A.Glen	FW190 destroyed	N Beauvais	1600
		F/O Prince E.Galitzine	FW190 prob.dest	SW Beauvais	1620
		F/O B.B.Newman	FW190 prob.dest	Beauvais	1620

The Ju88C was operated over the Bay of Biscay by V./KG 40 against RAF Coastal Command aircraft and ferry flights to and from the Middle East.

64 Sqn	Spit	FC	F/L J.A.Plagis	Bf109 destroyed	5m SW Rouen	1100±
66 Sqn	Spit	FC	F/L G.C.Elcombe	Bf110 destroyed	Off Pte St Mathieu	1330
			F/S G.C.Thomas	Bf110 destroyed	Off Pte St Mathieu	1330
91 Sqn	Spit	FC	F/L J.C.S.Doll	FW190 destroyed	Poix	1615±
			S/L N.A.Kynaston	FW190 destroyed	Poix	1615±
			F/L J.A.Maridor	FW190 destroyed	Poix	1615±
			F/L J.A.Maridor	FW190 damaged	Poix	1615±
129 Sqn	Spit	FC	F/O D.F.Ruchwaldy	FW190 destroyed	NW Amiens	1108
197 Sqn	Typh	FC	P/O E.O'Callaghan	Bf109 damaged	Trouville	1110±
302 Sqn	Spit	FC	F/O T.Rzyski	FW190 prob.dest	Amiens	1115
303 Sqn	Spit	FC	F/L T.Koc	FW190 damaged	Amiens	1115
306 Sqn	Spit	FC	F/S F.Berezowski	FW190 prob.dest	Beauvais	1600
			F/S Z.Kawnik	FW190 prob.dest	Beauvais	1600
			F/O W.Tronczynski	Bf109 damaged	Beauvais	1600
310 Sqn	Spit	FC	F/L V.Chocholin	Bf110 prob.dest	4m E Brest	1335
313 Sqn	Spit	FC	S/L J.Himr	Bf110 destroyed	4m E Brest	1335
			F/S A.Zalesky	Bf110 prob.dest	4m E Brest	1335
331 Sqn	Spit	FC	Lt B.Bjornstad	FW190 damaged	Somme estuary	1120
341 Sqn	Spit	FC	Cdt M.Boudier	FW190 destroyed	NNW Poix	1620
			Capt L.C.Martell	FW190 destroyed	15m S Le Treport	1620
			Lt S.P.N.Roos	FW190 destroyed	15m S Le Treport	1620
402 Sqn	Spit	FC	F/O W.G.Dodd	FW190 prob.dest	Beauvais	1700
			F/L J.D.Mitchner	FW190 prob.dest	Beauvais	1700
			Sgt J.N.Thorne	- shared -		
			Digby Wing	- shared -		
			F/L J.D.Mitchner	FW190 destroyed	Beauvais	1700#
			Digby Wing	- shared -		

403 Sqn Spit	FC	F/O G.F.Beurling	FW190 destroyed	Poix	1610
421 Sqn Spit	FC	F/L R.A.Buckham	FW190 destroyed	Poix	1610
		F/L R.A.Buckham	FW190 damaged	Poix	1610
486 Sqn Typh	FC	S/L D.J.Scott	FW190 damaged	4m SE Trouville	1100
		F/L A.E.Umbers	FW190 damaged	4m SE Trouville	1100
610 Sqn Spit	FC	F/S W.A.Nicholls F/O F.Venesoen	Bf110 destroyed - shared -	Pte St Mathieu	1340
		F/S N.Samuels	Bf110 destroyed	Pte St Mathieu	1340
		Unnamed pilot	Bf110 damaged	Pte St Mathieu	1340
127 Wg Spit	FC	W/C H.C.Godefroy	FW190 destroyed	Poix	1610
Dig Wg Spit	FC	W/C L.V.Chadburn 416 Squadron	FW190 prob.dest - shared -	Beauvais	1700
		W/C L.V.Chadburn 416 Squadron	FW190 destroyed - shared -	Beauvais	1700
Perr Wg Spit	FC	W/C E.F.J.Charles	Bf110 destroyed	10m W Brest	1330

25th September 1943

307 Sqn Mosq	FC	S/L J.Damsz	Ju88 destroyed	Biscay	1637
		S/L J.Damsz	Ju88 damaged	Biscay	1637
		W/O K.Jankowiak	Ju88 damaged	Biscay	1637
		F/S L.Steinke	Ju88 destroyed	Biscay	1637
		F/S L.Steinke	Ju88 prob.dest	Biscay	1637
		F/S L.Steinke	Ju88 damaged	Biscay	1637

Combat Report - 24th September 1943

I took off from Westhampnett at 1520 flying as Blue 1 in 41 Squadron. We made rendezvous with 72 Marauders and proceeded to Beauvais. My R/T was u/s and I heard no warnings of any E/A about, but when approaching target at about 15,000 ft - I saw about 10 F.W. 190's diving on my port side towards the bombers. I broke left and came in behind them and they pulled steeply to the right. Two of the E/A were lagging slightly and I took a quick squirt at the leader from about 300 yds and 45° deflection using cannon and m/g. I saw a large flash in the cockpit and he flicked over and collided with the E/A following him.
Both A/C disintegrated. There was a terrific mix up in the area but being unable to find any further Huns within range, I joined the last box of bombers and came out on their flank, landing at base at 16.40.
I claim 2 F.W. 190's destroyed.

A.A.Glen, Flight Lieutenant. 41 Squadron

On 25th September 307 Squadron Mosquito crews flew an Instep patrol to Biscay, meeting some of the Ju88C-6s of V./KG 40. Squadron Leader Jerzy Damsz (left) and Flight Sergeant Ludvik Steinke (right) each destroyed one. Steinke claimed another probably destroyed and they both claimed another damaged, as did Warrant Officer K.Janowiak.(centre)

26/27th September 1943

410 Sqn Mosq	FC	F/L M.A.Cybulski	Do217 destroyed	5m W Ijmuiden	2305

27th September 1943

41 Sqn	Spit	FC	Sgt P. Graham	FW190 damaged	15m NW Beauvais	1040
			F/O C.R.Birbeck	FW190 damaged	N Beauvais	1045±
			F/O C.R.Birbeck	Bf109 damaged	Beauvais-Dieppe	1130
91 Sqn	Spit	FC	F/L R.S.Easby	Bf109 destroyed	N Beauvais	1100±
			F/O G.H.Huntley	FW190 damaged	N Beauvais	1100±
			F/O A.G.Shaughnessy	Bf109 destroyed	N Beauvais	1100±
129 Sqn	Spit	FC	Sgt D.H.Nelson	Bf109 damaged	Beauvais	1100±
			P/O D.F.Ruchwaldy	Bf109 damaged	Beauvais	1100±
			F/L A.J.Hancock	Bf109 damaged	NW Dreux	1725
			Sgt D.H.Nelson	FW190 destroyed	5m NW Dreux	1725
			F/O D.F.Ruchwaldy	FW190 destroyed	3m SW Dreux	1725
			S/L P.V.K.Tripe	FW190 damaged	NW Dreux	1725
222 Sqn	Spit	FC	F/L R.B.Hesslyn	FW190 destroyed	Beauvais	1100±
			F/O O.Smik	FW190 destroyed	Beauvais	1100±
			F/O O.Smik	FW190 destroyed	Beauvais	1100±

Loading the guns of a 96 Squadron Beaufighter at Drem, autumn 1943.
(ww2images.com)

Sergeant Peter Graham of 41 Squadron was credited with an FW190 damaged on 27th February after he saw the pilot jettisoning the cockpit hood. (P.Graham)

222 Sqn Spit	FC	F/O O.Smik	FW190 damaged	Beauvais	1100±
		F/O O.Smik	Bf109 destroyed	Beauvais	1100±
		P/O H.E.Turney	FW190 damaged	Beauvais	1100±
		F/S S.G.Walton	FW190 damaged	Beauvais	1100±
		F/O O.Smik	Bf109 destroyed	Bernay	1730±
302 Sqn Spit	FC	Sgt A.Pietrzak	FW190 destroyed	10m W Le Treport	1100±
306 Sqn Spit	FC	W/O M.Machiowak	FW190 destroyed	Forges	1050
310 Sqn Spit	FC	F/L K.Drobohlav	FW190 prob.dest	W Beauvais	1059
313 Sqn Spit	FC	Sgt S.Hlucka	FW190 damaged	Beauvais A/D	1100
		F/L A.Hochmal	FW190 damaged	Beauvais A/D	1100
		F/O F.Masarik	FW190 damaged	15m NW Beauvais A/D	1105
		F/L O.Kucera	FW190 destroyed	Conches A/D	1730
331 Sqn Spit	FC	Capt S.Heglund	Bf109 destroyed	Beauvais	1048
402 Sqn Spit	FC	P/O B.E.Innes F/L J.D.Mitchner	FW190 prob.dest - shared -	Fecamp	1745
		P/O L.A.Moore Digby Wing	Bf109 damaged - shared -	Fecamp	1745
		F/L H.A.Simpson	FW190 prob.dest	Fecamp	1745
Dig Wg Spit	FC	W/C L.V.Chadburn	Bf109 destroyed	Fecamp	1745
		W/C L.V.Chadburn	FW190 prob.dest	Fecamp	1745
		W/C L.V.Chadburn 402 Squadron	Bf109 damaged - shared -	Fecamp	1745
Hch Wg Spit	FC	W/C W.V.Crawford -Compton	FW190 damaged	Beauvais	1100±
WH Wg Spit	FC	W/C R.H.Harries	Bf109 destroyed	N Beauvais	1100±

27/28th September 1943

141 Sqn Beau	FC	W/C J.R.D.Braham	Do217 destroyed	10m W Hannover	2135
418 Sqn Mosq	FC	F/L H.S.Lisson	E/A destroyed	Volkenröde A/D	2247
		F/L H.S.Lisson	Ju88 destroyed	Volkenröde A/D	2253
605 Sqn Mosq	FC	Sgt H.J.Collins	E/A destroyed	Vechta	2311
		Sgt H.J.Collins	E/A destroyed	Vechta	2315
		S/L T.A.Heath	Do217 destroyed	Parchim	2315
		W/C B.R.O'B.Hoare	Do217 destroyed	Detelsdorf	2318

29/30th September 1943

141 Sqn Beau	FC	W/C J.R.D.Braham	Bf110 destroyed	Zuider Zee	2045
		W/C J.R.D.Braham	Ju88 damaged	3m S Zwolle	2055

2nd October 1943

124 Sqn Spit	FC	F/S D.P.Kelly	FW190 prob.dest	30m S Isle of Wight	1545±
129 Sqn Spit	FC	F/O A.Bradshaw	Bf109 destroyed	S Aalsmeer	1135
		F/O D.C.Byrne	Bf109 destroyed	1m off Noordwijk	1135
		F/O A.J.Hancock	Bf109 destroyed	S Aalsmeer	1135
183 Sqn Typh	FC	F/L W.Dring	FW190 destroyed	Channel	1352
		F/O J.E.Mitchell	FW190 destroyed	Channel	1352
222 Sqn Spit	FC	F/L R.B.Hesslyn	Bf109 destroyed	Beauvais	1730
303 Sqn Spit	FC	W/O M.Popek	FW190 damaged	S Lille	1715
		F/O J.Stasik	FW190 damaged	S Lille	1715
331 Sqn Spit	FC	Maj R.A.Berg	Bf109 destroyed	Near Rouen	1725
		Lt F.S.Fearnley	Bf109 destroyed	Near Rouen	1725
		Capt S.Heglund	Bf109 destroyed	Near Rouen	1725
		Capt S.Heglund	FW190 damaged	Near Rouen	1725
		2/Lt T.Larssen	FW190 damaged	Near Rouen	1725
		Sgt O.F.Solvang	Bf109 damaged	Near Rouen	1725
332 Sqn Spit	FC	2/Lt O.G.Aanjesen	FW190 damaged	Gournay area	1725
341 Sqn Spit	FC	Cdt B.Duperier S/Lt W.Chevalier	FW190 destroyed - shared -	S Somme estuary	1445±
		Cdt B.Duperier	FW190 damaged	S Somme estuary	1445±
		Lt P.L.Laurent	FW190 destroyed	S Somme estuary	1445±

Two great fighter leaders: Charles Demoulin of 609 Squadron and Bernard Duperier of 341 Squadron (right). Demoulin claimed a Bf110 on 4th October and Duperier an FW190 shot down and another damaged on 2nd. Demoulin and Duperier would both survive - Demoulin as a prisoner.

402 Sqn Spit	FC	F/O W.G.Dodd	Bf109 destroyed	Coast near Ijmuiden	1125
		F/L J.D.Mitchner	Bf109 damaged	Coast near Ijmuiden	1125
		S/L G.W.Northcott	Bf109 damaged	Coast near Ijmuiden	1125
		Sgt J.N.Thorne	Bf109 damaged	Coast near Ijmuiden	1125
403 Sqn Spit	FC	F/L A.C.Coles	FW190 destroyed	Roye/Amy A/D	1725
		F/L A.C.Coles	FW190 destroyed	NE edge Roye/Amy AD	1725
412 Sqn Spit	FC	F/S H.W.Bowker	FW190 destroyed	4m NW Ault	1457
		F/L M.D.Boyd	FW190 damaged	4m NW Ault	1457
		F/S H.W.Bowker	FW190 destroyed	4m NW Ault	1459
421 Sqn Spit	FC	P/O W.F.Cook P/O K.R.Linton	FW190 destroyed - shared -	WSW Roye/Amy A/D	1725
		P/O J.S.Hicks	FW190 destroyed	WSW Roye/Amy A/D	1725
		S/L R.W.McNair	FW190 destroyed	Near St Nicholas	1125
		P/O H.F.Packard	FW190 destroyed	WSW Roye/Amy A/D	1725
453 Sqn Spit	FC	F/O L.J.Hanshill	FW190 damaged	15-20m S Oisemont	1755
456 Sqn Mosq	FC	S/L G.Panitz	Ju88 destroyed	Near Lake Biscarosse	1933
485 Sqn Spit	FC	F/S G.C.Couper W/O B.S.Wipiti	FW190 destroyed - shared -	S Somme estuary	1440
		F/O J.E.Mortimer	FW190 prob.dest	Somme area	1440
		F/O J.E.Mortimer	FW190 damaged	Somme area	1440
132 Wg Spit	FC	Maj K.Birksted	Bf109 destroyed	Near Rouen	1725
		Maj K.Birksted	Bf109 damaged	Near Rouen	1725
Dig Wg Spit	FC	W/C L.V.Chadburn	Bf109 destroyed	Coast near Ijmuiden	1125
Hch Wg Spit	FC	W/C W.V.Crawford -Compton	Bf109 destroyed	Off Noordwijk	1130

3/4th October 1943

25 Sqn Mosq	FC	F/L V.H.Linthune	Ju88 destroyed	Kassel	0030
68 Sqn Beau	FC	F/L P.F.Allen	Me410 destroyed	60m E Winterton	0040

4th October 1943

609 Sqn Typh	FC	S/L J.R.Baldwin	Bf109 destroyed	Juvincourt	1230±
		F/O C.J.G.De Moulin	Bf110 destroyed	Florennes	1230±
		F/L L.L.Henrion	Bf109 destroyed	Juvincourt	1230±

5th October 1943

247 Sqn Typh	FC	F/L C.E.Brayshaw	Fi156 destroyed	Boissets	1150
		F/L C.E.Brayshaw	Ju88 damaged	Nangis	1150±
		F/O P.A.Chappel	Fi156 destroyed	Boissets	1150±
609 Sqn Typh	FC	P/O L.W.F.Stark	Ju88 destroyed	Sevry	1430±
		P/O R.Van Lierde	Ju88 destroyed	Soissons	1730±

6/7th October 1943

| 488 Sqn Mosq | FC | P/O N.M.Knox | Do217 damaged | 5m W Canterbury | 2000 |

7th October 1943

198 Sqn Typh	FC	S/L J.M.Bryan	FW190 destroyed	Thielt	0743
		F/L V.Fittall	FW190 destroyed	Thielt	0743
		F/O A.R.F.Jonas	FW190 damaged	Thielt	0743
501 Sqn Spit	FC	Capt S.Fuchs	FW190 prob.dest	N Cayeaux	1035±
609 Sqn Typh	FC	F/L J.R.Baldwin	FW190 damaged	N Beauvais	1640±

7/8th October 1943

68 Sqn Beau	FC	P/O R.E.B.Sargent	Do217 destroyed	60m E Yarmouth	1945±
85 Sqn Mosq	FC	F/L W.H.Maguire	Me410 destroyed	10m S Hastings	2130
		Capt J.O.R.Bugge	Me410 destroyed	Gravesend	2210
		F/O B.J.Thwaites	Me410 damaged	Gravesend	2210
		Lt T.Weisteen	Me410 destroyed	Off Dungeness	2223
157 Sqn Mosq	FC	F/S W.A.Robertson	Me410 damaged	Shoeburyness	2215

8th October 1943

66 Sqn Spit	FC	F/O D.Baker	Bf110 destroyed	10m W Brest	1445
		F/L G.C.Elcombe	Bf110 destroyed	10-15m E Brest	1445
		S/L W.M.Foster	Bf110 prob.dest	10m W Brest	1445

On 8th October, Squadron leader Ken Lofts (left) led his 66 Squadron pilots in one of several combats against Bf110s of II./ZG 1 in the Western Approaches. The Germans lost eleven Messerschmitts, including that flown by Hauptmann Karl-Heinz Matern, the Gruppenkommandeur (centre). He survived the war, credited with at least four victories, but was killed in a flying accident in 1951. Right: A Bf110C of ZG 1 in late 1943.

66 Sqn	Spit	FC	S/L K.T.Lofts	Bf110 damaged	10m W Brest	1445
			F/O C.Reader	Bf110 prob.dest	10m W Brest	1445
402 Sqn	Spit	FC	F/L J.A.H.G. de Niverville	Do24 destroyed	80m E Lowestoft	1732
			F/O W.G.Dodd	- shared -		
			P/O L.A.Moore	- shared -		
			F/L R.H.S.Ewins	Bf110 destroyed	SW Scilly Isles	0845
			P/O C.R.Leith	Bf110 destroyed	SW Scilly Isles	0845
			P/O C.R.Leith	Bf110 destroyed	SW Scilly Isles	0845
			F/O P.V.McDade	Bf110 destroyed	SW Scilly Isles	0845
			F/O P.V.McDade	Bf110 destroyed	SW Scilly Isles	0845
610 Sqn	Spit	FC	F/S R.Hussey	Bf110 destroyed	SW Predannack	1445
			F/O V.K.Moody	Bf110 destroyed	SW Predannack	1445
			Unamed pilot	Bf110 damaged	SW Predannack	1445
132 Wg	Spit	FC	Maj K.Birksted	Bf109 destroyed	Near Rouen	1725
			Maj K.Birksted	Bf109 damaged	Near Rouen	1725

8/9th October 1943

85 Sqn	Mosq	FC	S/L E.N.Bunting	Ju188 destroyed	S Dover	2020
			F/O S.V.Holloway	Ju88 destroyed	S Bradwell Bay	2038
605 Sqn	Mosq	FC	Sgt H.J.Collins	Me210 damaged	Vechta	0253

12/13th October 1943

151 Sqn Mosq	FC	F/O A.D.Boyle	Me410 destroyed	30m NE Cromer		2136

13th October 1943

66 Sqn Spit	FC	F/S R.C.Casburn	Ju88 destroyed	70m SW Lands End	1750±
		F/O T.Hamer	- shared -		
		S/L K.TLofts	- shared -		
		Lt Thompson	- shared -		
		F/S V.Tidy	- shared -		
		F/O A,Varey	- shared -		

15th October 1943

257 Sqn Typh	FC	F/O S.J.Khin	FW190 destroyed	Poulmic	1630±
		F/S D.C.J.Calnan	- shared -		
		F/O S.J.Khin	FW190 damaged	Poulmic	1630±
266 Sqn Typh	FC	Sgt D.Drummond	FW190 destroyed	35m E Start Point	1300
		F/O J.N.Lucas	- shared -		
		F/S I.O.Hulley	FW190 dam	50m SSE Start Point	1555
		F/O J.N.Lucas	FW190 destroyed	40m SE Start Point	1555

15/16th October 1943

85 Sqn Mosq	FC	F/L W.H.Maguire	Ju88 destroyed	Near Woodbridge	2258
		F/L W.H.Maguire	Ju88 destroyed	S Clacton	2310
		F/O H.B.Thomas	Me410 destroyed	Birchington	2315

16th October 1943

609 Sqn Typh	FC	F/L J.R.Baldwin	Ju88 destroyed	20m S Paris	1650±
		S/L P.G.Thornton			
		-Brown	- shared -		
		P/O C.F.JDetal	Me410 destroyed	20m S Paris	1650±
		F/O L.E.Smith	- shared -		
		F/L L.E.Smith	Ju88 destroyed	20m S Paris	1650±
		S/L P.G.Thornton			
		-Brown	- shared -		

17th October 1943

124 Sqn Spit	FC	F/S A.D.Yeardley	FW190 destroyed	15m W Le Touquet	1640

Three from 29 Squadron: Flying Officer J.Hopkins, Flight Lieutenant J.E.Barry and Squadron Leader C.Kirkland discuss the night's operations. On the night of 20th October Barry destroyed an FW190 of I./SKG 10 for his first victory. He would end the war with four credited.
(K.Lowes via F.Pringle).

17/18th October 1943

85 Sqn	Mosq	FC	S/L E.N.Bunting	Me410 destroyed	Brentwood	0225

18th October 1943

91 Sqn	Spit	FC	Lt J.Andrieux	Bf109 destroyed	NW Amiens	1430±
132 Sqn	Spit	FC	Sgt J.H.Williams	Bf109 destroyed	Bethune/Aire	1420
			S/L F.F.Colloredo-Mansfeld	FW190 prob.dest	Bethune/Aire	1420
			F/S C.A.Joseph	Bf109 destroyed	Bethune/Aire	1420
421 Sqn	Spit	FC	P/O K.R.Linton	FW190 destroyed	W Lille	1450
485 Sqn	Spit	FC	F/L K.C.Lee	FW190 damaged	Near Poix	0940
			F/O J.G.Thompson	FW190 damaged	Near Poix	0940
602 Sqn	Spit	FC	F/L R.A.Sutherland	FW190 prob.dest	Bethune/Aire	1420

19th October 1943

91 Sqn	Spit	FC	F/O D.H.Davy	Bf109 damaged	Veulettes	1120
247 Sqn	Typh	FC	F/O A.S.Aitcheson	FW190 damaged	Off Le Havre	1105±
			F/O J.S.Slaney	- shared -		

20th October 1943

41 Sqn	Spit	FC	F/O P.Cowell	Bf109G destroyed	Near Beaumont-le-Roger	1005
			F/O B.B.Newman	Bf109G destroyed	Near Beaumont-le-Roger	1005

41 Sqn	Spit	FC	F/O R.T.H.Collis	Bf109G destroyed	N Rouen	1015
			F/O B.Fisher	Bf109G destroyed	Evreux	1015
91 Sqn	Spit	FC	F/S R.A.B.Blumer	Bf109 destroyed	Nr Beaumont	1015±
			F/L J.C.S.Doll	Bf109 destroyed	Nr Beaumont	1015±
			S/L N.A.Kynaston	FW190 destroyed	Nr Beaumont	1015±
			F/O R.S.Nash	Bf109 destroyed	Nr Beaumont	1015±
331 Sqn	Spit	FC	Maj A.Austeen	FW190 destroyed	Near St Quentin	1420
			Lt F.S.Fearnley	FW190 destroyed	Near St Quentin	1420
			Lt F.S.Fearnley	FW190 destroyed	Near St Quentin	1420
			Sgt O.Ulstein	FW190 damaged	Near St Quentin	1420
485 Sqn	Spit	FC	F/L P.H.Gaskin	Bf109 damaged	Ostend	0945
WH Wg	Spit	FC	W/C R.H.Harries	Bf109G destroyed	Rouen	1015±
			W/C R.H.Harries	Bf109G destroyed	Rouen	1015±

20/21st October 1943

| 29 Sqn | Mosq | FC | F/O E.Barry | FW190 destroyed | S Beachy Head | 0115 |
| 29 Sqn | Mosq | FC | F/L R.C.Pargeter | Me410 prob.dest | Channel | 0143 |

21st October 1943

| 1 Sqn | Typh | FC | F/S J.D.Fairburn | FW190 destroyed | 15m N St.Aubin | 0815 |
| | | | F/O J.W.Wiley | - shared - | | |

21/22nd October 1943

| 29 Sqn | Mosq | FC | F/O R.A.Crone | FW190 destroyed | Off St Aubin | 0340 |

Combat Report - 20th October 1943

I was flying as Blue 3 in Viceroy Sqdn, when the squadron was attacked by 20 E/A. I broke sharply to port and saw a F.W. 190 diving away on my starboard side. I followed this A/C down and opened fire at about 600 yds. I gave several bursts on the way down and, at about 150 - 200 yds, I gave a long burst of cannon and M.G. closing to 50 yds. The stbd. oleo leg dropped and I saw hits in the engine, which caught fire. The pilot baled out at 500 to 1000 ft and the A/C crashed in a field.
P.Cowell, Flying Officer. 41 Squadron.

The German fighter that Peter Cowell had engaged on 20th October was a Focke Wulf from 3./JG 2, from which Unteroffizier Rudolf Gerdtz baled out wounded. A second FW190 from this unit was attacked and shot down by Squadron Leader N.A.Kynaston of 91 Squadron. Oberfeldwebel Friedich May was killed.

On 21st October 1943, the Bf109G-6s of I/JG 3 arrived in France, led by Majpr Klaus Quaet-Faslem, a Ritterkreuztrager, credited with 48 kills, mainly in Russia. On 24th October his unit scrapped with Spitfires and Marauders and he was shot down and belly-landed his Messerschmitt near Lille, unhurt. It is likely that his opponents were Spitfires from 331 Squadron. (left) Bf109G-6 of JG 3.

22nd October 1943

129 Sqn Spit	FC	F/S E.W.Edwards	Bf109 damaged	Near Arras	1012
		S/L P.V.K.Tripe	Bf109 damaged	Near Arras	1012
		P/O M.F.S.Young	FW190 damaged	Near Arras	1012
222 Sqn Spit	FC	F/L D.F.Lenton	Bf109 destroyed	Amiens	1030±
331 Sqn Spit	FC	Maj A.Austeen	FW190 destroyed	Albert area	1000
		Maj A.Austeen	FW190 destroyed	Albert area	1000
		Lt B.Bjornstad	Bf109 destroyed	Albert area	1000
		Sgt P.P.M.Coucheron	FW190 prob.dest	Albert area	1000
		Capt S.Heglund	FW190 damaged	Albert area	1015
332 Sqn Spit	FC	Sgt J.Helland	FW190 destroyed	Albert Area	1000
400 Sqn Must	AC	F/L H.L.Morham	Do217 destroyed	Near Charleroi	1715
421 Sqn Spit	FC	F/O P.G.Johnson	FW190 damaged	NE Beauvais	1040
		P/O K.R.Linton	FW190 destroyed	NE Beauvais	1040
		F/O A.R.Mackenzie	FW190 destroyed	NE Beauvais	1040
132 Wg Spit	FC	Maj K.Birksted	FW190 destroyed	Albert area	1000

23rd October 1943

66 Sqn Spit	FC	F/L G.C.Elcombe	FW190 destroyed	10m N Ile de Batz	1125
		F/L J.A.Jackson	FW190 destroyed	10m N Ile de Batz	1125

23/24th October 1943

85 Sqn Mosq	FC	F/O J.D.R.Shaw	E/A prob.dest	Near Le Touquet	1950

24th October 1943

306 Sqn Spit	FC	F/O W.Potocki	FW190 damaged	8m SE Montdidier	1200
331 Sqn Spit	FC	Maj A.Austeen	Bf109G destroyed	10m E Abbeville	1210
		Maj A.Austeen	Bf109G damaged	10m E Abbeville	1210
		Maj A.Austeen	FW190 damaged	10m E Abbeville	1210
		Sgt R.Dogger	Bf109G destroyed	10m E Abbeville	1210
		Capt S.Heglund	Bf109 destroyed	10m E Abbeville	1210
		Capt S.Heglund	Bf109 damaged	10m E Abbeville	1210
		2/Lt K.Sandvig	FW190 damaged	10m E Abbeville	1210
		Sgt A.Schojdt	FW190 destroyed	10m E Abbeville	1210
332 Sqn Spit	FC	Lt T.O.Waerner	FW190 destroyed	10m E Abbeville	1210
400 Sqn Must	AC	F/O L.W.Seath	Hs126 destroyed	E Chartres	1130
		F/O L.W.Seath	He111 damaged	4m S Rouen	1130±
		F/O A.T.Carlson	FW190 destroyed	Hesdin-Frevent	1515
		F/O E.Garry	FW190 damaged	Hesdin-Frevent	1515
		F/O I.G.McLeod	- shared -		
		F/O J.P.Roberts	- shared -		
402 Sqn Spit	FC	S/L G.W.Northcott	FW190 destroyed	15m SW Amiens	1215
		P/O R.H.Preble	FW190 damaged	15m SW Amiens	1215
403 Sqn Spit	FC	F/O J.D.Browne	Bf109 destroyed	10m NE Abbeville	1215
		F/O J.D.Browne	Bf109 damaged	10m NE Abbeville	1215
421 Sqn Spit	FC	F/O R.G.Driver	FW190 damaged	10m SW Abbeville	1220
		S/L C.M.Magwood	FW190 damaged	Breilly area	1220
602 Sqn Spit	FC	P/O F.S.Sorge	Bf109 destroyed	Near Noordwijk	1640
		Squadron	Bf109 destroyed	Off Dutch coast	1640

30/31st October 1943

85 Sqn Mosq	FC	F/O R.L.T.Robb	Ju188 destroyed	20m SSE Rye	2015
85 Sqn Mosq	FC	F/O H.B.Thomas	Ju188 destroyed	20m S Shoreham	2040

31st October 1943

414 Sqn Must	AC	F/O R.C.J.Brown	Yale destroyed	Montlhery area	1550
		F/O L.F.May	- shared -		
		F/O L.F.May	Ju88 destroyed	Gournay area	1600
		F/O R.C.J.Brown	- shared -		

Chapter Two

Gathering Strength

The planned 'split-up' of Fighter Command now became a reality when 84 and 85 Groups of Second Tactical Air Force, together with the light and medium bombers of 2 Group and several reconnaissance units, commenced independent operations.This powerful entity comprised three squadrons of Bostons, five of Mitchells and four of Mosquito fighter-bombers; seven squadrons of Typhoons, twenty of Spitfire VBs and IXs with six more arriving during November; two of Hurricane IVs, and nine of Mustang Is. Three of the Spitfire units - Nos 19, 65 and 122 were shortly to have their aircraft replaced by the Mustang III. No nightfighters were included - these would join during 1944.

Another significant event was the creation of No 100 Group Bomber Command, taking six squadrons of nightfighters from Fighter Command to be used in the long-range bomber escort and intruding role. The new force was, in theory, formed on 23rd November, but actually became an entity in December. The planned units were 141, 169 and 239 Squadrons as high-level intruders and 85, 151 and 515 Squadrons as low-level intruders. The high-level squadrons were to 'escort' the bomber stream and, employing *Serrate* detection equipment, would hunt down the German nightfighters by homing in on their radar emissions. The low-level fighters were to patrol known *Luftwaffe* nightfighter bases, attacking the defenders as they took off and landed. The seed had already been sown earlier in the year, when the Beaufighter crews of 141 Squadron, equipped with *Serrate*, had begun to enjoy considerable success. In addition to the above units, Mosquitos of 23 and 515 Squadrons would join 100 Group in mid-1944

1st November 1943

1 Sqn	Typh	FC	P/O R.W.Hornall	Bf109 damaged	Off Grtiz Nez	1355
197 Sqn	Typh	FC	P/O E.O'Callaghan	Ju52 destroyed	Foret l'Evecques	1630±
501 Sqn	Spit	FC	Capt S.Fuchs Sgt J.L.Lilburn	Bf109 damaged - Shared -	S Calais	1340±

1/2nd November 1943

| 29 Sqn | Mosq | FC | F/L S.E.Hodsman | Ju188 destroyed | Combe | 1828 |

The hunter. A Mosquito NF II equipped with the 'Serrate' radar detector. Note the arrow-shaped transmitter in the nose and the receiving aerials in the wings. This equipment was designed to home on the radar transmission from Luftwaffe nightfighters.

Left: A Ju188 of KG 6 being bombed-up. Right: Flight Lieutenant Steve Hodsman of 29 Squadron intercepted one of these bombers on the night of 1st November and shot it down at Combe.

(Ken Lowes via Frank Pringle)

2nd November 1943

4 Sqn	Must	FC	F/O R.D.Browne	FW190 destroyed	Brussels	1300
			F/O G.Wonnacott	- Shared -		
609 Sqn	Typh	FC	P/O G.L.C.F.Jaspis	Bu133 destroyed	15m NE Paris	1100±
			P/O L.W.F.Stark	Ju88 destroyed	15m NE Paris	1100±

2/3rd November 1943

85 Sqn	Mosq	FC	F/L E.R.Hedgcoe	FW190 destroyed	S Canvey Island	1925

3rd November 1943

64 Sqn	Spit	FC	S/L M.G.L.M.Donnet	Bf109G prob.dest	Over Schipol	1600
129 Sqn	Spit	FC	F/O A.Bradshaw	Bf109 destroyed	Near Zandvoort	1556
132 Sqn	Spit	FC	F/O J.J.Burgess	Bf109 damaged	Ijmuiden	1620
			F/S R.B.Pullin	- Shared -		
402 Sqn	Spit	FC	F/L J.D.Mitchner	Bf109 destroyed	Near Ijmuiden	1600
			S/L G.W.Northcott	Bf109 destroyed	Near Ijmuiden	1600
416 Sqn	Spit	FC	F/L R.D.Booth	Bf109 destroyed	O/s Zandvoort	1600
			F/O W.H.Jacobs	Bf109 destroyed	O/s Zandvoort	1600
			F/L D.E.Noonan	Bf109 destroyed	Centre Zandvoort	1600
			F/L D.E.Noonan	Bf109 destroyed	O/s Zandvoort	1600
			F/L A.H.Sager	- Shared -		
			F/L A.H.Sager	Bf109 destroyed	O/s Zandvoort	1600

Flying Officer Russell Steward of 29 Squadron with his RO Flying Officer G.K.Main. On the night of 8th November they engaged an Me410 of 14./KG2 and shot it down into the sea off Beachy Head. Unteroffiziers H.Holzmann and W.Fischer were lost. (K.Lowes, via Frank Pringle)

421 Sqn Spit	FC	F/L A.E.Fleming	Bf109 prob.dest	Near St Andre	1105
		F/L F.J.Sherlock	FW190 destroyed	Near St Andre	1105
		F/L F.J.Sherlock	Bf109 damaged	Near St Andre	1105
		S/L C.M.Magwood	FW190 destroyed	N Fauville	1130
Dig Wg Spit	FC	W/C L.V.Chadburn	Bf109 destroyed	Near Ijmuiden	1600
		W/C L.V.Chadburn	Bf109 destroyed	Near Ijmuiden	1600

3/4th November 1943

157 Sqn Mosq FC	S/L R.F.Robinson	Do217 destroyed	Dusseldorf	2000
605 Sqn Mosq FC	F/O E.L.Williams	E/A damaged*	Venlo	2041
	F/O E.L.Williams	Bf109 damaged*	Venlo	2053

Note: possibly both on on ground

5th November 1943

| 168 Sqn Must FC | F/O J.D.Stubbs | Ju52 damaged | Crepy-en-Valois AD, | 1210± |

5/6th November 1943

| 410 Sqn Mosq FC | F/O C.F.Green | Me410 destroyed | 15m off Dungeness | 2104 |

6th November 1943

| 2 Sqn Must FC | F/O R.C.Cooper | Bf109 destroyed | 10m SW Douai | 1418 |
| | F/L C.E.Maitland | - Shared - | | |

6/7th November 1943

| 68 Sqn Beau FC | W/C D.Hayley-Bell | Me410 destroyed | 6m N Happisburgh | 0000± |
| 85 Sqn Mosq FC | S/L J.Selway | FW190 destroyed | S Hastings | 2355 |

8/9th November 1943

29 Sqn	Mosq	FC	F/O R.Steward	Me410 destroyed	S Beachy Head	2215
85 Sqn	Mosq	FC	S/L W.H.Maguire	Me410 destroyed	Eastbourne	2243
488 Sqn	Mosq	FC	F/O G.R.Reed	Me410 destroyed	15m N Manston	0000

9th November 1943

605 Sqn	Mosq	FC	S/L D.H.Blomeley	Bf110 destroyed	25m SW Aalborg	1359

11th November 1943

19 Sqn	Spit	FC	F/L T.H.Drinkwater	FW190 destroyed	Near St Pol	1300
122 Sqn	Spit	FC	Capt T.Jonsson	FW190 destroyed	Near St Pol	1300
231 Sqn	Must	FC	F/L A.E.Lee F/O F.G.Walsh	Do217 destroyed - Shared -	S Flers	1535±
400 Sqn	Must	FC	F/L H.L.Morham	Me210 damaged	Arras-Albert	1530
			F/L H.L.Morham F/O J.M.Robb	Me210 destroyed - Shared -	N Albert	1530
			F/L H.L.Morham F/O J.M.Robb	Me210 prob.dest - Shared -	Arras-Albert	1530

18/19th November 1943

FIU	Mosq	FC	W/C R.A.Chisholm	Bf110 destroyed	Mannheim	2130±

Combat Report - 11th November 1943

I was leading White section of 19 Sqdn., flying east at 17,000 feet near St. Pol, when I saw 190's and 109's mixing it with 122 Squadron. On flying nearer the scrapping I spotted one F.W. 190 break away, and dive rapidly west. I turned and using full boost and revs chased him down from 17,000 ft. and got in a couple of bursts from dead astern. The 190 pulled out at about 2,000 ft. and I turned to starboard with him and got in several deflection bursts at angle off of 10 degrees at a range of about 150 to 200 yards. I saw cannon strikes, but can't say what part of the e/a I hit as my windscreen fogged up. I had to pull over and cross on top of the 190 to avoid collision. We were then at less than 1,000 ft. I pulled up to about 3,000 ft., and looking down saw the 190 hit the ground and burst into flames. Visibility was poor and there was 5/10th's broken cloud.

T.H.Drinkwater, Flight Lieutenant. 19 Squadron.

Flight Lieutenant Tommy Drinkwater of 19 Squadron claimed an FW190 destroyed on 11th November as his sole confirmed kill. He would fall in combat on 18th May when leading the Squadron. (D.Sarkar)

On 11th November a pair of Tac/R Mustang pilots found several Me210 fighters - arguably the worst aircraft ever produced by Germany in WW2 - near Albert. Flight Lieutenant H.L.Morham of 400 Squadron (left) shared one destroyed and another probably so with Flying Officer J.M.Robb and then claimed a third damaged.

19th November 1943

129 Sqn	Spit	2TAF	F/O A.Bradshaw	FW190 destroyed	20m S Tricqueville	1430
			F/L A.J.Hancock DFC	Bf109 damaged	20m S Tricqueville	1430
332 Sqn	Spit	2TAF	Capt B.Raeder	Bf109G prob.dest	St Claire-Lisieux	1420
			Sgt J.Rosland	- Shared -		

20th November 1943

157 Sqn	Mosq	ADGB	F/O J.L.Clifton	Ju88 damaged	Biscay	1400±
			F/L G.O.L.Dyke	Ju88 prob.dest	N Cap Ortegal	1400±
			F/L G.O.L.Dyke	Ju88 damaged	N Cap Ortegal	1400±
			W/C J.A.Mackie	Ju290 destroyed	40m NW Esparto Pt	1400±
			W/C J.A.Mackie	Ju88 damaged	40m NW Esparto Pt	1400±
610 Sqn	Spit	ADGB	F/S W.P.Furler	FW190 damaged	Off Guernsey	1630±
			F/L P.J.Pound	FW190 damaged	Off Guernsey	1630±

20/21st November 1943

29 Sqn	Mosq	ADGB	F/L R.C.Pargeter	FW190 destroyed	Horsham	2049
151 Sqn	Mosq	ADGB	F/S J.Playford	Me410 destroyed	40m S Worthing	2028
			F/S J.Playford	FW190 prob.dest	40m S Worthing	2050

22nd November 1943

307 Sqn	Mosq	ADGB	F/S K.Jaworski	He177 destroyed	50m SW Egero, Shetlands	1239

23rd November 1943

64 Sqn	Spit	2TAF	F/L J.A.Plagis	FW190 destroyed	W Den Helder	1455
170 Sqn	Must	2TAF	S/L E.Cassidy	Bf109 destroyed	10m NW Den Helder	1455
			F/O B.C.Kelly	- Shared -		
			Sgt J.N.Thorne	- Shared -		

24th November 1943

170 Sqn	Must	2TAF	F/L R.F.C.Garvey	FW190 damaged	Near Doullens	1230±

25th November 1943

122 Sqn	Spit	2TAF	P/O J.L.Gilbert	Bf109 damaged	N Bethune	1600
332 Sqn	Spit	ADGB	2/Lt O.G.Aanjesen	Bf109G destroyed	10-15m SE Lille	1555

25/26th November 1943

488 Sqn	Mosq	ADGB	F/O P.F.L.Hall	Me410 destroyed	Off Calais	0315

26th November 1943

131 Sqn	Spit	ADGB	F/L R.W.F.Sampson	FW190 damaged	Barfleur	1035±
165 Sqn	Spit	ADGB	Lt A.H.Beane	FW190 prob.dest	Barfleur	1030
			Lt G.R.Gouby	FW190 destroyed	Barfleur	1030
			Lt G.R.Gouby	FW190 damaged	Barfleur	1030
			P/O M.Lorand	FW190 destroyed	Barfleur	1030
			P/O J.Quinn	FW190 prob.dest	Barfleur	1030
			P/O J.Quinn	FW190 damaged	Barfleur	1030
			P/O J.Quinn	FW190 damaged	Barfleur	1030
			P/O T.A.Vance	FW190 prob.dest	Barfleur	1030
			P/O T.A.Vance	FW190 damaged	Barfleur	1030
			P/O T.A.Vance	FW190 damaged	Barfleur	1030
307 Sqn	Mosq	ADGB	F/O A.Suskiewicz	Ju88 destroyed	190m N Shetlands	1300±
331 Sqn	Spit	ADGB	Sgt C.J.Stousland	Bf109F destroyed	S Bresles, nr Beauvais	1107
401 Sqn	Spit	2TAF	F/L J.E.Sheppard	FW190 destroyed	Achiet A/D-Albert	1215
416 Sqn	Spit	ADGB	F/L A.H.Sager	FW190 destroyed	Grevillers	1220

29th November 1943

129 Sqn	Spit	ADGB	F/O D.F.Ruchwaldy	FW190 damaged	S Chievres	0945
			F/O D.F.Ruchwaldy	FW190 destroyed	10m E Furnes	0954
			F/O D.F.Ruchwaldy	Bf109F destroyed	E Coxyde	1010
306 Sqn	Spit	2TAF	F/O W.Szajda	FW190 destroyed	Ath	0950
401 Sqn	Spit	2TAF	F/O L.M.Cameron	FW190 destroyed	Chievres A/D	1000
			F/O W.R.Tew	FW190 damaged	Chievres A/D	1000

On 23rd November a Coastal Command Beaufighter strike was sent to the area north of Texel. Three Beaufighters were lost to II./JG3, two credited to Leutnant Franz Ruhl (right). 170 Squadron Mustang pilots engaged the Luftwaffe and shot Ruhl down. He baled out safely. Ruhl would survive until December 1944, when he was lost to USAAF fighters. Two days later JG 3 pilots were engaged by Spitfires, losing two of 3 Staffel, one to 2nd Lieutenant O.G.Aanjesen of 332 Squadron. (right).

411 Sqn	Spit	2TAF	F/L D.R.Matheson	FW190 destroyed	SE Ostend	1000
412 Sqn	Spit	2TAF	F/L A.C.Coles	FW190 damaged	Chievres A/D	1000

30th November 1943

198 Sqn	Typh	ADGB	F/O C.R.Abbott	FW190 destroyed	Deelen	1300
			S/L J.M.Bryan	FW190 destroyed	Deelen	1300
			F/L V.C.Fittall	FW190 destroyed	Deelen	1300
			F/O J.A.Macdonald	FW190 damaged	Deelen	1300
			F/L V.Smith	Ju188 destroyed	Deelen	1300
			F/O J.F.Williams	FW190 destroyed	Deelen	1300
609 Sqn	Typh	ADGB	F/L R.Van Lierde	Bf110 destroyed	Hasselt	1315±

1st December 1943

129 Sqn	Spit	ADGB	F/O D.C.Byrne	FW190 damaged	S Ypres	1315
157 Sqn	Mosq	ADGB	F/L G.O.L.Dyke	Ju88 destroyed	230m W Lorient	1155
			F/L G.O.L.Dyke	Ju88 destroyed	230m W Lorient	1155
			F/O B.M.Whitlock	Ju88 destroyed	230m W Lorient	1155
193 Sqn	Typh	ADGB	F/O J.A.Pressland	Ju88 destroyed	Cap Chevre	1315±
			266 Squadron	- Shared -		
198 Sqn	Typh	ADGB	S/L J.R.Baldwin	FW190 destroyed	Harskamp, Arnhem	1300
			F/S J.Stanley	FW190 prob.dest	Near Arnhem	1300
266 Sqn	Typh	ADGB	F/O S.J.P.Blackwell	Ju52 destroyed	NW Ile de Croix	1315±
			F/L J.H.Deall	Ju88 destroyed	Cap Chevre	1315±
			F/O J.D.Miller	- Shared -		
			193 Squadron	- Shared -		
			F/O S.J.P.Blackwell	Ju88 destroyed	Ile de Croix	1315±
			F/S I.O.Hulley	- Shared -		
			S/L P.W.LeFevre	- Shared -		
			F/O W.V.Mollett	- Shared -		

411 Sqn	Spit	2TAF	F/L D.R.Matheson	FW190 destroyed	Croisilies	0950
			F/O S.A.Mills	FW190 destroyed	Croisilies	0950
412 Sqn	Spit	2TAF	S/L G.C.Keefer	FW190 prob.dest	S Knocke	1330
609 Sqn	Typh	ADGB	F/S G.K.E.Martin	Bf109 destroyed	Brussels	1315±

2nd December 1943

181 Sqn	Typh	2TAF	F/S K.C.Hanna	Do217 damaged	Near Brighton	1100±
453 Sqn	Spit	ADGB	F/L E.A.R.Esau	Ju88 destroyed	35m SSE Sumburgh	1450
			F/O L.McAuliffe	- Shared -		

4th December 1943

198 Sqn	Typh	ADGB	P/O C.R.Abbott	Do217 destroyed	Over Eindhoven	1500
			F/L V.Fittall	- Shared -		
			F/O K.F.C.Bowman	Do217 destroyed	Over Eindhoven	1500
			F/O J.F.H.Williams	- Shared -		
			F/O H.Freeman	Do217 destroyed	Over Eindhoven	1500
			F/O J.MacDonald	- Shared -		
			S/L J.R.Baldwin	Do217 destroyed	Over Eindhoven	1500
609 Sqn	Typh	ADGB	P/O C.F.J.Detal	Do217 destroyed	Eindhoven	1500
			P/O C.F.J.Detal	Do217 destroyed	Eindhoven	1500
			F/O A.S.Geerts	Do217 destroyed	Eindhoven	1500
			Sgt L.L.Henrion	Do217 destroyed	Over Eindhoven	1500
			F/O A.S.Ross	- Shared -		
			F/O A.S.Ross	Do217 destroyed	Eindhoven	1500
			S/L P.G.Thornton -Brown	Do217 destroyed	Over Eindhoven	1500
			F/O A.S.Ross	- Shared -		
			S/L P.G.Thornton -Brown	Do217 destroyed	Eindhoven	1500

9th December 1943

307 Sqn	Mosq	ADGB	F/O J.Pacholczyk	Ju88 destroyed	40m NNW Herma Ness Shetland	0850

10/11th December 1943

68 Sqn	Beau	ADGB	W/C D.Hayley-Bell	Do217 damaged	20m N Bradwell Bay	2025±
			W/C D.Hayley-Bell	Do217 damaged	20m N Bradwell Bay	2025±
410 Sqn	Mosq	ADGB	F/O R.D.Schultz	Do217 destroyed	Clacton-Dunkirk	1910
			F/O R.D.Schultz	Do217 destroyed	Clacton-Dunkirk	1925
			F/O R.D.Schultz	Do217 destroyed	Clacton-Dunkirk	1925
			F/O D.M.Norman	Do217 damaged	N Chelmsford	1940

Flying Officer R.D.Schultz with his navigator Flying Officer V.A.Williams of 410 Squadron (left) scored a notable success on the night of 10th December 1943 by shooting down three Do217s of KG 2 off the south coast of England within a space of fifteen minutes. (right) 132 Squadron being reviewed at Detling on 15th December.

12th December 1943

418 Sqn	Mosq	ADGB	F/L R.A.Kipp F/O J.R.F.Johnson	He111 destroyed - Shared -	S Bourges/Avord A/D	1555
			F/L R.A.Kipp F/O J.R.FJohnson	He111 prob.dest - Shared -	S Bourges/Avord A/D	1600

13th December 1943

411 Sqn	Spit	2TAF	F/L J.D.F.McFarlane P/O C.M.Steele F/O R.F.M.Walker P/O T.R.Wheler	Bf109 damaged - Shared - - Shared - - Shared -	Schipol A/D	1445
			F/L J.D.F.McFarlane P/O C.M.Steele F/O R.F.M.Walker P/O T.R.Wheler	Bf109 damaged - Shared - - Shared - - Shared -	Schipol A/D	1445

16/17th December 1943

141 Sqn	Mosq	BC	F/O F.F.Lambert	Bf110 damaged	Near Hoya A/D	1945

19/20th December 1943

488 Sqn	Mosq	ADGB	P/O D.N.Robinson	Me410 destroyed	Near Rye	0240

20th December 1943

331 Sqn	Spit	2TAF	Lt F.S.Fearnley	FW190 destroyed	Cambrai	1113
332 Sqn	Spit	2TAF	Lt O.Tidemand -Johansen	FW190 destroyed	Cambrai	1113
401 Sqn	Spit	2TAF	F/L L.M.Cameron	Ju88 destroyed	Brussels	1110
403 Sqn	Spit	2TAF	F/O R.T.Pentland	Fw190 damaged	Merville-Douai	1100

411 Sqn	Spit	2TAF	P/O J.Dunn	Do217 destroyed	Brussels city centre	1105
			F/O D.J.Givens	- Shared -		
421 Sqn	Spit	2TAF	P/O T.J.De Courcey	FW190 destroyed	Merville-Douai	1100
			F/L E.L.Gimbel	FW190 destroyed	Merville-Douai	1100
			S/L J.F.Lambert	Bf109 destroyed	Merville-Douai	1100
			F/L K.R.Linton	Bf109 destroyed	Merville-Douai	1100
			F/L K.R.Linton	FW190 damaged	Merville-Douai	1100
			F/L K.R.Linton	FW190 damaged	Merville-Douai	1100
			F/O A.R.Mackenzie	FW190 destroyed	Merville-Douai	1100
			F/O A.R.Mackenzie	FW190 destroyed	Merville-Douai	1100
			F/O A.R.Mackenzie	Bf109 prob.dest	Merville-Douai	1100
132 Wg	Spit	2TAF	Col K.Birksted	FW190 destroyed	Cambrai	1113

20/21st December 1943

418 Sqn	Mosq	ADGB	P/O J.T.Caine	E/A destroyed	Delme A/D, Metz	2140
			F/O H.E.Jones	Bf110 destroyed	Ansbach A/D	2110
			F/O R.H.Lee	E/A damaged	Boblingen A/D	2130±
605 Sqn	Mosq	ADGB	F/L M.Negus	E/A damaged	Handorf	2230

21st December 1943

132 Sqn	Spit	2TAF	F/L A.E.Tomblin	FW190 destroyed	Near Cambrai	1145
			F/L H.E.Walmsley	FW190 damaged	Near Cambrai	1145
			P/O J.H.Williams	FW190 damaged	Near Cambrai	1145
350 Sqn	Spit	ADGB	F/O A.Herreman	FW190 destroyed	5m SSW Boulogne	1010
403 Sqn	Spit	2TAF	F/O J.D.Hodgson	Ju87 destroyed	Peronne A/D	1155
			P/O W.J.Myers	- Shared -		
602 Sqn	Spit	2TAF	Capt P.G.J.Aubertin	FW190 prob.dest	Near Cambrai	1145
			S/L R.A.Sutherland	FW190 destroyed	Near Cambrai	1145

22nd December 1943

85 Sqn	Mosq	FC	F/L C.G.Houghton	Me410 prob.dest	Off Orfordness	2350
418 Sqn	Mosq	ADGB	F/L D.A.MacFadyen	E/A prob.dest	Orleans A/D	1915
605 Sqn	Mosq	FC	F/L C.E.Knowles	Do217 destroyed	Wunstorf	2208
			F/O A.G.Woods	E/A destroyed	Ardorf	2200
			F/O A.G.Woods	E/A damaged	Ardorf	2208
			S/L T.A.Heath	Ju88 destroyed	Wunstorf	2300

23rd December 1943

141 Sqn	Beau	BC	F/L H.C.Kelsey	Ju88 destroyed	nr Duren	0238
605 Sqn	Mosq	ADGB	F/L A.D.Wagner	E/A destroyed	Fassberg AD	0522

On 20th December 421 Squadron Spitfire pilots fought FW190s and Bf109s, Flight Lieutenant K.R.Linton (left) claiming a '109 shot down and two '190s damaged, while Andy Mackenzie (left in centre picture) claimed two Focke Wulfs destroyed and a '109 probably so. Next day Squadron Leader Pat Thornton-Brown (right), leading 609 Squadron, was one of two Typhoon pilots shot down by USAAF P-47 pilots. He was killed, possibly shot in his parachute by German troops. The Typhoon depicted shows the recognition stripes painted on to avoid this kind of event, but the Thunderbolt pilots never seemed to learn. In 1945 Hugh Fraser of 439 Squadron wrote in his logbook. "T-bolts as stupid as ever. One day I'm gonna blast 'em!"

25th December 1943

157 Sqn	Mosq	ADGB	S/L H.E.Tappin	He177 destroyed	250m SW Brest	1803
183 Sqn	Typh	ADGB	S/L W.Dring	FW200 destroyed	Kerlin Bastard	1500
			F/L R.Hartley	- Shared -		
			F/OC.N.Walley	- Shared -		

28th December 1943

350 Sqn	Spit	2TAF	F/O P.A.J.DSiroux	FW190 destroyed	Gueschart	1605

30th December 1943

266 Sqn	Typh	ADGB	F/O N.J.Lucas	Ju52 destroyed	W Ile de Croix	1430
			F/O W.V.Mollett	- Shared -		
341 Sqn	Spit	ADGB	S/Lt R.Borne	FW190 prob.dest	NW Ushant	1500
			Capt L.C.Martell	FW190 damaged	NW Ushant	1500
			Capt L.C.Martell	FW190 damaged	NW Ushant	1500
403 Sqn	Spit	2TAF	F/O H.R.Finley	Bf109 destroyed	W Albert	1340
			P/O C.Weaver III	Bf109 destroyed	SE Albert	1340

The Luftwaffe gave Squadron Leader Walter Dring (above) and his boys a present on Christmas day on a sweep to Kerlin Bastard airfield, western France. Here they claimed an FW200 destroyed, which actually appears to have been an He177 of II./KG 40. Oberfeldwebel Hans Behr and his crew died when their huge aircraft was shot down on take-off by the Typhoon pilots. (ww2images.com)

412 Sqn Spit	2TAF	F/L G.F.Beurling	Bf109 destroyed	7m W Compeigne	1335
		F/O W.H.Bliss	Bf109 damaged	7m W Compeigne	1335
		F/O D.C.Laubman	Bf109 damaged	Compeigne area	1335

31st December 1943

165 Sqn Spit	ADGB	S/L H.A.S.Johnston	FW190 destroyed	St Brieuc	1510
		P/O T.A.Vance	FW190 destroyed	St Brieuc	1510
		P/O T.A.Vance	FW190 destroyed	St Brieuc	1510
		F/O D.Warren	Bf109 destroyed	St Brieuc	1510
257 Sqn Typh	ADGB	F/O M.H.Yi	FW190 damaged	St Brieuc	1510

2nd January 1944

198 Sqn Typh	ADGB	S/L J.R.Baldwin	FW190 destroyed	W Paris	1515±
		F/L R.Dall	Bü131	Paris	1515
		F/L J.Scambler	- Shared -		
		F/L R.Dall	Bü131 damaged	near Paris	1515
		F/L J.Niblett	Me210 destroyed	St Quentin	1515
		F/O P.D.L.Roper	- Shared -		
609 Sqn Typh	ADGB	F/O L.E.J.M.Geerts	FW190 destroyed	40m W Charleville	1245±

An American, Claude Weaver III (left) had previously flown over Malta before joining 403 Squadron in England. He claimed his eleventh kill on 30th December, but was killed in action on 28th January with twelve confirmed victories credited. On 30th December Spitfire pilots from 412 Squadron fought Bf109s of II./JG 2 near Compeigne. The legendary George Beurling (right) claimed his 31st - and last - confirmed kill.

2/3rd January 1944

85 Sqn	Mosq	ADGB	W/C J.Cunningham	Me410 destroyed	Le Touquet	2359
96 Sqn	Mosq	ADGB	F/L N.S.Head	FW190 destroyed	Rye	2355
488 Sqn	Mosq	ADGB	F/O R.D.Bergemann	Me410 destroyed	15m S Dover	2359

3rd January 1944

198 Sqn	Typh	ADGB	F/O R.Armstrong	Bf109 damaged	Compeigne	1225±
			F/L R.Curtis	Bf109 destroyed	Compeigne	1225±
			F/L J.Dall	Bf109 damaged	Compeigne	1225±
609 Sqn	Typh	ADGB	F/O C.F.J.Detal	FW190 destroyed	Cambrai-Epinoy A/D	1340

4th January 1944

122 Sqn	Spit	2TAF	P/O E.A.Roemmele	FW190 prob.dest	SW Abbeville	1605
			F/O D.R.Stephens	FW190 prob.dest	SW Abbeville	1605
198 Sqn	Typh	ADGB	Sgt J.S.Fraser -Petthebridge	Do217 destroyed	Gilze-Rijn	1545±
411 Sqn	Spit	2TAF	F/L R.W.Orr	Bf109 damaged	W Rouen	1600±
609 Sqn	Typh	ADGB	F/L I.J.Davies	Do217 destroyed	Gilze-Rijn	1545±
			F/O C.F.J.Detal	Do217 destroyed	Gilze-Rijn	1545±
			F/O L.E.J.M.Geerts P/O L.W.F.Stark	Do217 destroyed - Shared -	Gilze-Rijn	1545±
			F/O W.F.Watts	Do217 destroyed	Gilze-Rijn	1545±

4/5th January 1944

85 Sqn	Mosq	ADGB	F/L E.R.Hedgecoe	Ju88 destroyed	off Le Treport	0258
96 Sqn	Mosq	ADGB	W/C E.D.Crew	Me410 damaged	off Beachy Head	0200±
			W/C E.D.Crew	Me410 destroyed	off Beachy Head	0204

5th January 1944

| 302 Sqn | Spit | ADGB | W/O S.Wojcik | FW190 damaged | SE Flers | 1230 |

6th January 1944

19 Sqn	Spit	2TAF	F/S R.A.Hutchinson	FW190 destroyed	8m NW Rouen	1210
			F/S R.A.Hutchinson	FW190 damaged	8m NW Rouen	1210
			F/S R.A.Hutchinson	FW190 damaged	8m NW Rouen	1210
122 Sqn	Spit	2TAF	F/O D.R.Stevens	FW190 damaged	8m NW Rouen	1210
			F/S J.Crossland	Bf109 damaged	Rouen area	1230±
401 Sqn	Spit	2TAF	F/O H.K.Hamilton	FW190 destroyed	Pavilly, E Rouen	1230
411 Sqn	Spit	2TAF	F/L R.W.Orr	FW190 destroyed	Pointe d'Ailly-E Rouen	1230

7th January 1944

19 Sqn	Spit	2TAF	F/L T.H.Drinkwater	FW190 damaged	St Pol area	1330
91 Sqn	Spit	ADGB	Lt J.Andrieux	FW190 destroyed	Montreuil	1545±
132 Sqn	Spit	2TAF	F/L H.E.Walmsley	FW190 destroyed	E Abbeville	1340
157 Sqn	Mosq	ADGB	F/O P.E.Huckin	Ju88 destroyed	SW Brest	1700±
602 Sqn	Spit	2TAF	P/O P.H.Clostermann	FW190 damaged	E Abbeville	1350
125 Wg	Spit	2TAF	W/C R.D.Yule	FW190 destroyed	Cambrai-Albert area	1325

8th January 1944

157 Sqn	Mosq	ADGB	S/L J.H.M.Chisholm F/O B.M.Whitlock	Ju88 damaged - Shared -	SW Brest	1620
174 Sqn	Typh	2TAF	F/L F.A.Grantham F/S G.J.Steel	Ju88 prob.dest - Shared -	Villaroche	1405
245 Sqn	Typh	2TAF	P/O K.J.A.Dickie 121 Wing	LeO451 destroyed - Shared -	Soissons	1400
121 Wg	Typh	2TAF	W/C R.T.P.Davidson 245 Squadron	LeO451 destroyed - Shared -	Soissons	1400

10th January 1944

| 609 Sqn | Typh | ADGB | P/O G.L.C.F.Jaspis | Ju88 destroyed | Brussels/Melsbroek | 1540± |

10/11th January 1944

| 605 Sqn | Mosq | ADGB | W/C B.R.O'B.Hoare | Ju188 destroyed | 4m E Chievres | 0334 |

Pilot Officer L.W.F. 'Pinky' Stark shared one of the Do217s destroyed at Gilze-Rijn on 4th January with Flying Officer L.E.J.M.Geerts. He would end the war with five confirmed kills, all with the Typhoon.

13th January 1944

198 Sqn	Typh	ADGB	S/L J.R.Baldwin	Goeland dest'd	15m S Poix	1520±
			W/OJ.Allen	Ar96 destroyed	Near St.Cyr en Arthies	1520
			F/L R.Dall	- Shared -		
			F/O J.MacDonald	- Shared -		
			F/O G.Plamonden	- Shared -		
			S/L J.M.Bryan	Goeland dest'd	Poix	1520±
			S/L J.M.Bryan	Bf109 destroyed	Near Rosieres	1520±
			F/O H.Freeman	- Shared -		
			F/L R.Dall	Ju88 destroyed	4m W St.Leger	1520±
			F/O J.MacDonald	Ju88 destroyed	N La Roche Guyon	1520±
			F/L J.Niblett	Bf109 destroyed	Near Rosieres	1520±
			F/O G.Plamonden	Ju88 destroyed	3m E Septeuil	1520±

14th January 1944

132 Sqn	Spit	2TAF	F/O H.S.Smith	FW190 destroyed	10m E Le Touquet	1150
308 Sqn	Spit	2TAF	F/S W.Korwel	FW190 damaged	10m SE St Omer	1200
602 Sqn	Spit	2TAF	F/L K.L.Charney	Bf109 destroyed	Boulogne-Hesdin-St Pol	1200
			P/OB.J.Dumbrell	Bf109 prob.dest	Boulogne-Hesdin-St Pol	1210
			F/S J.J.Remlinger	Bf109 damaged	Boulogne-Hesdin-St Pol	1200
125 Wg	Spit	2TAF	W/C R.D.Yule	Bf109 damaged	Abbeville area	1155
146 Wg	Typh	ADGB	W/C D.E.Gillam	FW190 damaged	Bretigny	1150±

14/15th January 1944

418 Sqn	Mosq	ADGB	F/L R.A.Kipp	Me210 damaged	Munster A/D	2120

15th January 1944

132 Sqn	Spit	2TAF	F/O J.J.Caulton	FW190 damaged	Near St Omer	1530±

15/16th January 1944

96 Sqn   Mosq   ADGB   S/L A.Parker-Rees   FW190 destroyed   Dungeness   2010±

16/17th January 1944

68 Sqn   Beau   ADGB   F/L D.E.Hickin   Ju88 destroyed   60m E Peterhead   0518

19th January 1944

307 Sqn   Mosq   ADGB   F/L R.Zwolinski   JuW34 destroyed   Stavanger   1130±

21st January 1944

193 Sqn   Typh   ADGB   F/L G.E.Cassie   Bf109 destroyed   Lannion A/D   1600±
                        F/O J.A.Inglis   - Shared -
266 Sqn   Typh   ADGB   S/L P.W.Lefevre   Bf109 destroyed   Lannion A/D   1600±
306 Sqn   Spit   2TAF   F/L ZDrybanski   Me210 destroyed   Hucqueliers   1230
403 Sqn   Spit   2TAF   F/LJ.D.Browne   FW190 damaged   Arras-Lens   1240
                        F/O H.R.Finley   FW190 destroyed   SW Lens   1240
                        F/O C.Weaver III   FW190 destroyed   ½m W Lens   1240
122 Wg   Spit   2TAF   W/C R.J.C.Grant   Me210 destroyed   St Pol   1305
                        122 Squadron*   - Shared -
Note: No individual pilot credits

21/22nd January 1944

29 Sqn   Mosq   ADGB   F/L A.C.Musgrove   FW190 damaged   Channel S Ford   2145
                       F/O B.C.Jarvis   FW190 destroyed   S Beachy Head   2200±
85 Sqn   Mosq   ADGB   F/LD.Dixon   Ju88 destroyed   15m S Dungeness   2210
                       F/O C.K.Nowell   He177 destroyed   6m SE Hastings   0429
96 Sqn   Mosq   ADGB   S/Lt J.A.Lawley
                         -Wakelin   Ju88 destroyed   Paddock Wood   0432
151 Sqn   Mosq   ADGB   W/O H.K.Kemp   He177 destroyed   Hindhead   2131
418 Sqn   Mosq   ADGB   Lt J.F.Luma (US)   Me210 destroyed   20m SW Wunstorf A/D 0017
488 Sqn   Mosq   ADGB   F/L J.A.S.Hall   Do217 destroyed   S Dungeness   2130
                        F/L J.A.S.Hall   Ju88 destroyed   NW Lympne   2145

22nd January 1944

268 Sqn   Must   2TAF   F/L A.Brees   FW190 prob.dest   Queox   1500±

On 24th January, Flying Officer W.G.Eagle, a Typhoon pilot from 198 Squadron, claimed to have engaged and destroyed three Bf109s over the North Sea to the north of Ameland. Presumably his victories were credited on camera gun evidence, but no trace of his opponents has yet been discovered. (ww2images.com)

23rd January 1944

266 Sqn	Typh	ADGB	F/L J.H.Deall	FW190 destroyed	2m SE Gael A/D	1516
			P/O G.M.R.Eastwood	- Shared -		
			S/L P.W.Lefevre	- Shared -		
			F/L A.V.Sanders	- Shared -		
306 Sqn	Spit	2TAF	F/O S.Tronczynski	FW190 destroyed	Gravelines	1540
331 Sqn	Spit	2TAF	2/Lt R.Dogger	FW190 destroyed	Breteuil	1545
332 Sqn	Spit	2TAF	Maj W.Christie	FW190 destroyed	Breteuil	1545
			Sgt N.Riung	- Shared -		
132 Wg	Spit	2TAF	Lt Col K.Birksted	FW190 destroyed	Breteuil	1545

24th January 1944

198 Sqn	Typh	ADGB	F/O W.G.Eagle	Bf109 destroyed	30m N Ameland	1115
			F/O W.G.Eagle	Bf109 destroyed	30m N Ameland	1115
			F/O W.G.Eagle	Bf109 destroyed	30m N Ameland	1115

27th January 1944

418 Sqn	Mosq	ADGB	W/C D.C.S.MacDonald	He111 destroyed	Bourges A/D	1625
			W/C D.C.S.MacDonald	He177 destroyed	E Avord A/D	1632
			F/L C.C.Scherf	FW200 destroyed	SE Avord A/D	1630
			F/O J.T.Caine	JuW34 destroyed	10m SE Bourges	1632
			F/L J.R.F.Johnson	- Shared -		
			F/L J.R.F.Johnson	Ju86 damaged	Clermont-Ferrand A/D	1654
			F/L J.R.F.Johnson	Ju88 destroyed	Clermont-Ferrand A/D	1656
			F/O J.T.Caine	Ju88 destroyed	4-5m from Clermont	1700
			F/LJ.R.F.Johnson	JuW34 destroyed	Clermont-Frerrand A/D	1703
			F/O J.T.Caine	- Shared -		
609 Sqn	Typh	ADGB	F/O C.F.J.Detal	Bf110 destroyed	Evere A/D	1640±
			F/O C.F.J.Detal	Bf109 destroyed	Brussels	1640±
			P/O L.W.FStark	Goeland dest'd	SSE Brussels	1640±

28th January 1944

403 Sqn	Spit	2TAF	F/O L.Foster	FW190 damaged	NE Amiens		1550
414 Sqn	Must	2TAF	F/OR.O.Brown	Ar96 destroyed	5m E Chartres		1235
			F/L G.Wonnacott	Ar96 destroyed	5m E Chartres		1235
			F/L G.W.Burroughs	- Shared -			
			F/L G.W.Burroughs	Bf109G destroyed	NE Chartres		1240
			F/L G.Wonnacott	Bf109E destroyed	NE Chartres		1240

28/29th January 1944

96 Sqn	Mosq	ADGB	S/L A.Parker-Rees	Me410 prob.dest	Ramsgate	2220±
141 Sqn	Mosq	BC	F/O H.E.White	Bf109 destroyed	40m W Berlin	0342
239 Sqn	Mosq	BC	F/O N. Munro	Bf110 destroyed	Near Briest	0300±

29th January 1944

247 Sqn	Typh	2TAF	F/O A.S.Aitcheson	FW200 destroyed	5m SE Chateaudun AD	1345
			P/O R.S.Colquhoun	- Shared -		
			F/O K.B.Sellick	- Shared -		
			124 Wing	- Shared -		
257 Sqn	Typh	ADGB	F/O J.N.P.Arkle	Bü131 destroyed	Paris	1500±
			F/O J.N.P.Arkle	Do217 destroyed	Fecamp	1500±
			F/O T.Clift	- Shared -		
			F/O D.A.Porter	- Shared -		
			W/O J.Wood	- Shared -		
			W/O J.Wood	Bü131 destroyed	Paris	1500±
124 Wg	Typh	2TAF	W/C E.Haabjoern	FW200 destroyed	5m SE Chateaudun AD	1345
			247 Squadron	- Shared -		

29/30th January 1944

68 Sqn	Beau	ADGB	F/S L.W.Neal	Ju188 destroyed	near Ipswich	2040
96 Sqn	Mosq	ADGB	F/O S.A.Hibbert	Ju88 prob.dest	near Biddenham	2115
410 Sqn	Mosq	ADGB	Lt R.P.Cross (RNVR)	Ju88 destroyed	Hadleigh -Needham Market	2044

30th January 1944

198 Sqn	Typh	ADGB	S/L J.R.Baldwin	FW190 destroyed	Rouen-La Roche	1300±
			S/L J.R.Baldwin	FW190 destroyed	Rouen-La Roche	1300±
			F/S R.C.A.Crouch	FW190 destroyed	Rouen-La Roche	1300±
			F/S R.C.A.Crouch	FW190 prob.dest	Rouen-La Roche	1300±
			F/L R.Dall	FW190 damaged	Rouen-La Roche	1300±

Squadron Leader RA Newbury of 610 Squadron leads a section of new Spitfire XIVs. There would be no combat successes until March however, but the 'XIV' was to give the Spitfire a new - and deadly - lease of life.

198 Sqn	Typh	ADGB	F/L R.Dall	FW190 damaged	Rouen-La Roche	1300±
			F/L J.Niblett	FW190 destroyed	Rouen-La Roche	1300±
			F/L J.Niblett	FW190 destroyed	Rouen-La Roche	1300±
			W/O J.Stanley	FW190 destroyed	Rouen-La Roche	1300±
			W/O J.Stanley	FW190 destroyed	Rouen-La Roche	1300±
			F/O J.F.Williams	FW190 destroyed	Rouen-La Roche	1300±
			F/O J.F.Williams	FW190 destroyed	Rouen-La Roche	1300±
609 Sqn	Typh	ADGB	F/O C.J.G.Demoulin	FW190 destroyed	Givors/Roye	1310±
			F/O C.J.G.Demoulin	FW190 destroyed	Givors/Roye	1310±
			P/O L.W.F.Stark	FW190 destroyed	Givors/Roye	1310±

30/31st January 1944

141 Sqn	Mosq	BC	F/L G.J.Rice	Bf110 destroyed	near Berlin	1930±
169 Sqn	Mosq	BC	S/L J.A.H.Cooper	Bf110 destroyed	Near Brandenburg	1920±

3/4th February 1944

68 Sqn	Beau	ADGB	F/O K.Seda	Ju88 destroyed	off Southwold	0550±
85 Sqn	Mosq	ADGB	Lt J.Raad	Ju88 damaged	SW Tonbridge	2054
85 Sqn	Mosq	ADGB	F/O H.B.Thomas	Do217 destroyed	20m E Naze	0450
410 Sqn	Mosq	ADGB	F/O E.S.P.Fox	Do217 destroyed	40m E Orfordness	0450
410 Sqn	Mosq	ADGB	F/O W.G.Dinsdale	Ju88 damaged	Near Stapleford Tawney	0515
418 Sqn	Mosq	ADGB	F/L J.C.Anderson	E/A destroyed	Tours A/D	2052
488 Sqn	Mosq	ADGB	F/O C.J.Vlotman	Do217 destroyed	40m E Foulness	0452
605 Sqn	Mosq	ADGB	F/L A.D.Wagner	E/A damaged	Chievres	0656

5/6th February 1944

169 Sqn	Mosq	BC	P/O W.H.Miller	Bf110 destroyed	N Sea W Katwijk	2100

8th February 1944

157 Sqn	Mosq	ADGB	S/L H.E.Tappin	BV222 destroyed	Biscarosse	2120
193 Sqn	Typh	ADGB	F/L P.H.Beake	FW190 destroyed	Gael	1300±
Har Wg	Typh	ADGB	W/C E.R.Baker	FW190 destroyed	Gael	1300±

9th February 1944

266 Sqn	Typh	ADGB	P/O D.Erasmus	Bf109 destroyed	SE Chartres	1130
			F/O N.J.Lucas	Do24 destroyed	Near Evreux	1130
			F/O J.D.Miller	- Shared -		

10th February 1944

266 Sqn	Typh	ADGB	F/L J.H.Deall	Ju88 destroyed	Bretigny	1430±
			P/O J.Haworth	Yale damaged	Villacoublay	1430±
			F/O D.McGibbon	Yale destroyed	Villacoublay	1430±
			F/O D.McGibbon	Yale destroyed	Villacoublay	1430±
			F/O D.McGibbon	Yale destroyed	Villacoublay	1430±
Har Wg	Typh	ADGB	W/C E.R.Baker	FW190 destroyed	Bretigny	1430±
			W/C E.R.Baker	Do217 destroyed	Bretigny	1430±

11th February 1944

263 Sqn	Typh	ADGB	S/L G.B.Warnes	Do217 destroyed	5m S Gael AD	1545±
331 Sqn	Spit	2TAF	Lt F.S.Fearnley	FW190 destroyed	40m SW Lille	1350
			2/Lt J.W.Garben	FW190 damaged	10m NW Dieppe	1400

11/12th February 1944

169 Sqn	Mosq	BC	F/O G.R.Shipley	Bf110 damaged	Dutch coast	2115±

12th February 1944

157 Sqn	Mosq	ADGB	F/L R.D.Doleman	FW200 destroyed	Biscay	1637
			F/O V.H.C.Hannwin	- Shared -		
			F/O V.H.C.Hannwin	FW200 damaged	Biscay	1637
			F/O B.M.Whitlock	- Shared -		
198 Sqn	Typh	ADGB	F/O H.Freeman	LeO451 destroyed	Near Arras	1645±
			F/L J.Niblett	LeO451 destroyed	Near Arras	1645±

Night aces: Squadron Leader J.D.Somerville of 410 Squadron (left) achieved his first successes on the night of 13th February. He would survive the war with seven credited victories. The magnificently moustached Bertie Hoare (centre) started night intruder missions in 1941. He claimed a 'damaged' on the night of 21st February and achieved a total of nine confirmed kills. He too survived the war, but was killed in a flying accident on 26th March 1947. (ww2images.com) James Luma (right in cap), an American pilot on temporasry transfer to the RCAF, peers through a large Flak hole in the fin of his Mosquito. He claimed an He177 on the night of 12th February and survived the war flying with the USAAF after scoring five confirmed kills with 418 Squadron.

12/13th February 1944

29 Sqn	Mosq	ADGB	F/O R.R.Densham	Me410 destroyed	Fecamp	2125±
418 Sqn	Mosq	ADGB	Lt J.F.Luma (US)	He177 destroyed	3m S Bordeaux	0200

13th February 1944

263 Sqn	Typh	ADGB	S/L G.B.Warnes	Bf109 destroyed	NW Chartres	1645±

13/14th February 1944

96 Sqn	Mosq	ADGB	W/C E.D.Crew	Ju188 destroyed	Whitstable	2043
410 Sqn	Mosq	ADGB	F/O R.D.Schultz	Ju188 destroyed	Off Clacton	2150
			S/L J.D.Somerville	Ju88 destroyed	Thames estuary	2039
			S/L J.D.Somerville	Ju188 damaged	Thames estuary	2110
605 Sqn	Mosq	ADGB	F/S F.Cassidy	E/A destroyed	Chievres	2205

14th February 1944

124 Sqn	Spit	ADGB	F/S D.P.Kelly	Bf109 destroyed	10m SE St Omer	1106
			F/S D.P.Kelly	Bf109 destroyed	15m S Lille	1120
			W/O A.E.Nelson	- Shared -		
			P/O A.D.Yeardley	FW190 damaged	10m SE Nieuport	1640±
401 Sqn	Spit	2TAF	F/O R.K.Hayward	Me210 destroyed	St Andre L'Eure A/D	1615

15/16th February 1944

141 Sqn	Mosq	BC	F/L J.C.N.Forshaw	Ju88 damaged	Berlin	2115±
			F/O H.E.White	He177 destroyed	Berlin	2140±

18/19th February 1944

418 Sqn	Mosq	ADGB	F/L R.A.Kipp	Me410 destroyed	Juvincourt A/D	0225
			F/L R.A.Kipp	Me410 destroyed	Juvincourt A/D	0226

19th February 1944

157 Sqn	Mosq	ADGB	F/L R.J.Coombs	Ju290 destroyed	30m N Ortigueira	1154
			F/L R.D.Doleman	- Shared -		
418 Sqn	Mosq	ADGB	F/L C.C.Scherf	E/A destroyed	St Hubert, Florennes	0317

19/20th February 1944

605 Sqn	Mosq	ADGB	Sgt V.J.Chipman	E/A destroyed	Handorf	0505

20th February 1944

602 Sqn	Spit	2TAF	P/O I.Blair	Bf109G destroyed	40m E Duncansby Hd	1800±

20/21st February 1944

25 Sqn	Mosq	ADGB	P/O J.R.Brockbank	Ju188 destroyed	Braintree	2210
25 Sqn	Mosq	ADGB	F/L J.Singleton	He177 destroyed	50m E Lowestoft	2236
85 Sqn	Mosq	ADGB	W/C J.Cunningham	Ju188 damaged	Staplehurst	2209
85 Sqn	Mosq	ADGB	F/L B.J.Thwaites	Ju188 prob.dest	Lydd	2200
239 Sqn	Mosq	BC	F/O T.Knight	Bf110 destroyed	nr Stuttgart	2330±
605 Sqn	Mosq	ADGB	W/C B.R.O'B.Hoare	E/A damaged	Soesterberg	2345

21st February 1944

96 Sqn	Mosq	ADGB	F/S T.N.Bryan	Me410 destroyed	0320±

22/23rd February 1944

25 Sqn	Mosq	ADGB	F/L A.S.H.Baillie	He177 destroyed	Yoxford	0012
85 Sqn	Mosq	ADGB	F/L B.A.Burbridge	Me410 destroyed	Off Dungeness	0045

85 Sqn	Mosq	ADGB	F/L D.Dixon	Ju188 prob.dest	Off Dungeness	0050±
			F/L D.Dixon	Ju188 damaged	Off Dungeness	0100±
			F/O E.R.Hedgcoe	Me410 destroyed	Off Dungeness	0032
96 Sqn	Mosq	ADGB	S/L G.L.Caldwell	Me410 destroyed	Near Uckfield	0015
410 Sqn	Mosq	ADGB	S/L C.A.S.Anderson	Ju88 destroyed	Off Suffolk	2343
			S/L C.A.S.Anderson	Ju188 destroyed	Off Suffolk	0003
418 Sqn	Mosq	ADGB	F/S H.Williams	E/A damaged	1m NW Coulommieres	0150
			F/S H.Williams	Me410 destroyed	2m N Coulommieres A/D	0153
605 Sqn	Mosq	ADGB	F/O B.F.Miller	E/A destroyed	Melsbroek	0145
			F/L W.A.Bird	E/A damaged	Eindhoven	0230

23/24th February 1944

| 85 Sqn | Mosq | ADGB | W/C J.Cunningham | Ju88 prob.dest | Beachy Head | 2220 |
| 605 Sqn | Mosq | ADGB | F/O E.L.Williams | Ju88 destroyed | Chievres | 0012 |

24th February 1944

3 Sqn	Typh	ADGB	F/S R.W.Cole	LeO451 destroyed	Near Louvain	1625±
			P/O R.Dryland	- Shared -		
			F/S R.W.Pottinger	- Shared -		

24/25th February 1944

29 Sqn	Mosq	ADGB	F/L E.Cox	He177 destroyed	Channel	2100±
			S/L C.Kirkland	Do217 destroyed	Dorking	2156
			F/O J.E.Barry	Me410 prob.dest	Willesborough	2233
			F/O J.E.Barry	Do217 destroyed	Willesborough	2233
			AA Command	- Shared -		
			F/L R.C.Pargeter	Ju88 destroyed	Framfield	2144
			F/L R.C.Pargeter	Me410 destroyed	NE Brighton	2150
			F/L R.C.Pargeter	Ju188 damaged	N West Malling	2159
			F/O W.W.Provan	Ju88 destroyed	Shorn Hartfield	2150
			F/O W.W.Provan	Ju188 destroyed	Shorn Hartfield	2230
			F/O W.W.Provan	Ju88 damaged	Shorn Hartfield	2241
85 Sqn	Mosq	ADGB	F/LB.J.Thwaites	Ju188 prob.dest	15m SSW West Malling	2225
96 Sqn	Mosq	ADGB	S/L A.Parker-Rees	He177 prob.dest	Sussex	2300
			F/L D.L.Ward	Me410 destroyed	Off Beachy Head	2130
418 Sqn	Mosq	ADGB	F/L D.A.McFadyen	Me410 destroyed	Würzburg A/D	0215

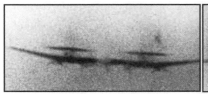 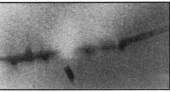

On 26th February 1944 Flight Lieutenants Charlie Scherf (right) and Howie Cleveland of 418 Squadron flew a Ranger mission to Tavaux airfield, where they destroyed this He111Z. Note the flying debris.

418 Sqn	Mosq	ADGB	F/L C.C.Scherf	Ju88 destroyed	Ansbach A/D	0230
			F/L C.C.Scherf	Ju88 destroyed	Ansbach A/D	0239
488 Sqn	Mosq	ADGB	F/L P.F.L.Hall	Do217 damaged	Near Plumpton	2225
			F/L P.F.L.Hall	He177 destroyed	Lemberhurst	2240
605 Sqn	Mosq	ADGB	F/L G.A.Holland	E/A damaged	Melsbroek AD	2330
FIU	Mosq	ADGB	Lt J.O.Armour RM	Ju188 damaged	Sussex	0300±

25th February 1944

124 Sqn	Spit	ADGB	P/O A.D.Yeardley	Ju88 destroyed	Boulogne	0930±
331 Sqn	Spit	ADGB	Lt F.S.Fearnley	He177 destroyed	5m NW St Trond A/D	1100
			Sgt E.Gundersen	- Shared -		
			F/S P.Thulin	- Shared -		
			Sgt E.Tjensvoll	- Shared -		

25/26th February 1944

169 Sqn	Mosq	BC	F/L R.G.Woodman	Bf110 destroyed	SW Mannheim	2335±
456 Sqn	Mosq	ADGB	F/O C.S.Samson	Ju88 destroyed	Rennes A/D	1912
605 Sqn	Mosq	ADGB	F/L G.A.Holland	Bf110 destroyed	Ober Olm	0300

26th February 1944

198 Sqn	Typh	ADGB	P/O G.E.A.Hardy	Bf110 destroyed	Off Dunkirk	0940
			P/O R.A.Lallemant	- Shared -		
245 Sqn	Typh	2TAF	F/O D.Maxwell	Fi156 destroyed	10m NW Laval	1455
			F/L J.W.H.Wilson	- Shared -		
418 Sqn	Mosq	ADGB	F/L H.D.Cleveland	He111Z destroyed	Tavaux A/D	1750
			F/L C.C.Scherf	- Shared -		
			F/L H.D.Cleveland	Go242 destroyed	Tavaux A/D	1750
			F/L C.C.Scherf	Go242 destroyed	Tavaux A/D	1750
609 Sqn	Typh	ADGB	P/O G.L.C.F.Jaspis	Ju88 destroyed	Near Fruges	1200±

The Luftwaffe lost one of its night aces on 26th February when Oberfeldwebel Heinz Vinke of 11./ NJG 1 flew a daylight mission over the English Channel. His Bf110 was engaged by Typhoon pilots of 198 Squadron, who correctly identified the Messerschmitt as a nightfighter. Pilot Officers R.A.Lallemant (right) and G.E.A.Hardy quickly shot the aircraft down into the sea off Dunkirk.

29th February 1944

609 Sqn	Typh	ADGB	W/O J.D.Buchanon	Ju188 destroyed	Villaroche A/D	1315±
			S/L J.C.Wells	- Shared -		
			W/O G.K.E.Martin	- Shared –		
			F/O C.J.G.Demoulin	- Shared –		
			F/L L.E.Smith	- Shared -		
			W/O J.D.Buchanon	Ju188 destroyed	Villaroche A/D	1315±
			F/O G.L.C.F.Jaspis	- Shared -		
			F/L J.Le Grand	- Shared -		
			W/O G.K.E.Martin		- Shared -	
			F/L L.E.Smith	- Shared -		
			S/L J.C.Wells	- Shared -		

29th February/1st March 1944

85 Sqn	Mosq	ADGB	F/L R.H.Farrell	He177 destroyed	S Beachy Head	2136
96 Sqn	Mosq	ADGB	F/L B.G.Primavesi	FW190 destroyed	S Beachy H	2045±

Chapter Three

Build-Up to Invasion

The task of the Second Tactical Air Force was now to attack German assets in the occupied territories since the American daylight onslaught had forced the bulk of the *Luftwaffe* back into Germany to defend the *Reich*. Indeed, the vast majority of air combats now involved nightfighter crews. These were mainly engaged upon night intruder and long range daylight *Ranger* operations. Occasionally, however, Second TAF fighter escorts met German fighters and normally gave a good account of themselves. The main danger now appeared to be *Flak*, which had now become truly horrendous.

One particular target for the RAF medium bombers was the increasing number of 'ski-sites', so-called due to their curious shape. These were actually projected launching sites for the Fieseler ramjet powered flying bomb that the Germans planned to use against London. The British, well aware of the German plan, intended to destroy or seriously damage every one of these sites thus preventing the onslaught, but they reckoned without the army of slave labour utilised by the Todt organisation. The sites were multiplying faster than they could be attacked and thus many Spitfire squadrons were 'converted' to the fighter-bomber role and joined their Typhoon comrades in this deadly and dangerous work.

There was one bright light for the RAF with the arrival of the Hawker Tempest, developed from the Typhoon and with a stunning low-level performance. These, however, would be in short supply until later in the year.

1st March 1944

308 Sqn Spit	2TAF	F/S T.Rybczynski	FW190 destroyed	Near Criel A/D	1610

1/2nd March 1944

96 Sqn Mosq	ADGB	F/O W.J.Gough	Me410 destroyed	50m SE Beachy Head	0330±
151 Sqn Mosq	ADGB	W/C G.H.Goodman	Ju88 destroyed	Off Isle of Wight	0235
		W/C G.H.Goodman	He177 destroyed	Off Isle of Wight	0305
		F/L A.J,Stevens	Ju88 destroyed	15m SE Selsey	0220
		S/L R.H.Harrison	Ju88 destroyed	30m S Bournemouth	0250
456 Sqn Mosq	ADGB	P/O R.W.Richardson	Do217 damaged	Ford	0305
605 Sqn Mosq	ADGB	F/S V.J.Chipman	Bf110 damaged	AD N Paris	0419
		S/L M.Negus	E/A destroyed	Laon	0420
		S/L M.Negus	E/A damaged	N Paris	0500±

5th March 1944

613 Sqn Mosq	2TAF	W/C J.R.D.Braham	He177 destroyed	Chateaudun	1500±

The new hope: the massive seven-ton Hawker Tempest. It was the fastest piston-engined aircraft to be operated by the RAF, but its performance began to decline above 10,000 feet. In the summer of 1944 it would be used very effectively against the flying bombs.

5/6th March 1944

515 Sqn Mosq	BC	W/C E.F.F.Lambert*	He177 destroyed	8m W Melun		2147
605 Sqn Mosq	ADGB	F/L A.D.Wagner	FW190 destroyed	Gardelegen		2333
		F/L A.D.Wagner	Me410 destroyed	Gardelegen		2347
		F/L A.D.Wagner	Me410 destroyed	Gardelegen		2356
		F/L A.D.Wagner	E/A damaged	Gardelegen		0001

Note: attached from 605 Sqn

6/7th March 1944

418 Sqn Mosq	ADGB	Lt J.F.Luma (US)	FW190 destroyed	Pau, nr Spanish Frontier	2242
605 Sqn Mosq	ADGB	F/O J.Reid	Bf110 destroyed	Gardelegen AD	2332

7th March 1944

401 Sqn Spit	2TAF	S/L L.M.Cameron	Bf109 damaged	N Beaumont-sur-Oise	1455
		F/O W.E.Cummings	Bf109 damaged	N Beaumont-sur-Oise	1455
		F/O W.T.Klersey	FW190 destroyed	N Beaumont-sur-Oise	1455
		F/L J.E.Sheppard	FW190 destroyed	N Beaumont-sur-Oise	1455
610 Sqn Spit	ADGB	F/S M.F.Harding	FW190 damaged	Lyme Bay	1750±

10th March 1944

157 Sqn Mosq	ADGB	Lt F.H.Sandiford	Ju88 destroyed	Off Brest	1712
		F/L R.J.V.Smyth	- Shared -		

14/15th March 1944

25 Sqn Mosq	ADGB	F/L J.Singleton	Ju88 destroyed	off Lowestoft	2330±
68 Sqn Beau	ADGB	W/C D.Hayley-Bell	Ju88 destroyed	Ilford	2315
96 Sqn Mosq	ADGB	F/L N.S.Head	Ju88 destroyed	Hildenborough	2305
		F/L N.S.Head	Ju188 destroyed	Channel	2330±
410 Sqn Mosq	ADGB	1/Lt A.A.Harrington	Ju188 destroyed	Hildenborough	2316
	ADGB	S/L W.P.Green	Ju88 prob.dest	Althorne	0052

On 15th March Spitfire pilots from 401 Squadron tangled with FW190s of III./JG 26 near Epinoy airfield. Bob Hayward (right) claimed one shot down and a second damaged. On the night of 19th March, Joe Singleton of 25 Squadron (far right) claimed a 'hat trick' by destroying three Ju88s over the North Sea to bring his final total to seven.

488 Sqn Mosq	ADGB	S/L E.N.Bunting	Ju188 destroyed	Great Leigh	2303
605 Sqn Mosq	ADGB	S/L M.Negus	Do217 destroyed	Eindhoven	0020
		S/L M.Negus	Do217 destroyed	Eindhoven	0020
		S/L R.A.Mitchell F/L A.G.Woods	Ju88 destroyed - Shared -	Boblingen A/D	0027
		S/L R.A.Mitchell F/L A.G.Woods	Ju88 destroyed - Shared -	Boblingen A/D	0027

15th March 1944

401 Sqn Spit	2TAF	F/O D.D.Ashleigh	FW190 destroyed	SE Cambrai-Epinoy AD	1100
		F/L A.F.Halcrow	FW190 destroyed	4m from Epinoy AD	1100
		F/O R.K.Hayward	FW190 destroyed	Cambrai-Epinoy /D	1100
		F/O R.K.Hayward	FW190 damaged	Cambrai-Epinoy AD	1100
		F/L J.E.Sheppard	FW190 destroyed	S Cambrai-Epinoy AD	1100

16th March 1944

174 Sqn Typh	2TAF	F/L F.A.Grantham	Ar96B destroyed	N Etampes	1650±
		P/O G.J.Steele W/O R.C.Hayes	Ar96B destroyed - Shared -	N Etampes	1650±
175 Sqn Typh	2TAF	P/O W.Cross	Ju188 destroyed	Villaroche	1634
		F/L H.Davies	Bf108 destroyed	S Fontainebleu	1635

18/19th March 1944

141 Sqn Mosq	BC	F/L J.C.N.Forshaw	Ju88 destroyed	nr Frankfurt	2055±
		F/O H.E.White	Ju88 destroyed	nr Frankfurt	2210
		F/O H.E.White	Ju88 destroyed	nr Frankfurt	2225

On 21st March two 418 Squadron Mosquito crews visited Luxeuil airfield, where James Luma and Don MacFadyen shot down a Ju188 and two Ju W34s. Don MacFadyen (right) ended the war with a score of seven, plus five V-1s shot down. Above: a 418 Squadron Mosquito FBVI prepares to take off.

19/20th March 1944

25 Sqn	Mosq	ADGB	F/L D.H.Greaves	Do217 destroyed	25m NNE Cromer	2128
			F/L D.H.Greaves	He177 destroyed	30m NNW Cromer	2148
			F/L J.Singleton	Ju188 destroyed	55m NNE Cromer	2120
			F/L J.Singleton	Ju188 destroyed	65m NNE Cromer	2127
			F/L J.Singleton	Ju188 destroyed	80m NNE Cromer	2133
264 Sqn	Mosq	ADGB	F/O R.L.J.Barbour	Do217 destroyed	3m SE Louth	2206
307 Sqn	Mosq	ADGB	P/O J.Brochocki	He177 destroyed	NE Skegness	2146
406 Sqn	Beau	ADGB	S/L D.J.Williams	He177 destroyed	15m W Guernsey	2332
605 Sqn	Mosq	ADGB	F/L G.A.Holland	Ju88 destroyed	Rheine	2345

20th March 1944

165 Sqn	Spit	ADGB	F/O D.C.Eva	Ju88 destroyed	Grandchamp	0045
			P/O J.N.Haslope	- Shared -		

20/21st March 1944

25 Sqn	Mosq	ADGB	F/L R.D.R.Davies	Ju188 destroyed	35M SW Lowestoft	0015
418 Sqn	Mosq	ADGB	F/L C.A.Walker	Bü131 destroyed	Melun A/D	2302

21st March 1944

418 Sqn	Mosq	ADGB	Lt J.F.Luma	JuW34 destroyed	Luxeuil A/D	1835
			Lt J.F.Luma	Ju52 destroyed	Luxeuil A/D	1850
			F/L D.A.McFadyen	JuW34 destroyed	Luxeuil A/D	1840

On 21/22nd March Squadron Leader E.N.Bunting of 488 Squadron (pointing) destroyed a 9./KG 30 Ju88 at Cavendish, Suffolk. He shot down a second Ju88 less than an hour later. His navigator, Flight Lieutenant C.P.Reed is shown far left, beside Flight Lieutenant J.A.S.Hall, who was also successful that night. ww2images.com)

21/22st March 1944

25 Sqn Mosq	ADGB	F/L R.D.R.Davies	Ju188 destroyed	25m SW Lowestoft	0033
85 Sqn Mosq	ADGB	F/O C.K.Nowell	Me410 damaged	Kent	0040
		F/L R.H.Farrell	Ju88 damaged	S Shoreham	0125
96 Sqn Mosq	ADGB	P/O W.J.Gough	FW190 damaged	Thames estuary	0050±
410 Sqn Mosq	ADGB	F/O S.B.Huppert	Ju88 destroyed	Sussex Coast	0055
456 Sqn Mosq	ADGB	Lt D.G.Thornley	FW190 damaged	50m S Beachy Head	0044
		F/O K.A.Roediger	Ju88 destroyed	Off Rye	0112
488 Sqn Mosq	ADGB	S/L E.N.Bunting	Ju88 destroyed	Near Clare	0045
		S/L E.N.Bunting	Ju188 destroyed	Great Wakering	0110
		F/L J.A.S.Hall	Ju88 destroyed	Earls Colne	0047
		F/S C.J.Vlotman	Ju88 destroyed	Off East Anglia	0020
		F/S C.J.Vlotman	E/A destroyed	Off Herne Bay	0055
604 Sqn Mosq	ADGB	F/L J.C.Surman	Ju88 destroyed	Letchington	0051
		F/L J.C.Surman	Ju88 damaged	Letchington	0108

22/23rd March 1944

96 Sqn Mosq	ADGB	F/L N.S.Head	FW190 destroyed	Off Hastings	2120
605 Sqn Mosq	ADGB	F/L G.J.Wright	E/A destroyed	Stade	0300±
		F/L G.J.Wright	E/A destroyed	Stade	2300±

23rd March 1944

312 Sqn Spit	2TAF	F/O L.Svetlik	FW190 destroyed	10m N Courtrai	1747
412 Sqn Spit	2TAF	F/O D.C.Laubman	Ju88 destroyed	Near Criel	1200
		F/L W.B.Needham	- Shared -		
610 Sqn Spit	ADGB	P/O W.A.Nicholls	FW190 damaged	Off Guernsey	1910±

The wreckage of a 4./KG 30 Ju88, shot down on the night of 21st March by Flying Officer S.B.Huppert of 410 Squadron at Latchingdon, Essex.

23/24th March 1944

85 Sqn	Mosq	ADGB	S/L B.J.Thwaites	FW190 destroyed	Off Hastings	0012
239 Sqn	Mosq	BC	S/L E.W.Kinchin	Bf110 destroyed	Frankfurt	2100±
605 Sqn	Mosq	ADGB	F/L G.A.Holland	FW190 destroyed	Neuburg	2232
			F/L G.A.Holland	E/A destroyed	Neuburg	2303

24th March 1944

613 Sqn	Mosq	2TAF	W/C J.R.D.Braham	JuW34 destroyed	6m SAalborg	1504
			W/C J.R.D.Braham	Ju52 destroyed	15m S Aalborg	1509

24/25th March 1944

25 Sqn	Mosq	ADGB	F/O V.H.Linthune	Ju188 destroyed	45m E Lowestoft	0042
85 Sqn	Mosq	ADGB	F/L B.A.Burbridge	Ju88 destroyed	Dover Straits	0020
			F/L B.A.Burbridge	Do217 prob.dest	Dover Straits	0052
			F/O E.R.Hedgecoe	Ju188 destroyed	Hastings	2323
141 Sqn	Mosq	BC	F/L H.C.Kelsey	FW190 destroyed	Berlin	2315±
410 Sqn	Mosq	ADGB	W/O W.F.Price	Me410 prob.dest	Off Knocke	0037
456 Sqn	Mosq	ADGB	W/C K.M.Hampshire	Ju88 destroyed	Walburton	2345
605 Sqn	Mosq	ADGB	W/C B.R.O'B.Hoare	Bf109 destroyed	Burg AD	2338
			S/L R.A.Mitchell	Ju88 damaged	Perleberg AD	2341
			F/L A.D.Wagner	Ju88 destroyed	Erfurt	2332
			F/L A.D.Wagner	He219 damaged	Erfurt	2355

26/27th March 1944

68 Sqn Beau	ADGB	F/O R.Russell	Ju188 destroyed	Coxley	0010
96 Sqn Mosq	ADGB	F/L K.Kennedy	FW190 destroyed	Off Dungeness	0000±
141 Sqn Mosq	BC	F/O H.E.White	Ju88 damaged	Ruhr	2215±
219 Sqn Mosq	ADGB	S/L H.V.Ellis	Ju88 destroyed	Cheddon, near Taunton	2357
406 Sqn Beau	ADGB	F/L H.D.McNabb	Ju88 destroyed	Clapton, Gloucs	2350
		P/O R.L.Green	Ju188 destroyed	20m S Plymouth	0020
456 Sqn Mosq	ADGB	W/C K.M.Hampshire	Ju88 destroyed	Near Beer	2343
		W/C K.M.Hampshire	Ju88 destroyed	Isle Brewers	2359
		S/L B.Howard	Ju88 destroyed	V.72	0118

27/28th March 1944

219 Sqn Mosq	ADGB	S/L H.V.Ellis	Ju88 destroyed	Near Yeovil	2357

30/31st March 1944

239 Sqn Mosq	BC	F/S J.Campbell	Ju88 destroyed	Nuremburg	0015

4th April 1944

613 Sqn Mosq	2TAF	W/C J.R.D.Braham	Bü131 destroyed	St Jean d'Angel	1546

5th April 1944

418 Sqn Mosq	ADGB	F/L C.C.Scherf	Po630 destroyed	Lyons	1815
		F/L C.C.Scherf	Fi156 destroyed	Lyons	1819

6th April 1944

266 Sqn Typh	2TAF	F/O G.M.R.Eastwood	Ju88 destroyed	4m S Rennes	1300
		F/S J.O.Hulley	- Shared -		

11th April 1944

151 Sqn Mosq	ADGB	W/C G.H.Goodman	Ju88 destroyed	Off St Nazaire	0930
		F/L D.S.Handley	Ju88 destroyed	Off St Nazaire esuary	0930
		F/O J.H.Etherton	Ju88 damaged	Off St Nazaire	0937
		F/O H.Turner	Ju88 destroyed	Off St Nazaire	0940

Another Ju88 reported missing: Wing Commander Keith Hampshire of 456 Squadron (right) with his navigator Flying Officer T.Condon, inspect the remains of a Junkers from 6./KG 6, shot down at Walburton, Sussex, on the night of 24th March. Two further Ju88s fell to their guns on the night of 26th. This crew would end the war with seven confirmed kills.

(ww2images.com)

151 Sqn	Mosq	ADGB	S/L R.H.Harrison	Ju88 destroyed	20m SW St Nazaire	1540
			S/L R.H.Harrison	Ju88 prob.dest	20m SW St Nazaire	1540
			F/S J.Playford	Ju88 destroyed	20m SW St Nazaire	1540
			F/S J.Playford	Ju88 destroyed	20m SW St Nazaire	1540
			F/S J.Playford	Ju88 damaged	20m SW St Nazaire	1540

11/12th April 1944

239 Sqn	Mosq	BC	S/L N.E.Reeves	Do217 destroyed	Aachen	2245±
418 Sqn	Mosq	ADGB	W/O M.H.Sims	Ju188 destroyed	Ober Olm	0040
			F/O H.E.Jones	FW190 destroyed	Furstenfeldbruck	0100

12/13th April 1944

418 Sqn	Mosq	ADGB	F/O G.N.Miller	He177 prob.dest	1m S Kolberg A/D	2230
			F/O G.N.Miller	He111 destroyed	Kolberg A/D	2238
			F/O G.N.Miller	E/A prob.dest	Kolberg A/D	2346
			F/O C.M.Jasper	FW190 destroyed	12m SE Verdun	2259
605 Sqn	Mosq	ADGB	F/L P.J.Garner	E/A prob.dest	Neuburg	0018

13th April 1944

305 Sqn	Mosq	2TAF	W/C J.R.D.Braham	He111 destroyed	Esbjerg	1515
			W/C J.R.D.Braham	FW58 destroyed	Aalborg	1610

13/14th April 1944

96 Sqn	Mosq	ADGB	S/L A.Parker-Rees	Ju88 destroyed	Off French coast	2220±
			F/L D.L.Ward	Me410 destroyed	Off Dungeness	0100±

On 18th April 263 Squadron Typhoon pilots caught a Do217 and an Me410 at Villaroche and destroyed them. The squadron pilots line up for a group photo with their CO, Squadron Leader D.H.Rutter, then a flight commander. (ww2images.com)

14th April 1944

418 Sqn Mosq ADGB	F/OJ.T.Caine	Ju52 destroyed	Off Sjaellands Pt,		
				Kattegat	1510
	S/L R.A.Kipp	Ju52 destroyed	Off Sjaellands Pt,		
				Kattegat	1510
	F/O J.T.Caine	Ju52 destroyed	Off Sjaellands Pt,		
				Kattegat	1511
	S/L R.A.Kipp	Ju52 destroyed	Off Sjaellands Pt,		
				Kattegat	1511

14/15th April 1944

96 Sqn Mosq ADGB	S/L A.Parker-Rees	Me410 destroyed	Off Dungeness	0138

16th April 1944

418 Sqn Mosq ADGB	F/L W.J.Harper	JuW34 destroyed	Luxeuil A/D	1747
	F/L W.J.Harper	JuW34 destroyed	Luxeuil A/D	1747
	F/L C.M.Jasper	Caudron destroyed	Luxeuil A/D	1747

18th April 1944

263 Sqn Typh ADGB	P/O F.Green	Do217 destroyed	Villaroche	1620

 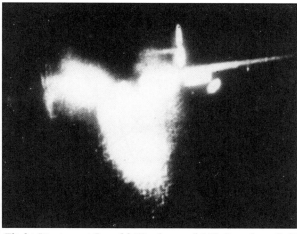

Flight Lieutenant Ronald Woodman of 169 Squadron (left) claimed his second victory on the night of 18th April by shooting down a Bf110 of 9./NJG 4 flown by Hauptmann Kurt Fladrich a Luftwaffe ace who survived. Five nights later, on 22/23rd. he destroyed another Bf110, this believed from the Schulstaffel of NJG 6, that crashed near Bonn. Oberfahrnrich Walter Daiser and his Bordfunker were killed. The Mosquitos operating over Germany by night had begun to sting. (Right) A Bf110 being shot down by a Mosquito.

263 Sqn Typh	ADGB	F/S W.A.Handley	- Shared -		
		P/O J.E.Purkis	- Shared -		
		F/L D.H.Rutter	- Shared -		
		F/S J.Thould	Me410 destroyed	Villaroche	1620
266 Sqn Typh	2TAF	F/L A.V.Sanders	Ju188 destroyed	Need Oar Point	0745
		F/S D.H.Dodd	- Shared –		

18/19th April 1944

25 Sqn	Mosq	ADGB	F/L R.M.Carr	Ju88 prob.dest	off Southwold	0030
			F/L R.M.Carr	Ju188 destroyed	off Southwold	0115
			P/O K.V.Panter	Me410 destroyed	Off Holland	0435
			P/O B.Travers	Do217 prob.dest	60m off Yarmouth	0114
85 Sqn	Mosq	ADGB	W/C C.M.Miller	Ju188 destroyed	Ivychurch	0130
			S/LB.A.Burbridge	Ju188 destroyed	Off Sangatte	0133
96 Sqn	Mosq	ADGB	W/C E.D.Crew	Me410 destroyed	Brighton	0050
			P/O C.J.O.Allen	Ju88 destroyed	Near Cranbrook	0115±
			S/L W.P.Green	Ju88 destroyed	10m N Margate	0140±
169 Sqn	Mosq	BC	F/L R.G.Woodman	Bf110 destroyed	Compeigne	2330±
410 Sqn	Mosq	ADGB	F/O L.R.Snowdon	Ju188 damaged	Near Braintree	0058
			F/O S.B.Huppert	He177 destroyed	Saffron Waldron	0100

On 23rd April, four Mustang pilots of 122 Squadron flew a Ranger to Tavaux airfield in France. Here they found a number of He111s, which were immediately attacked. Six were claimed destroyed and a seventh damaged without loss. The records of IV./KG 27 show the loss of at least four Heinkels with another two damaged. The aircraft above appears to be that flown by Unteroffizier Hans Langbehn, that was crash-landed on the airfield with three casualties.

488 Sqn Mosq	ADGB	W/O R.F.D.Bourke	Ju88 destroyed	16m SE Trimley	0048
488 Sqn Mosq	ADGB	F/L J.A.S.Hall	Ju88 destroyed	60m E Bradwell	0111
605 Sqn Mosq	ADGB	F/L G.E.Allison	FW190 destroyed	Rheine	0333

19th April 1944

| 443 Sqn Spit | 2TAF | S/L H.W.McLeod | Do217 destroyed | E Louvain | 1850 |

19/20th April 1944

| 456 Sqn Mosq | ADGB | F/L C.L.Brooks | Me410 destroyed | S Horsham | 2228 |

20th April 1944

| 151 Sqn Mosq | ADGB | W/C G.H.Goodman | JuW34 destroyed | Biscarosse | 1700 |

20/21st April 1944

25 Sqn Mosq	ADGB	F/S D.J.Carter	Ju188 destroyed	30m E Spurn Head	0008
141 Sqn Mosq	BC	F/O H.E.White	Do217 destroyed	N Paris	0000
169 Sqn Mosq	BC	F/L G.F.Cremer	Bf110 destroyed	Ruhr	0230±
264 Sqn Mosq	ADGB	F/O H.J.Corre	He177 destroyed	40m E Spurn Head	2355
605 Sqn Mosq	ADGB	P/O R.C.Walton	Do217 damaged	Gilze-Rijn AD	0122
605 Sqn Mosq	ADGB	P/O H.J.Collins	E/A damaged	Juvincourt	0205

The four successful 122 Squadron Mustang pilots compare notes:(l to r) Flight Lieutenant L.A.P. Burra-Robinson, Pilot Officers E.A.Roemmele, J.Crossland and Flight Lieutenant A.F.Pavey.

21st April 1944

616 Sqn Spit	ADGB	F/O A.G.P.Jennings		FW190 destroyed	landing Maupertus	1230±
		P/O J.Clerc		- Shared -		

22nd April 1944

19 Sqn Must	2TAF	W/C G.R.A.McG. Johnston		Bf109F damaged	S Laon	1730
		W/C G.R.A.McG. Johnston		Bf109F destroyed	S Laon	1730
		F/S B.M.Vassiliades		Bf109 destroyed	Nancy area	1730
65 Sqn Must	2TAF	F/O N.E.S.Mutter		Bf109 destroyed	S Laon	1730
504 Sqn Spit	ADGB	F/O J.Waslyk		Ju88 destroyed	30m SE Ronaldsway	2200±
		F/S J.N.Thorne		- Shared -		

22/23rd April 1944

169 Sqn Mosq	BC	F/L R.G.Woodman		Bf110 destroyed	Bonn, E Ruhr	0130±
169 Sqn Mosq	BC	P/O W.H.Miller		Bf110 destroyed	Köln	0145±
605 Sqn Mosq	ADGB	F/L G.J.Wright		E/A damaged	Langensalza	0323

23rd April 1944

122 Sqn Must	2TAF	F/L L.A.P.Burra -Robinson		He111 destroyed	Tavaux AD	1630±
		F/L L.A.P.Burra -Robinson		He111 destroyed	Tavaux AD	1630±

122 Sqn Must	2TAF	F/L L.A.P.Burra -Robinson	He111 destroyed	Tavaux AD	1630±
		P/O J.Crossland	- Shared -		
		F/L A.F.Pavey	- Shared -		
		P/O E.A.Roemmele	- Shared -		
		P/O J.Crossland	He111 destroyed	Tavaux AD	1630±
		P/O J.Crossland	He111 destroyed	Tavaux AD	1630±
		P/O E.A.Roemmele	- Shared -		
		F/L A.F.Pavey	He111 destroyed	Tavaux AD	1630±
		F/L A.F.Pavey	He111 damaged	Tavaux AD	1630±

23/24rd April 1944

125 Sqn Mosq	ADGB	P/O W.A.Beadle	Ju188 destroyed	Near Swanage	0147
		S/L E.G.Barwell	Ju188 destroyed	Warminster	0150
		F/L V.P.Key	Ju188 destroyed	S Portland	0200
		S/L L.W.G.Gill	Ju88 damaged	Winterbourne Houghton	0205
		F/L R.W.Leggett	Ju88 damaged	Near Blandford	0220
141 Sqn Mosq	BC	F/L G.J.Rice	FW190 destroyed	Flensburg	0041
406 Sqn Beau	ADGB	W/O G.F.MacEwen	Ju88 destroyed	35m E Start Point	0229
456 Sqn Mosq	ADGB	W/C K.M.Hampshire	Ju188 destroyed	Off Swanage	0210

24th April 1944

401 Sqn Spit	2TAF	F/O R.K.Hayward	Bf110 destroyed	SW Laon	1947
		F/O D.D.Ashleigh	- Shared -		
		F/O T.WDowbiggin	Bf110 destroyed	6m E Laon	1948

24/25th April 1944

605 Sqn Mosq	ADGB	F/L A.D.Wagner	Ju88 destroyed	Neuburg	0232

25th April 1944

441 Sqn Spit	2TAF	F/O J.W.Fleming	FW190 destroyed	Near Laon	0820
		F/O L.A.Plummer	- Shared -		
		S/L G.U.Hill	FW190 destroyed	Near Laon	0820
		P/O R.H.Sparling	- Shared -		
443 Sqn Spit	2TAF	F/L H.Russell	FW190 destroyed	Near Laon	0820
		F/L D.M.Walz	FW190 destroyed	Near Laon	0820
144 Wg Spit	2TAF	W/C J.E.Johnson	FW190 destroyed	Near Laon	0820
		W/C J.E.Johnson	FW190 destroyed	Near Laon	0820

On the night of 26th April, Bill Breithaupt of 239 Squadron (left) destroyed a Bf110 over the Ruhr. He would fall in combat on 12/13th September while engaging a Bf110 of NJG 6. On 13/14th September Howie Cleveland (centre) of 418 Squadron claimed an unidentified aircraft destroyed at Croix de Matz, while Roy Lelong (right) of 605 Squadron claimed a 'probable' at Ober Olm airfield.

25/26th April 1944

85 Sqn	Mosq	ADGB	F/L B.A.Burbridge	Me410 destroyed	7m S Selsey	0507
125 Sqn	Mosq	ADGB	F/L V.P.Key	Do217 destroyed	S Isle of Wight	0455
456 Sqn	Mosq	ADGB	F/L W.R.V.Lewis	Ju88 destroyed	Near Beachy Head	2357
			F/O G.R.Houston	Ju188 destroyed	S Selsey	0457
			F/O K.A.Roediger	Ju188 destroyed	15m SW Selsey	0516
605 Sqn	Mosq	ADGB	F/S V.J.Chipman	E/A damaged	Laon/Athies	0153

26th April 1944

132 Sqn	Spit	2TAF	S/L A.G.Page	JuW34 destroyed	12m S Duren	1455
			F/S J.E.Ford	- Shared -		
			F/S D.J.Watkins	- Shared -		
			F/OR.O.Webster	- Shared -		

26/27th April 1944

125 Sqn	Mosq	ADGB	W/C J.G.Topham	Ju188 destroyed	10m S St Catherines Pt	0200
239 Sqn	Mosq	BC	F/O W.R.Breithaupt	Bf110 destroyed	Essen	0150
418 Sqn	Mosq	ADGB	W/O M.H.Sims	E/A destroyed	Schweinfurt AD	0335
515 Sqn	Mosq	BC	W/O T.S Ecclestone	E/A destroyed	landing Le Culot	0310
			W/O T.S.Ecclestone	Ju88 destroyed	landing Brussels-Evere	0315

27th April 1944

65 Sqn	Must	ADGB	F/L R.Barrett	FW190 destroyed	Mourmelon AD	1220

On 29th April, Geoffrey Page of 132 Squadron (far right) led six Spitfires on a sweep over Holland. They discovered a Bf110 nightfighter of NJG1 in the Deelen circuit and attacked. One Spitfire overshot the target and was shot down, killing Flying Officer R.B.Pullin. Flying Officer J.O.Caulton then tried a head-on pass - a near-fatal error, for he too was shot down by the Luftwaffe ace, Hauptmann Hans-Joachim Jabs. Page then led the remainder of his pilot in to attack and Jabs belly-landed his '110 at Deelen. After the war Jabs became firm friends with both Page and Caulton.

27/28th April 1944

85 Sqn	Mosq	ADGB	Capt M.Ree	He177 destroyed	Dieppe	2315
169 Sqn	Mosq	BC	P/O P.Johnson	Bf110 destroyed	SE Strasbourg	0245±
239 Sqn	Mosq	BC	F/O R.Depper	Bf110 destroyed	Montzon-Aulnoye	0215±
			F/O R.Depper	Ju88 destroyed	Montzon-Aulnoye	0220±
418 Sqn	Mosq	ADGB	S/L H.D.Cleveland	E/A destroyed	Croix de Matz	0350
605 Sqn	Mosq	ADGB	F/OA.J.Craven	E/A damaged	Venlo AD	0240
			F/O R.E.Lelong	E/A prob.dest	Ober Olm AD	0323

28th April 1944

19 Sqn	Must	2TAF	F/S A.J.Fellows	Ar196 destroyed	Near L'Aigle	1540
			F/S B.Vassiliades	- Shared -		
			F/S W.T.Warren	- Shared -		
197 Sqn	Typh	ADGB	F/L K.J.Harding	French trpt a/c		0845±
			F/S L.S.Clarke	- Shared -		
441 Sqn	Spit	2TAF	F/L T.A.Brannagan	Caudron destroyed	La Neuve Lyre	2000
			F/L L.A.Moore	- Shared -		

28/29th April 1944

239 Sqn	Mosq	BC	S/L N.E.Reeves	Bf110 destroyed	Montzon-Aulnoye	0200±
456 Sqn	Mosq	ADGB	W/C K.M.Hampshire	Do217 prob.dest	86m off Durrington	0036

On the night of 2nd May, Bob Kipp of 418 Squadron (above) caught four FW190s while intruding over Germany. Also shown above is his Mosquito 'Black Rufe' sporting his victory markings for both air and ground kills. He ended the war with ten confirmed air-to-air victories.

29th April 1944

132 Sqn Spit	2TAF	S/LA.G.Page	Bf110 destroyed	Deelen	1530
		F/S W.S.Armour	- Shared -		
		F/O J.J.Caulton	- Shared -		
193 Sqn Typh	2TAF	F/L A.S.Ross	LeO45 destroyed	nr Lisieux	0755±
		257 Squadron	- Shared -		
257 Sqn Typh	2TAF	F/O D.A.Porter	LeO45 destroyed	nr Lisieux	0755±
		P/O B.J.Spragg	- Shared –		
		193 Squadron	- Shared -		
305 Sqn Mosq	2TAF	W/C J.R.DBraham	FW190 destroyed	NW Poitiers	1802

29/30th April 1944

68 Sqn Beau	ADGB	F/L J.Capka	Ju88 prob.dest	off Morlaix	0400±
406 Sqn Beau	ADGB	Lt S.I.Kvam (US)	Ju88 destroyed	40m S Start Point	0310
406 Sqn Beau	ADGB	S/L D.J.Williams	Do217 destroyed	Y-26	0354
		S/LD.J.Williams	Do217 destroyed	Y-15	0405

2/3rd May 1944

418 Sqn Mosq	ADGB	S/L R.A.Kipp	FW190 destroyed	15m SW Ammersee	0040
		S/L R.A.Kipp	FW190 destroyed	2m from Gunzburg	0140
		S/L R.A.Kipp	FW190 destroyed	Sarrebourg	0205
		S/L R.A.Kipp	FW190 destroyed	Sarrebourg	0205

Wing Commander Geoffrey Goodman of 151 Squadron (left) with his navigator Flying Officer W.F.Thomas. On 4th May they flew a Day Ranger to Dijon, where they discovered a formation of He111s and claimed four destroyed to bring his final score to nine.

4th May 1944

151 Sqn Mosq	ADGB	W/C G.H.Goodman	He111 destroyed	Dijon	1727
		W/C G.H.Goodman	He111 destroyed	Dijon	1729
		W/C G.H.Goodman	He111 destroyed	Dijon	1732
		W/C G.H.Goodman	He111 destroyed	Dijon	1735

5th May 1944

441 Sqn Spit	2TAF	P/O T.C.Gamey	FW190 destroyed	Near Mons	0820
		P/O F.A.W.J.Wilson	FW190 destroyed	Near Mons	0820
443 Sqn Spit	2TAF	S/L H.W.McLeod	FW190 destroyed	S Brussels	0830
144 Wg Spit	2TAF	W/C J.E.Johnson	FW190 destroyed	Near Douai	0820

6th May 1944

151 Sqn Mosq	ADGB	S/L C.A.Cooke	FW190 destroyed	15m SSW Bourges	1750

6/7th May 1944

605 Sqn Mosq	ADGB	W/CN.V.Starr	Bf110 destroyed	St Dizier AD	0317

On 7th May Flight Lieutenant Russ Orr (right) of 411 Squadron surprised a pair of 3./JG 26 FW190 pilots as they climbed away from Laon/Athies airfield. He shot them both down in flames, killing Obergefreiter Thomas Schwertl and Oberfahnrich Erich Scheyda (far right). Scheyda had been credited with 20 victories.

7th May 1944

21 Sqn	Mosq	2TAF	W/C J.R.D.Braham	Ju88 destroyed	30m N Copenhagen	1050
403 Sqn	Spit	2TAF	F/L J.D.Hodgson	FW190 damaged	Near Mons	1000
			F/L J.D.Lindsay	FW190 damaged	Near Mons	1000
			F/L J.D.Lindsay	Bf109 destroyed	Near Mons	1000
411 Sqn	Spit	2TAF	F/L R.W.Orr	FW190 destroyed	6-8m E Laon	0845±
			F/L R.W.Orr	FW190 destroyed	6-8m E Laon	0845±

7/8th May 1944

169 Sqn	Mosq	BC	F/O R.G.Woodman	Bf110 destroyed	nr Lille	0330±
605 Sqn	Mosq	ADGB	S/L J.F.Evans	He177 damaged	Laon	0150

8th May 1944

421 Sqn	Spit	2TAF	F/O P.G.Johnson	Bf110 destroyed	SSE Cambrai	0700

8/9th May 1944

418 Sqn	Mosq	ADGB	F/O E.E.Jones	Ju290 destroyed	Illesheim A/D	0105
			F/O D.E.Roberts	FW190 destroyed	Oberpfaffenhausen AD	0132
605 Sqn	Mosq	ADGB	F/O R.E.Lelong	Ju88 destroyed	Crailsheim AD	0300
			F/O R.E.Lelong	FW190 damaged	Crailsheim AD	0300

10th May 1944

412 Sqn	Spit	2TAF	F/L E.C.R.Likeness	FW190 destroyed	S Rheims	1340
			S/L J.E.Sheppard	FW190 destroyed	S Rheims	1340

| 602 Sqn | Spit | 2TAF | S/L R.A.Sutherland | FW190 destroyed | Near Neufchatel | 1115 |
| | | | S/L R.A.Sutherland | FW190 prob.dest | Near Neufchatel | 1115 |

10/11th May 1944

| 239 Sqn | Mosq | BC | P/O V.Bridges | Bf110 destroyed | Charleroi | 0035± |

11/12th May 1944

141 Sqn	Mosq	BC	F/L H.E.White	Ju88 destroyed	N Amiens	2350
			F/L L.J.G.LeBoutte	Ju88 destroyed	SW Brussels	0030
151 Sqn	Mosq	ADGB	S/L R.H.Harrison	Ju88 destroyed	50m S St Andre	0150

12th May 1944

| 107 Sqn | Mosq | 2TAF | W/C J.R.D.Braham | FW190 destroyed | 10m WSW Aalborg | 1155 |

12/13th May 1944

239 Sqn	Mosq	BC	F/O V.Bridges	Ju88 destroyed	Wittem	0050±
			F/O W.R.Breithaupt	Bf110 destroyed	Hasselt-Louvain	0120
605 Sqn	Mosq	ADGB	F/L J.Rhodes	Do217 destroyed	Wertheim	0214

14th May 1944

| 418 Sqn | Mosq | ADGB | F/O C.M.Jasper | He111 destroyed | Nancy-Croix de Metz | 1011 |

14/15th May 1944

68 Sqn	Beau	ADGB	S/L M.J.Mansfeld	Do217 destroyed	Channel	0200±
			S/L M.J.Mansfeld	Do217 destroyed	Channel	0200±
			F/S J.H.Peters	He111 destroyed	Channel	0200±
125 Sqn	Mosq	ADGB	F/L R.C.White	Me410 damaged	10m N Portland Bill	0155
			S/L L.W.G.Gill	Ju88 destroyed	N Cherbourg	0215
264 Sqn	Mosq	ADGB	F/L C.M.Ramsay	Ju188 destroyed	Alton	2208
406 Sqn	Mosq	ADGB	F/L H.D.McNabb	Ju88 prob.dest	20m SE Guernsey	0120
			F/L H.D.McNabb	E/A damaged	20m SE Guernsey	0210
			P/O W.G.Mushchett	Ju88 destroyed	Coast nr Portland Bill	0148
			P/O W.G.Mushchett	Ju88 destroyed	Coast nr Portland Bill	0151
			P/O W.G.Mushchett	Ju88 prob.dest	Coast near Portland Bill	0153
			W/C R.C.Fumerton	Ju88 destroyed	20m SE Portland	0150

On the night of 14th May, Squadron Leader M.J.Mansfeld of 68 Squadron (far right) claimed two Do217s shot down in a night of heavy German losses and some RAF overclaiming. On 16th, Charlie Scherf of 418 Squadron had a field day, destroying five German aircraft on a Ranger to North  Germany. His companion, Howie Cleveland, got one more, but then went down to Flak - his navigator was killed and Cleveland and was interned in Sweden.

406 Sqn Mosq	ADGB	P/O D.J.M.McConnell	He177 prob.dest	SE Channel Is	0240	
		P/O D.J.M.McConnell	Ju188 destroyed	SE Channel Is	0323	
418 Sqn Mosq	ADGB	S/L R.A.Kipp	He177 destroyed	Mont de Marsan A/D	0122	
456 Sqn Mosq	ADGB	F/O D.W.Arnold	Ju88 destroyed	Near Medstead	0020	
		F/O A.S.McEvoy	Ju188 destroyed	Near Netheravon	0200	
488 Sqn Mosq	ADGB	F/O R.G.Jeffs	Ju88 destroyed	SE Yeovil	0148	
		F/O R.G.Jeffs	Do217 prob.dest	S Sturminster	0204	
		F/L J.A.S.Hall	Ju188 destroyed	Hensbridge NE Exeter	0155	
		F/S R.W.Mitchell	Ju188 damaged	Near Ilchester	0240	
604 Sqn Mosq	ADGB	F/O R.M.T.M.B. MacDonald	Ju88 damaged	NE Poole	0200	
		F/S J.C.Surman	Do217 destroyed	20m S Needles	0250	

15th May 1944

403 Sqn Spit	2TAF	F/O A.J.Bryan	FW190 destroyed	Courtrai	1030
		F/O J.D.Orr	- Shared -		
		F/O C.P.Thornton	- Shared -		
		F/L E.C.Williams	- Shared -		

15/16th May 1944

68 Sqn Beau	ADGB	F/O G.Wild	Ju88 destroyed	25m SW Portland	0100±
169 Sqn Mosq	BC	F/O W.H.Miller	Ju88 destroyed	Elbe estuary	0100±
		F/O W.H.Miller	Ju88 destroyed	Elbe estuary	0110±
		F/O W.H.Miller	Bf110 destroyed	Heide	0145±
264 Sqn Mosq	ADGB	S/L P.B.Elwell	Me410 destroyed	30m S IoWight	0015
406 Sqn Mosq	ADGB	P/O D.J.M.McConnell	He177 destroyed	30m SW Portland	0125±

456 Sqn Mosq	ADGB	F/O D.W.Arnold		Ju88 destroyed	Medstead	0025
604 Sqn Mosq	ADGB	W/C M.H.Constable -Maxwell		Ju188 destroyed	S Isle of Wight	0025

16th May 1944

418 Sqn Mosq	ADGB	S/L C.C.Scherf	He111 destroyed	Gedser Head	1705
		S/L C.C.Scherf	FW190 destroyed	Zingst	1725
		S/L C.C.Scherf	He177 destroyed	Kubitzen Bay	1730
		S/L C.C.Scherf	Hs123 destroyed	Kubitzen Bay	1734
		S/L C.C.Scherf	Ju86P destroyed	Stralsund	1737
		S/L H.D.Cleveland	He111 destroyed	Near Kiel Bay	1735

17th May 1944

65 Sqn Must	2TAF	F/L B.G.Collyns	Ju88 destroyed	Near Aalborg	1200
		S/L D.F.Westenra 122 Wing	- Shared - - Shared -		
		F/L B.B.Collyns	Ju88 destroyed	Near Aalborg	1200
		S/L D.F.Westenra	Ju88 destroyed	Near Aalborg	1200
		F/S R.T.Williams	JuW34 destroyed	Near Aalborg	1200
		F/S R.T.Williams	JuW34 destroyed	Near Aalborg	1200
		F/S R.T.Williams U/k Mustang	He177 destroyed - Shared -	Near Aalborg	1200
122 Sqn Must	2TAF	F/S W.P.Kelly F/O M.H.Pinches	JuW34 destroyed - Shared -	Near Aalborg	1200
		F/S W.P.Kelly	Bf109 destroyed	Near Aalborg	1200
		F/S W.P.Kelly	Bf109 destroyed	Near Aalborg	1200
		F/S W.P.Kelly	Doi217 prob.dest	Near Aalborg	1200
		F/S W.P.Kelly	FW190 damaged	Near Aalborg	1200
		Lt K. Nyerod	JuW34 destroyed	Near Aalborg	1200
		Lt K. Nyerod	JuW34 damaged	Near Aalborg	1200
		F/O M.H.Pinches	He177 destroyed	Near Aalborg	1200
		F/O M.H.Pinches	Ju188 destroyed	Near Aalborg	1200
		F/O M.H.Pinches	Ar96 damaged	Near Aalborg	1200
		F/O M.H.Pinches	Ar96 damaged	Near Aalborg	1200
122 Wg Must	2TAF	W/C G.R.A.McG. Johnston	Ju88 destroyed	Near Aalborg	1200
		W/C G.R.A.McG Johnston 65 Squadron	Ju88 destroyed - Shared -	Near Aalborg	1200

On 17th May the Mustang III pilots from 65 and 122 Squadrons flew a Ranger to Aalborg, on the Danish coast. Here they found a plethora of Luftwaffe aircraft and ripped into them, destroying or badly damaging five Ju88s of IV./KG 30, four Bf109s from the Alarmstaffel of JG 11, an He177 of 4./KG 100, a Ju W34 of Zielstaffel IV./FZG 1 and a Ju88 of I./KG 26. Flight Lieutenant Basil Collyns of 65 Squadron (right) was credited with a Ju88 destroyed and a second shared. Two Mustangs were lost, the one above, flown by Flight Sergeant R.T.Williams, falling to Unteroffizier Siegfried Rudinschat of 10./JG 11. Hptm Siegfried Simsch from the same unit shot down Flight Lieutenant R.Barrett, but his claim was not confirmed. Williams evaded capture. 'Buck' Collyns would be lost on 20th August, believed victim to Gefreiter Erich Schafer of 4./JG 11. He had been credited with five victories at the time of his death.

18th May 1944

164 Sqn Typh	2TAF	F/S L.Plows		Bf109 destroyed	Gisors-Pontoise	1605±
		F/L A.G.Todd		- Shared -		
		183 Squadron		- Shared -		
183 Sqn Typh	2TAF	F/L F.H.Pollock		Bf109 destroyed	Gisors-Pontoise	1605±
		136 Wing		- Shared -		
		F/L F.H.Pollock		Bf109 destroyed	Gisors-Pontoise	1605±
		164 Squadron		- Shared -		
306 Sqn Must	2TAF	F/O A.Beyer		He111 destroyed	12m NE Nevers	1740
		F/S J.Pomietlarz		- Shared -		
		F/L W.Potocki		- Shared -		
		F/O S.Tronczynski		- Shared -		
136 Wg Typh	2TAF	W/C J.M.Bryan		Bf109 destroyed	Gisors-Pontoise	1605±
		183 Squadron		- Shared -		

19th May 1944

403 Sqn Spit	2TAF	F/L D.Hodgson		FW190 destroyed	Beaumont-sur-Oise AD	1830±
		F/L J.D.Lindsay		FW190 destroyed	N Auneuil	1830±
		F/L R.H.Smith		- Shared -		

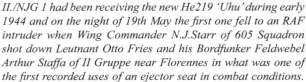

II./NJG 1 had been receiving the new He219 'Uhu' during early 1944 and on the night of 19th May the first one fell to an RAF intruder when Wing Commander N.J.Starr of 605 Squadron shot down Leutnant Otto Fries and his Bordfunker Feldwebel Arthur Staffa of II Gruppe near Florennes in what was one of the first recorded uses of an ejector seat in combat conditions.
This crew would eject again in 1945, shot down by Flight Lieutenant K.D.Vaughan of 85 Squadron. Of the Mosquitos, Fries was to say later, "The Mosquitos would attack us on take-off, chase us into the bomber streams, through the bomber streams and then chase us home and bomb us as we landed. We were shot down twice and blown off the runway several times by bombing."

19/20th May 1944

605 Sqn Mosq	ADGB	W/C N.J.Starr	He219 destroyed	Florennes	0152

21st May 1944

19 Sqn Must	2TAF	W/O M.H.Bell	LeO45 destroyed	S Viborg	1645
		F/L A.C.Shirref	- Shared -		
		W/O L.T.Woodward	- Shared –		
		418 Squadron		- Shared -	
418 Sqn Mosq	ADGB	F/L J.B.Kerr	LeO45 destroyed	S Viborg	1645
		19 Squadron	- Shared -		
		F/L J.B.Kerr	LeO45 destroyed	S Viborg	1645

21/22nd May 1944

605 Sqn Mosq	ADGB	F/O E.L.Williams	E/A damaged	Eindhoven	0317

22nd May 1944

416 Sqn Spit	2TAF	F/L R.D.Forbes			
		-Roberts	FW190 destroyed	Etrepagny AD	0800±
		F/L W.F.Mason	FW190 destroyed	Etrepagny AD	0800±

The Poles of 315 'City of Deblin' Squadron had received their new Mustang IIIs in March and soon made their presence felt over France in Ranger missions. Tadeusz Jankowski, (left) Janusz Marciniak (centre) and Maciej Kirste (right) were all successful on 25th May over

Bourges airfield. All three pilots would achieve two victores apiece, but only Kirste would survive the war. Marciniak fell in combat near Dreux on 23rd June 1944 and Jankowski was killed on 20th September in support of the Arnhem operation. (Kirste - ww2images.com)

416 Sqn Spit	2TAF	F/O A.R.McFadden	Bf109 destroyed	Etrepagny AD	0800±
		P/O W.H.Palmer	FW190 destroyed	Etrepagny AD	0800±
		F/L G.R.Patterson	FW190 destroyed	Etrepagny AD	0800±
410 RSUSpit	2TAF	F/O H.W.Bowker	FW190 destroyed	S Selsey	1100±
		F/O H.W.Bowker	FW190 destroyed	S Selsey	1100±

22/23rd May 1944

29 Sqn Mosq	ADGB	F/O R.A.Crone	E/A damaged	Coulommieres	0200±
125 Sqn Mosq	ADGB	F/O K.O'Sullivan	Ju188 destroyed	50m S St Catherines Pt	0020
		F/L G.F.Simcock	Ju88 destroyed	17m S St Catherines Pt	0045
169 Sqn Mosq	BC	W/C N.B.R.Bromley	Bf110 destroyed	Groningen area	0100±
239 Sqn Mosq	BC	F/L D.L.Hughes	Bf110 destroyed	Dortmund	0115±
456 Sqn Mosq	ADGB	W/C K.M.Hampshire	Ju88 destroyed	30m S Isle of Wight	0023
		P/O I.W.Sanderson	Ju88 destroyed	30m S Isle of Wight	0024

24 May 1944

401 Sqn Spit	2TAF	S/L L.M.Cameron	FW190 destroyed	Nivelles	2015

24/25th May 1944

219 Sqn Mosq	ADGB	P/O D.T.Tull	Ju88 prob.dest	55m NE Orfordness	0338
239 Sqn Mosq	BC	F/L D.L.Hughes	Bf110 destroyed	40m NW Aachen	0015±
		F/O W.R.Breithaupt	Ju88 destroyed	15m ESE Bonn	0125
		F/O W.R.Breithaupt	Bf109 damaged	NW Aachen	0125±
239 Sqn Mosq	BC	F/L D.J.Raby	Bf110 destroyed	Aachen	0145±
605 Sqn Mosq	ADGB	F/L I.F.Pengelly	E/A damaged	Westerbeek/Hooge	0137

25th May 1944

315 Sqn Must	2TAF	F/S T.Jankowski	Ar96B destroyed	Bourges	1915
		F/O M.Kirste	- Shared -		
		F/O J.Polak	- Shared -		
		F/L J.Marciniak	Ar96B destroyed	Bourges	1915

27/28th May 1944

141 Sqn Mosq	BC	F/L H.E.White	Bf109 destroyed	W Aachen	0235
239 Sqn Mosq	BC	F/L N.A.Reeves	Bf110 destroyed	Leeuwarden	0140±
		F/O R.K.Bailey	Bf110 destroyed*	Leeuwarden	u/k

Note: Crew FTR and PoW. Victory never confirmed by RAF.

410 Sqn Mosq	ADGB	P/O L.J.Kearney	Ju88 destroyed	Lille	0400

28th May 1944

605 Sqn Mosq	ADGB	S/L G.J.Wright	Ju52 destroyed	Heligoland	0940
		S/L G.J.Wright	Ju52 destroyed	Heligoland	0954
		F/L L.W.H.Welch	Ju52 destroyed	Heligoland	0954

28/29th May 1944

25 Sqn Mosq	ADGB	W/C C.M.Wight -Boycott	Me410 destroyed	55m E Cromer	0400±

29th May 1944

183 Sqn Typh	2TAF	F/O A.R.Taylor	Bf109 destroyed	40m S Isle of Wight	1530±
		F/O A.R.Taylor	Bf109 destroyed	40m S Isle of Wight	1530±

29/30th May 1944

151 Sqn Mosq	ADGB	F/O B. Kneath	He111 destroyed	10m S Falmouth	0040
456 Sqn Mosq	ADGB	W/C K.M.Hampshire	Me410 prob.dest	Channel	0145±

30th May 1944

118 Sqn Spit	ADGB	F/O J.J.Parker	Ju88 destroyed	25m E Kirkwall	1739
		W/O A.Taylor	- Shared -		

31st May/1st June 1944

239 Sqn Mosq	BC	F/O V.Bridges	Bf110 destroyed	nr Trappes, Paris	0100±

1st June 1944

122 Sqn Must	2TAF	S/L E.L.Joyce	He111 destroyed	N Alte Mellum	0740
418 Sqn Mosq	ADGB	F/L T.G.Anderson	Do217 destroyed	5m N Plan de Dieu A/D	0757

1/2nd June 1944

418 Sqn Mosq	ADGB	P/O M.H.Sims	JuW34 destroyed	Baden-Baden A/D	2134
239 Sqn Mosq	BC	F/O D.Welfare	Bf110 destroyed	W Paris	0230±

2/3rd June 1944

219 Sqn Mosq	ADGB	P/O D.T.Tull	He219 destroyed	Dutch Isles	0220±
239 Sqn Mosq	BC	F/L T.L.Wright	Bf110 destroyed	4900N 0050E	0130

5/6th June 1944

25 Sqn Mosq	ADGB	F/L R.D.R.Davies	Bf110 destroyed	Schiermonnikoog.	0045
239 Sqn Mosq	BC	F/O W.R.Breithaupt	Ju88 destroyed	10m S Norderney	0053
		F/O D.Welfare	Bf110 destroyed	N Aachen	0120±
409 Sqn Mosq	2TAF	F/O H.F.Pearce	Ju188 destroyed	NW Somme	0223
605 Sqn Mosq	ADGB	F/O R.E.Lelong	Me410 destroyed	SE Evreux	0148

Chapter Four

Normandy and Beyond

D-Day - the date for the invasion of France - had arrived and the fighter pilots and aircrews of the 2nd TAF, together with their USAAF comrades, now had a formidable task. By day, this was to (a) achieve air supremacy over the English Channel and the beachheads. (b) to prevent movement of German reinforcements and particularly the armour from its holding positions near Calais. (c) to provide close air support for advancing Allied troops. (d) to provide escorts for daylight bomber operations. By night, the main tasks were to (a) prevent *Luftwaffe* night attacks on the beachhead and naval shipping. (b) to maintain intruder patrols around known *Luftwaffe* night-flying bases. (c) to continue road and rail transport interdiction. (d) to continue long-range patrols against *Luftwaffe* nightfighter bases and, for the 100 Group *Serrate* crews, to continue the hunt for German nightfighters.

These tasks were made easier initially by the almost complete absence of German fighter activity in France, caused by the Allied *Point Blank* offensive against Germany. This caused the *Oberkommando der Luftwaffe* to pull its fighter forces back into Germany for the defence of the *Reich*. Thus air supremacy was to be achieved immediately and, due to the massive numerical superiority of the Allies, this would never change. The fighter-bombers too would reign supreme, so much so that German units dared not move in daylight without attracting attention from the swarms of Typhoons and American Thunderbolts and Lightnings that roamed freely over the battlefield and the approaches.

The ADGB fighters, now a mere shadow of the strength displayed by 2nd TAF, were to engage in a deadly fight from the middle of June, when the German V-1 offensive against London began.

6th June 1944 - 'D-Day'

Sqn		Pilot	Claim	Location	Time
122 Sqn Must	2TAF	P/O K.A.Galloway	FW190 damaged	N Caen	2130±
129 Sqn Must	2TAF	F/L A.J.Hancock	FW190 destroyed	15m SW Caen	2115
		W/O W.E.Rigby	- Shared -		
164 Sqn Typh	2TAF	S/L P.H.Beake	FW190 destroyed	5m N Caen	1835
165 Sqn Spit	ADGB	F/L J.G.Clouston	Ju88 destroyed	S Baud	2055
		P/O D.Moffat-Wilson	- Shared -		
		W/O J.M.Walton	- Shared –		
		Predannack Wg	- Shared -		
349 Sqn Spit	2TAF	F/O H.Bailley	Ju88 damaged	3m NNW Caen	1545
		F/L A.A.Van der Velde	- Shared -		
		F/L G.M.H.Seydel	Ju88 damaged	3m E Ryes	1545
		Sgt D.Blair	- Shared -		
		F/S J.C.I.Van Melkot	Ju88 destroyed	4m S Caen	1545
		Sgt J.Bragard	- Shared -		
		F/O J.Moreau	Ju88 destroyed	6m NE Caen	1545
		F/O M.J.Sans	- Shared -		
		F/S J.Moureau	Ju88 destroyed	6m NE Caen	1545
		F/O M.Siraut	Ju88 damaged	5m N Caen	1545

485 Sqn Spit	2TAF	F/O J.A.Houlton	Ju88 destroyed	Beachhead-Caen	1545
		F/S E.G.Atkins	Ju88 destroyed	Beachhead-Caen	1545
		F/O J.A.Houlton	- Shared -		
		F/L K.J.MacDonald	- Shared -		
		F/O M.G.Maystom	- Shared -		
Pre Wg Spit	ADGB	W/C D.G.Smallwood	Ju88 destroyed	S Baud	2055
		165 Squadron	- Shared -		

6/7th June 1944

29 Sqn Mosq	ADGB	F/LG.E.Allison	E/A destroyed	Coulommieres	2340
		F/LG.E.Allison	Ju52 destroyed	Coulommieres	2352
		F/LR.Beynon	E/A destroyed	Melun AD	0032
307 Sqn Mosq	ADGB	W/O K.Oleszczuk	Ju88 damaged	10m S Leeuwarden A/D	0128
418 Sqn Mosq	ADGB	F/L D.A.McFayden	Ju52 destroyed	N Coulommieres A/D	2345
		F/L S.H.R.Cotterill	Ju52 destroyed	2m W Chateaudun	0012
		F/L S.H.R.Cotterill	Ju52 destroyed	Orleans A/D	0015
		F/L S.H.R.Cotterill	Ju188 destroyed	S Orleans	0023
		F/L S.H.R.Cotterill	Ju52 destroyed	Orleans A/D	0032
		W/O J.J.P.McGale	Ju52 damaged	Beaugency	0255
		F/O F.M.Sawyer	E/A damaged	Coulommieres	0237
456 Sqn Mosq	ADGB	F/O R.G.Pratt	He177 destroyed	N Cherbourg	0125
		F/O F.S.Stevens	He177 destroyed	N Cherbourg	0256
		F/O F.S.Stevens	He177 destroyed	N Cherbourg	0314
		W/C K.M.Hampshire	He177 destroyed	3m E Barfleur	0349
605 Sqn Mosq	ADGB	F/O E.L.Williams	Ju88 destroyed	Orleans	0158
		W/C N.V.Starr	E/A damaged	Dreux	0234

7th June 1944

129 Sqn Must	2TAF	F/O M.Twomey	FW190 destroyed	Evreux-Bernay	0640
132 Sqn Spit	2TAF	F/L D.J.Hawkins	Bf109 damaged	Near Cap Barfleur	0920
306 Sqn Must	2TAF	F/O A.Beyer	Bf109F destroyed	Near Pont Audemer	1035
		F/L R.Budrewicz	Bf109F destroyed	Near Pont Audemer	1035
		F/S J.Czezowski	Bf109F prob.dest	Near Pont Audemer	1035
		S/L S.H.Lapka	Bf109F destroyed	Near Pont Audemer	1035
		F/S J.Pomietlerz	Bf109F damaged	Near Pont Audemer	1035
		F/L J.Siekierski	Bf109F destroyed	Near Pont Audemer	1035
		F/L J.Siekierski	Bf109F damaged	Near Pont Audemer	1035
		F/L G.Sologub	Bf109F destroyed	Near Pont Audemer	1035

Stan Cotterill of 418 Squadron, pictured here with his navigator Flying Officer McKenna, made his mark on the night of 6th June by destroying three Ju52s and a Ju188 over and around Orleans airfield, all within the space of twenty minutes. He was lost on 17th October 1944 while returning from a Day Ranger to Vienna. During the V-1 offensive he was credited with four flying bombs destroyed.

306 Sqn Must	2TAF	F/L J.Jelinski	Bf109F damaged	10m E Argentan	1805
		F/S W.Nowczyk	Bf109F destroyed	10m E Argentan	1805
		F/O H.Pietrzak	Bf109F destroyed	10m E Argentan	1805
		F/O H.Pietrzak	Bf109F destroyed	10m E Argentan	1805
		F/O H.Pietrzak	Bf109F damaged	10m E Argentan	1805
		F/L W.Potocki	Bf109F destroyed	10m E Argentan	1805
		F/L W.Potocki	Bf109F destroyed	10m E Argentan	1805
		F/S S.Rudowski	Bf109F destroyed	10m E Argentan	1805
		F/S S.Rudowski	Bf109F damaged	10m E Argentan	1805
312 Sqn Spit	2TAF	F/S J.Konvicka	FW190 damaged	20m SW Rouen	1345
		F/O V.Kopocek	FW190 damaged	20m SW Rouen	1345
315 Sqn Must	2TAF	F/L A.S.Sworniowski	FW 190 destroyed	3m W Argentan	0700
		F/S T.Berka	Bf109 destroyed	15m SE Rouen	1010
		F/S R.Idrjan	Bf109 destroyed	15m SE Rouen	1010
		F/O M.Kirste	Bf109F destroyed	15m SE Rouen	1010
		F/L J.Marciniak	Bf109F destroyed	15m SE Rouen	1010
		F/L J.Marciniak	Bf109F prob.dest	15m SE Rouen	1010
349 Sqn Spit	2TAF	F/L G.M.H.Seydel	FW190 damaged	5m SSW Caen	0635
401 Sqn Spit	2TAF	F/O G.D.Billings	Ju88 destroyed	Beachhead	0920
		F/L G.B.Murray F/O W.A.Bishop	Ju88 destroyed - Shared -	Near Caen	0920
		F/L R.H.Cull	Ju88 destroyed	Gold Beach	0920
		F/L A.F.Halcrow	Ju88 prob.dest	Gold Beach	0920
		F/O D.F.Husband	Ju88 destroyed	N Caen	0930
		S/L L.M.Cameron	Ju88 destroyed	3m inland Gold Beach	0950
		S/L L.M.Cameron	Ju88 destroyed	3m inland Gold Beach	0950
		F/O W.T.Klersey	FW190 destroeyd	NW Caen	1330
		F/L R.R.Bouskill	FW190 damaged	Near Le Havre	1345
		F/L W.R.Tew	FW190 damaged	U-2060	1340

On 7th June the Germans frantically attempted to bring their fighters and fighter-bombers back to France to repel the invasion - but it was too late. Three pilots who were successful during the heavy actions of the 7th were Gerry Billings of 401 Squadron (left)pictured following his destruction of a Ju88. Andrezej Beyer of 306 Squadron (centre) got a Bf109F and would later destroy five V-1s, and George Burroughs (right), a Tac/R Mustang pilot who 'shared' a Ju52 with his wingman north of Mortaigne.

411 Sqn Spit	2TAF	S/L G.D.Robertson	FW190 destroeyd	4m N Caen	1915
		F/L G.W.Johnson	Bf109 destroyed	3m N Caen	1920
412 Sqn Spit	2TAF	F/O P.M.Charron	Ju88 destroyed	Beachhead-Caen	0920
		F/L H.L.Phillips	Ju88 damaged	Beachhead	0920
		F/O J.P.M.Laureys	Ju88 damaged	NW Caen	0930
414 Sqn Must	2TAF	F/L G.W.Burroughs	Ju52 destroyed	N Martagne	0630
		F/O R.A.Bromley	- Shared -		
443 Sqn Spit	2TAF	F/L H.Russell	Bf109 destroyed	N Caen	1700
		F/O G.F.Ockenden	- Shared -		
		F/L W.A.Prest	Bf109 damaged	E Caen	1700±
126 Wg Spit	2TAF	W/C G.C.Keefer	Ju88 destroyed	NW Caen	0920
		W/C G.C.Keefer	FW190 destroyed	Eastern Beachhead	1842
145 Wg Spit	2TAF	W/C W.V.Crawford -Compton	Ju88 destroyed	W Caen	0950

7/8th June 1944

25 Sqn	Mosq	ADGB	F/L D.H.Greaves	Me410 destroyed	off Happisburgh	0015
29 Sqn	Mosq	ADGB	F/O F.E.Pringle	E/A damaged	S Dreux	2355
			F/O F.E.Pringle	E?A destroyed	Dreux AD	0035
			F/L J.E.Barry	Ju188 destroyed	Nr Marolles	0108
			F/L J.E.Barry	Ju188 destroyed	W Bretigny AD	0115
219 Sqn	Mosq	2TAF	S/LP.L.Burke	Ju188 destroyed	Off Harwich	2359
			P/O D.T.Tull	Me410 destroyed	10m E Harwich	0030
307 Sqn	Mosq	ADGB	W/O K.Oleszczuk	Ju88 damaged	10m S Leeuwarden A/D	0128
406 Sqn	Beau	ADGB	P/O R.L.Green	Do217 destroyed	2m N Lannion	0040
418 Sqn	Mosq	ADGB	F/L J.B.Kerr	Ju52 destroyed	F-3801	0144

Tempests went into action early in the invasion campaign. 3 Squadron claimed its first kills west of Rouen on 8th June, probably against III./JG 3.

456 Sqn Mosq	ADGB	S/L B.Howard	He177 destroyed	Off Cherbourg	0105
		S/L B.Howard	He177 destroyed	Off Cherbourg	0125
		P/O R.D.Hodgen	He177 destroyed	Off Cherbourg	0155
604 Sqn Mosq	2TAF	F/L J.C.I.Hooper	Bf110 destroyed	N Laval	0155

8th June 1944

3 Sqn	Temp	ADGB	F/L A.R.Moore	Bf109 destroyed	W Rouen	1250
			F/O G.A.Whitman	Bf109 destroyed	W Rouen	1250
65 Sqn	Must	2TAF	F/L R.A.E.Milton	FW190 destroyed	Gace/Dreux	0600
			F/L R.L.Sutherland	FW190 destroyed	Gace/Dreux	0600
			S/L D.F.Westenra	FW190 destroyed	Gace/Dreux	0600
164 Sqn	Typh	2TAF	F/L A.G.Todd F/S R.J.M.Wilson	Bf109 destroyed - Shared -	10-15m S Caen	1320
222 Sqn	Spit	2TAF	F/L R.F.Bass	FW190 destroyed	East Beach	2000±
			F/L R.F.Bass F/O A.A.McIntyre	Bf109 damaged - Shared -	East Beach	2000±
			F/O W.F.Bern	FW190 damaged	East Beach	2000±
			F/O A.W.Burge	FW190 destroeyd	East Beach	2000±
			F/O A.W.Burge	Bf109 damaged	East Beach	2000±
			S/L D.G.S.R.Cox	FW190 damaged	East Beach	2000±
			F/L G.C.D.Green	FW190 damaged	East Beach	2000±
			F/S G.G.Walters	FW190 destroeyd	East Beach	2000±
310 Sqn	Spit	2TAF	F/O O.Smik	FW190 destroyed	S Lisieux	1340
312 Sqn	Spit	2TAF	F/O V.Kopocek	FW190 damaged	10-15m SE Caen	1335
			F/O V.Kopocek	FW190 damaged	10-15m SE Caen	1335

312 Sqn Spit	2TAF	P/O F.Mlejnecky	FW190 damaged	10-15m SE Caen	1335
		W/O A.Skach	FW190 damaged	10-15m SE Caen	1335
		Sgt V.Angetter	FW190 destroyed	5m N Courselles-s-Mer	1340
349 Sqn Spit	2TAF	W/O D.Clarke F/L G.M.H.Seydel	FW190 destroyed - Shared -	4m S Trouville	0625
485 Sqn Spit	2TAF	F/O J.F.P.Yeatman	FW190 destroeyd	3m SE St Aubin	0658
		P/O H.W.B.Patterson	Bf109 destroyed	8m SSE Caen	2030
		P/O F.Transom	Bf109 destroyed	15m W Caen	2030
		W/O H.M.Esdaile	FW190 damaged	Near Caen	2035
		F/O J.A.Houlton	Bf109 destroyed	15m W Caen	2035
		S/L J.B.Niven	FW190 damaged	10m E Caen	2035
		F/O A.B,.Stead	FW190 destroeyd	15m ESE Caen	2046
501 Sqn Spit	ADGB	P/O R.H.Bennett	Bf109 prob.dest	Off Cabourg	0540
		S/L D.C.Fairbanks	Bf109 destroyed	Off Cabourg	0540
		S/L D.C.Fairbanks	Bf109 damaged	Off Cabourg	0540
		F/L L.P.Griffiths	Bf109 destroyed	Off Cabourg	0540

Combat Report - 8th June 1944

I was leading the Newchurch Tempest wing on a Fighter sweep to the Caen area of the beachhead via Rouen, Bernay and Argentan. We took off from Newchurch at 12.25 hours, and crossed the French coast at Pte d'Ailly at 10,000 ft. When we were a few miles to the West of Rouen at 12.50 hours over scattered cloud, I saw five aircraft in line astern at about 5,000 ft, turning from East to North. Leaving 486 (N.Z.) Squadron up above as top cover, I took No. 3 Squadron down to investigate. I closed in behind the aircraft at 370 I.A.S., and recognized them as ME.109G's. They were travelling at approximately 300 m.p.h. and did not realize they were being bounced until just before I opened fire, when the e/a broke to port and dived for cloud with violent evasive action. I selected the fourth or last e/a, I am not sure which, and opened fire with a 2/3 second burst, starting with 30° deflection, and changing according to the e/a's evasive action.

I opened fire at about 500 yards range closing to pointblank, and saw strikes at the end of the burst on the starboard side of the fuselage. The e/a immediately poured smoke and flames. I had to break to starboard in order to avoid collision and then to port when I saw clearly the e/a enveloped in flames in an inverted dive. I broke to starboard as I finished my attack and heard a loud bang and saw a strike on my starboard wing. My No. 2 who subsequently saw my e/a disintegrate and the starboard wing break off, saw two ME.109's diving down out of sun at him and myself. My U/C warning lights went on so I handed over to S/Ldr. Dredge, of No. 3 Squadron, and set course for base where I landed at 13.30 hrs. The aircraft I destroyed was camouflaged mottled chocolate and brown and no national markings were visible.

I claim one ME. 109G destroyed.

R. P. Beamont, Wing Commander 150 (Newchurch) Wing

The FW190F was to be employed in great numbers as a low-level fighter-bomber, but suffered hugely against the Allied fighter cover.

134 Wg Spit	2TAF	W/C J.Cermak	FW190 destroeyd	Mezidon	1335
		W/C J.Cermak	FW190 damaged	Mezidon	1335
136 Wg Typh	2TAF	W/C J.M.Bryan	Bf109 damaged	10-15m S Caen	1310±
		W/C J.M.Bryan	Bf109 damaged	10-15m S Caen	1310±
150 Wg Temp	ADGB	W/C R.P.Beamont	Bf109 destroyed	W Rouen	1250
WH Wg Spit	ADGB	W/C J.M.Checketts	Bf109F damaged	Mouth of R Orne	0610

8/9th June 1944

29 Sqn Mosq	ADGB	F/O R.A.Wigglesworth	Ju88 destroyed	Beachhead	0206
141 Sqn Mosq	BC	F/O A.C.Gallacher	E/A destroyed	Rennes	0030±
FIU Mosq	ADGB	F/L J.N.Howard			
		-Williams	He177 damaged	Etampes	0128

9/10th June 1944

29 Sqn Mosq	ADGB	S/L R.C.Pargeter	Ju88 destroyed	Lisieux	0225
		Lt D.R.O.Price	Ju188 destroyed	Melun	0330±
169 Sqn Mosq	BC	W/C N.B.R.Bromley	Do217 destroyed	S Paris	0200±
409 Sqn Mosq	ADGB	S/L A.S.Jephson	Ju188 destroyed	30m S Le Havre	0315±
410 Sqn Mosq	ADGB	F/OR.L.Snowden	Ju188 destroyed	Beachhead	0355
456 Sqn Mosq	ADGB	F/L R.B.Cowper	Do217 destroyed	Near Cap Levy	0400
		F/L R.B.Cowper	He177 destroyed	Near Beaumont	0405

10th June 1944

19 Sqn Must	2TAF	F/S T.A.Carson	Bf109 destroyed	10m S Caen	1020
		W/O H.Holmes	Bf109 destroyed	10m S Caen	1020
		W/O A.Sima	- Shared -		
		F/L D.P.Lamb	Bf109 damaged	10m S Caen	1020
65 Sqn Must	2TAF	F/L B.G.Collyns	Bf109 destroyed	S Caen	1010±

65 Sqn Must	2TAF	F/L R.L.Stillwell	Bf109 damaged	S Caen	1010±
		F/L R.A.E.Milton	Bf109 destroyed	Battle area	1045
		F/L R.A.Milton	Bf109 damaged	near Breteuil	1045
		F/S W.P.Kelly	Bf109 destroyed	near Breteuil	1850
130 Sqn Spit	ADGB	F/L G.V.Scott	Ju188 destroyed	Near Benouville	0540
222 Sqn Spit	2TAF	F/L G.W.Varley	FW190 destroyed	Cabourg	0700±
312 Sqn Spit	2TAF	Sgt J.Konvicka	Bf109 prob.dest	By collision Caen	1350
401 Sqn Spit	2TAF	F/L A.A.Williams 411 Squadron	FW190 destroyed - Shared -	Dreux	2110
411 Sqn Spit	2TAF	F/L H.J.Nixon 401 Squadron	FW190 destroyed - Shared -	Dreux	2110
414 Sqn Must	2TAF	F/OB.B.Mossing	FW190 damaged	N Mezidon	1445

10/11th June 1944

130 Sqn Spit	ADGB	F/L G.A.Mathieson	Ju188 destroyed	Beachhead	2250±
		F/L G.A.Mathieson	Ju88 destroyed	5m SE St Mere Eglise	2315
264 Sqn Mosq	ADGB	F/L H.J.Corre	Ju88 destroyed	10m E St Mere Eglise	0355
		F/L H.J.Corre	FW190 prob.dest	N R.Orne	0422
409 Sqn Mosq	ADGB	F/O R.L.Fullerton	Ju188 destroyed	Seine area	0224
		F/O C.J.Preece	Ju188 destroyed	Bretteville	0334
		F/O C.J.Preece	Ju188 destroyed	Falaise	0415
456 Sqn Mosq	ADGB	P/O I.W.Sanderson	He177 destroyed	30m S Shoreham	0331
		S/L G.L.Howitt	He177 prob.dest	Channel	0405
605 Sqn Mosq	ADGB	W/C N.J.Starr	Me410 destroyed	Chateaudun	0229
		F/O R.E.Lelong	Ju188 destroyed	Coulommieres	0238
611 Sqn Spit	ADGB	S/L W.A.Douglas	Ju88 destroyed	Carentan	0030±
		Sgt J.Marquis	Ju88 destroyed	Carentan	0030±

11th June 1944

485 Sqn Spit	ADGB	F/O J.A.Houlton F/L W.A.Newenham	Bf109 destroyed - Shared -	Beachhead	1200±
		F/O J.A,Houlton F/L W.A.Newenham	Bf109 destroyed - Shared -	Beachhead	1200±

11/12th June 1944

85 Sqn Mosq	BC	W/C C.M.Miller	Bf110 destroyed	Melun AD	0035
		F/L M.Phillips	Bf110 destroyed	nr Paris	0100

Successful on 8th June were Johnny Checketts, leading the Westhampnett Spitfire Wing, who got a Bf109 damaged and Flight Lieutenant L.P.Griffiths a '109 shot down (Griffiths: Dan Johnson).

239 Sqn Mosq	BC	F/L D.Welfare	Bf110 destroyed	N.Paris	0030±
409 Sqn Mosq	ADGB	F/O A.W.Sterrenberg	Do217 destroyed	Alencon	0005
		F/O K.Livingstone	Ju188 destroyed	Near Carentan	0417

12th June 1944

124 Sqn Spit	ADGB	F/L P.V.Ayerst F/L W.J.Hibbert	Bf109G destroyed - Shared -	20m E North Foreland	1910
131 Sqn Spit	ADGB	F/O R.K.Parry	Bf109 destroyed	1m W Laval AD	1415
315 Sqn Must	ADGB	F/S J.Bargielowski	FW190 destroyed	8m SE Sens	1240
		F/S J.Bargielowski	FW190 destroyed	8m SE Sens	1240
		S/L E.Horbaczewski	FW190 destroyed	8m SE Sens	1240
		F/O M.Kirste	FW190 destroyed	8m SE Sens	1240
340 Sqn Spit	2TAF	Capt O.Massert	FW190 destroyed	NW Caen	1440
485 Sqn Spit	2TAF	F/O J.A.Houlton	Bf109 destroyed	2m SW Aunay-s-Odon	0640
		F/L W.A.Newenham	Bf109 destroyed	2m SW Aunay-s-Odon	0640
616 Sqn Spit	ADGB	F/L J.M.Cleland	FW190 destroyed	Laval	1445
		F/L J.M.Cleland	FW190 destroyed	Laval	1445
		F/L G.A.Harrison	Bf109 destroyed	Laval (by collision)	1445
		W/O R.A.Hart	Bf109 destroyed	Laval	1445

12/13th June 1944

157 Sqn Mosq	BC	S/LJ.G.Benson	Ju88 destroyed	Foret de Compeigne	0152
264 Sqn Mosq	ADGB	F/L R.L.Beverley	Ju188 destroyed	Beachhead	0355
		F/L M.M.Davison	Ju188 destroyed	Falaise	0435
410 Sqn Mosq	ADGB	F/O J.Maday	Ju88 damaged	Near Baueux	0006
		P/O L.J.Kearney	He177 destroyed	15m NE Le Havre	0130
		W/O W.F.Price	Do217 destroyed	25m SE Caen	0210
		W/O W.F.Price	Do217 destroyed	25m SE Caen	0230

On 12th June, Squadron Leader Eugenius Horbaczewski (left) led the Mustangs of 315 Squadron against FW190s near Sens. He claimed one destroyed as did Flying Officer M.Kirste, but Jakub Bargielowski (centre) got two. A still from his camera-gun is shown right, with a '190 going down.

410 Sqn Mosq	ADGB	F/O R.L.Snowdon	Ju88 destroyed	S Caen, near Lisieux	0405
456 Sqn Mosq	ADGB	W/C K.M.Hampshire	Ju88 destroyed	N Port-en-Bassin	0418
488 Sqn Mosq	ADGB	S/L E.N.Bunting	Ju88 destroyed	W Caen-Bayeux	0425
604 Sqn Mosq	ADGB	F/O R.A.Miller	He177 destroyed	Beachhead	0215
		F/L J.C.I.Hooper	Ju88 destroyed	Cherbourg	0403
605 Sqn Mosq	ADGB	F/O E.L.Williams	Ju88 prob.dest	Chievres	0229
		F/O E.L.Williams	E/A damaged	Chievres	0230

13th June 1944

315 Sqn Must	2TAF	F/L H.Stefankiewicz	FW190 destroyed	5m NE Flers	1945

13/14th June 1944

169 Sqn Mosq	BC	W/O L.W.Turner	Ju88 destroyed	Near Paris	0115±
264 Sqn Mosq	ADGB	F/L I.H.Cosby	He177 destroyed	40m NNE FDT.216	0208
409 Sqn Mosq	ADGB	W/C J.W.Reid	He177 destroyed	20-25m N Le Havre	0145
410 Sqn Mosq	ADGB	F/L C.E.Edinger	Ju88 damaged	Beachhead	0338
		S/L I.A.March	Ju88 destroyed	49°30'N, 00°30'E	0353
456 Sqn Mosq	ADGB	P/O S.J.Williams	He177 destroyed	Off Fecamp	0215
		Lt D.G.Thornley	He129 damaged	Off Fecamp	0230
604 Sqn Mosq	ADGB	F/L F.C.Ellis	He177 destroyed	17m ENE Barfleur	0208

On 12th June Olivier Massert of 340 Squadron gained his second victory. He would become a prisoner on 13th March 1945. On the same day Lloyd Chadburn, the 127 Wing Leader (far right), was killed when he collided with his wingman, Flight Lieutenant F.Clark, over Rainville.

14th June 1944

Sqn	Type	Force	Crew	Claim	Location	Time
19 Sqn	Must	2TAF	W/O M.H.Bell	Bf109 destroyed	10m SW Rouen	1230±
			F/O J.Paton	Bf109 destroyed	10m SW Rouen	1230±
			P/O F.D.Schofield	- Shared -		
			W/O A.Sima	- Shared -		
			F/S C.R.Wells	- Shared -		
65 Sqn	Must	2TAF	F/O C.P.Ashworth	Bf109 destroyed	10m SW Rouen	1210
			F/O J.M.W.Lloyd	Bf109 damaged	10m SW Rouen	1210
			F/O J.M.W.Lloyd	Bf109 damaged	10m SW Rouen	1210
			F/L R.L.Stillwell	FW190 damaged	10m SW Rouen	1210
80 Sqn	Spit	ADGB	Maj B.A.Bjornstad	Bf109 damaged	Dieppe-Paris	1145±
			F/L D.M.Wiseman	- Shared -		
332 Sqn	Spit	2TAF	2/Lt R.Kolling	Me410 damaged	W Le Havre	2250
			2/Lt J.Rosland	- Shared -		
			2/Lt O.Tidemand -Johansen	- Shared -		
418 Sqn	Mosq	ADGB	P/O M.H.Sims	JuW34 destroyed	S end Bagenkop Island	1534
			S/L R.A.Kipp	He111 destroyed	S end Bagenkop Island	1537
443 Sqn	Spit	2TAF	S/L H.W.McLeod	Do217 destroyed	SW Le Havre	2245
			F/O R.A.Hodgins	Do217 destroyed	NE Le Havre	2250
611 Sqn	Spit	ADGB	Lt J.J.Carre	Bf109 prob.dest	S Caen	1530±
			Lt J.J.Carre	Bf109 damaged	S Caen	1530±
			W/O F.Delery	Bf109 damaged	S Caen	1530±
			S/L W.A.Douglas	Bf109 destroyed	S Caen	1530±
			F/O K.T.King	Bf109 destroyed	S Caen	1530±
			F/S J.Marquis	Bf109 damaged	S Caen	1530±
			F/L C.S.McGregor	Bf109 destroyed	S Caen	1530±
			F/S M.K.S.Wilson	- Shared -		

Russ Bannock (left) of 418 Squadron - on left with navigator 'Bob' Bruce - claimed his first kill on 14/15th June. He would then concentrate on V-1 interceptions and, after 18 destroyed, he returned to intruding, claiming a further eight victories. Bannock's Mosquito was 'Hairless Joe' (centre). Seconded from the Royal Navy complete with beard, Douglas Price (right) flew with 29 Squadron and claimed three kills. His first claim was for a Ju88 'damaged' on 14th/15th June. (K.Lowes, via Frank Pringle)

14/15th June 1944

29 Sqn	Mosq	ADGB	S/Lt D.R.O.Price	Ju88 damaged	Coulommieres	0300±
85 Sqn	Mosq	BC	F/O H.B.Thomas	Ju88 destroyed	nr Criel	0016
			F/L B.A.Burbridge	Ju188 destroyed	SW Nivelles	0127
141 Sqn	Mosq	BC	W/O H.W.Welham	Me410 destroyed	N Lille	0140
157 Sqn	Mosq	BC	F/L J.Tweedale	Ju88 destroyed	N Lille	0149
219 Sqn	Mosq	ADGB	F/L M.J.Gloster	Ju88 destroyed	North Sea	0302
264 Sqn	Mosq	ADGB	F/L H.J.Corre	Ju188 destroyed	25m W Le Havre	0016
409 Sqn	Mosq	ADGB	F/L W.L.Marr	Ju188 damaged	7-8m N Le Havre	2355
410 Sqn	Mosq	ADGB	F/L W.G.Dinsdale	Ju88 destroyed	25m SE Caen	2340
418 Sqn	Mosq	ADGB	S/L R.Bannock	Bf110 destroyed	Avord A/D	0143
456 Sqn	Mosq	ADGB	F/L R.B.Cowper	Ju88 destroyed	Channel	0041
488 Sqn	Mosq	ADGB	F/L P.F.L.Hall	Ju88 destroyed	5-10m SW St Lo	0230
604 Sqn	Mosq	ADGB	F/O T.R.Wood	FW190 prob.dest	St Mere Eglise -Pte de Percee	0400
			F/O T.R.Wood	FW190 destroyed	St Mere Eglise	0430
FIU	Mosq	ADGB	W/C C.H.Hartley	Bf110 dest	Lens-Bethune	0130

15th June 1944

66 Sqn	Spit	2TAF	F/O C.Brown	FW190 damaged	Evreux	0645
			P/O R.C.Casburn W/O V.Lonnen	FW190 destroyed - Shared -	Evreux	0645
			F/L J.A.Jackson	FW190 destroyed	Evreux	0645
			S/L H.A.S.Johnston	FW190 destroyed	Evreux	0645
			F/O J.H.Waterhouse	Bf109 damaged	Evreux	0645

604 Squadron played an important part in the night defence of the beachhead. The CO, Michael Constable-Maxwell flew with 56 Squadron during 1940 and would end the war with at least six confirmed victories.

331 Sqn Spit	2TAF	Lt R.Dogger	FW190 destroyed	Evreux	0645
		2/Lt O.F.Solvang	FW190 destroyed	S Evreux A/D	0645
		Sgt A.Steen	FW190 damaged	NE Evreux A/D	0645
332 Sqn Spit	2TAF	2/Lt E.Sunde	FW190 damaged	4m SE Evreux	0640
		Maj W.Christie	FW190 destroyed	Evreux	0645
		Maj W.Christie	Bf109 damaged	Evreux	0645
		Lt H.R.Isachsen	FW190 damaged	Evreux	0645
		Lt H.R.Isachsen	FW190 damaged	Evreux	0645
		2/Lt R.Keim	Bf109 damaged	E Evreux	0645
		2/Lt R.Kolling	FW190 destroyed	E Evreux	0645
		F/S A.Sohr	FW190 damaged	E Evreux	0645
		Capt E.Westly	FW190 destroyed	2m SE Evreux	0645
421 Sqn Spit	2TAF	F/O J.N.Bamford	Bf109 destroyed	Caen-15m S Caen	1950
		F/O J.N.Bamford	Bf109 destroyed	Caen-15m S Caen	1950
		F/O J.N.Bamford	Bf109 prob.dest	Caen-15m S Caen	1950
		F/O W.F.Cook	Bf109 destroyed	Caen-15m S Caen	1950
		F/L C.D.Grant	Bf109 damaged	Caen-15m S Caen	1950
		F/L J.F.McElroy	Bf109 damaged	Caen-15m S Caen	1950
		F/L J.N.Paterson	Bf109 destroyed	Caen-15m S Caen	1950
		F/L J.N.Paterson	Bf109 prob.dest	Caen-15m S Caen	1950
		F/L W.N.Stronach	Bf109 destroyed	Caen-15m S Caen	1950
		F/O W.Warfield	Bf109 destroyed	Caen-15m S Caen	1950
		F/O W.Warfield	Bf109 destroyed	Caen-15m S Caen	1950
602 Sqn Spit	2TAF	S/Lt P.H.Clostermann	Bf109 prob.dest	Dreux A/D	1140

15/16th June 1944

29 Sqn	Mosq	ADGB	F/O W.W.Provan	E/A damaged	Coulommieres	0200
85 Sqn	Mosq	BC	S/L F.S.Gonsalves	Bf110 destroyed	St Trond AD	0147
			S/L F.S.Gonsalves	Bf110 damaged	St Trond AD	0147

157 Sqn Mosq	BC	F/L J.O.Mathews	Ju88 damaged	Cormeilles	0105
		F/L J.O.Mathews	Ju88 destroyed	Creil	0110
264 Sqn Mosq	ADGB	S/L F.J.A.Chase	Ju88 damaged	6m E Granville	0030
FIU Mosq	ADGB	Lt P.Twiss	Ju88 destroyed	Beachhead	0130±

16th June 1944

403 Sqn Spit	2TAF	F/O G.R.Nadon	Bf109 destroyed	Lisieux	0640
		F/O J.D.Orr	Bf109 destroyed	Lisieux	0640
		F/O J.D.Orr	Bf109 damaged	Lisieux	0640
		F/O W.H.Rhodes	Bf109 destroyed	Lisieux	0640
		F/O W.H.Rhodes	Bf109 damaged	Lisieux	0640
		F/L J.D.Lindsay	Bf109 damaged	NW Caen	1115
443 Sqn Spit	2TAF	F/L D.M.Walz	Bf109G destroyed	4m S St Croix-sur-Mere	0620
		F/L W.A.Prest	FW190 damaged	W Rouen	1215
		S/L H.W.McLeod	Bf109G destroyed	NE Caen	2050
453 Sqn Spit	2TAF	F/L V.A.Lancaster W/O C.A.Rice	Bf109 destroyed - Shared -	4m E Caen	2043
		F/O K.K.Lawrence W/O C.A.Seeney	Bf109 destroyed - Shared -	4m E Caen	2043
		F/L P.V.McDade	Bf109 prob.dest	4m E Caen	2043
		F/O D.S.Murray	Bf109 damaged	4m E Caen	2043
		S/L D.H.Smith	Bf109 damaged	4m E Caen	2043
602 Sqn Spit	2TAF	S/Lt P.H.Clostermann	Bf109 prob.dest	E Orne Canal	1125
		S/Lt P.H.Clostermann	FW190 destroyed	S Carpiquet AD	1130
144 Wg Spit	2TAF	W/C J.E.Johnson	FW190 destroyed	NE Villers-Bocage	2110

16/17th June 1944

29 Sqn Mosq	ADGB	F/O R.A.Crone	Do217 destroyed	St Trond AD	0215
		F/O R.A.Crone	E/A destroyed	St Trond	0245
85 Sqn Mosq	BC	F/O P.S.Kendall	Bf110 destroyed	Eindhoven-Soesturburg	0140±
169 Sqn Mosq	BC	F/O W.H.Miller	Ju88 destroyed	Pas de Calais	0200±
219 Sqn Mosq	ADGB	F/O O.P.Faraday	Me410 destroyed	30m SE Dungeness	2358
264 Sqn Mosq	ADGB	F/L M.M.Davison	Ju188 destroyed	La Hoye des Puits	2359
409 Sqn Mosq	ADGB	W/O D.J.MacDonald	Ju188 damaged	St Sauveur	0115
410 Sqn Mosq	ADGB	F/O I.S.Girvan	Ju88 destroyed	SE Valenges	0010
488 Sqn Mosq	ADGB	S/L E.N.Bunting DFC	FW190 destroyed	S St Lô	0423

Fighting Norwegians. (l to r) Odd Flood Solvang of 331 Squadron, Erik Westly and Werner Christie of 332 Squadron. All would survive the war, Solvang with two confirmed kills, Westly with four and Christie with at least nine. All three were successful over and around Evreux on 15th June.

17th June 1944

26 Sqn	Spit	2TAF	F/L B.Lees	Bf109 damaged	S Houlgate	0645
			F/L J.Roberts	- Shared -		
65 Sqn	Must	2TAF	F/O C.P.Ashworth	FW190 destroyed	Alencon area	1550
			F/S G.C.Dinsdale	- Shared -		
122 Sqn	Must	2TAF	P/O J.N.Thorne	Bf109 destroyed	Dreux - Chartres	1930
			F/OA.V.Hargreaves	Bf109 destroyed	S Dreux	2045
			F/L J.T.Reynolds	- Shared -		
			F/OR.E.Tickner	- Shared -		
			F/O M.H.Pinches	Bf109 destroyed	S Dreux	2045
306 Sqn	Must	2TAF	F/OA.Beyer	FW190 destroyed	10m SW Nogent	2200
			F/S J.Pomietlarz	- Shared -		
			F/L Z.Jelinski	FW190 destroyed	10m SW Nogent	2200
			F/L W.Potocki	- Shared -		
310 Sqn	Spit	2TAF	F/O O.Smik	FW190 destroyed	Caen	1910
			F/O O.Smik	FW190 destroyed	12m SE Caen	1910
			F/O F.Vindis	- Shared -		
403 Sqn	Spit	2TAF	F/O W.H.Rhodes	FW190 damaged	5m SE St Lo	1905
453 Sqn	Spit	ADGB	S/L D.G.Andrews	FW190 prob.dest*	Beachhead	u/k

Note: Provenance doubtful

611 Sqn	Spit	ADGB	Lt R.G.Gouby	FW190 destroyed	Carentan	1925±
			F/S T.Ward	FW190 destroyed	Carentan	1925±

17/18th June 1944

29 Sqn	Mosq	ADGB	F/S F.C.Johnson	Ju88 destroyed	Inland from Beachhead	0040
219 Sqn	Mosq	ADGB	F/L G.R.I.Parker	Ju188 prob.dest	18m N Ostend	0355

239 Sqn Mosq	BC	F/L G.F.Poulton	Ju88 destroyed	Near Eindhoven	0120±
		F/L G.E.Poulton	Ju88 damaged	Near Eindhoven	0130±
264 Sqn Mosq	ADGB	F/O J.C.Duffy	Ju188 destroyed	S Bayeux	2330
		F/O J.P.Brooke	Ju188 destroyed	Cherbourg	0130
		F/O J.P.Brooke	Ju188 destroyed	Near W coast Cherbourg	0140
		F/L I.H.Cosby	FW190 destroyed	T.9040	0409
		F/L M.M.Davison	FW190 destroyed	Beachhead T.9727	0530±
410 Sqn Mosq	ADGB	F/L C.E.Edinger	Ju188 destroyed	6m off Le Havre	0010
		S/L I.A.March	Ju88 destroyed	S Caen	0240
488 Sqn Mosq	ADGB	F/L P.F.L.Hall	Ju88 destroyed	30m S Beachhead	0230
		F/O D.N.Robinson	FW190 destroyed	Near Gavray, Cherbourg	0421

18th June 1944

2 Sqn Must	2TAF	F/O L.W.Burt	Bf109 damaged	Montagne	1545
132 Sqn Spit	2TAF	S/L A.G.Page	FW190 damaged	Near Connelles	1535
		F/O B.F.Collings	- Shared -		
268 Sqn Must	2TAF	F/L W.N.Tuele	FW190 destroyed	La Merlemault	2045

18/19th June 1944

125 Sqn Mosq	ADGB	W/C J.G.Topham	Ju88 destroyed	V.65	2355
		W/C J.G.Topham	Ju88 destroyed	5m N Centre Beach	0020
409 Sqn Mosq	2TAF	S/L J.A.Hatch	Do217 damaged	Beachhead	0155
410 Sqn Mosq	2TAF	Lt A.A.Harrington	Ju88 destroyed	Vire	0042
		F/O G.E.Edwards	Ju88 destroyed	Vire	0050

19/20th June 1944

264 Sqn Mosq	ADGB	S/L F.J.A.Chase	Ju88 destroyed	Off Le Havre	0335
409 Sqn Mosq	ADGB	W/C J.W.Reid	Ju88 damaged	Near Rouen	0235
488 Sqn Mosq	ADGB	P/O C.J.Vlotman	FW190 destroyed	5m S Falaise	0220

20th June 1944

19 Sqn Must	2TAF	F/S T.A.Carson	FW190 prob.dest	Near Dreux	1630
		P/O F.D.Schofield	FW190 damaged	Near Dreux	1630
		F/S T.A.Carson	- Shared -		
		F/L B.G.Collyns	FW190 damaged	Near Dreux	1630
		F/L D.P.Lamb	FW190 destroyed	Near Dreux	1630

Three remarkable pilots.  *Peter Twiss of the Fleet Air Arm (left) claimed one confirmed and one damaged whilst flying Fulmars in the Middle East area. He moved to the FIU and got two night victories over the beachhead, one on 15/16th June. On 10th March 1956 he became the fastest man alive by flying the Fairey FD 2 at 1,132 mph. John McElroy of 421 Squadron (centre) was another Middle East veteran, claiming at least seven kills over Malta before reaching England. He ended the war with a total of at least ten and later flew for Israel where, in 1948, he shot down three more aircraft including two RAF Spitfires. He claimed a Bf109 damaged on 15th June. Wally McLeod, CO of 443 Squadron (right) claimed a Bf109 destroyed on 16th, his 16th kill, having scored heavily in Malta. A master of brevity, one Combat Report read "Saw 4 Me109s below. Shot one down." He was killed in acton on 27th September with his score standing at 21.*

19 Sqn Must	2TAF	P/O E.R.Davies	FW190 - Shared -			
		S/L W.McM.Gilmour	FW190 destroyed	Near Dreux		1630
		S/L W.McM.Gilmour	FW190 damaged	Near Dreux		1630
		F/L D.P.Lamb	FW190 damaged	Near Dreux		1630
		F/L P.B.Plumridge	FW190 damaged	Near Dreux		1630
317 Sqn Spit	2TAF	F/S L.Winski	FW190 destroyed	Near Airel		1600
317 Sqn Spit	2TAF	F/L H.Knapik	FW190 prob.dest	Foret des Boards,	N Caen	1605
		F/S T.Wojciechowski	FW190 prob.dest	Foret des Boards,	N Caen	1605
331 Sqn Spit	2TAF	2/Lt P.M.Coucheron	Bf109G destroyed	E Douvres		0605
		Capt N.K.Jorstad	- Shared -			
		Lt K.M.Kopperud	- Shared -			
131 Wg Spit	2TAF	W/C J.Kowalski	FW190 prob.dest	Near Airel		1600

20/21st June 1944

125 Sqn Mosq	ADGB	F/O R.C.Daly	Ju88 damaged	15m NW Le Havre	0003
151 Sqn Mosq	ADGB	F/L L.Gregory	He111 destroyed	20m SW Bretigny	0030
409 Sqn Mosq	2TAF	F/L M.C.Taylor	Ju88 prob.dest	4m NW Caen	0210

21st June 1944

19 Sqn Must	2TAF	F/L J.M.Hayward	Bf109 destroyed	Conches	1840
		F/L D.P.Lamb	Bf109 destroyed	Conches	1840

19 Sqn Must	2TAF	F/O J.Paton	Bf109 destroyed	Conches	1840
		W/O A.Sima	Bf109 damaged	Conches	1840
		F/S B.Vassilliades	Bf109 destroyed	Conches	1840
515 Sqn Mosq	BC	S/L P.W.Rabone	Bf110 destroyed	Eelde AD	1515

21/22nd June 1944

29 Sqn Mosq	ADGB	F/L D.R.O.Price	Bf110 destroyed	St Trond	0240±
		F/L D.R.O.Price	Do217 damaged	St Trond area	0240±
239 Sqn Mosq	BC	F/O R.Depper	He177 destroyed	Ruhr	0100±

22nd June 1944

151 Sqn Mosq	ADGB	F/L L.Gregory	FW200 damaged	Cognac	1630
		F/O B.C.Gray	- Shared -		
341 Sqn Spit	2TAF	Lt M.Mailfert	FW190 prob.dest	Utah Beach	1145
441 Sqn Spit	2TAF	F/O W.W.LBrown	FW190 destroyed	SE Domfront	1440
		F/O W.R.Chowen	- Shared -		
		F/S R.A.McMillan	- Shared -		
		F/O J.W.Fleming	FW190 destroyed	SE Domfront	1440
442 Sqn Spit	2TAF	S/L B.D.Russel	FW190 destroyed	Near Argentan	1435
		F/L J.T.Marriott	- Shared -		
		F/O R.W.Weeks	Bf109 destroyed	Near Argentan	1435
		P/O F.B.Young	Bf109 destroyed	10m SW Argentan	1435
144 Wg Spit	2TAF	W/C J.E.Johnson	Bf109 destroyed	7m W Argentan	1435

22/23rd June 1944

29 Sqn Mosq	ADGB	F/S R.Beynon	Ju188 destroyed	10m NE Bourges	0132
125 Sqn Mosq	ADGB	F/O W.J.Grey	Ju88 destroyed	Fecamp-Le Havre	2315
		F/O W.J.Grey	Ju88 destroyed	Fecamp-Le Havre	2330
		F/O W.J.Grey	Ju88 prob.dest	Fecamp-Le Havre	2345
		S/Lt M.H.J.Petrie	Ju88 destroyed	Near Le Havre	2320
		S/Lt M.H.J.Petrie	Ju88 destroyed	Near Le Havre	2340
		F/O E.MGosse	Ju88 prob.dest	Cherbourg	2350
264 Sqn Mosq	ADGB	F/S J.Pickering	Ju188 destroyed	5m S Ford	0150
456 Sqn Mosq	ADGB	F/O F.S.Stevens	Ju88 prob.dest	80m S Worthing	0030
488 Sqn Mosq	ADGB	P/O O.J.McCabe	Ju188 destroyed	E Bayeux	0012
604 Sqn Mosq	ADGB	F/L P.V.G.Sandeman	Ju188 destroyed	Cherbourg	2355

On 20th June 'Mac' Gilmour (left) led his 19 Squadron pilots into a Staffel of FW190s near Dreux. The Mustang pilots claimed two destroyed - one by Gilmour - and several more probably destroyed or damaged, one by Flight Lieutenant P.B.Plumridge, (far right) - ww2images.com

23rd June 1944

132 Sqn Spit	2TAF	S/L A.G.Page	FW190 destroyed	E Caen	1150
229 Sqn Spit	ADGB	F/S K.E.Clark	FW190 damaged	Beachhead	1700±
		F/L R.H.Small	FW190 destroyed	Beachhead	1700±
306 Sqn Must	2TAF	P/O J.Bzowski	Bf109F destroyed	Verneuil	1200
		F/S J.Czezowski	FW190 destroyed	2-3m N Verneuil	1200
		F/S J.Czezowski	FW190 damaged	Verneuil	1200
		F/S J.Czezowski	FW190 damaged	Verneuil	1200
		F/S S.Letki	FW190 destroyed	Verneuil	1200
		F/S J.Pomietlarz	Bf109 destroyed	Verneuil	1200
		F/L W.Potocki	Bf109F destroyed	Verneuil	1200
		F/L W.Potocki	Bf109F destroyed	Verneuil	1200
		F/L G.Sollegub	FW190 destroyed	Verneuil	1200
403 Sqn Spit	2TAF	F/L M.J.Gordon	FW190 destroyed	NE Caen	1640
		F/L M.J.Gordon	FW190 damaged	NE Caen	1640
		F/L P.Logan	FW190 destroyed	NE Caen	1640
		F/L P.Logan	FW190 damaged	NE Caen	1640
		F/O B.K.Oliver	FW190 damaged	NE Caen	1640
414 Sqn Must	2TAF	S/L C.H.Stover	FW190 damaged	Caen area	1300±
421 Sqn Spit	2TAF	F/O R.C.McRoberts	FW190 damaged	20m E Caen	1235
		F/O A.C.Brandon	FW190 damaged	Le Merlerault	2150
		F/O R.G.Driver	Bf109 damaged	Le Merlerault	2150
		F/O R.G.Driver	Bf109 damaged	Le Merlerault	2150

421 Sqn Spit	2TAF	F/L P.G.Johnson	FW190 destroyed	Le Merlerault	2150
		F/O G.L.Mayson	FW190 destroyed	Le Merlerault	2150
		F/L J.F.McElroy	FW190 destroyed	Le Merlerault	2150
		F/L R.C.Wilson	FW190 destroyed	Le Merlerault	2150
		F/L R.C.Wilson	FW190 damaged	Le Merlerault	2150
443 Sqn Spit	2TAF	S/L H.W.McLeod	FW190 destroyed	½m N Alencon	2145
		S/L H.W.McLeod	FW190 destroyed	½m N Alencon	2145
		F/L W.V.Shenk	FW190 damaged	Near Alencon	2200
602 Sqn Spit	2TAF	F/L T.A.Burke	Bf109 destroyed	Caen	1150
		F/L T.A.Burke	Bf109 damaged	Caen	1150
		F/L K.L.Charney	Bf109 prob.dest	SW Caen	1150
		P/O J.S.McConachie	Bf109 damaged	Caen	1150
		F/OG.L.Robinson	FW190 destroyed	Caen	1150
609 Sqn Typh	2TAF	W/O J.D.Buchanon	Bf109 damaged	Near Dreux	1100±
		F/O R.K.Gibson	Bf109 damaged	Near Dreux	1100±
		F/O R.K.Holmes	Bf109 damaged	Near Dreux	1100±
		F/L E.R.ARoberts	Bf109 destroyed	Near Dreux	1100±
		F/O R.S.Royston	Bf109 damaged	Near Dreux	1100±

23/24th June 1944

25 Sqn Mosq	ADGB	W/C C.M.Wight			
		-Boycott	Ju88 destroyed	NW Orfordness	0010±
85 Sqn Mosq	BC	F/L B.A.Burbridge	Ju88 destroyed	Coulommieres	0315±
125 Sqn Mosq	ADGB	F/L R.W.Leggett	Ju88 destroyed	Somme estuary	0100
264 Sqn Mosq	ADGB	F/O J.C.Trigg	Ju88 destroyed	20m ENE Rouen	0120
409 Sqn Mosq	ADGB	F/O W.H.Vincent	Ju188 destroyed	15m NW Caen	2400
410 Sqn Mosq	ADGB	W/O R.Jones	Ju188 destroyed	15 min NNW Beachh'd	0209
604 Sqn Mosq	ADGB	F/O J.SSmith	Ju88 destroyed	10m W Le Havre	0420

24th June 1944

19 Sqn Must	2TAF	W/O M.H.Bell	FW190 destroyed	Near Dreux	0720
		W/O H.Holmes	FW190 destroyed	Near Dreux	0720
		F/O J.M.Maynard	FW190 destroyed	Near Dreux	0720
		F/O J.E.Staples	FW190 damaged	Near Dreux	0720
		F/S B.Vassiliades	FW190 destroyed	Near Dreux	0720
		F/S B.Vassiliades	Bf109 destroyed	Near Dreux	0720

On 22nd June II./JG 2 lost its high-scoring Gruppenkommandeur Major Josef Wurmheller (left) to Flying Officer J.W.Fleming, a 441 Squadron Spitfire pilot. Next day the Mustang pilots of 306 Squadron were successful near Verneuil, fighting Bf109s and FW190s at noon and claiming seven destroyed, one each by Jan Pomietlarz (centre) and Grzegorz Sollogub (right), whose fifth and last kill this was to be.

19 Sqn Must	2TAF	F/S B.Vassiliades	He111 damaged	Near Dreux		0720
65 Sqn Must	2TAF	F/L B.P.W.Clapin F/O P.S.Taylor	FW190 destroyed - Shared -	SE Dreux		0720
		F/O T.E.Jonssen	FW190 destroyed	SE Dreux		0720
		F/O T.E.Jonssen	FW190 destroyed	SE Dreux		0720
122 Sqn Must	2TAF	F/O C.L.F.Tallalla	FW190 destroyed	Near Dreux		0720
306 Sqn Must	2TAF	F/S W.Nowoczyn	FW190 damaged	Tilliers		1205
		F/L K.Sporny	Bf109 destroyed	Tilliers		1205
		F/L K.Sporny	FW190 damaged	Tilliers		1205
315 Sqn Must	2TAF	F/S J.Bargielowski	Bf109F damaged	Tilliers		1205
		F/O M.Kirste	Bf109 damaged	Tilliers		1205
		F/O M.Kirste	Bf109 damaged	Tilliers		1205
		F/O J.Polak	Bf109F destroyed	Tilliers		1205
		F/O J.Polak	Bf109F destroyed	Tilliers		1205
		F/L J.Schmidt	FW190 destroyed	Tilliers		1205
331 Sqn Spit	2TAF	F/S J.P.Ditlev -Simonsen	Bf109G damaged	Caen		0835
		2/Lt J.W.Garben	Bf109G destroyed	5m NW Caen		0835
		2/Lt J.W.Garben	Bf109G destroyed	5m NW Caen		0835
		2/Lt O.F.Solvang	Bf109G destroyed	NW Caen		0835
122 Wg Must	2TAF	W/C G.R.A.McG. Johnston	FW190 destroyed	Near Dreux		0730
132 Wg Spit	2TAF	Lt Col R.A.Berg	Bf109G destroyed	5m NW Caen		0835
133 Wg Must	2TAF	W/C S.F.Skalski	Bf109F destroyed	By collision Tilliers		1205
		W/C S.F.Skalski	Bf109F destroyed	By collision Tilliers		1205

On 24th June 65 Squadron Mustang pilots fought FW190s of III./JG 54. Flying Officer T.E.Jonssen (left) claimed two and Peter Taylor (centre) shared a third. Two were actually lost, but four Mustangs failed to return. A day ealier Tac/R pilot Squadron Leader C.H. Stover fought FW190s near Caen, claiming one damaged, but he and his wingman were both shot down and wounded by Bf109 pilots from JG 3.

24/25th June 1944

125 Sqn	Mosq	ADGB	S/L E.G.Barwell	Ju88 destroyed	Off Pointe de la Percee	2320
			P/O W.A.Beadle	Ju88 destroyed	15-20m W Le Havre	0053
239 Sqn	Mosq	BC	F/L D.Welfare	Ju88 destroyed	Paris-Amiens	0120±
264 Sqn	Mosq	ADGB	S/L P.B.Elwell	FW190 destroyed	10m N Le Havre	2315
			S/L P.B.Elwell	FW190 prob.dest	N Le Havre	2315
409 Sqn	Mosq	ADGB	W/O W.G.Kirkwood	Ju188 destroyed	10m N Le Havre	0040
410 Sqn	Mosq	ADGB	F/L S.B.Huppert	Ju188 damaged	W Coutances	0145
488 Sqn	Mosq	ADGB	F/L G.E.Jameson	Me410 destroyed	20m SW Bayeux	0407

25th June 1944

126 Wg	Spit	2TAF	W/C G.C.Keefer	Bf110 destroyed	5m S Caen	0545±

25/26th June 1944

125 Sqn	Mosq	ADGB	F/L G.F.Simcock	Ju88 destroyed	N Seine estuary	0105
409 Sqn	Mosq	ADGB	F/L D.T.Steele	Do217 damaged	20m SE Le Havre	0045
			F/L D.T.Steele	Ju188 destroyed	20m SE Le Havre	0050

27th June 1944

26 Sqn	Spit	2TAF	F/S S.F.Nurse	FW190 damaged	Guerville	1715
65 Sqn	Must	2TAF	F/S W.P.Kelly	Bf109 damaged	Alencon-Dreux	1600
			F/O J.M.W.Lloyd	Bf109 destroyed	Alencon-Dreux	1600
122 Sqn	Must	2TAF	F/L A.F.Pavey	FW190 destroyed	Bernay	2130
			F/L A.F.Pavey	FW190 destroyed	Bernay	2130
122 Sqn	Must	2TAF	F/O E.A.Roemmele	FW190 damaged	Bernay	2130

Ex-patriate Mustang pilots in action on 24th June: Cyril 'Jimmy' Talalla of 122 Squadron (left) came from Ceylon, and is pictured early in the war being introduced to Queen Elizabeth. He was commissioned and survived the war with three confirmed kills. Jerzy Schmidt of 306 Squadron (centre) was credited with two victories, but died on 6th December when he ditched his Mustang in the North Sea. Basilios 'Basil' Vassiliades of 19 Squadron (right) of Greek stock would be credited with five victories, but was killed on 25th March 1945 when his 3 Squadron Tempest was shot down by Flak.

332 Sqn Spit	2TAF	Lt O.G.Aanjesen	Bf109 destroyed	Dreux	2105
411 Sqn Spit	2TAF	F/L G.W.Johnson	FW190 damaged	SE Caen	1350
		F/L G.W.Johnson	FW190 damaged	SE Caen	1350
		W/O J.A.Kerr	FW190 damaged	Caen-Falaise	1350
		S/L G.D.Robertson	FW190 destroyed	SW Bretteville	1350
418 Sqn Mosq	ADGB	F/L C.M.Jasper	Ju88 destroyed	2m N Rostock	1752
442 Sqn Spit	2TAF	F/O S.M.McLarty	Bf109 destroyed	S Lisieux	1235
		F/O S.M.McLarty	Bf109 destroyed	Near Lisieux	1235
		F/L H.J.Dowding	Bf109 destroyed	Near Lisieux	1250
		F/L H.J. Dowding	Bf109 destroyed	SW Mezidon	1250
453 Sqn Spit	2TAF	F/L V.A.Lancaster	FW190 prob.dest	W Martinville	1050
		F/L V.A.Lancaster	FW190 damaged	W Martinville	1050
		F/O J.F.Olver	FW190 damaged	W Martinville	1050
		F/S R.Peters	FW190 damaged	W Martinville	1050
		W/O C.A.Rice	FW190 damaged	W Martinville	1050
453 Sqn Spit	2TAF	F/L V.A.Lancaster	FW190 prob.dest	15m W Caen	2100
122 Wg Must	2TAF	W/C G.R.A.McG. Johnston	Bf109 destroyed	Alencon-Dreux	1600±
126 Wg Spit	2TAF	W/C G.C.Keefer	Bf109 destroyed	Near Beaumont	1550

27/28th June 1944

141 Sqn Mosq	BC	W/O H.Welham	Ju88 destroyed	S Tilburg	0005
		S/L G.J.Rice	Ju88 destroyed	Cambrai	0122
239 Sqn Mosq	BC	F/L D.Welfare	Me410 destroyed	E Paris	0200±
		F/L D.R.Howard	Ju88 destroyed	Nr Brussels	0240±
		W/C P.M.J.Evans	FW190 destroyed	Nr Brussels	0300±
264 Sqn Mosq	ADGB	F/L A.Turner	Ju188 destroyed	20m W Le Havre	0400
515 Sqn Mosq	BC	P/O C.W.Chown	Ju88 destroyed	Eindhoven	0213
FIU Mosq	ADGB	F/L J.N,Howard -Williams	Ju88 destroyed	W Chateaudun	0230±

28th June 1944

127 Sqn Spit	ADGB	W/O C.Bell	FW190 damaged	Beachhead	1725±
		F/L E.O.Doyle	FW190 damaged	Beachhead	1725±
401 Sqn Spit	2TAF	F/L A.F.Halcrow	FW190 destroyed	10m S Caen	0930
		F/L R.M.Stayner	FW190 destroyed	15m SW Caen	0930
		F/L I.F.Kennedy	FW190 destroyed	10m E Domfront	2140
		F/O W.T.Klersey	FW190 destroyed	10m E Domfront	2140
		F/O W.T.Klersey	FW190 destroyed	10m E Domfront	2140
		F/L W.R.Tew	FW190 destroyed	10m E Domfront	2140
403 Sqn Spit	2TAF	F/L A.R.MacKenzie	FW190 destroyed	Evreux	0615
411 Sqn Spit	2TAF	F/O T.R.Wheler	Bf109 destroyed	20m S Le Havre	1315±
		F/O T.R.Wheler	Bf109 damaged	20m S Le Havre	1315±
		F/L R.K.Hayward	FW190 damaged	S Le Havre	1315±
		F/L H.C.Trainor	Bf109 destroyed	20m S Le Havre	1315±
		F/L D.J.Givens	Bf109 damaged	5m SE Caen	2000±
		F/L R.K.Hayward	FW190 destroyed	5m SE Caen	2000±
		F/L R.K.Hayward	FW190 destroyed	5m SE Caen	2000±
		F/L G.W.Johnson	FW190 destroyed	5m SE Caen	2000±
		F/L H.C.Trainor	FW190 destroyed	2m NE Lisieux	2000±
412 Sqn Spit	2TAF	F/O W.J.Banks	Bf109 destroyed	NE Bernay	0615±
		F/L C.W.Fox	FW190 damaged	NE Bernay	0615±
416 Sqn Spit	2TAF	F/O G.H.Farquharson	Bf109 destroyed	Caen	1125
		F/L D.E.Noonan	FW190 destroyed	E Caen	1125
		F/L J.B.B.Rainville	FW190 destroyed	Caen	1125
		F/L F.R.Patterson	FW190 destroyed	Caen	1600
		F/L D.R.Cuthbertson	FW190 damaged	Caen	1630

On 16th June, Mike Herrick (left), a six-victory ace who had fought as a night fighter pilot over the UK and by day in the far east, was shot down and killed by Robert Spreckels of JG 1 (centre). Nine days later, on 25th, Spreckels scored again by bringing down another Mosquito, this flown by 'Bob' Braham, the most highly decorated fighter pilot of the RAF. Braham and 'Sticks' Gregory survived as PoWs and Braham and Spreckels shared a beer some years after the event and in peacetime.

421 Sqn Spit	2TAF	F/O A.C.Brandon	Bf109 damaged	Caen	1800
		F/O J.M.Flood	Bf109 damaged	Caen	1800
		F/L J.F.McElroy	Bf109 destroyed	Caen	1800
		F/L H.P.M.Zary	Bf109 destroyed	Near Caen	1800
442 Sqn Spit	2TAF	P/O N.A.Burns	Bf109 damaged	Caen	1130
		F/O D.W.Goodwin	Bf109 destroyed	S Caen	1130
		F/O J.B.O'Sullivan	Bf109 prob.dest	S Caen	1130
		F/O J.G.L.Robillard	Bf109 destroyed	SW Caen	1130
		S/L H.J.Dowding	FW190 damaged	3m S Cabourg	1705
		F/O S.M.McLarty	FW190 damaged	SE Cabourg	1705
		P/O B.E.Middleton	FW190 damaged	SE Cabourg	1705
443 Sqn Spit	2TAF	F/O W.A.C.Gilbert	FW190 damaged	2m NE Falaise	1135
		F/L W.V.Shenk	FW190 damaged	2m NE Falaise	1135
		F/O G.R.Stephen	FW190 destroyed	2m NE Falaise	1135
144 Wg Spit	2TAF	W/C J.E.Johnson	Bf109 destroyed	S Caen	1130
		W/C J.E.Johnson	Bf109 destroyed	S Caen	1130

28/29th June 1944

169 Sqn Mosq	BC	P/O H.Reed	Bf110 destroyed	Nr Mucke	0020±
409 Sqn Mosq	ADGB	W/O W.G.Kirkwood	Ju188 destroyed	20-25m N Bayeux	0020
488 Sqn Mosq	ADGB	F/L G.E.Jameson	Ju88 destroyed	10m NE Caen	0040

On 28th June Irving 'Hap' Kennedy of 401 Squadron (above) got his ninth kill (of ten) and Joseph 'Larry' Robillard achieved his fifth (of seven). Both survived the war.

29th June 1944

193 Sqn Typh	2TAF	F/O G.L.Bilz	Bf109 damaged	Conches area	1145
		F/O J.G.Brown	Bf109 damaged	Conches area	1145
		F/O W.M.JBulleid	Bf109 destroyed	Conches area	1145
		F/S G.A.Gough	Bf109 destroyed	Conches area	1145
		F/O C.E.Hall	Bf109 damaged	Conches area	1145
		F/L A.S.Smith	Bf109 destroyed	Conches area	1145
		F/O E.Statters	Bf109 damaged	Conches area	1145
222 Sqn Spit	2TAF	F/L D.W.Beedham	FW190 destroyed	SW Lisieux	0830±
340 Sqn Spit	2TAF	Lt J.Guignard	FW190 destroyed	Montfort-Evreux	1950
403 Sqn Spit	2TAF	F/L J.D.Lindsay	Bf109 destroyed	10m SE Caen	1345
411 Sqn Spit	2TAF	F/L H.C.Trainor	Bf109 destroyed	5m E Caen	1615±
485 Sqn Spit	2TAF	F/O J.A.Houlton	Bf109 damaged	15m S Caen	0830
602 Sqn Spit	2TAF	S/Lt P.H.Clostermann	FW190 destroyed	Nr Rouen	1940
122 Wg Must	2TAF	W/C G.R.A.McG. Johnston	Bf109 destroyed	NW l'Aigle	0915
145 Wg Spit	2TAF	W/C W.V.Crawford -Compton	FW190 destroyed	Nr Beaumont-le-Roger	1950
		W/C W.V.Crawford -Compton	FW190 destroyed	Nr Beaumont-le-Roger	1950
146 Wg Typh	2TAF	W/C J.R.Baldwin	Bf109 destroyed	Conches area	1145
		W/C J.R.Baldwin	Bf109 destroyed	Conches area	1145
		W/C J.R.Baldwin	Bf109 damaged	Conches area	1145

And still the Canadians scored. On 29th Hugh Trainor (left) achieved his fourth (increased to eight before being captured on 19th September) and James Lindsay (centre) his third. In 1952 he would add two MiG-15s to his WW2 score of six. On 30th Graham Robertson of 411 Squadron (right) got his third (pictured in 1941 after his first fight). (ww2images.com)

29/30th June 1944

264 Sqn Mosq	ADGB	F/O R.L.J.Barbour	Ju188 destroyed	5m N Grandchamp	0030

30th June 1944

341 Sqn Spit	2TAF	Capt J.Andrieux	Bf109F destroyed	Lisieux-Cabourg	2035
		Lt L.Giradon	Bf109F destroyed	Lisieux-Cabourg	2035
401 Sqn Spit	2TAF	F/L R.M.Stayner	Bf109 destroyed	5m E Caen	1440±
403 Sqn Spit	2TAF	F/L H.R.Finlay	Bf109 damaged	Falaise-Lisieux	1300
		F/O J.D.Orr	Bf109 destroyed	Near Bayeux	2040
411 Sqn Spit	2TAF	S/L G.D.Robertson	FW190 destroyed	15m W Falaise	1640±
421 Sqn Spit	2TAF	F/L P.G.Johnson	Bf109 destroyed	15m N Bernay	0705
		F/L P.G.Johnson	Bf109 damaged	15m N Bernay	0705
		F/L R.C.Wilson	Bf109 destroyed	15m N Bernay	0705
		F/L P.G.Johnson	Bf109 destroyed	E Lisieux	2030
		F/L P.G.Johnson	Bf109 destroyed	E Lisieux	2030
		F/O R.C.McRoberts	Bf109 destroyed	E Lisieux	2035
441 Sqn Spit	2TAF	S/L J.D.Browne	FW190 destroyed	Near Gace	1235
		F/L A.Johnstone	Bf109 destroyed	Near Gace	1235
		F/L A.Johnstone	Bf109G damaged	Near Gace	1235
		F/L G.E.Mott	FW190 destroyed	E Gace	1235
		F/L H.C.Trainor	Bf109 destroyed	Thury-Harcourt	2105±

The great Don Kingaby refused to keep himself out of harm's way. Whilst on the staff of Fighter Command HQ, he sometimes managed to fly the occasional combat sortie. On 30th June, whilst flying as a 'guest' with 501 Squadron, he gained his 21st and last combat success, shared with Flying Officer C.R.Stockton. (ww2images.com)

442 Sqn Spit	2TAF	F/L A.W.Roseland F/O G.G.Millar	FW190 destroyed - Shared -	1m ENE Villers-Bocage	1100
		F/L A.W.Roseland	FW190 destroyed	1m ENE Villers-Bocage	1100
		F/O F.B.Young	FW190 destroyed	1m ENE Villers-Bocage	1100
		F/L D.E.Trott	FW190 destroyed	W Falaise	1730
		P/O G.A.Costello	Bf109 destroyed	W Falaise	1730
		F/L D.H.Dover	FW190 destroyed	W Falaise	1730
501 Sqn Spit	ADGB	W/C D.E.Kingaby* F/O R.C.Stockburn	Bf109 destroyed - Shared -	Cazelle	1130±

Note: Flying as 'guest'.

515 Sqn Mosq	BC	S/L L.P.Rabone	He111 destroyed	Jagel/Schleswig	1530
		S/L L.P.Rabone	Ju W34 destroyed	Jagel/Schleswig	1534
602 Sqn Spit	2TAF	S/Lt P.H.Clostermann	Bf109 prob.dest	Vire	1500
144 Wg Spit	2TAF	W/C J.E.Johnson	Bf109 destroyed	E Gace	1235

30th June/1st July 1944

239 Sqn Mosq	BC	F/L D.J.Raby	Ju88 destroyed	Le Havre	u/k

1st July 1944

132 Sqn Spit	2TAF	S/L A.G.Page F/S W.G.Thom	FW190 destroyed - Shared -	20-30m SE Caen	1545
		W/O D.J.Watkins	Bf109 damaged	20-30m SE Caen	1545
401 Sqn Spit	2TAF	F/L R.H.Cull	FW190 damaged	5m E Caen	1630±
411 Sqn Spit	2TAF	F/L R.K.Hayward	Bf109 damaged	5m E Caen	1400±
		S/L G.D.Robertson	Bf109 damaged	5m E Caen	1400±
		F/L H.C.Trainor	Bf109 prob.dest	5m E Caen	1400±

Left: Typhoon pilots of 198 Squadron taxiing out for a rocket strike. Right: Rockets leaving the rails, about to 'ruin somebody's entire day'. The missiles were so 'touchy' that the arming pins were not removed until the aircraft was on the runway, about to take-off.

2nd July 1944

Sqn			Pilot	Claim	Location	Time
65 Sqn	Must	2TAF	F/S G.C.Dinsdale	Bf109 destroyed	S Mezidon	1945
			F/S G.C.Dinsdale	Bf109 damaged	S Mezidon	1945
			F/S W.P.Kelly	Bf109 prob.dest	S Mezidon	1945
			F/S W.P.Kelly	Bf109 damaged	S Mezidon	1945
132 Sqn	Spit	2TAF	F/L D.J.Hawkins	FW190 damaged	Potigny area	1610
			F/S T.Lindsay	FW190 damaged	Potigny area	1610
401 Sqn	Spit	2TAF	F/L I.F.Kennedy	Bf109 destroyed	Near Bernay	1550±
			F/O W.T.Klersey	Bf109 destroyed	S Caen	1550±
403 Sqn	Spit	2TAF	W/O J.A.L.Wilcocks	Bf109 damaged	E Caen	1442
			S/L E.P.Wood	FW190 prob.dest	E Caen	1500
			S/L E.P.Wood	FW190 damaged	E Caen	1500
			S/L E.P.Wood	FW190 damaged	E Caen	1500
			F/L M.J.Gordon	Bf109 destroyed	12m SW Caen	1500
			F/L M.J.Gordon	Bf109 destroyed	12m SW Caen	1500
			F/L W.J.Hill F/O R.B.Greene	Bf109 destroyed - Shared -	10m SE Caen	1500
			F/L J.D.Lindsay	Bf109 destroyed	12m SW Caen	1500
			F/L J.D.Lindsay	Bf109 destroyed	12m SW Caen	1500
			F/L J.D.Lindsay	Bf109 destroyed	12m SW Caen	1500
			F/L A.R.MacKenzie	Bf109 destroyed	½m E Caen	1500
			F/L A.R.MacKenzie	Bf109 damaged	E Caen	1500
			F/O F.W.Thomson	FW190 damaged	E Caen	1508
411 Sqn	Spit	2TAF	F/O E.G.Lapp	FW190 destroyed	5m E Caen	0630±

412 Sqn Spit	2TAF	F/O J.N.Goldberg	Bf109 damaged	20m SE Caen	1215±
		P/O R.C.Jamieson	FW190 destroyed	20m SE Lisieux	1215±
		P/O R.C.Jamieson	FW190 damaged	20m SE Lisieux	1215±
		F/O D.CLaubman	FW190 destroyed	20m SE Caen	1215±
		F/O D.C.Laubman	FW190 destroyed	20m SE Caen	1215±
		F/L H.L.Phillips	FW190 damaged	20m SE Caen	1215±
		F/O G.T.Schwalm	FW190 damaged	20m SE Lisieux	1215±
		F/O G.T.Schwalm	FW190 damaged	20m SE Lisieux	1215±
412 Sqn Spit	2TAF	S/L J.E.Sheppard	FW190 destroyed	20m SE Lisieux	1215±
441 Sqn Spit	2TAF	F/O A.J.McDonald	FW190 destroyed	W Lisieux	1250
		F/O R.G.Lake	FW190 destroyed	3m W Lisieux	1310
		F/O R.G.Lake	Bf109 destroyed	3m W Lisieux	1310
		F/L L.A.Moore F/O R.G.Lake	Bf109 destroyed - Shared -	3m W Lisieux	1310
		F/L L.A.Moore	Bf109 destroyed	3m W Lisieux	1310
		F/L L.A.Moore	Bf109 destroyed	3m W Lisieux	1310
442 Sqn Spit	2TAF	F/L A.W.Roseland	FW190 destroyed	2m W Lisieux	1315
453 Sqn Spit	2TAF	F/S A.W.Dowding F/L P.V.McDade F/O J.F.Olver	FW190 destroyed - Shared - - Shared -	Argentan	2100
		F/L G.Roberts F/O J.F.Olver	FW190 destroyed - Shared -	S Argentan	2105
602 Sqn Spit	2TAF	F/L F. Woolley	FW190 damaged	5m S Cabourg	1600
		F/L K.LCharney	FW190 destroyed	5m S Cabourg	1603
		Sgt P.H.Clostermann	FW190 destroyed	5m S Cabourg	1605
		Sgt P.H.Clostermann	FW190 damaged	5m S Cabourg	1605
		Sgt P.H.Clostermann	FW190 damaged	5m S Cabourg	1605
		Sgt P.H.Clostermann	FW190 damaged	5m S Cabourg	1605
		Sgt P.H.Clostermann	FW190 damaged	5m S Cabourg	1605
		Capt P.G.J.Aubertin	FW190 damaged	S Cabourg	1605
602 Sqn Spit	2TAF	F/L T.A.Burke	Bf109 damaged	10m SE Caen	1930
602 Sqn Spit	2TAF	F/O B.JDumbrell	FW190 prob.dest	20m S Bayeux	2045
		F/O B.JDumbrell	FW190 damaged	20m S Bayeux	2045
		F/L A.R.Stewart	FW90 damaged	SE Caen	2045
		F/L D.A.W.Manson	FW190 damaged	15m SW Bayeux	2050

Sergeant Pierre Clostermann congratulates Ken Charney on their victories on 2nd July. The unit also claimed another six FW190s damaged, three by Clostermann. (ww2images.com)

2/3rd July 1944

604 Sqn Mosq	ADGB	F/O R.A.Miller	Ju188 destroyed	10m N Ouistreham	0125
		W/C M.H.Constable -Maxwell	Ju88 destroyed	10m N Ouistreham	0135

3rd July 944

317 Sqn Spit	ADGB	F/S L.Winski	FW190 destroyed	Beachhead	2200±

3/4th July 1944

141 Sqn Beau	FC	F/O H.E.White	Bf110 damaged	Aachen	0115
157 Sqn Mosq	FC	F/L J.G.Benson	Do217 destroyed	St Trond	0039
264 Sqn Mosq	ADGB	F/L I.H.Cosby	Ju188 destroyed	10m E Barfleur	0101
		F/S P.N.Lee	Ju188 damaged	Beachy Head	0100±
410 Sqn Mosq	ADGB	F/L C.E.Edinger	Ju188 destroyed	NE Raz de Pierce	0105
604 Sqn Mosq	ADGB	S/L D.C.Furse	Ju88 destroyed	20m NNW Le Havre	0055

4th July 1944

66 Sqn Spit	2TAF	F/O R.C.Casburn F/L A.B.Kolubinski	Bf109G destroyed - Shared -	Near Dreux AD	2115
		F/L J.A.Jackson	Bf109 damaged	Near Dreux AD	2115
		F/L P.L.Gibbs	FW190 damaged	20m NW Dreux	2120
340 Sqn Spit	2TAF	Lt J.Homolle	FW190 damaged	4m SE Caen	1515
		Lt J.Homolle	FW190 damaged	4m SE Caen	1515
		Sgt F.Lagarde	FW190 damaged	4m SE Caen	1515
		Sgt C.C.Rosa	FW190 damaged	4m SE Caen	1515

411 Sqn Spit	2TAF	F/L H.C.Trainor	Bf109 destroyed	2-3m E Caen	1820±
		F/L H.C.Trainor	Bf109 destroyed	2-3m E Caen	1820±
		F/L A.B.Whiteford	Bf109 damaged	8m S Caen	1820±
		F/L R.K.Hayward	FW190 destroyed	SE Caen	1820±
		F/L R.K.Hayward	FW190 damaged	SE Caen	1820±
		F/L R.K.Hayward	FW190 damaged	SE Caen	1820±
		F/L R.S.Hyndman	Bf109 damaged	5-6m SE Caen	1820±
		S/L G.D.Robertson	Do217 destroyed	N Cabourg	2230
		F/L H.C.Trainor	- Shared -		
414 Sqn Must	2TAF	F/O J.C.Younge	FW190 destroyed	La Mangeliere	1320
602 Sqn Spit	2TAF	W/O F.JFarrell	FW190 damaged	E Vire	1920
		Capt T.Jonssen	FW190 damaged	E Falaise	1930
		F/L T.A.Burke	FW190 damaged	SE Caen	1945

4/5th July 1944

21 Sqn Mosq	ADGB	F/O R.M.Seage	Do217 damaged	Loire area	0130±
125 Sqn Mosq	ADGB	S/L L.W.G.Gill	Do217 destroyed	20m SW Le Havre	0010
		F/L V.P.Key	Ju88 damaged	Channel	0100
141 Sqn Mosq	BC	F/L J.D.Peterkin	Me410 destroyed	Nr Orleans	0027
169 Sqn Mosq	BC	F/L J.S.Fifield	Ju88 destroyed	Villeneuve	0120±
239 Sqn Mosq	BC	S/L N.A.Reeves	Bf110 destroyed	NW Paris	0200±
418 Sqn Mosq	ADGB	F/L J.B.Kerr	Ju88 destroyed	15m W Chateaudun	0110
456 Sqn Mosq	ADGB	F/L R.B.Cowper	He177 destroyed	V-2058	0054
		F/O E.C.Radford	He177 destroyed	W-04	0104
		P/O S.J.Williams	Do217 destroyed	70m S Newhaven	0011
		P/O I.W.Sanderson	He177 destroyed	V2945	0121
515 Sqn Mosq	BC	W/O R.E.Preston	Ju88 destroyed	Nr Coulommieres	0250

5th July 1944

122 Sqn Must	2TAF	F/L A.F.Pavey	Bf109 destroyed	6m E Vernon	1345
		F/O A.W.Minchin	- Shared -		
		F/O C.Tallala	- Shared -		
132 Sqn Spit	2TAF	F/L M.Graham	Bf109 destroyed	E Caen	1530
		F/L D.J.Hawkins	Bf109 destroyed	5m N Cabourg	2100
		F/O W.A.Doyle	- Shared -		
		F/L O.J.Eskil	- Shared -		
401 Sqn Spit	2TAF	F/O R.M.Davenport	FW190 destroyed	NW Chartres	1200±

'Doodle-bug Buster'. Peter Graham's Spitfire XII EB-B of 41 Squadron in the summer of 1944. The unit would not come into its own until the autumn, when it moved out to the continent.

- Alan Hillman

403 Sqn Spit	2TAF	F/L J.D.Lindsay	FW190 damaged	Lisieux	1150
		F/O J.D.Orr	FW190 damaged	12m S Lisieux	1150
412 Sqn Spit	2TAF	F/O D.C.Laubman	FW190 destroyed	W Chartes	1200±
421 Sqn Spit	2TAF	S/L W.A.G.Conrad	Bf109 damaged	10m NE Bernay	1605
		P/O O.E.Libby	Bf109 damaged	10m NE Bernay	1605
		F/O R.C.McRoberts	Bf109 destroyed	10m NE Bernay	1605
		F/O R.C.McRoberts	Bf109 destroyed	10m NE Bernay	1605
441 Sqn Spit	2TAF	S/L T.A.Brannagan	FW190 destroyed	Near Alencon	1840
		S/L T.A.Brannagan	FW190 damaged	Near Alencon	1840
		F/O W.R.Chowen	FW190 destroyed	Near Alencon	1840
		F/L G.E.Mott F/O W.R.Chowen	FW190 destroyed - Shared -	Near Alencon	1840
		P/O W.D.Hill	FW190 damaged	Near Alencon	1840
		F/O D.H.Kimball	FW190 destroyed	Near Alencon	1840
		P/O B.M.Mackenzie	FW190 damaged	Near Alencon	1840
		F/L G.E.Mott	FW190 destroyed	Near Alencon	1840
		F/O J.W.Neil	FW190 destroyed	Near Alencon	1840
144 Wg Spit	2TAF	W/C J.E.Johnson	FW190 destroyed	Near Alencon	1840
		W/C J.E.Johnson	FW190 destroyed	Near Alencon	1840

5/6th July 1944

169 Sqn Mosq	BC	F/O P.G.Bailey	Ju88 destroyed	S Paris	0100±
		F/L C.M.Ramsay	Ju88 destroyed	8m S Falaise	0235±
		F/L C.M.Ramsay	Me410 destroyed	10m S Evreux	0245±
264 Sqn Mosq	ADGB	F/O J.C.Trigg	Ju188 destroyed	S Briouze	0125
456 Sqn Mosq	ADGB	F/L C.L.Brooks	He177 destroyed	Beachhead	0030
604 Sqn Mosq	ADGB	W/O J.H.Moore	Me410 destroyed	WSW Caen	0235

6th July 1944

66 Sqn	Spit	2TAF	S/L W.M.Foster	Bf109 destroyed	10m from Chartres	1320
			S/L W.M.Foster	Bf109 damaged	10m from Chartres	1320
			F/L J.G.Pattinson	Bf109 destroyed	10m from Chartres	1320
331 Sqn	Spit	2TAF	Maj M.Y.Gran Lt K.L.'l'Abbe-Lund	Bf109 destroyed - Shared -	20m NW Chartres	1320
			2/Lt E.Gundersen	Bf109 destroyed	20m NW Chartres	1320
			Cpt N.K.Jorstad	FW190 destroyed	20m NW Chartres	1320
			Cpt N.K.Jorstad	Bf109 destroyed	20m NW Chartres	1320
332 Sqn	Spit	2TAF	Capt J.Tvedte	FW190 destroyed	20m NW Chartres	1320
132 Wg	Spit	2TAF	Lt Col R.A.Berg	Bf109G destroyed	5m NW Caen	1320
			Lt Col R.A.Berg	Bf109G destroyed	20m NW Chartres	1320

6/7th July 1944

605 Sqn	Mosq	ADGB	F/L I.F.Pengelly	He177 damaged	Schwabisch Hall	0213
			F/L I.F.Pengelly	E/A damaged	Creilsheim	0225

7th July1944

132 Sqn	Spit	2TAF	F/O N.V.Chevers	FW190 destroyed	5m SE Cabourg	1150±
			F/O F.Campbell	FW190 damaged	SE Lisieux	1645
			F/O F.Campbell	FW190 destroyed	SE Lisieux	1645
			F/O F.Campbell	Bf109 destroyed	SE Lisieux	1645
			F/O B.F.Collings	Bf109 destroyed	SE Lisieux	1645
			F/O W.A.Doyle	Bf109 damaged	SE Lisieux	1645
			W/O R.C.Harden	FW190 destroyed	SE Lisieux	1645
			S/L A.G.Page	Bf109 destroyed	SE Lisieux	1645
			W/O V.C.Parker	FW190 destroyed	SE Lisieux	1645
			F/L A.G.Russell	Bf109 prob.dest	SE Lisieux	1645
			F/L A.G.Russell	Bf109 damaged	SE Lisieux	1645
			F/L A.G.Russell	Bf109 damaged	SE Lisieux	1645
401 Sqn	Spit	2TAF	F/L W.R.McRae	Bf109 destroyed	3m W Lisieux	1110±
			F/O A.L.Sinclair	FW190 destroyed	Lisieux	1140
			F/O A.L.Sinclair	Bf109 destroyed	Lisieux	1140
			F/L W.R.Tew	Bf109 destroyed	Falaise	2100±
			F/OE.T.Gardner	Bf109 damaged	Troarn	2100±

Geoffrey Page (2nd from left) briefs his pilots. On 7th July he claimed his seventh victory and would increase his score to ten, with five more shared, by the armistice.

411 Sqn Spit	2TAF	F/L H.J.Nixon	FW190 damaged	6m E Caen	1710±
412 Sqn Spit	2TAF	F/O W.J.Banks	Bf109 destroyed	NE Bernay	0710±
		P/O D.R.C.Jamieson	Bf109 destroyed	NE Bernay	0710±
		F/O W.B.Randall	FW190 damaged	Near Argentan	1450±
		F/O G.T.Schwalm	FW190 destroyed	Near Argentan	1450±
		F/L R.I.A.Smith DFC	FW190 destroyed	Near Argentan	1450±

7/8th July 1944

29 Sqn Mosq	ADGB	F/O J.E.Bennett	E/A destroyed	landing at Brussels	0147
141 Sqn Mosq	BC	S/L G.J.Rice	Bf110 destroyed	8m NW Amiens	0050
239 Sqn Mosq	BC	F/L V.Bridges	Bf110 destroyed	Charleroi	0110±
		W/C P.M.J.Evans	FW190 destroyed	Pas de Calais	0115±
		S/L J.S.Booth	Bf110 destroyed	Paris	0115±
		S/L J.S.Booth	Bf110 destroyed	Paris	0120±
409 Sqn Mosq	ADGB	F/O H.F.Pearce	Ju188 destroyed	10m SE Beauvais	0050
		F/O H.F.Pearce	Ju88 destroyed	20m SW Beauvais	0105
410 Sqn Mosq	ADGB	F/L S.B.Huppert	Ju88 destroyed	Channel	0100
		S/L I.A.March	Me410 destroyed	SW o/s Paris	0127
418 Sqn Mosq	ADGB	F/L F.M.Sawyer	Ju88 destroyed	Mayen A/D	0158
FIU Mosq	ADGB	F/L J.N.Howard -Williams	Ju188 destroyed	Coulommieres	0130±

8th July 1944

19 Sqn Must	2TAF	F/L D.P.Lamb	Bf109 destroyed	Near Alencon	1045
		F/O J.M.Maynard	- Shared -		
		F/S B.Vassiliades	- Shared -		
		F/L D.P.Lamb	Bf109 destroyed	Near Alencon	1045
		F/O J.M.Maynard	- Shared -		
		F/S B.Vassiliades	- Shared -		

8/9th July 1944

604 Sqn Mosq	ADGB	W/C M.H.Constable -Maxwell	Do217 prob.dest	10m W Le Havre	0130
		W/C M.H.Constable -Maxwell	Ju88 destroyed	S bank R Seine	0135

9th July 1944

340 Sqn Spit	2TAF	Cdt J.A.M.Fournier	Bf109 destroyed	5m NNE Bernay	1335
341 Sqn Spit	2TAF	Capt M.Boudier	Bf109 destroyed	Bernay	2000±
453 Sqn Spit	2TAF	W/O J.A.Boulton	FW190 destroyed	W Lisieux	1330
		W/O K.F.Daff	Bf109 destroyed	W Lisieux	1330
		F/S A.W.Dowding	Bf109 damaged	W Lisieux	1330
		P/O K.C.Kinross	Bf109 damaged	W Lisieux	1330
		F/L G.Roberts	FW190 damaged	W Lisieux	1330
		W/O C.A.Seeney	FW190 damaged	W Lisieux	1330
		W/O C.A.Seeney	FW190 damaged	W Lisieux	1330
		S/L D.H.Smith	Bf109 prob.dest	W Lisieux	1330
		S/L D.H.Smith	FW190 damaged	W Lisieux	1330
		W/O J.Steward	FW190 destroyed	W Lisieux	1330
145 Wg Spit	2TAF	W/C W.V.Crawford -Compton	Bf109F destroyed	5m N Bernay	1335

9/10th July 1944

264 Sqn Mosq	ADGB	S/L F.J.A.Chase	Ju88 destroyed	25m NE Bayeux	0125

10th July 1944

19 Sqn Must	2TAF	W/O T.A.Carson	Bf109 damaged	SE Caen	1610
		F/O E.R.Davies	Bf109 damaged	SE Caen	1610
		S/L W.McM.Gilmour	Bf109 destroyed	SE Caen	1610
		F/O R.H.Heath	Bf109 damaged	SE Caen	1610
		F/O J.Paton	Bf109 destroyed	SE Caen	1610
		F/O J.E.Staples	FW190 damaged	SE Caen	1610
412 Sqn Spit	2TAF	F/O W.J.Banks	Bf109 destroyed	Mortagne area	0910±
421 Sqn Spit	2TAF	P/O J.M.Calvert	Bf109 prob.dest	Pont l'Evecque	1815
		F/O R.C.McRoberts	Bf109 damaged	Pont l'Evecque	1815
		F/O G.M.Smith	Bf109 destroyed	Pont l'Evecque	1815
		F/O G.M.Smith	Bf109 damaged	Pont l'Evecque	1815
453 Sqn Spit	2TAF	W/O F.F.Cowpe 125 Wing	FW190 destroyed - Shared -	7m E Caen	1915

Jeremy Howard-Williams (seated right) flew with 604 Squadron and eventually with the Fighter Interception Unit. His second victory came on the night of 7th June 1944. He ended the war with three confirmed night kills.
(Chris Goss)

125 Wg Spit	2TAF	W/C A.G.Page 453 Squadron	FW190 destroyed - Shared -	7m E Caen	1915

12/13th July 1944

157 Sqn Mosq	BC	F/L J.O.Mathews	Ju88 destroyed	10m S Etampes	0214
219 Sqn Mosq	ADGB	S/L P.L.Burke	Ju188 destroyed	Argentan	0100±
264 Sqn Mosq	ADGB	F/OR.L.J.Barbour	Ju188 destroyed	Seine estuary nr Bernay	0116
409 Sqn Mosq	ADGB	S/L J.A.Hatch	Bf110 damaged	Juvincourt	0240

13th July 1944

122 Sqn Must	2TAF	F/O M.H.Pinches	Bf109 damaged	Evreux area	1130
122 Sqn Must	2TAF	P/O J.N.Thorne	FW190 damaged	Near Gisors	1845
132 Sqn Spit	2TAF	S/L K.L.Charney DFC	FW190 damaged	10m S Lisieux	1825
		S/L K.L.Charney DFC	Bf109 damaged	10m SE Cabourg	1825
257 Sqn Typh	2TAF	S/L W.C.Ahrens	Bf109 damaged	S Lisieux	1825
		F/O R.Logan	Bf109 damaged	S Lisieux	1825
		F/S M.E.Marriott	Bf109 prob.dest	S Lisieux	1825
		F/O W.B.Richardson	Bf109 damaged	S Lisieux	1825
		F/S A.Shannon	Bf109 destroyed	S Lisieux	1825
		F/O R.WSnell	Bf109 damaged	S Lisieux	1825
401 Sqn Spit	2TAF	F/L W.T.Klersey	FW190 damaged	E Caen	1715±
441 Sqn Spit	2TAF	S/L T.A.Brannagan	FW190 destroyed	2m N L'Aigle	2035
		S/L T.A.Brannagan	FW190 destroyed	2m N L'Aigle	2035
		F/L J.C.Copeland	FW190 destroyed	2m N L'Aigle	2035
		F/O D.H.Kimball	FW190 destroyed	2m N L'Aigle	2035
		F/O B.M.MacKenzie	FW190 destroyed	2m N L'Aigle	2035
		F/L G.E.Mott	FW190 destroyed	2m N L'Aigle	2035

441 Sqn Spit	2TAF	F/O W.J.Myers	FW190 destroyed	2m N L'Aigle	2035
		F/O W.J.Myers	FW190 destroyed	2m N L'Aigle	2035
		F/O W.J.Myers	FW190 destroyed	2m N L'Aigle	2035
		F/O L.A.Plummer	FW190 destroyed	2m N L'Aigle	2035
442 Sqn Spit	2TAF	F/O S.M.McLarty	Bf109 damaged	SE Cabourg	2025±
443 Sqn Spit	2TAF	F/L W.A.Prest	FW190 damaged	N Falaise	1840
146 Wg Typh	2TAF	W/C J.R.Baldwin	Bf109G destroyed	S Lisieux	1825

14th July 1944

132 Sqn Spit	2TAF	S/L K.L.Charney	FW190 destroyed	Argentan area	1435
401 Sqn Spit	2TAF	F/O T.P.Jarvis	Bf109 destroyed	S Caen	2000±
		F/O C.P.B.Wyman	Bf109 destroyed	S Caen	2000±
411 Sqn Spit	2TAF	F/O R.M.Cook	FW190 damaged	NW Caen	1440
		F/O J.N.L.Harrison	FW190 destroyed	NW Caen	1440
		F/O A.M.Tooley	FW190 damaged	NW Caen	1440
		F/O T.R.Wheler	FW190 destroyed	5m NW Caen	1440
416 Sqn Spit	2TAF	F/O A.J.Fraser	FW190 damaged	1m N Villiers	1320
		F/L D.E.Noonan	Bf109 destroyed	1m N Villiers	1320
		F/L D.E.Noonan F/O A.J.Fraser	Bf109 destroyed - Shared -	1m N Villiers	1320
		F/S R.E.Chambers	Bf109 damaged	Pont l'Evecque area	1430
		F/O M.R.Sharun	Bf109 destroyed	N Caen	1430
		F/O J.B.Gould	Bf109 destroyed	Pont l'Evecque area	1430
		F/L G.R.Patterson	Bf109 destroyed	Near Crepon	1930
		F/L R.D.Forbes -Roberts	FW190 destroyed	Near Crepon	1930
515 Sqn Mosq	BC	F/L A.E.Callard	Ju W34 destroyed	Stralsund	1120
125 Wg Spit	2TAF	W/C A.G.Page	FW190 destroyed	Argentan area	1435
		W/C A.G.Page	FW190 damaged	Argentan area	1435

14/15th July 1944

29 Sqn Mosq	ADGB	F/O F.E.Pringle	E/A damaged	Orly	0225
157 Sqn Mosq	BC	Lt F.H.Sandiford	Bf110 destroyed	NE Juvincourt	0153
169 Sqn Mosq	BC	F/L J.S.Fifield	Ju88 damaged	S Brussels	0145±
		W/O L.W.Turner	Bf109 destroyed	30m SW Lille	0145±
219 Sqn Mosq	ADGB	S/L P.L.Burke	Ju188 destroyed	SW Caen	2345±
FIU	Mosq ADGB	Lt J.O.Armour RM	Do217 destroyed	10m W Antwerp	0100±

15th July 1944

122 Sqn Must	2TAF	F/O A.V.Hargreaves	Ju188 destroyed	S Conflans	2105
		F/O M.H.Pinches	- Shared -		
		F/O R.Tickner	- Shared -		
412 Sqn Spit	2TAF	F/O L.F.Berryman	FW190 destroyed	5m SE Caen	0710±
602 Sqn Spit	2TAF	S/L J.J.Le Roux	FW190 destroyed	SE Caen	0810±
		S/L J.J.Le Roux	Bf109 destroyed		2100±

15/16th July 1944

219 Sqn Mosq	ADGB	S/L H.V.Ellis	Ju188 prob.dest	25m W Le Havre	0035

16th July 1944

403 Sqn Spit	2TAF	F/L J.E.Collier	Bf109 destroyed	8m NNW Argentan	2015
		F/O H.V.Boyle	Bf109 destroyed	8m NW Argentan	2020
		F/O H.V.Boyle	Bf109 destroyed	8m NW Argentan	2020
		F/O H.V.Boyle	Bf109 damaged	8m NW Argentan	2020
		P/O M.L.Garland	Bf109 damaged	8m NW Argentan	2020
		F/L A.R.MacKenzie	Bf109 destroyed	8m NW Argentan	2020
		F/L A.R.MacKenzie	Bf109 destroyed	8m NW Argentan	2020
421 Sqn Spit	2TAF	F/L J.N.Patterson	Bf109 destroyed	Near Caen	1820
602 Sqn Spit	2TAF	S/L J.J.Le Roux	FW190 destroyed	10m NW Bayeux	0715
		Asp J.Remlinger	FW190 damaged	10m NW Bayeux	0715

17th July 1944

401 Sqn Spit	2TAF	F/L R.H.Cull	Bf109 damaged	E Bretteville-sur-Oden	2035
		F/L W.S.Johnson	Bf109 damaged	Near Carpiquet A/D	2035
		F/L W.T.Klersey	Do217 destroyed	NE Caen	2230±
		F/O R.M.Davenport	Do217 destroyed	N Cabourg	2230±
		F/L A.A.Williams	Do217 damaged	Sea W Le Havre	2230±
411 Sqn Spit	2TAF	S/L G.D.Robertson	Bf109 destroyed	NE Lisieux	1645±
441 Sqn Spit	2TAF	F/L W.W.L.Brown	FW190 destroyed	SW Verneuil	1655
		F/L W.W.L.Brown	FW190 destroyed	SW Verneuil	1655
		F/O D.H.Kimball	FW190 destroyed	Dreux-Chartes	1655
602 Sqn Spit	2TAF	S/LJ.J.Le Roux	Bf109 destroyed	Nr Flers	1615±
		S/LJ.J.Le Roux	Bf109 damaged	Nr Flers	1615±

602 Sq	Spit	2TAF	Capt T.Jonssen	Bf109 destroyed	S Caen	2015
			F/L T.A.Burke	FW190 destroyed	SW Cabourg	2015
			Capt T.Jonssen	Bf109 destroyed	S Caen	2015
			F/O M.D.Morgan	Bf109 destroyed	S Carpiquet	2015
			F/O M.D.Morgan	Bf109 damaged	S Carpiquet	2015
			F/O B.J.Oliver	FW190 destroyed	S Caen	2015

17/18th July 1944

418 Sqn	Mosq	ADGB	S/L R.Bannock	E/A damaged	Altenburg A/D	0152
			S/L R.Bannock	E/A destroyed	Altenburg A/D	0204
602 Sqn	Spit	2TAF	S/L J.J.Le Roux	Bf109 destroyed	Caen-Cabourg	2230
			S/L J.J.Le Roux	Bf109 damaged	Caen-Cabourg	2230
604 Sqn	Mosq	ADGB	F/L G.A.Hayhurst	Ju88 destroyed	15m S Cap Cararet	0035
605 Sqn	Mosq	ADGB	W/C N.V.Starr	E/A destroyed	Schwabisch Hall	0141

18th July 1944

441 Sqn	Spit	2TAF	F/L J.C.Copeland	Bf109 destroyed	Flers	0935
			F/L A.Johnstone	- Shared -		
			F/L G.E.Mott	Bf109 destroyed	E Tourourve	0935

18/19th July 1944

29 Sqn	Mosq	ADGB	W/O A.R.C.Cresswell	E/A destroyed	Bonn	0200±
141 Sqn	Mosq	BC	F/O A.C.Gallacher	Me410 damaged	Beacon 'Karl'	0025±
169 Sqn	Mosq	BC	F/L R.J.Dix	Ju88 damaged	S Brussels	0115±
409 Sqn	Mosq	ADGB	W/C W.G.Kirkwood	Ju88 destroyed	N Caen	2315
			F/O A.S.McPhail	Do217 destroyed	S Caen	2315
418 Sqn	Mosq	ADGB	F/L C.J.Evans	E/A prob.dest	Oberpfaffenhofen A/D	0140
			F/L L.E.Evans	FW190 prob.dest	Lechfeld A/D	0210

19th July 1944

131 Sqn	Spit	ADGB	F/O G.A.Edwards	Bf109 destroyed	Alencon	1550
			616 Squadron	- Shared -		
266 Sqn	Typh	2TAF	P/O I.H.Forrester	Bf109 destroyed	3m N Lisieux	2030±
616 Sqn	Spit	ADGB	P/O I.Wilson	Bf109 destroyed	Alencon	1550
			131 Squadron	- Shared -		

19/20th July 1944

219 Sqn	Mosq	ADGB	F/O D.W.B.Farrar	Ju188 destroyed	15m WSW Le Havre	0010
604 Sqn	Mosq	ADGB	F/L R.A.Miller	FW190 damaged	Coutances	0015

Squadron Leader J.J. 'Chris' Le Roux of 602 Squadron (left) added to his score on 14th and 15th July.
He would disappear on 29th August on a transfer flight, with his score standing at 18. Frank Pringle
of 29 Squadron claimed a 'damaged' on 14/15th and would survive at a score of three destroyed.

- Pringle

20th July 1944

132 Sqn Spit	2TAF	F/L D.J.Hawkins	Bf109 damaged	St Julien	1540
401 Sqn Spit	2TAF	F/L A.F.Halcrow	FW190 destroyed	Conde-sur-Noireau	1330±
		F/L R.M.Stayner	FW190 destroyed	8m S Argentan	1330±
412 Sqn Spit	2TAF	F/O D.R.C.Jamieson	FW190 destroyed	S La Hogue	1600±
442 Sqn Spit	2TAF	F/O G.R.Blair	FW190 destroyed	SE St Lo	1315±
		F/L W.A.Olmsted	FW190 destroyed	SE St Lo	1315±
		F/L W.A.Olmsted	FW190 destroyed	SE St Lo	1315±
443 Sqn Spit	2TAF	S/L H.W.McLeod	FW190 destroyed	NW Bernay	1530
		F/L J.G.L.Robillard	FW190 destroyed	Bernay -Beaumont le Roger	1550
602 Sqn Spit	2TAF	F/L B.J.Oliver	FW190 destroyed	Ecouchie	1330
125 Wg Spit	2TAF	W/C A.G.Page	Bf109 destroyed	St Julian	1540
144 Wg Spit	2TAF	W/C J.E.Johnson	FW190 damaged	S Argentan	1330±

20/21st July 1944

141 Sqn Mosq	BC	P/O M.J.G.Lagouge	Bf110 damaged	5020N 0207E	0035
169 Sqn Mosq	BC	W/C N.B.R.Bromley	Bf110 destroyed	N Lille	0220±
		F/L J.S.Fifield	Bf110 destroyed	E Ruhr	0300±
		P/O H.Reed	Ju88 destroyed	Nr Homburg	0045±

The night stalker: The Mosquito NF II was used as a high level night intruder by 100 Group in defence of the bomber stream.

21st July 1944

406 Sqn Mosq	ADGB	S/L D.J.Williams	Do217 destroyed	WSW Ushant	1315
		S/L D.J.Williams Coastal Command	Do217 destroyed - Shared -	WSW Ushant	1315
		F/O W.H.Meakin	Do217 destroyed	WSW Ushant	1315
		F/O W.H.Meakin	Do217 destroyed	WSW Ushant	1315
		F/O W.H.Meakin	Do217 destroyed	WSW Ushant	1315

22nd July 1944

418 Sqn Mosq	ADGB	P/O W.E.Bowhay	Ju52 destroyed	6m W Putnitz A/D	1415
		F/L C.J.Evans	Ju52 destroyed	6m W Putnitz A/D	1415

23/24th July 1944

29 Sqn Mosq	ADGB	F/L A.C.Musgrove	Ju188 destroyed	Leeuwarden	0230±
141 Sqn Mosq	BC	P/O I.D.Gregory	Ju88 destroyed	SW Beauvais	0100
169 Sqn Mosq	BC	F/L R.J.Dix	Bf110 destroyed	Nr Kiel	0130±

24th July 1944

126 Sqn Spit	ADGB	F/L R.Collis	Bf109 destroyed	E Angers	1930
		S/L J.A.Plagis	Bf109 destroyed	E Angers	1930
412 Sqn Spit	2TAF	F/O W.J.Banks	Bf109 destroyed	E Lisieux	1530±
		F/O W.J.Banks	Bf109 destroyed	E Lisieux	1530±
		F/O W.J.Banks	FW190 destroyed	E Lisieux	1530±
		F/O D.R.C.Jamieson	Bf109 destroyed	E Lisieux	1530±

On 24th, Wilfred Banks of 412 Squadron claimed two Bf109s and an FW190 to bring his score to six. He survived the war with a total of nine confirmed victories.

412 Sqn Spit	2TAF	F/OD.R.C.Jamieson	Bf109 destroyed	E Lisieux	1530±
		F/L O.M.Linton	FW190 destroyed	E Lisieux	1530±
		F/L O.M.Linton	FW190 destroyed	E Lisieux	1530±
453 Sqn Spit	2TAF	F/L P.V.McDade	Bf109 destroyed	Cambremer	2000
		F/L G.Roberts	FW190 destroyed	Cambremer	2000
		P/O J.W.Scott	FW190 damaged	SE Cabourg	2000
		P/O J.W.Scott	FW190 damaged	SE Cabourg	2000

24/25th July 1944

409 Sqn Mosq	ADGB	W/O D.J.MacDonald	Ju88 destroyed	NE Le Havre	2310

25th July 1944

19 Sqn Must	2TAF	W/O M.H.Bell	FW190 destroyed	E Lisieux	1615
		W/O T.A.Carson	FW190 destroyed	E Lisieux	1615
65 Sqn Must	2TAF	F/O T.E.Jonsson	Bf109 destroyed	St Leger	1130±
		F/O T.E.Jonsson	Bf109 damaged	St Leger	1130±
		F/S W.P.Kelly	Bf109 destroyed	St Leger	1130
		F/S O.H.Robinson	Bf109 destroyed	St Leger	1130
122 Sqn Must	2TAF	P/O R.Benoit 122 Wing	FW190 destroyed - Shared -	St Leger	1130
		P/O A.F.Cush	FW190 destroyed	St Leger	1130
		F/OH.H.Pavey	FW190 damaged	St Leger	1130
		F/O A.VHargreaves	FW190 damaged	SE Evreux	1900
		F/O M.H.Pinches	FW190 destroyed	SE Evreux	1900
		F/O M.H.Pinches	FW190 damaged	SE Evreux	1900

122 Sqn Must	2TAF	F/O M.H.Pinches	FW190 damaged	SE Evreux	1900
		F/O S.K.Walker	FW190 destroyed	SE Evreux	1900
421 Sqn Spit	2TAF	F/O W.F.Cook	Bf109 destroyed	Near les Andelys	1100
		F/O W.F.Cook	Bf109 damaged	Near les Andelys	1100
		P/O O.H.Levere	Bf109 destroyed	Near les Andelys	1100
		F/O J.W.Neil	Bf109 prob.dest	Near les Andelys	1100
		F/O G.M.Smith	Bf109 damaged	Near les Andelys	1100
		F/L L.R.Thorne	Bf109 damaged	Near les Andelys	1100
		F/L H.P.M.Zary	Bf109 destroyed	Near les Andelys	1100
		F/L H.P.M.Zary	Bf109 destroyed	Near les Andelys	1100
		F/L H.P.M.Zary	Bf109 destroyed	Near les Andelys	1100
453 Sqn Spit	2TAF	F/L G.Roberts W/O F.F.Coupe	FW190 destroyed - Shared -	6m E Falaise	1115
		W/O K.F.Daff	Bf109 destroyed	5m SW Lisieux	1540
		W/O A.H.J.Harris	Bf109 prob.dest	5m SW Lisieux	1540
		W/O A.H.J.Harris F/O C.R.Leith	Bf109 destroyed - Shared -	5m SW Lisieux	1540
		F/O J.F.Olver	Bf109 prob.dest	5m SW Lisieux	1540
122 Wg Must	2TAF	W/C G.R.A.McG. Johnston 122 Squadron	FW190 destroyed - Shared -	St Leger	1130
125 Wg Spit	2TAF	W/C R.H.Harries	FW190 destroyed	L'Aigle	2000±

25/26th July 1944

23 Sqn Mosq	BC	F/L D.J.Griffiths	E/A destroyed	Laon Couvron	0350±
219 Sqn Mosq	ADGB	F/L D.L.Ryalls	Do217 damaged	15m SW Le Havre	2335
		F/O D.T.Tull	Ju88 destroyed	20m ENE Rouen	0100±
409 Sqn Mosq	ADGB	W/C J.R.Reid	Ju88 destroyed	SW Rouen	0001
515 Sqn Mosq	BC	S/L H.B.Martin	Me410 destroyed	Off Knocke	0350

26th July 1944

33 Sqn Spit	2TAF	F/L G.Mason	Bf109 destroyed	Near Alencon	1035
		F/L G.Mason	FW190 destroyed	Near Alencon	1035
122 Sqn Must	2TAF	F/O H.H.Cush	FW190 destroyed	Near L'Aigle	1850
		F/L A.E.Lee	- Shared -		
		F/L A.F.Pavey	FW190 destroyed	Near L'Aigle	1850
		F/L A.F.Pavey	FW190 prob.dest	Near L'Aigle	1850

The Mustang III proved to be a highly efficient fighter-bomber, but equally deadly in air combat. On 26th July 122 Squadron pilots fought FW190s, possibly from JG 2, and claimed six shot down. They would claim four more next day. Here one of their pilots prepares for a fighter-bomber sortie.

122 Sqn Must	2TAF	F/L A.F.Pavey	FW190 damaged	Near L'Aigle		1850
		F/L A.F.Pavey	FW190 damaged	Near L'Aigle		1850
		F/L A.F.Pavey	FW190 damaged	Near L'Aigle		1850
		S/L R.L.Stillwell	FW190 destroyed	Near L'Aigle		1850
		F/S J.K.Stockbridge	FW190 damaged	Near L'Aigle		1850
		P/O J.N.Thorne	FW190 destroyed	Near L'Aigle		1850
		P/O J.N.Thorne	FW190 destroyed	Near L'Aigle		1850
		P/O J.N.Thorne	FW190 damaged	Near L'Aigle		1850
		F/L M.J.Wright	FW190 destroyed	Near L'Aigle		1850
132 Sqn Spit	2TAF	P/O N.V.Chevers	Bf109 prob.dest	20m E Caen		1415
		P/O N.V.Chevers	FW190 damaged	20m E Caen		1415
		F/O B.F.Collings	Bf109 damaged	20m E Caen		1415
		F/S W.G.Thom	FW190 damaged	20m E Caen		1415
349 Sqn Spit	2TAF	F/O J.Ester	Bf109 damaged	E Alencon		1035
		F/L G.M.H.Seydel	Bf109 destroyed	E Alencon		1035
		F/L P.A.J.D.Siroux	Bf109 destroyed	Near Alencon		1035
		F/S D.A.Smerdon	Bf109 damaged	E Alencon		1035
		F/O A.Uydens	Bf109 damaged	E Alencon		1035
443 Sqn Spit	2TAF	F/O G.R.Stephen	FW190 destroyed	6m NW Dreux		1935

26/27th July 1944

23 Sqn Mosq	ADGB	W/C A.M.Murphy	Ju88 damaged	Chateaudun-Orleans	0300±
29 Sqn Mosq	ADGB	F/O F.E.Pringle	Ju188 destroyed	Melun	0132
219 Sqn Mosq	ADGB	F/O A.Hollingsworth	Ju188 damaged	60m S Paris	0215
409 Sqn Mosq	ADGB	S/L R.S.Jephson	Ju88 destroyed	Caen	0210
604 Sqn Mosq	ADGB	F/O J.C.Truscott	Ju88 destroyed	Off Granville	2335

27th July 1944

64 Sqn	Spit	ADGB	F/L D.A.Drew	Bf109 destroyed	W Nantes	2010
122 Sqn	Must	2TAF	F/O M.H.Pinches	FW190 destroyed	Pont l'Evecque	0715
			F/O M.H.Pinches	FW190 damaged	Pont l'Evecque	0715
			F/O M.H.Pinches	FW190 damaged	Pont l'Evecque	0715
			F/O M.H.Pinches F/O R.E.Tickner	FW190 destroyed - Shared -	Pont l'Evecque	0715
			S/L R.L.Stillwell	FW190 destroyed	Pont l'Evecque	0715
			F/O M.H.Tickner	FW190 destroyed	Pont l'Evecque	0715
			F/L M.J.Wright	FW190 damaged	Pont l'Evecque	0715
401 Sqn	Spit	2TAF	F/O G.A.Bell	Bf109 destroyed	10m SW Caen	0720±
			F/L A.F.Halcrow	Bf109 destroyed	10m SW Caen	0720±
			P/O M.H.Havers	Bf109 destroyed	10m SW Caen	0720±
			F/L G.W.Johnson	Bf109 destroyed	5m SW Caen	0720±
			F/L W.R.McRae	Bf109 destroyed	10m SW Caen	0720±
			F/L A.E.Morrison	FW190 destroyed	10m SW Caen	0720±
			S/L H.C.Trainor	Bf109 destroyed	10m SW Caen	0720±
			F/O C.P.B.Wyman	Bf109 destroyed	10m SE Caen	0720±
			F/O C.P.B.Wyman	FW190 damaged	10m SE Caen	0720±
			F/L T.P.Jarvis	FW190 damaged	16m SE Caen	1910
			F/L R.R.Bouskill	FW190 destroyed	16m SE Caen	1910
416 Sqn	Spit	2TAF	F/S R.E.Chambers F/L D.W.Hayworth	FW190 damaged - Shared -	3-4m NE Alencon	0730
			S/L J.F.McElroy	FW190 destroyed	3-4m NE Alencon	0730
			F/L D.E.Noonan	FW190 destroyed	3-4m NE Alencon	0730
441 Sqn	Spit	2TAF	F/O D.H.Kimball	FW190 destroyed	SE Caen	0726
			F/L G.E.Mott	FW190 destroyed	SE Caen	0726
442 Sqn	Spit	2TAF	P/O W.S.Curtis	FW190 damaged	Near Lisieux	1515
			P/O H.F.Morse	Bf109 damaged	Near Dreux	1515
			F/L W.A.Olmsted	Bf109 prob.dest	Near Dreux	1515
			F/O W.R.Weeks	Bf109 damaged	Near Lisieux	1515

27/28th July 1944

604 Sqn	Mosq	ADGB	F/L R.A.Miller	Ju88 destroyed	3m E Breteuil	0037

As the beachhead consolidated and expanded, the Luftwaffe threw in eveything it had against the overwhelming Allied air superiority. Most opponents seemed to be FW190s, but the Bf109Gs were still in evidence. On 27th Flight Lieutenant Bill Olmsted of 442 Squadron (left) claimed a Bf109 probably destroyed and would survive the war with three confirmed kills. Right: Harry White and Michael Allen of 141 Squadron proved to be one of the units top teams, bringing their score to twelve confirmed on 28/29th July. (via M.Allen)

28th July 1944

416 Sqn Spit	2TAF	F/L D.J.England	Bf109 destroyed	W Caen	1850
		F/O A.J.Fraser	Bf109 damaged	W Caen	1850
		F/O M.R.Sharun	Bf109 destroyed	W Caen	1850
		F/L N.G.Russell	FW190 destroyed	W Riseux	1945
453 Sqn Spit	2TAF	P/O C.A.Rice	FW190 damaged	E Bayeux	1643

28/29th July 1944

141 Sqn Mosq	BC	F/L H.E.White	Ju88 destroyed	S Metz	0042
		F/L H.E.White	Ju88 destroyed	SE Neufchateau	0052
		P/O L.D.Gregory	Ju88 destroyed	16m NW Metz	0045
		W/C C.V.Winn	Ju88 damaged	Beacon 'Trappe'	0050±
410 Sqn Mosq	ADGB	F/L W.A.Dexter	Ju88 destroyed	30m E Tessy	0116
488 Sqn Mosq	ADGB	F/L P.F.Hall	Ju88 destroyed	Lessay	2259
		F/O D.N.Robinson	Ju188 destroyed	15m N Mayenne	0118
604 Sqn Mosq	ADGB	F/L J.P.Meadows	Ju88 destroyed	Lisieux	0145
605 Sqn Mosq	ADGB	F/O R.E.Lelong	E/A damaged	Creilsheim	0233
		F/O R.E.Lelong	E/A damaged	Creilsheim	0240

On 29/30th July 'Jamie' Jameson and his navigator Norman Crookes of 488 Squadron claimed four kills in twenty minutes to bring their score to nine. They would end the war as the top New Zealand night fighter crew with eleven destroyed. (Chris Goss)

29th July 1944

65 Sqn	Must	2TAF	F/O C.P.Ashworth	Bf109 damaged	Near Conches A/D	0725
			F/O T.E.Jonsson	Bf109 destroyed	Near Conches A/D	0725
			F/S W.P.Kelly	Bf109 damaged	Near Conches A/D	0725
			S/L D.P.Lamb	Bf109 destroyed	Near Conches A/D	0725

29/30th July 1944

264 Sqn	Mosq	ADGB	S/L F.J.A.Chase	Ju188 destroyed	15m SE St Lo	0505
410 Sqn	Mosq	ADGB	P/O D.M.MacKenzie	Ju88 destroyed	70-80m from Beacon HY	0500
488 Sqn	Mosq	ADGB	F/L G.E.Jameson	Ju88 destroyed	5-6m S Caen	0505
			F/L G.E.Jameson	Ju88 destroyed	5-6m S Caen	0509
			F/L G.E.Jameson	Ju88 destroyed	5-6m S Liseux	0515
			F/L G.E.Jameson	Do217 destroyed	5-6m S Liseux	0525

30th July 1944

151 Sqn	Mosq	ADGB	F/L J.H.Etherton	Ju188 damaged	300m SW Belle Isle	1645
315 Sqn	Must	ADGB	F/L M.Cwynar P/O G.Swiston	Bf109F destroyed - Shared -	30m W Lister A/D	1845
			F/L M.Cwynar	Bf109F destroyed	30m W Lister A/D	1845
			S/L E.Horbaczewski	Bf109F destroyed	30m W Lister A/D	1845
			S/L E.Horbaczewski P/O E.Nowosielski	Bf109F destroyed - Shared	30m W Lister A/D	1845
			W/O R.Idrian	Bf110 destroyed	30m W Lister A/D	1845

Michal Cwynar of 315 Squadron claimed his fifth and last victory on July 30th.

315 Sqn Must	ADGB	W/O T.Jankowski	Bf109F destroyed	30m W Lister A/D	1845
		W/O T.Jankowski	FW190 destroyed	30m W Lister A/D	1845
		P/OG.Swiston	Bf109F destroyed	30m W Lister A/D	1845
443 Sqn Spit	2TAF	F/O W.J.Bentley	Bf109 destroyed	20m SE Dreux	1540
		F/O R.A.Hodgins	Bf109 damaged	E Alencon	1540
		S/L H.W.McLeod	Bf109 destroyed	SW Dreux	1540

30/31st July 1944

29 Sqn Mosq	ADGB	F/O F.E.Pringle	Ju88 destroyed	Near Melun	0134
219 Sqn Mosq	ADGB	S/L H.V.Ellis	Ju188 destroyed	5m S Le Havre	0045
409 Sqn Mosq	ADGB	W/O W.G.Kirkwood	Ju88 destroyed	Near Vire	0045
604 Sqn Mosq	ADGB	S/L B.Maitland -Thompson	Ju88 destroyed	35m S Cherbourg	0100

31st July 1944

401 Sqn Spit	2TAF	F/L W.T.Klersey	FW190 destroyed	NW Domfront	1255
		S/L H.C.Trainor	FW190 destroyed	E Domfront	1255
602 Sqn Spit	2TAF	S/L J.JLe Roux	FW190 destroyed	8m SW Vire	1730

Chapter Five

Breakout

The beachhead was by now consolidated beyond the capability of the German forces to halt its expansion. The *Luftwaffe* had, in sheer desperation, thrown in every available aircraft in a futile attempt to halt the inexorable advances of the Allied forces. *Operation Cobra* had commenced on 25th July and, by 31st, German resistance was fast collapsing under the ground and aerial onslaught. On 1st August General George S.Patton assumed command of the US Third Army and immediately ordered a massive advance towards Brittany. Although the Germans fought bitterly, the few counter attacks they would make had little or no effect on the Allied advance. The German fighters and fighter-bombers were shot down in droves and the only limited successes enjoyed by the *Luftwaffe* would be at night - but the night bombers were also to pay a high price.

1st August 1944

64 Sqn	Spit	ADGB	F/O O'Neil	Bf109 destroyed	N Angers	1650
HB Wg	Spit	ADGB	W/C H.A.C.Bird -Wilson	Bf109 destroyed	Varades-Angenis	1650

1/2nd August 1944

410 Sqn	Mosq	ADGB	S/L J.D.Somerville	Ju188 destroyed	NE Tessy	0100
488 Sqn	Mosq	ADGB	F/L P.F.L.Hall	Ju88 destroyed	10m E St Lo	0101
604 Sqn	Mosq	ADGB	F/L F.C.Ellis	Ju188 destroyed	SE Caen	0245±

2nd August 1944

412 Sqn	Spit	2TAF	F/O T.M.Saunderson	FW190 destroyed	W Ecouches	1430
453 Sqn	Spit	2TAF	F/O J.H.Ferguson	Bf109 damaged	Tenchebray area	1500

2/3rd August 1944

264 Sqn	Mosq	ADGB	S/L F.J.A.Chase	Ju88 destroyed	10m W Argentan	0030
410 Sqn	Mosq	ADGB	S/L J.D.Somerville	Do217 destroyed	6m NW Pontorson	2255
			F/L B.E.Plumer	Ju188 destroyed	25m S Beacon FM	0040
488 Sqn	Mosq	ADGB	F/L A.E.Browne	Do217 destroyed	Beach at Avranches	2305
			W/O T.G.C.MacKay	Ju188 destroyed	5-10m S Avranches	0052

3rd August 1944

401 Sqn	Spit	2TAF	F/O R.R.Bouskill	Bf109 destroyed	10m SE Domfront	1240±

Squadron Leader Jack Sheppard of 412 Squadron was not popular amongst his men, both pilots and ground staff. On 2nd August he fell to Unteroffizier Anton Schöppler (right) - and the squadron celebrated. Sheppard was captured, but managed to escape, evade and return, halting the general mood of elation! Toni Schöppler would later became an ace with the Me262. (A.Schöppler)

401 Sqn	Spit	2TAF	F/L R.H.Cull	Bf109 destroyed	10m SE Domfront	1240±
			F/L G.W.Johnson	Bf109 destroyed	10m SE Domfront	1240±
403 Sqn	Spit	2TAF	F/L J.D. Lindsay	Bf109 damaged	E L'Aigle	1945±
			F/L J.D.Lindsay	Bf109 destroyed	NW Dreux	1945±

3/4th August 1944

219 Sqn	Mosq	ADGB	F/L P.G.K.Williamson	Ju188 destroyed	Seine	0025
			F/L P.G.K.Williamson	Ju188 destroyed	Le Havre	0040
264 Sqn	Mosq	ADGB	F/L R.L.Beverley	Ju88 destroyed	SW Vire	0032
			F/L I.H.Cosby	Ju88 destroyed	8m SW Vire	0140
409 Sqn	Mosq	ADGB	F/L E.N.Spiller	Ju188 destroyed	SE Le Havre	0045
			W/O D.J.MacDonald	Ju188 destroyed	SE Caen	0050
410 Sqn	Mosq	ADGB	F/L W.G.Dinsdale	Bf110 destroyed	10m NE Avranches	0050
488 Sqn	Mosq	ADGB	W/O G.S.Patrick	Ju88 destroyed	2m W Avranches	2354
			F/L G.E.Jameson	Ju88 destroyed	8m N St L-Bayeux	0035
604 Sqn	Mosq	ADGB	F/L R.J.Foster	Do217 destroyed	S Granville	2315

4/5th August 1944

29 Sqn	Mosq	ADGB	S/L R.C.Pargeter	Ju188 destroyed	Near Orly	0220
409 Sqn	Mosq	ADGB	P/O F.E.Haley	Ju188 prob.dest	St Vaast, SW Caen	0105
			W/O N.Joss	Ju188 destroyed	Mont St Michel	0355
488 Sqn	Mosq	ADGB	F/O A.L.Shaw	Ju188 destroyed	10m NE St Lô	0055
			F/O A.L.Shaw	Ju88 damaged	10m NE St Lô	0105
			W/C R.C.Haine	Ju88 destroyed	8m ENE Vire	0105

On the night of 6th August, Flight Lieuenant John Surman of 604 Squadron (left - Chris Goss) was credited with the destruction of two Do217s and a Bf110, the latter flown by Hauptmann Helmut Bergmann of NJG 4 whose score stood at 31 confirmed victories. No trace of Bergmann or his crew was ever found.

5/6th August 1944

488 Sqn Mosq	ADGB	F/L P.F.L.Hall	Do217 destroyed	Beachhead	0052
		F/S T.A.MacLean	Do217 destroyed	10m W Angers	0217
		F/S T.A.MacLean	Do217 damaged	10m W Angers	0227
604 Sqn Mosq	2TAF	F/L J.J.M.Haddon	Ju88 destroyed	Rennes	0020
		F/L J.J.M.Haddon	Ju188 destroyed	Rennes	2359

6th August 1944

131 Sqn Spit	ADGB	F/O R.K.Parry	FW190 destroyed	Argentan	1630
		W/O H.A.Patton	FW190 destroyed	Le Mans area	1630
331 Sqn Spit	2TAF	2/Lt E.Gundersen 2/Lt T.Tjensvold	FW190 destroyed - Shared -	Beaumont-sur-Oise area	1225
		Lt K.L.L'Abbe-Lund	Bf109G destroyed	Beaumont-sur-Oise area	1225
		Capt N.Ringdal	Bf109 destroyed	Beaumont-sur-Oise area	1225
		Capt N.Ringdal	Bf109 damaged	Beaumont-sur-Oise area	1225

6/7th August 1944

219 Sqn Mosq	ADGB	F/L P.G.K.Williamson	Ju188 destroyed	Argentan	0002
410 Sqn Mosq	ADGB	S/L J.D.Somerville	Ju88 destroyed	St Hilaire area	0215
488 Sqn Mosq	ADGB	F/L G.E.Jameson	Ju88 damaged	5m W Vire	2343
		F/L G.E.Jameson	Ju88 destroyed	15m E Avranches	0015
		F/L A.E.Browne	Ju188 destroyed	SW Avranches	0251
		F/L A.E.Browne	E/A destroyed	W Rennes	0306
		F/L A.E.Browne	E/A destroyed	SW Rennes	0331
604 Sqn Mosq	2TAF	W/C F.D.Hughes	Ju188 destroyed	S Avranches	0100

604 Sqn Mosq	2TAF	F/L J.C.Surman	Do217 destroyed	u/k		0105
		F/L J.C.Surman	Do217 destroyed	T.6310		0153
		F/L J.C.Surman	Bf110 destroyed	T.5220		0305
		F/O R.M.T.M.B. MacDonald	Ju188 destroyed	NW Vire		0305

7th August 1944

131 Sqn Spit	ADGB	S/L R.W.F.Sampson	FW190 destroyed	20m N La Fleche	1520
		F/L O.J.Waterhouse	FW190 destroyed	SE Le Mans	1535
CH Wg Spit	ADGB	W/C P.M.Brothers	FW190 destroyed	20m N La Fleche	1520

7/8th August 1944

219 Sqn Mosq	ADGB	F/L D.L.Ryalls	Ju188 destroyed	S Flers	0407
264 Sqn Mosq	ADGB	F/L M.M.Davison	Ju88 destroyed	Near Crepon	2305
409 Sqn Mosq	ADGB	W/O R.S.Henke	Ju188 destroyed	Beny Bocage area	0230
410 Sqn Mosq	ADGB	F/L R.M.G.Currie	Ju88 destroyed	SW Rennes	2315
604 Sqn Mosq	ADGB	F/O R.M.T.M.B. MacDonald	Ju188 destroyed	E Nantes	2320
		F/L J.R.Cross	Ju188 destroyed	E Falaise	2325
		F/L J.R.Cross	Ju88 destroyed	Conde	0005
		F/O J.S.Smith	Do217 destroyed	Rennes	0100
		F/O J.S.Smith	Do217 destroyed	Rennes	0112
FIU	Mosq	ADGB Lt P.Twiss	Ju88 destroyed	8m NE Melun	0105

8th August 1944

19 Sqn Must	2TAF	S/L W.W.J.Loud	Bf109 destroyed	Near Chartres	1920
		F/O P.T.Glanville	- Shared -		
		F/O J.A.Scott	- Shared -		
		F/S B.Vassiliades	Bf109 destroyed	Near Chartres	1920
		F/S B.Vassiliades	Bf109 destroyed	Near Chartres	1920
310 Sqn Spit	ADGB	Sgt A.Elbogen	Do217 destroyed	5m E Nijmegen	1900
		F/O S.J.J.Masek	- Shared -		
443 Sqn Spit	2TAF	F/O A.J.Horrell	Bf109 destroyed	10m SE Argentan	1435
		F/O W.J.Sherman	- Shared		
		F/L G.W.A.Troke	- Shared -		
		F/O D.W.J.Wegg	- Shared		

Two great Canadian fighter leaders: Left: Don Laubman of 412 Sqn claimed his fifth success on 10th August and survived the war with a score of fourteen. Right: Dal Russell, commanding 127 Wing, also scored on 10th and survived the war with two and five shared confirmed destroyed.

8/9th August 1944

219 Sqn Mosq	ADGB	F/L M.J.Gloster	Ju188 destroyed	Vire	0054
		F/L M.J.Gloster	Ju188 destroyed	Evreux	0148
239 Sqn Mosq	BC	F/L D.J.Raby	Bf110 destroyed		2355
		F/O D.Welfare	FW190 destroyed	St. Quentin	0020
264 Sqn Mosq	ADGB	F/S P.N.Lee	Ju188 prob.dest	N Caen	0130±
409 Sqn Mosq	ADGB	W/O N.Joss	Ju188 damaged	E Avranches	2330
604 Sqn Mosq	2TAF	F/O T.R.Wood	Do217 destroyed	4m W Carentan	0430

9th August 1944

19 Sqn Must	2TAF	F/O E.Clayton	FW190 destroyed	Near Aunay	1800
		F/L B.G.Collyns	FW190 destroyed	Near Aunay	1800
		W/O S.J.Larsen	- Shared -		
		F/L B.G.Collyns	FW190 destroyed	Near Aunay	1800
		F/O P.B.Plumridge	FW190 destroyed	Near Aunay	1800
430 Sqn Must	2TAF	F/L R.F.Gill	FW190 damaged	8m NW Alencon	0950

9/10th August 1944

169 Sqn Mosq	BC	F/L R.G.Woodman	FW190 destroyed	Nr Abbeville	2345
219 Sqn Mosq	ADGB	F/L M.J.Gloster	FW190 destroyed	E Evreux	2253
239 Sqn Mosq	BC	F/O D.Welfare	Bf109 damaged	N Paris	0025±

10th August 1944

65 Sqn Must	ADGB	S/L D.P.Lamb	Bf109 destroyed	6m SE Dreux	1930
308 Sqn Spit	ADGB	W/O W.Korwel	Bf109 destroyed	Vire-Falaise	2130
		W/O W.Korwel	Bf109 destroyed	Vire-Falaise	2130

412 Sqn Spit	ADGB	S/L D.H.Dover	Bf109 damaged	5m E Alencon	1645
		F/O D.C.Laubman	Bf109 destroyed	3m E Mamers	1645
		F/O T.M.Saunderson	- Shared -		
		F/O D.C.Laubman	Bf109 destroyed	4-5m SE Nogent	1645
		F/O C.R.Symons	Bf109 destroyed	SE Alencon	1645
126 Wg Spit	ADGB	W/C B.D.Russel	Bf109 damaged	Alencon	1645

10/11th August 1944

169 Sqn Mosq	BC	F/O W.H.Miller	Bf109 destroyed	Dijon	0045
219 Sqn Mosq	ADGB	F/L G.R.I.Parker	Ju88 destroyed	10mk SW Le Havre	2229
		F/L G.R.I.Parker	FW190 destroyed	15m S Le Havre	2249
		F/O H.Twidall	FW190 damaged	S Caen	2235
264 Sqn Mosq	ADGB	F/O J.Daber	Ju188 destroyed	Seine Bay	2325
		S/L F.J.A.Chase	Ju188 destroyed	E Le Havre	2344
409 Sqn Mosq	ADGB	S/L J.A.Hatch	FW190 destroyed	Montfort	2240
		F/L R.L.Fullerton	Ju88 prob.dest	Bolbec	2355
		F/O F.K.Collins	Do217 destroyed	Thury-Harcourt	0310
410 Sqn Mosq	ADGB	W/C G.A.Hiltz	Ju88 destroyed	10m NE Pointe de la Percee	0010

11/12th August 1944

141 Sqn Mosq	BC	F/L J.V.Thatcher	Bf110 prob.dest	20m S Paris	2350
219 Sqn Mosq	ADGB	F/L D.L.Ryalls	Ju88 destroyed	15m W Rouen	0405
409 Sqn Mosq	ADGB	W/O R.S.Henke	FW190 destroyed	Les Bain, 3m S Cabourg	2215
604 Sqn Mosq	2TAF	F/L R.A.Miller	Do217 prob.dest	U.14	0003

12th August 1944

66 Sqn Spit	2TAF	S/L W.M.Foster	FW190 destroyed	Nr Argentan	1420
		F/L J.G.Pattinson	FW190 destroyed	S Argentan	1420
340 Sqn Spit	2TAF	Sgt L.Trouillet	Bf109 destroyed	N Tours	1410
		Sgt L.Trouillet	Bf109 damaged	N Tours	1410
411 Sqn Spit	2TAF	F/O J.J.Boyle	Bf109 destroyed	SE Alencon	1850±
		F/O H.A.Crawford	Bf109 destroyed	SE Alencon	1850±
		F/L E.G.Lapp	Bf109 destroyed	SE Alencon	1850±
		F/O G.F.Mercer	Bf109 destroyed	SE Alencon	1850±
		F/L A.M.Tooley	Bf109 damaged	SE Alencon	1850±
		F/O T.M.Saunderson	Bf109 damaged	Neufchatel	1850±

Three nationalities, one object. Former London butcher Bill Loud (left) claimed his third and last kill on 15th August. Canadian Edward Lapp (centre) got his second on 12th and Rhodesian John Plagis (right) brought his score to fifteen on 14th August.

12/13th August 1944

169 Sqn	Mosq	BC	F/O W.H.Miller	He219 destroyed	Nr Aachen	u/k
418 Sqn	Mosq	ADGB	F/O J.J.Harvie	Ju88 damaged	Echterdingen AD	0343
FIU	Mosq	ADGB	F/O C.A.Bailey	Ju88 destroyed	2m E Munster AD	0225±

14th August 1944

126 Sqn	Spit	ADGB	F/O J.L.Flinterman	FW190 destroyed	12m SW Melun	1730
			F/O J.L.Flinterman	Bf109 destroyed	12m SW Melun	1730
			S/L J.A.Plagis	FW190 destroyed	12m SW Melun	1730
			S/L J.A.Plagis	Bf109 destroyed	12m SW Melun	1730
			S/L J.A.Plagis	Bf109 damaged	12m SW Melun	1730
			F/S J.D.Rae	Bf109 prob.dest	10m SW Melun	1730
			F/O J.R.B.Porter F/S J.D.Rae	Bf109 damaged	10m SW Melun - Shared -	1730
			P/O E.A.Riseley	Bf109 destroyed	10m SW Melun	1730
			P/O E.A.Riseley	Bf109 prob.dest	10m SW Melun	1730
229 Sqn	Spit	ADGB	F/L S.McAndrew	FW190 prob.dest	Near Wesel	1650
316 Sqn	Must	ADGB	S/L B.Arct	Bf109E destroyed	5m NW Chalons-s-Marne	2020
			F/L A.Cholajda	Bf109 destroyed	5m NW Chalons-s-Marne	2020
			F/L A.Cholajda	FW190 destroyed	5m NW Chalons-s-Marne	2020
			W/O J.Feruga	Bf109 destroyed	5m NW Chalons-s-Marne	2020

14/15th August 1944

409 Sqn	Mosq	ADGB	F/O F.K.Collins	Ju88 destroyed	8m S Caen	2220
410 Sqn	Mosq	ADGB	S/L J.D.Somerville	Ju88 destroyed	15m W Le Havre	2325
488 Sqn	Mosq	ADGB	F/L J.A.S.Hall	Ju88 destroyed	20-30m S Caen	0025

15th August 1944

122 Sqn	Must	2TAF	W/O C.R.Castleton	Bf109 destroyed	Dreux	1215
			F/O C.Tallala	FW190 damaged	Dreux	1215
			F/O J.N.Thorne	Bf109 damaged	Dreux	1215
19 Sqn	Must	2TAF	F/L B.G.Collyns	FW190 damaged	L'Aigle	0815
			F/L B.G.Collyns	FW190 damaged	L'Aigle	0815
			F/O P.T.Glanville	Bf109 damaged	L'Aigle	0815
			S/L W.W.J.Loud	Bf109 destroyed	L'Aigle	0815
			P/O A.Sima	FW190 damaged	L'Aigle	0815
19 Sqn	Must	2TAF	F/L B.G.Collyns	Bf109 prob.dest	SE Dreux	1240

15/16th August 1944

219 Sqn	Mosq	ADGB	F/L L.Stephenson	Ju188 destroyed	Caen	2300±
			F/L G.R.I.Parker	Ju88 destroyed	15m W Le Havre	0103
			F/L G.R.I.Parker	Ju88 damaged	10m W Le Havre	0225

16/17th August 1944

141 Sqn	Mosq	BC	W/O E.A.Lampkin	Bf110 destroyed	Ringkjobing Fjord	0240
151 Sqn	Mosq	ADGB	F/O G.F.Ayrton	Ju188 destroyed	6m SW Bretigny	0329
219 Sqn	Mosq	ADGB	F/L M.J.Gloster	Ju188 destroyed	W Le Havre	0001
409 Sqn	Mosq	2TAF	W/O D.J.MacDonald	Ju188 destroyed	Near Berigny	2235
			W/O N.Joss	Ju188 damaged	Parigny, Seine estuary	2245
488 Sqn	Mosq	2TAF	F/L W.R.Cook	Ju188 damaged	20m N Orne	2245
			P/O O.J.McCabe	Ju88 destroyed	6m S Caen	2300±

17th August 1944

184 Sqn	Typh	2TAF	W/O J. Richardson	FW190 damaged	NE Livarot	1915±
			S/L J.W.Wilson	FW190 damaged	NE Livarot	1915±
197 Sqn	Typh	2TAF	F/S P.G.Mason	FW190 damaged	Near Vimoutiers	1900±
266 Sqn	Typh	ADGB	F/L D.M.Gibbon	FW190 damaged	Near Vimoutiers	1900±
			F/S E.Palte	FW190 damaged	Near Vimoutiers	1900±
317 Sqn	Spit	2TAF	F/L K.Budzik	FW190 damaged	Near Lisieux	1920
			F/S W.Fajks	FW190 damaged	Near Lisieux	1920
			W/O W.Fraczek	FW190 damaged	Near Lisieux	1920

On 18th August Squadron Leader Horbaczewski led his 315 Squadron Mustang pilots to Beauvais, where they caught the Focke Wulfs of III./JG 26 on take-off. At least ten were shot down, with eight pilots killed. Among the successful Polish pilots were (from left) Bozydar Nowosielski, Henryk Pietrzak, Tadeusz Slon, Kazimierz Kijak and Eugenius Harbaczewski. The sole loss was that of Horbaczewski, who was killed, possibly by Oberfeldwebel Wilhelm Mayer of 5 Staffel.

317 Sqn Spit	2TAF	F/S S.Maciejowski	FW190 damaged	Near Lisieux	1920
		F/L T.Owczarski	FW190 damaged	Near Lisieux	1920
401 Sqn Spit	2TAF	F/L R.R.Bouskill	FW190 destroyed	L'Aigle-Bernay	1930±
		F/L R.H.Cull	FW190 damaged	L'Aigle-Bernay	1930±
		F/O G.A.Hardy	FW190 damaged	L'Aigle-Bernay	1930±
416 Sqn Spit	2TAF	F/L D.R.Cuthbertson	FW190 destroyed	SE Lisieux	1910

18th August 944

151 Sqn Mosq	ADGB	Lt J.A.Cramp	Do24 destroyed	Dijon	0800±
		Lt J.A.Cramp	Bf108 damaged	Chalons	0800±
315 Sqn Must	ADGB	F/S J.Bargielowski	FW190 destroyed	Nr Beauvais A/D	0830
		F/S J.Bargielowski	FW190 destroyed	Nr Beauvais A/D	0830
		F/S J.Bargielowski	FW190 damaged	Nr Beauvais A/D	0830
		F/S J.Bargielowski	FW190 damaged	Nr Beauvais A/D	0830
		S/L E.Horbaczewski	FW190 destroyed	Nr Beauvais A/D	0830
		S/L E.Horbaczewski	FW190 destroyed	Nr Beauvais A/D	0830
		S/L E.Horbaczewski	FW190 destroyed	Nr Beauvais A/D	0830
		F/S K.Kijak	FW190 destroyed	Nr Beauvais A/D	0830
		F/S K.Kijak	FW190 damaged	Nr Beauvais A/D	0830
		F/O B.Nowosielski	FW190 destroyed	Nr Beauvais A/D	0830
		F/L H.Pietrzak	FW190 destroyed	Nr Beauvais A/D	0830
		F/L H.Pietrzak	FW190 destroyed	Nr Beauvais A/D	0830
		F/L H.Pietrzak	FW190 destroyed	Nr Beauvais A/D	0830
		F/L J.Schmidt	FW190 destroyed	Nr Beauvais A/D	0830
		F/S K.Siwek	FW190 destroyed	Nr Beauvais A/D	0830

315 Sqn Must	ADGB	F/S K.Siwek	FW190 destroyed	Nr Beauvais A/D	0830
		F/S K.Siwek	FW190 destroyed	Nr Beauvais A/D	0830
		W/O T.Slon	FW190 destroyed	Nr Beauvais A/D	0830
		P/O G.Swiston	FW190 prob.dest	Nr Beauvais A/D	0830
		P/O G.Swiston	FW190 destroyed	Nr Beauvais A/D	0830

18/19th August 1944

409 Sqn Mosq	2TAF	S/L J.A.Hatch	Ju188 destroyed	Nr Routot	2305
		S/L J.A.Hatch	Ju88 destroyed	Nr Autheuil	2320
488 Sqn Mosq	2TAF	F/O R.G.Jeffs	Do217 destroyed	10-15m S Rouen	2343

19th August 1944

19 Sqn Must	2TAF	W/O M.H.Bell	FW190 destroyed	NW Bernay	0945
		F/L N.W.Wood	FW190 damaged	NW Bernay	0945
168 Sqn Must	2TAF	F/L D.Clark	Ju188 damaged	4m E Vernon	0730
		F/L G.R.Turner	- Shared -		
350 Sqn Spit	ADGB	F/L A.M.Plisnier	Ju88 destroyed	O/s Brussels	0805
401 Sqn Spit	2TAF	F/L G.W.Johnson	Bf109 destroyed	E Bernay	0845±
		F/L G.W.Johnson	FW190 damaged	Bernay area	0845±
		F/L J.C.Lee	FW190 destroyed	Bernay area	0845±

19/20th August 1944

409 Sqn Mosq	2TAF	S/L R.F.Hatton	Do217 destroyed	Neufchatel area	0020
410 Sqn Mosq	2TAF	F/O J.L.Fullerton	Ju88 destroyed	Beachhead nr Hottot	0015
		F/O J.L.Fullerton	Ju88 destroyed	4m E Mezidon	0025

20th August 1944

19 Sqn Must	2TAF	F/S W.G.Abbott	FW190 destroyed	E Paris nr Rouvres	1920
		W/O T.A.Carson	Bf109 damaged	E Paris nr Rouvres	1920
		F/L B.G.Collyns	FW190 destroyed	E Paris nr Rouvres	1920
65 Sqn Must	2TAF	F/L L.A.P.Burra -Robinson	FW190 destroyed	20m E Paris	1955
		F/L L.A.P.Burra -Robinson	FW190 destroyed	20m E Paris	1955
		F/L L.A.P.Burra -Robinson	FW190 destroyed	20m E Paris	1955
		F/O D.W.Davis	FW190 damaged	20m E Paris	1955

Left: Line-up of 315 Squadron Mustangs. Right: Horbaczewski's mount being armed. This aircraft failed to return from the slaughter of JG 26 on 18th August.

65 Sqn Must	2TAF	S/L D.P.Lamb	FW190 damaged	20m E Paris		1955
		S/L D.P.Lamb	FW190 destroyed	20m E Paris		1955
		F/O R.A.Walley	- Shared -			
		W/O H.Smith	FW190 damaged	20m E Paris		1955
		F/O P.S.Taylor	FW190 damaged	20m E Paris		1955
		F/O J.E.Staples	FW190 destroyed	E Paris nr Rouvres		1920
		F/O J.E.Staples	FW190 destroyed	E Paris nr Rouvres		1920
		F/L J.H.Taylor	Bf109 damaged	E Paris nr Rouvres		1920
		F/S C.R.Wells	FW190 destroyed	E Paris nr Rouvres		1920
		F/S C.R.Wells	FW190 damaged	E Paris nr Rouvres		1920
401 Sqn Spit	2TAF	F/O R.M.Davenport	FW190 destroyed	W Evreux		2000±
		F/O R.M.Davenport	FW190 damaged	W Evreux		2000±
		F/O D.F.Husband	FW190 destroyed	W Evreux		2000±
412 Sqn Spit	2TAF	F/L C.W.Fox	FW190 damaged	SE Orbec		1550±
		F/L O.M.Linton	Bf109 damaged	SE Orbec		1550±
122 Wg Must	2TAF	W/C G.R.A.M. Johnson	Bf109 damaged	E Paris nr Rouvres		1920

20/21st August 1944

409 Sqn Mosq	2TAF	F/O M.G.Kent	Ju88 damaged	2m W Cricqueville	2400
488 Sqn Mosq	2TAF	F/O D.N.Robinson	Ju188 destroyed	15m E Caen	2355

23rd August 1944

421 Sqn Spit	2TAF	F/L B.T.Gilmour	FW190 destroyed	Near Senlis	1335
		F/L T.H.Hoare	FW190 destroyed	Near Senlis	1335
		F/O R.E.Holness	FW190 destroyed	Near Senlis	1335
		F/O J.W.Neil	FW190 destroyed	Near Senlis	1335

421 Sqn Spit	2TAF	F/L E.S.Smith	Bf109 destroyed	Near Senlis	1335
		F/L E.S.Smith	Bf109 destroyed	Near Senlis	1335
		F/L W.N.Stronach	FW190 damaged	Near Senlis	1335
443 Sqn Spit	2TAF	F/O E.H.Fairfield	FW190 damaged	Near Senlis	1335
		F/O A.J.Horrell	FW190 destroyed	Near Senlis	1335
		F/O G.F.Ockenden	Bf109 destroyed	Near Senlis	1335
		F/O G.F.Ockenden	Bf109 destroyed	Near Senlis	1335
		F/O G.F.Ockenden	FW190 damaged	Near Senlis	1335
		F/L J.G.L.Robillard	Bf109 destroyed	Near Senlis	1335
127 Wg Spit	2TAF	W/C J.E.Johnson	FW190 destroyed	Near Senlis	1335
		W/C J.E.Johnson	FW190 destroyed	Near Senlis	1335

23/24th August 1944

29 Sqn Mosq	ADGB	W/O A.R.C.Cresswell	E/A damaged	Eindhoven	0057
409 Sqn Mosq	2TAF	F/L G.Sproule	Ju188 damaged	Evreux	2320

25th August 1944

127 Sqn Spit	2TAF	S/L C.F.Bradley	FW190 destroyed	3m S Boos	2000±

25/26th August 1944

29 Sqn Mosq	ADGB	F/O J.B.Foster	Ju88 damaged	60m ENE Bonn	0230

26th August 1944

416 Sqn Spit	2TAF	F/L D.W.A.Harling	FW190 destroyed	Near Forges	0950
		F/O G.A.Cameron	Bf109 damaged	Near Forges	1000
		F/O M.R.Sharun	Bf109 destroyed	Near Forges	1000
421 Sqn Spit	2TAF	F/O W.Warfield	FW190 destroyed	Gournay area	0945
430 Sqn Must	2TAF	F/O J.A.Lowndes	FW190 destroyed	4m N Vernon	2010
453 Sqn Spit	2TAF	F/O W.H.Carter	Bf109 prob.dest	NE Paris	0954
		W/O K.F.Daff	Bf109 prob.dest	NE Paris	0954
		S/L D.H.Smith	Bf109 prob.dest	NE Paris	0954
602 Sqn Spit	2TAF	F/O F.W.Farfan	FW190 destroyed	W Beauvais	0900
		F/S J.R.Karasek	FW190 destroyed	W Beauvais	0900
		F/L A.O.Pullman	FW190 damaged	W Beauvais	0900

On 23rd August Wing Commander 'Johnnie' Johnson led 127 Wing pilots to the Senlis area, engaging FW190s and Bf109s. Johnson claimed two but sustained damage to his Spitfire - for the first time - while Flying Officer G.G.Ockenden of 443 Squadron (centre) claimed two more. That night Warrant Officer A.R.Cresswell of 29 Squadron added a 'damaged' to his score. (via F.Pringle)

26/27th August 1944

169 Sqn	Mosq	BC	W/O L.W.Turner	Ju88 destroyed	Nr Bremen	0057

27th August 1944

19 Sqn	Must	2TAF	F/L E.S.Hughes	Bf109 destroyed	4m E Rouen	1450
			F/L E.S.Hughes	Bf109 prob.dest	4m E Rouen	1450
			F/L D.B.MacNeil	Bf109 damaged	4m E Rouen	1450
			F/L R.H.McLeod F/O J.E.Staples	Bf109 destroyed - Shared -	4m E Rouen	1450
			F/O A.B.Wheeler	Bf109 destroyed	4m E Rouen	1450

27/28th August 1944

25 Sqn	Mosq	ADGB	P/O B.Travers	Bf109 destroyed	Pas de Calais	0125

28th August 944

403 Sqn	Spit	2TAF	F/L J.D.Orr	FW190 destroyed	SE Amiens	1440

28/29th August 1944

604 Sqn	Mosq	2TAF	F/L P.V.G.Sandeman	He177 destroyed*	N Paris	2330

Note: Collided

605 Sqn	Mosq	ADGB	F/O R.E.Lelong	E/A destroyed	Chievres AD	0048

On 3rd September Hptm Emil Lang (left) led a section of FW190s away from St Trond. At the same time Flight Lieutenant Terry Spencer (2nd from left) led his section of 41 Squadron Spitfire XIVs down through cloud and emerged at 800 feet just above and behind the FW190s. Lang, a 170 victory 'Experte' was at once shot down by Spencer and was killed. Leutnant Alfred Gross another 'Experte' credited with 51 victories, shot down Warrant Officer Chattin (killed) before he too was shot down by Pat Coleman (far right). He baled out badly wounded. He died of his injuries shortly after the war ended.

29/30th August 1944

| 239 Sqn Mosq | BC | F/L D.L.Hughes | Ju88 destroyed | 5m E Malchin, Nr Stettin | 0205 |

30th August 1944

345 Sqn Spit	ADGB	Sgt/Ch G.Dromatakis	Do217 destroyed	Eindhoven	1845
		Sgt G.Juventin	- Shared -		
		Adj/Ch R.Maurel	- Shared -		
		Adj R.Porchon	- Shared -		

31st August/1st September 1944

| 219 Sqn Mosq | ADGB | F/L E.A.Campbell | Ju188 destroyed | NE Avranches | 0005 |
| 410 Sqn Mosq | ADGB | F/O J.Maday | Ju88 destroyed | Beachhead | 0002 |

1/2nd September 1944

| 410 Sqn Mosq | 2TAF | F/L I.E.MacTavish | FW190 destroyed | 5m NE Le Havre | 2335 |
| 488 Sqn Mosq | 2TAF | W/C R.C.Haine | Ju188 destroyed | 10-15m W Le Havre | 2325 |

3rd September 1944

41 Sqn Spit	ADGB	W/O P.T.Coleman	FW190 destroyed	Tirlemont	1330
		F/L T.Spencer	FW190 destroyed	Tirlemont	1330
418 Sqn Mosq	ADGB	F/L S.H.R.Cotterill	Bf109 damaged	3m SE Anklam A/D	1628

6/7th September 1944

| 515 Sqn Mosq | BC | W/C F.F.Lambert | Bf109 destroyed | Odder, Den | 2328 |

Left: Any landing you walk away from... Bill Stowe walked away from his bent 41 Squadron Spit' on 11 September (D.Johnson). Right: Three night intruder pilots get some rest. Flight Lieutenants J.O.Mathews, J.G.Benson and R.D.Doleman of 157 Squadron. Doleman destroyed a Bf110 of 2./NJG6 on 12/13th September, while Benson got two Ju188s on the previous night.

11/12th September 1944

141 Sqn	Mosq	BC	F/L P.A.Bates	Bf110 destroyed	SW Mannheim	0104
157 Sqn	Mosq	BC	S/L J.G.Benson	Ju188 destroyed	Zeeland	2255
			S/L J.G.Benson	Ju188 destroyed	Zeeland	2302
85 Sqn	Mosq	BC	S/L B.A.Burbridge	Ju188 destroyed	Baltic Sea	2237
			F/L P.S.Kendall	Bf109G destroyed	Soesterburg	0115
FIU	Mosq	ADGB	F/O D.T.Tull	Ju88 destroyed	Near Ansbach	0050±

12/13th September 1944

29 Sqn	Mosq	ADGB	F/O W.W.Provan	Bf110 destroyed	SE Frankfurt	2330±
157 Sqn	Mosq	BC	P/O B.D.Gale	Ju188 damaged	Erfurt	2330
			F/L R.D.Doleman	Bf110 destroyed	4958N 0900E	2350
219 Sqn	Mosq	2TAF	F/L L.Stephenson	Ju88 destroyed	10m NE Erkelenz	2359
239 Sqn	Mosq	BC	F/O W.R.Breithaupt	Bf110 destroyed	Rauschhack	2330±
418 Sqn	Mosq	ADGB	S/L R.Bannock	E/A T/e destroyed	Kitzingen	0221

13th September 1944

85 Sqn	Mosq	BC	F/L W.House	Bf110 destroyed	Koblenz area	2327
140 Sqn	Mosq	2TAF	F/L C.T.Butt	Bf109 destroyed	Salzwedel by collision	1715
157 Sqn	Mosq	BC	S/L J.G.Benson	Ju88 damaged	W Bonn	2347

16/17th September 1944

410 Sqn	Mosq	ADGB	F/L C.E.Edinger	E/A destroyed	Off Dutch Isles	0150
FIU	Mosq	ADGB	F/L E.R.Hedgecoe	T/e E/A destroyed	landing at Ardorf	0100±

Chapter Six

To The Rhine

The strategy employed by the Allied forces had now borne fruit. Montgomery's assaults upon Caen had kept the German armour heavily engaged, allowing Patton to strike southwest and north up the Cotentin peninsula. Caen had then finally fallen and the Germans had retreated to the east, a huge amount of personnel and material being caught and destroyed in the Falaise pocket. The prize was, of course the port of Antwerp and although the British had advanced steadily into Belgium the vital port would not be in British hands for some time. However, Montgomery had now come up with a radical plan to attack Germany directly by the use of paratroop forces to capture vital bridges and provide a corridor for the armour of 30 Corps to advance straight to and across the Rhine at Arnhem. This ambitious plan, ultimately doomed to failure, commenced on 17th September.

17th September 1944

19 Sqn	Must	2TAF	F/L E.S.Hughes	FW190 destroyed	W Emmerich	1700
			F/O J.M.Maynard	FW190 damaged	W Emmerich	1700
			F/O J.A.Scott F/O J.D.Beckett	Bf109 damaged - Shared -	W Emmerich	1700
			F/O J.E.Staples	FW190 damaged	W Emmerich	1700
			F/O J.E.Staples	FW190 damaged	W Emmerich	1700
65 Sqn	Must	2TAF	F/L J.W.Foster	FW190 destroyed	SE Arnhem	1600
602 Sqn	Spit	2TAF	F/S J.R.Karasek	FW190D damaged	N Nijmegen	1645
			F/L A.O.Pullman	FW190D damaged	N Nijmegen	1645

17/18th September 1944

29 Sqn	Mosq	ADGB	Lt D.R.O.Price	Bf110 destroyed	SW Münster	2200±
85 Sqn	Mosq	BC	F/L A.J.Owen	Bf110 destroyed	u/k	2200±
			F/L A.J.Owen	Bf110 destroyed	u/k	2200±

18th September 1944

401 Sqn	Spit	2TAF	F/O R.M.Davenport	FW190 destroyed	5m NW Venlo	1200±
			Lt Cdr A.C.Wallace	FW190 damaged	5m NW Venlo	1200±
441 Sqn	Spit	2TAF	P/O G.E.Heasman	Bf109 destroyed	W Nijmegen	1215
			S/L R.H.Walker F/L A.Johnstone	Bf109 destroyed - Shared -	W Nijmegen	1215
			F/L R.G.Lake	Bf109 destroyed	20m N Aachen-Duren	1525

Alan Owen of 85 Squadron (Left, right in photo) claimed a pair of Bf110s on the night of 17th September and added a 'damaged' on the 23rd. Ross Gray of 418 Squadron, here with his navigator Frank Smith, (centre) also got a 'double', this during a Day Ranger to Bad Aibling on 21st. Jan Smigielski of 306 Squadron (right), involved in the Market Garden air cover, claimed an FW190 damaged over Arnhem on 25th.

18/19th September 1944

157 Sqn	Mosq	BC	W/O B.Miller	Ju188 damaged	Handorf AD	2125

21st September 1944

91 Sqn	Spit	ADGB	P/O F.A.Lewis	FW190 damaged	Eindhoven	1800±
322 Sqn	Spit	ADGB	F/O P.A.Cramerus	FW190 damaged	NE Eindhoven	1630
			F/O G.F.J.Jongbloed	FW190 damaged	NE Eindhoven	1630
414 Sqn	Spit	2TAF	F/L D.I.Hall	FW190 destroyed	36563	1440
418 Sqn	Mosq	ADGB	S/L R.G.Gray	S/e destroyed	Bad Aibling A/D	1250
			S/L R.G.Gray	E/A s/e destroyed	Bad Aibling A/D	1250

23/24th September 1944

85 Sqn	Mosq	BC	F/L A.J.Owen	Bf110 damaged	S Munster	2245±
219 Sqn	Mosq	2TAF	W/C W.P.Green	Bf110 destroyed	10m NE Koln	2215
FIU	Mosq	ADGB	F/O D.T.Tull	Bf110 destroyed	20m NW Paderborn	0000±

24/25th September 1944

25 Sqn	Mosq	ADGB	F/O R.A.Henley	He111 prob.dest	50m W Amsterdam	2150
			W/C L.J.Mitchell	He111 prob.dest	60m E Coltishall	0515
409 Sqn	Mosq	2TAF	W/O L.E.Fitchett	He111 destroyed	Maastricht	0500

25th September 1944

118 Sqn	Spit	ADGB	F/L K.C.M.Giddings 142 Wing	Bf109 destroyed - Shared -	Arnhem	1700
122 Sqn	Must	2TAF	W/O C.R.Castleton	FW190 damaged	Near Nijmegen	1640
			F/S E.A.Evans	Bf109 damaged	Near Nijmegen	1640
			F/L D.RStevens	FW190 destroyed	Near Nijmegen	1640
			F/L C.Tallalla	Bf109 destroyed	Near Nijmegen	1640
			F/L M.J.Wright	Bf109 destroyed	Near Nijmegen	1640
129 Sqn	Must	ADGB	F/L J.P.Bassett	FW190 destroyed	Arnhem	1745±
			F/O G.R.Dickson	FW190 damaged	Arnhem	1745±
			F/L P.N.Howard	FW190 damaged	Arnhem	1745±
			F/O M.Humphries	FW190 destroyed	Arnhem	1745±
			F/L D.C.Parker	FW190 destroyed	Arnhem	1745±
132 Sqn	Spit	2TAF	F/L D.J.Hawkins	FW190 damaged	Near Nijmegen	1640
			F/S T.Lindsay	FW190 destroyed	Near Nijmegen	1640
			F/S T.Lindsay	FW190 damaged	Near Nijmegen	1640
			W/O J.R.McKinnon	FW190 damaged	Near Nijmegen	1640
			W/O J.R.McKinnon	FW190 damaged	Near Nijmegen	1640
			F/O H.Wilkinson	FW190 damaged	Near Nijmegen	1640
			F/O H.Wilkinson	FW190 damaged	Near Nijmegen	1640
182 Sqn	Typh	2TAF	F/L E.T.Brough	FW190 prob.dest	Near Kleve	0605±
			F/O H.M.S.Pattullo	FW190 damaged	Near Kleve	1605±
306 Sqn	Must	ADGB	F/O J.Smigielski	FW190 damaged	Arnhem	1730±
315 Sqn	Must	ADGB	F/L H.Pietrzak prob. 118 Squadron	FW190 destroyed - Shared -	Arnhem area	1700±
401 Sqn	Spit	2TAF	F/L R.R.Bouskill	FW190 destroyed	6m NW Nijmegen	1530±
			F/L R.R.Bouskill	Bf109 damaged	6m NW Nijmegen	1530±
			F/L G.W.Johnson	Bf109 destroyed	5m NE Nijmegen	1530±
			F/L G.W.Johnson	Bf109 destroyed	5m NE Nijmegen	1530±
			F/L G.W.Johnson	Bf109 damaged	5m NE Nijmegen	1530±
412 Sqn	Spit	2TAF	F/L D.C.Laubman	FW190 destroyed	Nijmegen	1600
			F/O H.W.McLeod	FW190 destroyed	Nijmegen	1600
416 Sqn	Spit	2TAF	F/L A.J.Fraser	FW190 destroyed	Arnhem	1640
			F/O W.H.Palmer	FW190 destroyed	10m N Arnhem	1640
			F/L N.G.Russell	FW190 destroyed	2m N Arnhem	1640
421 Sqn	Spit	2TAF	F/L J.D.Mitchner	Bf109 destroyed	Arnhem	1555
			F/L J.D.Mitchner	FW190 destroyed	Near Nijmegen	1555

Right: Jan Zumbach, Polish fighter pilot 'first-to-last' ended the war leading the Mustangs of 133 Wing. He claimed an FW190 'probable' on 25th September and Russ Bouskill of 401 Squadron (far right) got his fourth. He claimed one more before being killed on 2nd October.

421 Sqn	Spit	2TAF	S/L W.A.Prest	Bf109 destroyed	Near Nijmegen	1555
441 Sqn	Spit	2TAF	F/O H.E.Derraugh	Bf109 destroyed	Nijmegen area	1525
			F/O H.E.Derraugh	Bf109 damaged	Nijmegen area	1525
			F/O D.H.Kimball	Bf109 destroyed	Nijmegen area	1525
			F/O D.H.Kimball	Bf109 destroyed	Nijmegen area	1525
			S/L R.H.Walker	Bf109 damaged	Nijmegen area	1525
			S/L R.H.Walker	Bf109 damaged	Nijmegen area	1525
			F/O J.A.McIntosh	Bf109 damaged	Nijmegen area	1540
133 Wg	Must	ADGB	W/C J.Zumbach	FW190 prob.dest	Arnhem	1730±
142 Wg	Spit	ADGB	W/C J.M.Checketts 118 Squadron	Bf109 destroyed - Shared -	Arnhem	1700

26th September 1944

65 Sqn	Must	2TAF	F/L P.M.Banks	Bf109 destroyed	Munster	1740
			W/O C.C.Carson	Bf109 damaged	Munster	1740
			F/O J.M.W.Lloyd	Bf109 damaged	Munster	1740
132 Sqn	Spit	2TAF	F/L M.Graham	Bf109 destroyed	W Arnhem	1315
			F/S J.E.R.Beavan	Bf109 prob.dest	W Arnhem	1330
			F/S A.J.Bary	Bf109 damaged	W Arnhem	1335
			F/O F.Campbell	Me262 damaged	Nijmegen	1830
175 Sqn	Typh	2TAF	F/L H.Ambrose	Bf109 prob.dest	Arnhem-Apeldoorn	1300
			F/L H.Ambrose	Bf109 damaged	Apeldoorn	1300
412 Sqn	Spit	2TAF	F/L R.I.A.Smith	Bf109 destroyed	5-10m E Nijmegen	1330±
			F/L R.I.A.Smith	Bf109 destroyed	5-10m E Nijmegen	1330±
			F/O P.E.Hurtubise	Bf109 destroyed	NE Nijmegen	1330±
			F/L D.C.Laubman	FW190 destroyed	NE Nijmegen	1330±
			F/L D.C.Laubman	Bf109 destroyed	NE Nijmegen	1330±
			F/O W.J.Banks	FW190 destroyed	NE Arnhem	1330±

412 Sqn	Spit	2TAF	F/O W.J.Banks	FW190 destroyed	NE Arnhem		1330±
			F/O P.M.Charron	FW190 destroyed	NE Arnhem		1330±
			F/O W.H.Bellingham	Bf109 damaged	SE Nijmegen		1620±
			F/O P.M.Charron	Bf109 destroyed	E Nijmegen		1620±
			F/O P.M.Charron	Bf109 damaged	E Nijmegen		1620±
			F/L D.C.Laubman	FW190 destroyed	6m S Nijmegen -5m N Venlo		1620±
416 Sqn	Spit	2TAF	F/L J.B.McColl	FW190 destroyed	NE Arnhem		1245
			F/L J.H.Sager	FW190 damaged	10m E Arnhem		1320
			W/O W.L.Saunders	FW190 damaged	E Arnhem		1320
			W/O W.L.Saunders	FW190 destroyed	10m E Arnhem		1320
439 Sqn	Typh	2TAF	W/O W.A.Gray	FW190 damaged	Near Nijmegen		1910
			F/O J.H.Stitt	Ju88 destroyed	Near Nijmegen		1910
125 Wg	Spit	2TAF	W/C A.G.Page	Bf109 destroyed	5m SE Nijmegen		1630

26/27th September 1944

25 Sqn	Mosq	ADGB	W/C C.M.Wight -Boycott	Ju188 destroyed	50m E Southend	2110
151 Sqn	Mosq	BC	S/L H.F.Morley	He111 destroyed	Zellhausen AD	u/k
410 Sqn	Mosq	2TAF	Lt A.A.Harrington	Ju87 destroyed	12m N Aachen	2136

27th September 1944

19 Sqn	Must	2TAF	F/L J.Paton	FW190 damaged	E.Nijmegen	1630
122 Sqn	Must	2TAF	F/O H.H.Cush	Bf109 destroyed	Nijmegen area	1745
174 Sqn	Typh	2TAF	F/S K.C.McKenzie	FW190 damaged	Arnhem area	0925±
411 Sqn	Spit	2TAF	F/O G.F.Mercer	FW190 destroyed	E Nijmegen	0920±
			F/O G.F.Mercer	FW190 damaged	E Nijmegen	0920±
			F/L J.M.Portz	FW190 destroyed	Nijmegen	0920±
			F/L J.M.Portz	FW190 damaged	Nijmegen	0920±
			F/O L.G.D Pow	FW190 destroyed	Nijmegen	0920±
			F/O W.A.Reid	FW190 damaged	E Nijmegen	0920±
			F/L E.G.Lapp	FW190 destroyed	Nijmegen	0920±
			F/O E.G.Ireland	FW190 destroyed	E Nijmegen	0920±
			F/L J.M.McConnell	FW190 destroyed	E Nijmegen	0920±
			F/L E.G.Lapp	FW190 destroyed	Nijmegen	0920±
			F/L E.G.Lapp F/O R.M.Cook	Me410 destroyed - Shared -	Near Nijmegen	1330±

On the night of 26th, Mike Wight-Boycott of 29 Squadron (left) claimed his seventh and last kill. Hauptmann Walter Krupinski (centre) claimed a Spitfire during the September 27th battles, while JG 26 actually lost eight Focke Wulfs with their pilots. Lloyd Berryman of 412 Squadron (right) claimed three Bf109s later in the day.

412 Sqn	Spit	2TAF	F/L R.I.A.Smith	Bf109 destroyed	NE Nijmegen on Rhine bank	0830±
			F/L R.I.A.Smith	Bf109 destroyed	NE Nijmegen	0830±
			F/L D.C.Laubman	Bf109 destroyed	NE Nijmegenm	0830±
			F/L D.C.Laubman	Bf109 destroyed	W Nijmegen	0830±
			F/O L.F.Berryman	Bf109 destroyed	NE Nijmegen	0830±
			F/O L.F.Berryman	Bf109 destroyed	4m N Arnhem	0830±
			F/L D.C.Laubman	Bf109 destroyed	E Nijmegen	1240±
			F/L D.C.Laubman	Bf109 damaged	E Nijmegen	1240±
			F/L J.W.Banks	Bf109 prob.dest	Cleve	1240±
			F/L J.W.Banks	FW190 damaged	Cleve	1240±
			F/O L.F.Berryman	Bf109 destroyed	SW Nijmegen	1240±
			F/O L.F.Berryman	FW190 damaged	SW Nijmegen	1240±
			F/L C.W.Fox	FW190 destroyed	Arnhem-Nijmegen	1240±
			F/L C.W.Fox	FW190 destroyed	Arnhem-Nijmegen	1240±
			F/L C.W.Fox	FW190 damaged	Arnhem-Nijmegen	1240±
			F/L C.W.Fox	Bf109 damaged	Arnhem-Nijmegen	1240±
			F/O D.R.C.Jamieson	FW190 destroyed	Borkenberge A/D	1625±
			F/O D.R.C.Jamieson	FW190 destroyed	Borkenberge A/D	1625±
			F/L D.C.Laubman	FW190 destroyed	20m E Nijmegen	1625±
			F/L D.C.Laubman	FW190 damaged	20m E Nijmegen	1625±
			F/L J.B.Doak	FW190 destroyed	Borkenberge A/D	1625±
416 Sqn	Spit	2TAF	F/O G.A.Cameron	Bf109 damaged	Near Emmerich	1305
			F/O G.A.Cameron	Bf109 damaged	Near Emmerich	1305

416 Sqn	Spit	2TAF	F/L D.R.Cuthbertson	FW190 destroyed	Near Emmerich	1305
			F/O R.R.St Georges	Bf109 damaged	Near Emmerich	1305
			F/L D.W.A.Harling	FW190 destroyed	W Bocholt	1305
			F/L D.W.A.Harling	Bf109 destroyed	W Bocholt	1305
			F/L D.W.A.Harling	Bf109 damaged	W Bocholt	1305
			F/L W.F.Mason	FW190 damaged	Near Emmerich	1305
			F/L J.B.B.Rainville	FW190 destroyed	Near Emmerich	1305
			F/L N.G.Russell	FW190 damaged	Near Emmerich	1305
			F/L A.H.Sager	Bf109 destroyed	W Bocholt	1305
			F/L A.H.Sager	Bf109 destroyed	Outskirts of Emmerich	1305
418 Sqn	Mosq	ADGB	S/L R.Bannock	Bf108 destroyed	Parow A/D	0615
			S/L R.Bannock	Bf108 destroyed	Parow A/D	0616
421 Sqn	Spit	2TAF	P/O T.J.DeCourcey	Bf109 damaged	10-20m E Arnhem	0830
			F/L J.D.Mitchner	Bf109 destroyed	10-20m E Arnhem	0830
			F/O J.M.Calvert	Bf109 destroyed	W Dorsten	0845
			P/O W.L.McDonald	Bf109 destroyed	Haltern	0845
438 Sqn	Typh	2TAF	F/O H.G.Upham	Bf109 destroyed	10m E Nijmegen	1730
441 Sqn	Spit	2TAF	P/O S.Bregman	Bf109 destroyed	10m W Arnhem	0825
			F/L J.C.Copeland	Bf109 destroyed	10m W Arnhem	0825
			F/L R.G.Lake	Bf109 destroyed	10m W Arnhem	0825
443 Sqn	Spit	2TAF	F/L H.P.Fuller	Bf109 destroyed	Rees-on-Rhine	1250
			F/O W.A.C.Gilbert	Bf109 destroyed	Rees-on-Rhine	1250
			F/O R.A.Hodgins	Bf109 prob.dest	Rees-on-Rhine	1250
			F/L E.B.Stovel	Bf109 destroyed	Rees-on-Rhine	1250
			F/L E.B.Stovel	Bf109 prob.dest	Rees-on-Rhine	1250
			F/L D.M.Walz	Bf109 destroyed	Rees-on-Rhine	1250
453 Sqn	Spit	2TAF	W/O R.Lyall	Bf109 destroyed	10m NE Nijmegen	0930
			F/L W.R.Bennett	Bf109 destroyed	2m NE Arnhem	1245
			F/L W.R.Bennett	Bf109 prob.dest	2m NE Arnhem	1245
			F/L W.R.Bennett	Bf109 damaged	2m NE Arnhem	1245
			F/O C.R.Leith	Bf109 destroyed	2m NE Arnhem	1245
			F/O N.J.Marsh	Bf109 destroyed	2m NE Arnhem	1245
			W/O C.A.M.Taylor	Bf109 destroyed	2m NE Arnhem	1245
			W/O C.A.M.Taylor	Bf109 damaged	2m NE Arnhem	1245
			W/O C.A.M.Taylor	Bf109 damaged	2m NE Arnhem	1245
127 Wg	Spit	2TAF	W/C J.E.Johnson	Bf109 destroyed	Rees-on-Rhine	1250

On 27th September, Spitfire pilots of 416 Squadron fought Bf109s of JG 77 near Bocholt, where Hauptmann Franz Hrdlicka (left), a 43-victory Experte, was shot down and wounded. His victor was either Dave Harling (centre) or Art Sager (right).

27/28th September 1944

85 Sqn	Mosq	BC	F/L A.J.Owen	Ju188 prob.dest	SW Kaiserlautern	0210
418 Sqn	Mosq	ADGB	F/L E.A.Johnson	Ju88 destroyed	WSW Hailfingen	0125

28th September 1944

341 Sqn	Spit	2TAF	Sgt J.Dabos	Bf109 destroyed	Wesel	1630
			P/O P.Gallay	Bf109 destroyed	Wesel	1630
411 Sqn	Spit	2TAF	F/O R.M.Cook	FW190 damaged	Near Nijmegen	0710±
			F/O B.Eskow	FW190 damaged	Near Nijmegen	0710±
			F/O M.G.Graham	FW190 destroyed	Near Nijmegen	0710±
			F/L E.G.Lapp	FW190 damaged	Near Nijmegen	0710±
			F/L J.M.Portz	FW190 destroyed	Near Nijmegen	0710±
416 Sqn	Spit	2TAF	F/L J.B.McColl	Me262 damaged	Nijmegen	1010
442 Sqn	Spit	2TAF	F/O S.M.McClarty	FW190 damaged	NE Nijmegen	0945

28/29th September 1944

25 Sqn	Mosq	ADGB	W/C L.J.Mitchell	He111 destroyed	40m off Lowestoft	0520
			W/C L.J.Mitchell	He111 destroyed	40m off Lowestoft	0545
85 Sqn	Mosq	BC	F/L M.Phillips	Ju188 destroyed	Lamprecht	0209
219 Sqn	Mosq	ADGB	F/L G.R.I.Parker	Ju87 destroyed	Hasselt	2000

29th September 1944

Sqn			Pilot	Claim	Location	Time
56 Sqn	Temp	2TAF	S/L D.V.C.Cotes-Preedy	FW190 destroyed	Near Emmerich	1145
			W/O D.S.McKenzie	FW190 damaged	Near Emmerich	1145
			F/L A.R.Moore	FW190 destroyed	Near Emmerich	1145
			F/O D.E.Ness	FW190 destroyed	Near Emmerich	1145
			F/O D.E.Ness	FW190 destroyed	Near Emmerich	1145
			F/O J.J.Payton	FW190 prob.dest	Near Emmerich	1145
340 Sqn	Spit	2TAF	Lt J.Guignard	Bf109 prob.dest	Near Nijmegen	1045
401 Sqn	Spit	2TAF	F/O G.A.Bell	Bf109 damaged	2m SE Nijmegen	1025±
			F/L R.R.Bouskill	Bf109 destroyed	10m SE Nijmegen	1025±
			F/L R.R.Bouskill	Bf109 damaged	10m SE Nijmegen	1025±
			F/L H.J.Everard	Bf109 destroyed	15m SE Nijmegen	1025±
			F/L H.J.Everard	Bf109 destroyed	15m SE Nijmegen	1025±
			F/L H.J.Everard	Bf109 damaged	15m SE Nijmegen	1025±
			F/O J.C.Hughes	Bf109 destroyed	10m SE Nijmegen	1025±
			F/O J.C.Hughes	Bf109 destroyed	10m SE Nijmegen	1025±
			F/O D.F.Husband	Bf109 destroyed	7m SE Nijmegen	1025±
			F/O D.F.Husband	Bf109 destroyed	7m SE Nijmegen	1025±
			F/L E.B.Sheeby	Bf109 damaged	Near Nijmegen	1025±
			F/L E.B.Sheeby	FW190 damaged	Near Nijmegen	1025±
			S/L R.I.A.Smith	Bf109 destroyed	10m SE Nijmegen	1025±
			S/L R.I.A.Smith	Bf109 destroyed	10m SE Nijmegen	1025±
412 Sqn	Spit	2TAF	F/O W.A.Aziz	FW190 destroyed	NE Nijmegen	1115±
			P/O W.C.Busby	FW190 destroyed	E Nijmegen	1115±
			F/O D.R.C.Jamieson	FW190 destroyed	E Nijmegen	1115±
			F/O E.L.Prizer	FW190 damaged	10m SE Cleve	1115±
416 Sqn	Spit	2TAF	F/L D.W.A.Harling	FW190 destroyed	Emmerich	1145
			F/L J.B.McColl	FW190 destroyed	E Nijmegen	1145
			F/L J.D.Mitchner	FW190 destroyed	10m NE Nijmegen	1145
			F/L J.D.Mitchner	FW190 destroyed	10m NE Nijmegen	1145
			F/L L.L.Nault	FW190 damaged	Emmerich	1145
			F/O W.H.Palmer	FW190 destroyed	Emmerich	1145
			P/O W.G.O.Roddie	FW190 destroyed	10m E Nijmegen	1145
			F/L N.G.Russell	FW190 destroyed	Emmerich	1145
421 Sqn	Spit	2TAF	F/L L.Foster	Bf109 destroyed	NE Nijmegen	1030
			F/L B.T.Gilmour	Bf109 damaged	NE Nijmegen	1030

Left: A pair of Spitfire LFIXs of 443 Squadron take off from a forward base (ww2images.com). Right: Bf109G-6s of JG 27 were frequently encountered over the Arnhem - Nijmegen area in late September.

421 Sqn	Spit	2TAF	F/O K.M.Langmuir	Bf109 destroyed	NE Nijmegen	1030
			F/L G.M.Smith	Bf109 destroyed	NE Nijmegen	1030
			F/L G.M.Smith	Bf109 destroyed	NE Nijmegen	1030
438 Sqn	Typh	2TAF	F/S R.G.Fox	Bf109 damaged	6m E Nijmegen	1035
443 Sqn	Spit	2TAF	F/O A.J.Horrell	FW190 destroyed	E Nijmegen	1030
			F/O D.W.J.Wegg	Bf109 damaged	E Nijmegen	1030
			F/O F.R.Kearns	Bf109 damaged	NE Nijmegen	1030
			F/O G.F.Ockenden	Bf109 destroyed	5m NE Nijmegen	1030
			F/O G.F.Ockenden	Bf109 destroyed	5m NE Nijmegen	1030
			F/O R.A.Hodgins	Bf109 destroyed	Nijmegen	1035
			F/O R.A.Hodgins	Bf109 destroyed	Nijmegen	1035
			F/L G.W.A.Troke	Bf109 destroyed	E Nijmegen	1105
			F/L G.W.A.Troke	Bf109 destroyed	E Nijmegen	1105
			F/L G.W.A.Troke	Bf109 damaged	E Nijmegen	1105

29/30th September 1944

157 Sqn	Mosq	BC	F/L P.W.Vincent	Me410 destroyed	Darmstadt area	0035

30th September 1944

416 Sqn	Spit	2TAF	S/L J.F.McElroy F/L D.W.A.Harling	Bf109 destroyed - Shared -	Nijmegen	1345
418 Sqn	Mosq	ADGB	S/L R.G.Gray	FW190 destroyed	Erding	1430
			S/L R.G.Gray	FW190 damaged	Horsching	1430
			F/L D.E.Forsythe	FW190 destroyed	Eggebeck	1545
			F/L H.E.Miller	Bf109 destroyed	12m S Aalborg	1622
441 Sqn	Spit	2TAF	F/L R.G.Lake	Me262 damaged	15m E Nijmegen	1100
486 Sqn	Temp	2TAF	F/L S.S.Williams	Bf109F destroyed	Didam	1640

1/2nd October 1944

85 Sqn	Mosq	BC	F/L A.J.Owen		Ju88 destroyed	20m E Mulhouse	2120

2nd October 1944

401 Sqn	Spit	2TAF	F/O A.L.Sinclair		FW190 damaged	S Nijmegen	1230±
421 Sqn	Spit	2TAF	F/O J.M.Calvert		FW190 prob.dest	Arnhem-Nijmegen	1100
			F/O J.M.Calvert		FW190 damaged	Arnhem-Nijmegen	1100
			F/O W.F.Cook		Bf109 damaged	N Arnhem	1100
			F/L B.T.Gilmour		Bf109 destroyed	Arnhem-Nijmegen	1100
			F/L B.T.Gilmour		FW190 destroyed	Arnhem-Nijmegen	1100
			F/L B.T.Gilmour		FW190 damaged	Arnhem-Nijmegen	1100
			W/O S.C.Price		FW190 damaged	Arnhem-Nijmegen	1100
			F/L G.M.Smith		FW190 damaged	5m E Nijmegen	1100
442 Sqn	Spit	2TAF	F/O F.B.Young		Me262 damaged	Nijmegen	1800±
605 Sqn	Mosq	ADGB	F/O R.E.Lelong		BV138 damaged	Jasmunder Bay	1421
150 Wg	Temp	2TAF	W/C R.P.Beamont		FW190 destroyed	Near Nijmegen	1215

2/3rd October 1944

219 Sqn	Mosq	2TAF	W/C W.P.Green		Ju87 destroyed	8-10m SE Nijmegen	2040
			W/C W.P.Green		Ju87 destroyed	7_8m E Nijmegen	2050
			W/C W.P.Green		Ju87 destroyed	7-10m E Nijmegen	2100
			F/L J.R.Gardner		FW190 destroyed	3-4m E Nijmegen	2210

3rd October 1944

326 Sqn	Spit	1TAF	Lt M Billotet		Ju88 destroyed	Luxeuil-Tuttlingen	1715±

In mid-1944 a new enemy had appeared, the fast and deadly Messerschmitt 262 (opposite). During late September four Canadian Spitfire pilots had engaged Me262s, but succeeded only in claiming damage. On 5th October Squadron Leader Rod Smith of 401 Squadron (above left) led the first 'Spitfire shootdown' of a jet from KG(J)./51, killing the German pilot, Hauptmann Hans-Christof Buttmann. Right: RAF personnel inspect the wreckage near Nijmegen. (R.I.A.Smith)

326 Sqn	Spit	1TAF	Capt P.Le Borgne	Bf109G destroyed	Fribourg	1715±
			Sgt/ChA.Girard	- Shared -		
			Sgt M.Turull	- Shared -		
			S/Lt P.Boillot	- Shared -		
			Lt A.Fouchier	- Shared -		
			PM R.Bedard	- Shared -		
			PMG.Billotet	Ju88 destroyed	Fribourg	1715±

5th October 1944

401 Sqn	Spit	2TAF	S/L R.I.A.Smith	Me262 destroyed	2m SW Nijmegen	1500
			F/O J.MacKay	- Shared -		
			F/L R.M.Davenport	- Shared -		
			F/L H.J.Everard	- Shared -		
			F/O A.L.Sinclair	- Shared -		
403 Sqn	Spit	2TAF	S/L E.P.Wood	Bf109 destroyed	NW Arnhem	1520
			S/L E.P.Wood	Bf109 destroyed	NW Arnhem	1520
			P/O M.Reeves	Bf109 destroyed	Near Osterbeek	1525
			S/L E.P.Wood	Bf109 destroyed	Near Osterbeek	1525
			P/O R.C.Shannon	- Shared -		
			P/O F.W.Thomson	Bf109 destroyed	Near Osterbeek	1525
			F/L S.A.Tosh	Bf109 damaged	Near Osterbeek	1525

5/6th October 1944

25 Sqn	Mosq	ADGB	F/L J.F.R.Jones	He111 destroyed	45m E Lowestoft	1945
409 Sqn	Mosq	2TAF	S/L S.J.Fulton	Bf110 destroyed	SW Hamm	2255

6th October 1944

56 Sqn	Temp	2TAF	F/S L.Jackson	FW190 destroyed	N Nijmegen	1530
			P/O A.S.Miller	FW190 destroyed	N Nijmegen	1530
402 Sqn	Spit	2TAF	F/L J.B.Lawrence	Bf109 destroyed	SE Nijmegen	1520
			F/L A.R.Speare	FW190 destroyed	SE Nijmegen	1520
			F/O W.D.Whittaker	Bf109 destroyed	SE Nijmegen	1520
			S/L E.P.Wood	Bf109 destroyed	Nijmegen	1520
442 Sqn	Spit	2TAF	F/O D.W.Goodwin	FW190 destroyed	E Nijmegen	1500±
			F/O E.T.Hoare	Bf109 destroyed	E Nijmegen	1500±
			F/L W.E.Jowsey	FW190 prob.dest	E Cleve	1500±
			F/L N.A.Keene	FW190 damaged	E Nijmegen	1500±
			F/L W.M.MacLean	FW190 damaged	E Nijmegen	1500±
			F/O S.M.McClarty	Bf109 destroyed	E Nijmegen	1500±
			F/O W.R.Weeks	FW190 damaged	E Nijmegen	1500±

6/7th October 1944

25 Sqn	Mosq	ADGB	F/L A.E.Marshall	He111 destroyed	50m E Southwold	1956
141 Sqn	Mosq	BC	F/L A.C.Gallacher	Ju88 destroyed	4m S Leeuwarden	2122
219 Sqn	Mosq	2TAF	F/L G.R.I.Parker	Bf110 destroyed	N Arnhem	0053
			F/L J.C.E.Atkins	Ju87 destroyed	80m SEBrussels	0140
409 Sqn	Mosq	2TAF	P/O F.E.Haley	Ju188 destroyed	Near Kolberg	2120
			F/O R.H.Finlayson	Bf110 destroyed	Near Sittard	2320
410 Sqn	Mosq	2TAF	F/L C.E.Edinger	Ju88 destroyed	2m SW Hannut	1940
			F/L B.E.Plumer	Bf110 destroyed	Venlo	2320
456 Sqn	Mosq	ADGB	W/O J.L.Mulhall	Ju88 destroyed	Zaltbommel, 20m W Nijmegen	2305
605 Sqn	Mosq	ADGB	F/L I.F.Pengelly	E/A destroyed	Bonn	2249

7th October 1944

442 Sqn	Spit	2TAF	F/O G.A.Costello	FW190 damaged	5m E Cleve	1635±
			F/O J.P.Lumsden	FW190 destroyed	5m E Cleve	1635±
			F/O L.H.Wilson	FW190 damaged	5m E Cleve	1635±
			F/O F.B.Young	FW190 destroyed	5m E Cleve	1635±
			F/O F.B.Young	FW190 destroyed	5m E Cleve	1635±

The Tempest units really began to make their presence felt in October. On 13th Bob Cole of 3 Squadron (far right) destroyed an Me262 and an 80 Squadron pilot damaged a second. However a day earlier the capable and aggressive Roland Beamont was shot down and captured during a strafe of Rheine airfield.

7/8th October 1944

25 Sqn	Mosq	ADGB	F/O B.Travers	He111 damaged	60m E Lowestoft	1956
157 Sqn	Mosq	BC	F/L J.O.Mathews	Bf110 destroyed	W Neumünster	2050
410 Sqn	Mosq	2TAF	F/O J.L.Fullerton	Ju88 destroyed	15m NE Hasselt	2157

8th October 1944

326 Sqn	Spit	1TAF	PMG.Billotet Capt C.Mangin	Bf109 prob.dest - Shared -	Turckheim	1300±
			Lt J-M.Doillon	Bf109 destroyed	Turckheim	1300±
			PMG.Billotet Capt C.Mangin	Bf109 destroyed - Shared -	Colmar	1300±
515 Sqn	Mosq	BC	F/L F.T.L'Amie	Bf109 destroyed	Eggebeck, Den	1342

9th October 1944

611 Sqn	Spit	ADGB	F/S K.Mack	Ju188 destroyed	100m ENE Hermaness	0938

13th October 1944

3 Sqn	Temp	2TAF	F/S R.W.Cole	Me262 destroyed	Nr Grave AD	1210±
80 Sqn	Temp	2TAF	F/L A.Seager	Me262 damaged	15m SE Nijmegen	1405

14th October 1944

316 Sqn	Must	ADGB	W/O A.Pietrzak	Bf109 destroyed	10m NW Duisberg	0840

14/15th October 1044

85 Sqn	Mosq	BC	S/L B.A.Burbridge	Ju88G destroyed	Guterslohe AD	0345
			S/L B.A.Burbridge	Ju88G destroyed	Guterslohe AD	0345

Roland Beamont's Tempest 'R-B' (left). The sheer size of the aircraft is shown by the effort required to move this 80 Squadron machine.

125 Sqn	Mosq	ADGB	F/O G.S.Irving	He219 destroyed	SW Munster		0005
239 Sqn	Mosq	BC	F/L D.R.Howard	FW190 destroyed	Ameland		0350±
FIU	Mosq	ADGB	F/O D.T.Tull	Ju88G destroyed	Paderborn		0400

15/16th October 1944

85 Sqn	Mosq	BC	F/L C.K.Nowell	Bf110 destroyed	10m SE Schleswig	2125
605 Sqn	Mosq	ADGB	F/OA.T.Linn	FW190 damaged	Lubeck/Blankensee	2133

18th October 1944

316 Sqn	Must	FC	F/L S.Karnkowski	Bf109F destroyed	10m NE Aalborg	1205
			F/L S.Karnkowski W/O A.Pietrzak	Bf109F destroyed - Shared -	10m NE Aalborg	1205
			F/L Z.Nentwich	Bf109F destroyed	10m NE Aalborg	1205
			W/O A.Pietrzak	Bf109F destroyed	10m NE Aalborg	1205
			F/L J.Walawski	Bf109F destroyed	10m NE Aalborg	1205
			F/L J.Walawski	Bf109F destroyed	10m NE Aalborg	1205
133 Wg	Must	FC	W/C K.Rutkowski 316 Squadron	Bf109F destroyed - shared -	10m NE Aalborg	1205

19/20th October 1944

85 Sqn	Mosq	BC	S/L B.A.Burbridge	Ju188 destroyed	Metz	2220
141 Sqn	Mosq	BC	F/O J.C.Barton	Ju88 destroyed	30m NW Nuremburg	2152
			F/L G.D.Bates	Ju88 destroyed	10m SE Karlsruhe	2057
157 Sqn	Mosq	BC	S/L R.D.Doleman	Ju88 damaged	Near Biblis AD	2102
			S/L R.D.Doleman	Ju88 destroyed	4920N 0902E	2150
239 Sqn	Mosq	BC	W/O P.O.Falconer	Bf110 destroyed	Strasbourg	2315±
FIU	Mosq	FC	F/L Jones	E/A damaged	Frankfurt	u/k

On 18th October Wing Commander Kazimierz Rutkowski led his 316 Squadron Mustang pilots out to Aalborg. Six Bf109s were found and all were claimed destroyed without loss. Successful pilots included Flight Lieutenants J.Walawski, S.Karnkowski and Wing Commander Rutkowski - all claimed successes, However, the formation that they had surprised comprised Bf109Gs and Ar96s of I./JG 102, a training unit. These were probably unarmed. Three Messerschmitts and two Arados crashed or crash-landed, but the sole pilot casualty was Hauptmann Werner Haugk, a Ritterkreuztrager, whose 'Gustav' crashed into the sea and he perished. Although Haugk has been credited variously with between nine and twenty victories, not a single victory can be discovered in Luftwaffe records.

21st October 1944

3 Sqn	Temp	2TAF	F/L G.A.Duff	Me262 damaged	5m NE Nijmegen	1038
			F/O R.Dryland	- Shared -		
			S/L A.E.Umbers	Me262 damaged	Nijmegen	1505

25/26th October 1944

125 Sqn	Mosq	FC	F/O W.A.Beadle	He111 destroyed	50m E Yarmouth	1923
FIU	Beau	FC	F/O D.T.Tull	He111 destroyed	40m E Lowestoft	1945

28th October 1944

412 Sqn	Spit	2TAF	F/L D.C.Laubman	FW190 destroyed	Hohenbudberg	1420±
			F/L D.C.Laubman	FW190 destroyed	Hohenbudberg	1420±
			P/O W.C.Busby	Bf109 prob.dest	S Borken	1600±
			F/O P.M.Charron	Bf109 destroyed	Altenberge	1600±
			F/O P.M.Charron	Bf109 destroyed	Altenberge	1600±
486 Sqn	Temp	2TAF	F/O R.J.Danzey	Me262 damaged	S Volkel	1555

191

29th October 1944

403 Sqn	Spit	2TAF	F/L W.J.Hill	FW190 destroyed	Venlo	1455
			F/L W.J.Hill	FW190 destroyed	Venlo	1455
			F/L W.J.Hill	FW190 damaged	Venlo	1455
			P/O M.Reeves	FW190 destroyed	Venlo	1455
			P/O M.Reeves	FW190 damaged	Venlo	1455
515 Sqn	Mosq	BC	F/L F.T.L'Amie	FW190 destroyed	30m SSW Stuttgart	1528
			F/L F.T.L'Amie	Ju W34 destroyed	Straubing	1632
			F/O T.A.K.Groves	Bf110 destroyed	Ingolstadt	1550

29/30th October 1944

239 Sqn	Mosq	BC	F/L D.R.Howard	He111 destroyed	Dummer See	1950±
410 Sqn	Mosq	2TAF	Lt A.A.Harrington	FW190 destroyed	Near St Anton	1855

30/31st October 1944

125 Sqn	Mosq	FC	S/L L.V.G.Gill	He111 destroyed	North Sea	0755
			S/L L.V.G.Gill	He111 prob.dest	North Sea	0806

31st October/1st November 1944

85 Sqn	Mosq	BC	W/O W. Alderton	Ju88 destroyed	Frankfurt-Limburg	1953

1/2nd November 1944

418 Sqn	Mosq	FC	F/L H.E.Miller	Ju88G destroyed	Near Ober Olm	2038

2nd November 1944

65 Sqn	Must	FC	F/L D.M.Davidson	FW190 damaged	Minden	1600±
			F/L P.J.Hearne	FW190 destroyed	Minden	1600±
274 Sqn	Temp	2TAF	F/L L.A.,Wood	Me262 damaged	5m S Nijmegen	1505
			S/L J.R.Heap	Me262 damaged	Nijmegen	1510
			F/O G.Mann	Me262 damaged	Nijmegen	1510
442 Sqn	Spit	2TAF	F/O J.P.W.Francis	FW190 destroyed	SE Coesfeld	1645±
			F/L M.E.Jowsey	FW190 destroyed	SE Coesfeld	1645±

2/3rd November 1944

29 Sqn	Mosq	FC	F/O W.W.Provan	Bf110 destroyed	Handorf	2010

On the night of 4th November Squadron Leader Branse Burbridge, of 85 Squadron, with his navigator Flight Lieutenant Bill Skelton, claimed four victories around Bonn-Hangelar airfield. One was claimed as a Bf110, but was almost certainly an He219 of I./NJG 1 flown by Oberfeldwebel Wilhelm Morlock, (far left) who was killed. This team would go on to become the top-scoring nightfighter crew of the RAF.

3rd November 1944

122 Wg	Temp	2TAF	W/C J.B.Wray	Me262 prob.dest	Venraj-Geldern	1505

4/5th November 1944

85 Sqn	Mosq	BC	S/L B.A.Burbridge	Ju88G destroyed	30m E Bonn	1909
			S/L B.A.Burbridge	Ju88 destroyed	5m SE Bonn AD	2005
			S/L B.A.Burbridge	Bf110 destroyed	N Hangelar AD	2032
			S/L B.A.Burbridge	Ju88 destroyed	N Hangelar AD	2040
			F/L A.J.Owen	Ju88 destroyed	SE Bielefeld	1947
151 Sqn	Mosq	FC	P/O R. Oddy	Ju87 destroyed	85m NE Nijmegen	2245
157 Sqn	Mosq	BC	W/C K.H.P.Beauchamp	Bf110 destroyed	Osnabruck area	2030
169 Sqn	Mosq	BC	S/L R.G.Woodman	Bf110 destroyed*	Bochum	2000±

Note: Not claimed, credited post-war.

239 Sqn	Mosq	BC	F/L J.N.W.Young	Bf110 destroyed	Bochum	1920±
488 Sqn	Mosq	2TAF	W/O J.W. Marshall	Bf110 destroyed	20m E Arnhem	1858
FIDS	Beau	FC	S/L J.N.Howard -Williams	He111 destroyed	40-50m E Winterton	1940

5/6th November 1944

68 Sqn	Mosq	FC	F/S L.W.Neal	He111 destroyed	27m E Harwich	2100±

6/7th November 1944

85 Sqn	Mosq	BC	Cpt T.Weisteen	Ju88 prob.dest	15m NW Koblenz	1949
			S/L F.S.Gonsalves	Ju188 destroyed	5543N 0652E	2000
			F/L B.R.Keele	Bf110 destroyed	E Bonn AD	2110
151 Sqn	Mosq	FC	F/O H.Turner	Ju188 destroyed	30m E Munster	2030
157 Sqn	Mosq	BC	S/L R.D.Doleman	Bf110 destroyed	E Koblenz	1850
			F/L H.P.Kelway	Ju188 prob.dest	Osnabruck-Minden	2038
239 Sqn	Mosq	BC	F/O G.E.Jameson	Ju188 destroyed	Osnabrück	2100±

9/10th November 1944

25 Sqn	Mosq	FC	F/L J.Lomas	He111 destroyed	40m E Clacton	1910

10/11th November 1944

25 Sqn	Mosq	FC	F/L D.H.Greaves	He111 destroyed	70m E Lowestoft	0130
68 Sqn	Mosq	FC	W/O K.R. Cookson	He111 destroyed	50m E Lowstoft	0200±
125 Sqn	Mosq	FC	F/L G.F.Simcock	He111 prob.dest	60m E Southwold	2000±
157 Sqn	Mosq	BC	S/L J.G.Benson	Ju88 destroyed	Frankfurt-Koblenz	2130
169 Sqn	Mosq	BC	F/O R.G.Woodman	Ju88 damaged	E Kassel	2125

11/12th November 1944

68 Sqn	Mosq	FC	F/S A.R.Brooking	He111 destroyed	North Sea	0200±
85 Sqn	Mosq	BC	F/O A.J.Owen	FW190 destroyed	30m SE Hamburg	1909
157 Sqn	Mosq	BC	F/L J.O. Matthews	Ju88 damaged	Bonn area	2015

18/19th November 1944

219 Sqn	Mosq	2TAF	F/L J.C.E.Atkins	Ju87 destroyed	NE Aachen	0230

19th November 1944

486 Sqn	Temp	2TAF	F/L K.G.Taylor-Cannon	Me262 prob.dest	Rheine A/D	1125
			P/O O.D.Eagleson	- Shared -		
			P/O J.Steedman	Me262 damaged	Rheine A/D	1125

19/20th November 1944

456 Sqn	Mosq	FC	F/O D.W.Arnold	He111 destroyed	75m E Lowestoft	2023

On the 19th Flight Lieutenant Keith Taylor-Cannon of 486 Sqn had shared an Me262 'probable' at Rheine and followed this on 26th by sharing a Ju188 destroyed at Handorf. He died - believed shot by Volkssturm troops - on 13th April 1945 after falling to Flak. His victory total was four confirmed. Arthur Moore of 56 Squadron (right) ended the war with four, including an He219 of I./NJG 1 on 28th. Earlier, he had been credited with destroying 23 V-1 flying bombs.

20/21st November 1944

157 Sqn	Mosq	BC	F/L J.O.Matthews	Ju88 damaged	Frankfurt area	1933

21st November 1944

3 Sqn	Temp	2TAF	F/O R.Dryland	Me262 damaged	Near Rheine	1038
			F/L G.A.Duff	- Shared -		
401 Sqn	Spit	2TAF	F/L W.C.Connell	FW190 destroyed	Near Wesel	0930±
			F/L E.B.Sheehy	- Shared -		
			F/O K.C.Gallinger	FW190 damaged	Near Wesel	0930±
			F/O D.F.Husband	FW190 damaged	Near Wesel	0930±
411 Sqn	Spit	2TAF	F/L H.A.Crawford	FW190 destroyed	8-10m N Geldern	0930

21/22nd November 1944

29 Sqn	Mosq	FC	P/O R.Beynon	Ju188 destroyed	N Steyr	2100±
85 Sqn	Mosq	BC	S/L B.A.Burbridge	Bf110 destroyed	10m E Mannheim	1947
			S/L B.A.Burbridge	Ju88 destroyed	Bonn AD	2134
157 Sqn	Mosq	BC	F/O K.Bartholomew	Ju188 destroyed	5140N 0625E	1846

24/25th November 1944

456 Sqn	Mosq	FC	F/O F.S.Stevens	He111 destroyed	10m off Texel	0810

25/26th November 1944

409 Sqn	Mosq	2TAF	F/O R.I.E.Britten	Ju88 destroyed	Rheindahlen	1955
			F/O R.I.E.Britten	Ju188 damaged	Krefeld	2013
410 Sqn	Mosq	2TAF	Lt A.A.Harrington	Ju88G destroyed	Jackerath	2019
			Lt A.A.Harrington	Ju88 destroyed	N Hunxe	2026
			Lt A.A.Harrington	Ju88G destroyed	Near Muntz	2028

26th November 1944

80 Sqn	Temp	2TAF	F/OF.B.Findlay	Me262 damaged	Helmond	1040
			F/L D.L.Price	Me262 damaged	Helmond	1040
412 Sqn	Spit	2TAF	F/O F.T.Murray	FW190 destroyed	Near Venlo	1610
486 Sqn	Temp	2TAF	P/O J.Steedman	Ju188 prob.dest	Appr Handorf AD	0835
			F/L K.G.Taylor-Cannon	Ju188 destroyed	Appr Handorf AD	0835
			F/L S.S.Williams	- Shared -		

26/27th November 1944

409 Sqn	Mosq	2TAF	W/O R.A.Boorman	Ju87 damaged	Near Venlo	1830
			F/L W.H.McPhail	Ju87 damaged	Roermond	2155

28th November 1944

56 Sqn	Temp	2TAF	F/L A.R.Moore	He219 destroyed	Munster	0820
			P/O J.S.Ferguson	He219 damaged	Munster	0820
			F/O W.J.Green	- Shared -		
			F/S A.M.L.Kennaugh		- Shared -	
			F/L A.R.Moore	- Shared -		
			P/O H.Shaw	- Shared -		

29/30th November 1944

409 Sqn	Mosq	2TAF	W/O E.F.Cole	Ju88 destroyed	Beek	1900
			W/O E.F.Cole	Ju88 destroyed	Bracht	1930

30th November 1944

169 Sqn	Mosq	BC	W/C H.C.Kelsey	He177 destroyed	Liegnitz	u/k

30th November/1st December 1944

157 Sqn	Mosq	BC	F/L R.J.V.Smyth	Ju188 destroyed	5030N 0920E	2040

2nd December 1944

85 Sqn	Mosq	BC	Capt T.Weisteen	Bf110 destroyed	E Hagen	2136
157 Sqn	Mosq	BC	F/L W.Taylor	Ju88 destroyed	Osnabruck	2210

3rd December 1944

80 Sqn	Temp	2TAF	F/L R.W.A.McKichan	Bf109 damaged	4m S Rheine A/D	0930

Bf109s and FW190s were being encountered in roughly equal numbers during late September. Most of the combats were at very low level and the Messerschmitts tended to have rather the worst of things against the mainly Canadian Spitfire pilots. Here two Bf109G pilots are in the process of having their days ruined by Allied fighter pilots.

80 Sqn	Temp	2TAF	F/O J.W.Garland	Me262 destroyed	S Rheine A/D		0940
411 Sqn	Spit	2TAF	S/L E.G.Lapp F/L E.T.Gardner	Bf109 destroyed - Shared -	Venlo		1245±
412 Sqn	Spit	2TAF	F/O W.A.Aziz	Bf109 damaged	NW Krefeld		0920±

3/4th December 1944

85 Sqn	Mosq	BC	F/L E.R.Hedgecoe	Ju88 prob.dest	Guterslohe		u/k

4/5th December 1944

85 Sqn	Mosq	BC	F/L A.J.Owen	Ju88 destroyed	Nr Krefeld		1955
			F/L R.T.Goucher	Bf110 destroyed	Karlsruhe		2010
			F/L R.T.Goucher	Bf110 destroyed	Germesheim		2024
			Capt S.Heglund	Bf110 destroyed	Detmold AD		2054
157 Sqn	Mosq	BC	F/OB.D.Gale	Ju188 destroyed	Bochum area		1915
			F/L J.O.Mathews	Ju88 destroyed	Dortmund AD		2000
			F/L W.Taylor	Bf110 destroyed	Limburg		2028
219 Sqn	Mosq	2TAF	F/L L.Stephenson	Bf110 destroyed	10m NW Krefeld		2030

5th December 1944

91 Sqn	Spit	FC	P/O J.A.Faulkner	Bf109 destroyed	NE Wesel		1200±
			F/L W.C.Marshall	Bf109 destroyed	NE Wesel		1200±
			F/L W.C.Marshall	Bf109 destroyed	NE Wesel		1200±
			F/O E.Topham	Bf109 damaged	NE Wesel		1200±

(Left) Flight Lieutenant Edward Hedgecoe and his 'nav' Flying Officer Norman Bamford of 85 Squadron continued to punish the Luftwaffe by night. On 6th December they accounted for Hauptmann Hans-Heinz Augenstein, a 41-victory Experte of NJG 1 (centre). It was their seventh kill. On the night of 30th November Flight Lieutenant R.J.V.Smyth of 157 Squadron claimed a Ju188 destroyed. (ww2images.com)

182 Sqn	Typh	2TAF	S/L G.J.Gray F/S R.Lockyer	Bf109 destroyed - Shared -	15m S Munster	1130
			Lt J.I.A.Watt	Bf109 damaged	15m S Munster	1130
274 Sqn	Temp	2TAF	F/L R.B.Cole F/O G.Mann	Me262 damaged - Shared -	10 miles N Rheine	1425
412 Sqn	Spit	2TAF	F/L W.J.Banks	Bf109 prob.dest	SE Wesel	1140±
			F/L W.J.Banks	Bf109 prob.dest	SE Wesel	1140±
			F/O C.W.H.Clitheroe	Bf109 prob.dest	SE SE Wesel	1140±
			F/O F.T.Murray	Bf109 destroyed	10m SE SE Wesel	1140±
			F/O F.T.Murray	Bf109 destroyed	10m SE SE Wesel	1140±
			F/O F.T.Murray	Bf109 prob.dest	10m SE SE Wesel	1140±

5/6th December 1944

29 Sqn	Mosq	FC	P/O R.A.Wigglesworth	Bf110 damaged	Near Handorf	2210

6/7th December 1944

85 Sqn	Mosq	BC	F/L E.R.Hedgecoe	Bf110 destroyed	20-30m W Münster	2005
			F/L E.R.Hedgecoe	Bf110 damaged	Münster-Osnabruck	2005
157 Sqn	Mosq	BC	F/L J.O.Matthews	Bf110 destroyed	Nr Limburg	1955
			F/L J.O.Matthews	Ju88 destroyed	15m SW Giessen	2050
			S/L R.D.Doleman	Bf110 destroyed	nr Kitzingen	2040
			S/L R.D.Doleman	Ju88 destroyed	Kitzingen	2040
BSDU	Mosq	BC	S/L N.A.Reeves	Bf110 destroyed	W Giessen	2040±

On 7th December 315 Squadron Mustang pilots flew another Ranger, meeting fighters of JG 5 near Gossen Island. Again they overclaimed, four Bf109s were shot down but no FW190s. Warrant Officer Andrzej Czerwinski (right) was killed, but his attacker was himself then shot down by Flight Sergeant Jakub Bargielowski.

7th December 1944

315 Sqn	Must	FC	F/S J.Bargielowski	Bf109 destroyed	10m WSW Gossen Is	1421
			W/O B.Czerwinski	Bf109 destroyed	10m WSW Gossen Is	1421
			W/O R.Idrian	FW190 destroyed	W tip Gossen Is	1421
			W/O R.Idrian	FW190 destroyed	W tip Gossen Island	1421
			F/L K.Stembrowicz	FW190 prob.dest	10m WSW Gossen Is	1421
			F/L F.Wiza	Bf109 destroyed	10m WSW Gossen Is	1421
			F/L F.Wiza	Bf109 destroyed	10m WSW Gossen Is	1421
133 Wg	Must	FC	W/C K.Rutkowski	FW190 prob.dest	10m WSW Gossen Is	1421

8th December 1944

56 Sqn	Temp	2TAF	W/O D.C.H.Rex	FW190 damaged	N Rheine	1005
			F/O K.Watts	FW190 destroyed	N Rheine	1005
80 Sqn	Temp	2TAF	F/L J.M.Weston	Bf109 destroyed	2m NE Bielefeld	1615
127 Sqn	Spit	2TAF	F/S P.Attwood	Bf109 destroyed	Nr Neede	1215±
			F/S Griffin	- Shared -		
130 Sqn	Spit	2TAF	F/S G.W.Hudson	FW190 damaged	Burgsteinfurt	1505
			F/O K.M.Lowe	FW190 destroyed	Burgsteinfurt	1505
			P/O F.C.Riley	Bf109 destroyed	Burgsteinfurt	1505
			W/O J.W.Turnbull	FW190 damaged	Burgsteinfurt	1510
			W/O J.W.Turnbull	FW190 damaged	Burgsteinfurt	1510
			F/L H.Walmsley	Bf109 destroyed	Burgsteinfurt	1510
181 Sqn	Typh	2TAF	F/L H.R.Isachsen	FW190 destroyed	W Dummer Lake	1100±
403 Sqn	Spit	2TAF	F/L L.Foster	Bf109 destroyed	5m SE Wesel	1410
416 Sqn	Spit	2TAF	F/O A.G.Borland	Bf109 damaged	Rheine-Munster	1410
			S/L J.DMitchner	Bf109 destroyed	Near Munster	1410

10th December 1944

56 Sqn	Temp	2 TAF	F/S L.Jackson	Me262 damaged	Nijmegen area	1535
401 Sqn	Spit	2 TAF	F/O G.D.A.T.Cameron	FW190 prob.dest	N Enschede	1440±
			F/O G.D.A.T.Cameron	FW190 damaged	N Enschede	1440±
			F/O D.F.Church	Bf109 destroyed	NE Hengelo	1440±

11th December 1944

56 Sqn	Temp	2TAF	P/O H.Shaw	Bf109 destroyed	Near Rheine	1455
			S/L P.R.St Quentin	Bf109 destroyed	Near Rheine	1455
122 Sqn	Must	FC	F/L D.R.Stephens	Bf109 destroyed	S Haltern	1355

12th December 1944

65 Sqn	Must	FC	S/L L.A.P.Burra-Robinson	Bf109 damaged	Dortmund	1420±
			F/O J.Butler	Bf109 prob.dest	Dortmund	1420±
			F/L C.O.E.Hamilton-Williams	Bf109 damaged	Dortmund	1420±
			F/L P.J.Hearne	Bf109 destroyed	Dortmund	1420±
			F/L P.J.Hearne	Bf109 prob.dest	Dortmund	1420±
			F/L P.J.Hearne	Bf109 damaged	Dortmund	1420±
129 Sqn	Must	FC	F/O E.W.Edwards	Bf109 destroyed	Coesfeld	1400
			F/O E.W.Edwards	Bf109 destroyed	Coesfeld	1400
			F/O E.W.Edwards	Bf109 damaged	Coesfeld	1400
			F/O E.W.Edwards	Bf109 damaged	Coesfeld	1400
			F/L J.Walowski	Bf109 destroyed	12m NW Dortmund	1400

12/13th December 1944

85 Sqn	Mosq	BC	S/L B.A.Burbridge	Ju88 destroyed	Guterslohe AD	1853
			S/L B.A.Burbridge	Bf110 destroyed	2m W Essen	1957
			Capt E.P.Fossum	Ju88 destroyed	5135N 0805E	1920
157 Sqn	Mosq	BC	W/C K.H.P.Beauchamp	Bf110 damaged	Aschaffenburg area	2037
FIU	Mosq	FC	F/L E.R.Hedgecoe	Bf110 destroyed	S Hagen	1930
			F/L E.R.Hedgecoe	Bf110 destroyed	Essen	2002

On 17th December John Wray, the 122 Wing Leader, became the only RAF pilot, to down two Me262s, when he shot down Leutnant Wolfgang Lubking of 6./KG(J)51 into the Rhine River. He had previously brought down an aircraft from Kommando Nowotny on 3rd November (claimed as a 'probable'). Richard Goucher of 85 Squadron (far right) got his third kill of five that night, bringing down a Bf110 of II./NJG 5.

14th December 1944

56 Sqn	Temp	2TAF	F/O D.E.Ness	Bf109 destroyed	S Rheine	1430
			F/L J.D.Ross	Bf109 destroyed	S Rheine	1430
			P/O H.Shaw	Bf109 destroyed	S Rheine	1430
401 Sqn	Spit	2TAF	F/O D.F.Church	Bf109 damaged	NW Rheine	1520±
			F/L L.W.Woods	Bf109 damaged	Near Rheine	1520±
412 Sqn	Spit	2TAF	F/L R.N.Earle	Bf109 destroyed	Coesfeld-Dulmen	1425±
			S/L J.N.Newell	Bf109 destroyed	Coesfeld-Dulmen	1425±
			F/L F.H.Richards	Bf109 destroyed	Coesfeld-Dulmen	1425±

17th December 1944

3 Sqn	Temp	2TAF	F/S M.J.A.Rose	Bf109 destroyed	6m E Lingen	1035
			F/L B.C.MacKenzie	Bf109 damaged	15m E Nijmegen	1050
56 Sqn	Temp	2TAF	F/L J.D.Ross P/O H.Shaw	Bf109 destroyed - Shared -	Near Grave	1055
			F/S L.Jackson F/O K.Watts	Bf109 destroyed - Shared -	Near Grave	1055
56 Sqn	Temp	2TAF	W/O J.F.Alexander	Bf109 damaged	NE Munster	1415
			F/S J.A.Bosley F/L A.R.Moore	Bf109 destroyed - Shared -	NE Munster	1415
			F/L J.D.Ross P/O H.Shaw	He219 destroyed - Shared -	Handorf A/D	1415
			F/L A.R.Moore F/L J.D.Ross	Bf109 destroyed - Shared -	NE Munster	1415
274 Sqn	Temp	2TAF	S/L D.C.Fairbanks	Bf109 destroyed	Burgsteinfurt	1030
			S/L D.C.Fairbanks	Bf109 destroyed	10m SE Emmerich	1045
			F/L W.J.Hibbert	Bf109 destroyed	10m SE Emmerich	1045
			S/L D.C.Fairbanks	Bf109 damaged	E Nijmegan	1100

122 Wg	Temp	2TAF	W/C J.B.Wray	Me262 destroyed	Helmond-Rheine, nr Wesel	1110

17/18th December 1944

85 Sqn	Mosq	BC	F/L R.T.Goucher	Bf110 destroyed	40m from Uim	1959
125 Sqn	Mosq	FC	P/O K.D.Goodyear	He111 damaged	40m NE Orfordness	0547
157 Sqn	Mosq	BC	S/L J.G.Benson	Ju88 damaged	Wiesbaden AD	2034
			F/S J.A.,Leigh	Bf110 damaged	30m NNE Ulm	2042±
			W/O D.A.Taylor	Bf110 destroyed	5114N 0635E	0700

18th December 1944

66 Sqn	Spit	2TAF	W/O B.Deakes	Bf109 damaged	15-20m SE Koln	1510
			P/O R.Dunn	Bf109 damaged	15-20m SE Koln	1510
			P/O M.Silver	Bf109 destroyed	15-20m SE Koln	1510
			F/S L.Streeter	Bf109 damaged	15-20m SE Koln	1510
			F/L D.C.Warren	Bf109 damaged	15-20m SE Koln	1510

18/19th December 1944

157 Sqn	Mosq	BC	F/L W.Taylor	He219 destroyed	Nr Osnabrück	0220
409 Sqn	Mosq	2TAF	F/O F.E.Haley	Bf110 destroyed	Gerresheim	0020
			F/L R.H. Finlayson	Ju88 destroyed	Groin	0114
			W/C J.D.Somerville	Ju88 destroyed	Kaiserworth	0408
410 Sqn	Mosq	2TAF	F/L C.E.Edinger	Ju88 destroyed	S Bonninghardt	1953

21/22nd December 1944

157 Sqn	Mosq	BC	W/C K.H.P.Beauchamp	Ju88 destroyed	N Frankfurt	1919

22/23rd December 1944

85 Sqn	Mosq	BC	S/L B.A.Burbridge	Bf110 destroyed	Koblenz-Guterslohe	1937
			F/L A.J.Owen	Ju88 destroyed	Nr Saarbrücken	1821
			F/L A.J.Owen	Ju88 destroyed	Nr Saarbrücken	1828
			F/L A.J.Owen	Bf110 destroyed	Nr Saarbrücken	1905
125 Sqn	Mosq	FC	F/L R.W.Leggett	He111 destroyed	80m E Cromer	0705
157 Sqn	Mosq	BC	S/L R.D.Doleman	Ju88 destroyed	Nr Limburg	1935
219 Sqn	Mosq	2TAF	W/C W.P.Green	Ju188 destroyed	Verviers area	0025

Above: A 488 Squadron Mosquito on a Dutch airfield during the icy winter of 1944/45. Right: Wing Commander Ron Watts, CO of 488 Squadron. He claimed his second kill on the night of 23/24th December.

23rd December 1944

65 Sqn	Must	FC	F/O W.L.Black	FW190 damaged	Köln	1300±
			S/L L.A.P.Burra			
			-Robinson	FW190 damaged	Köln	1300±
			F/O J.Butler	FW190 destroyed	Köln	1300±
411 Sqn	Spit	2TAF	F/L J.J.Boyle	Me262 damaged	Nr Heesch AD	1405±

23/24th December 1944

68 Sqn	Mosq	FC	F/S A.Bullus	He111 damaged	30m NW Cromer	0630±
85 Sqn	Mosq	BC	F/L G.C.Chapman	Bf110 destroyed	Mannheim-Mainz	1832
157 Sqn	Mosq	BC	F/L R.J.V.Smyth	Ju88 destroyed	10m NE Koblenz	1845
			S/L J.G.Benson	Ju88 prob.dest	Neuenkirchen	1906
219 Sqn	Mosq	2TAF	F/O W.B.Allison	Ju88 destroyed	W Asperden	1835
			F/O W.B.Allison	Ju188 damaged	E Koln	1855
			W/C W.P.Green	Ju188 destroyed	S Huy	2240
			F/O R.L.Young	Ju88 damaged	N Bonninghardt	0255
409 Sqn	Mosq	2TAF	F/L W.H.McPhail	Ju188 destroyed	Near Venlo	2205
410 Sqn	Mosq	2TAF	F/O D.M.MacKenzie	Ju88 destroyed	Wickrath	0500
			F/O D.M.MacKenzie	Ju88 destroyed	Grefath	0546
488 Sqn	Mosq	2TAF	W/C R.G.Watts	Ju188 destroyed	3m N 'Voicebox'	1943
			F/L K.W.Stewart	Ju88 destroyed	10m W Maeseyck	1956
			F/L K.W.Stewart	Ju88 destroyed	10m W Maeseyck	2040
			F/L J.A.S.Hall	Ju88 destroyed	US Sector	2145
			F/L R.G.Jeffs	Ju88 damaged	Near Malmedy	0250

24th December 1944

3 Sqn	Temp	2TAF	F/O R.Dryland	FW190D destroyed	S Malmedy	1230
			F/L K.A.Thiele	Bf109 destroyed	S Malmedy	1230
274 Sqn	Temp	2TAF	S/L E.D.Mackie	FW190 destroyed	Eindhoven	1245
326 Sqn	Spit	1TAF	Capt C.J.G.Gauthier S/Lt P.Boillot	Bf109 destroyed - Shared -	Rottweil	1300±
			Capt C.J.G.Gauthier S/Lt N.de Balmain	Bf109 destroyed - Shared -	Rottweil	1300±
			Capt P.Le Borgne Sgt J.Carrier LV J.Vibert	FW190 destroyed - Shared - - Shared -	Fribourg	1300±
412 Sqn	Spit	2TAF	F/L M.D.Boyd	FW190 destroyed	15m SSE Venlo	1225
			S/L D.H.Dover	FW190 damaged	S Zulpich	1225
			S/L D.H.Dover	FW190 damaged	S Zulpich	1225
			F/L R.N.Earle	FW190 damaged	Near Zulpich	1225
			F/L C.W.Fox	FW190 destroyed	Near Zulpich	1225
414 Sqn	Spit	2TAF	F/L D.I.Hall	Bf109 destroyed	Near Krefeld	1200
			F/L D.I.Hall	Bf109 destroyed	Near Krefeld	1200
414 Sqn	Spit	2TAF	F/L W.Sawers	Bf109 destroyed	Neuss-Koln	1535
			F/L W.Sawers	Bf109 destroyed	Neuss-Koln	1535
			F/L W.Sawers	Bf109 destroyed	Neuss-Koln	1535
			F/L W.Sawers	Bf109 damaged	Neuss-Koln	1535
			F/L W.Sawers	Bf109 damaged	Neuss-Koln	1535
143 Wg	Typh	2TAF	W/C F.G.Grant	FW190 damaged	2-4m NW Aachen	1215

24/25th December 1944

85 Sqn	Mosq	BC	Capt S.Heglund	Bf110 destroyed	Wiesbaden	1856
157 Sqn	Mosq	BC	S/L J.G.Benson	Bf110 destroyed	5038N 0725E	1836
			F/L J.O.Mathews	Ju88G destroyed	3m S Köln	1900
			S/L R.D.Doleman	Bf110 destroyed	13m NW Köln	1905
			S/L R.D.Doleman	Bf110 destroyed	Duisburg	1921
219 Sqn	Mosq	2TAF	F/L L.Stephenson	Bf110 destroyed	Nr Hasselweiler	0246
			F/L G.R.I.Parker	Ju188 destroyed	34m E Arnhem	0300
			F/L G.R.I.Parker	Ju188 destroyed	12m E Eindhoven	0335
406 Sqn	Mosq	FC	W/C R.Bannock	Ju88 destroyed	3m NW Paderborn AD	2015
410 Sqn	Mosq	2TAF	F/L C.E.Edinger	Ju87 destroyed	Wassenberg	1955
			S/L I.E.MacTavish	Ju87 destroyed	Near Walbeck	2328

On 23rd December Flight Lieutenant John 'Jack' Boyle of 411 Sqn claimed damage to an Me262. On the 25th he became the first Spitfire pilot to bring one down. Tempest pilot John Garland of 80 Sqn (far right) brought down a '262 on 3rd December and followed this on 27th by destroying an FW190.

410 Sqn Mosq	2TAF	F/O J.A.Watt	Ju88 destroyed	Near Puffendt	0618
488 Sqn Mosq	2TAF	P/O T.A.Mallon	Ju188 damaged	E-4192	0040
604 Sqn Mosq	FC	F/L R.J.Foster	He219 destroyed	55m E Bocholt	1920

25th December 1944

80 Sqn Temp	2TAF	P/O R.J.Verran 122 Wing	Ar234 damage - Shared -	Near Liege	0915
193 Sqn Typh	2TAF	F/O W.M.J.Bulleid	FW190 destroyed	Coesfeld	1145
		F/L A.S.Smith	FW190 damaged	Coesfeld	1145
401 Sqn Spit	2TAF	F/L W.C.Connell F/S A.K.Woodill	Bf109 destroyed - Shared -	Duisburg	1200±
		F/L J.MacKay	Bf109 destroyed	Duisburg	1200±
402 Sqn Spit	2TAF	F/L D.Sherk	FW190 destroyed	20m SE Aachen	1505±
403 Sqn Spit	2TAF	S/L J.E.Collier	Me262 destroyed	15m SW Aachen	1525
411 Sqn Spit	2TAF	F/L J.J.Boyle	Me262 destroyed	Heesch-Erp	1200±
486 Sqn Temp	2TAF	F/O R.D.Bremner P/O J.H.Stafford	Me262 destroyed - Shared -	S Aachen	1525
122 Wg Temp	2TAF	W/C J.B.Wray 80 Squadron	Ar234 damaged - Shared -	Near Liege	0915

25/26th December 1944

| 219 Sqn Mosq | 2TAF | F/L E.A.Campbell | Bf110 destroyed | Nr Bergen | 2020 |

26th December 1944

411 Sqn Spit	2TAF	F/L E.G.Ireland	Me262 damaged	NW Julich	1350
421 Sqn Spit	2TAF	S/L J.D.Browne	Bf109 destroyed	Trier	1145
		F/O T.J.De Courcey	Bf109 destroyed	Trier	1145
135 Wg Spit	2TAF	W/C R.H.Harries	Me262 damaged	S Stavelot	1530

26/27th December 1944

219 Sqn Mosq	2TAF	W/C W.P.Green	Ju87 destroyed	Liege	1935
406 Sqn Mosq	FC	F/O E.A.Oswald	Ju88 damaged	Neubiberg AD	2120
488 Sqn Mosq	2TAF	F/L H.D.C.Webbe	Ju188 prob.dest	Nr Moers	0115

27th December 1944

80 Sqn	Temp	2TAF	F/O D.S.Angier	FW190 destroyed	6m NW Rheine	1200
			W/O G.W.Dopson	FW190 destroyed	6m NW Rheine	1200
			F/O J.W.Garland	FW190 destroyed	6m NW Rheine	1200
			F/L R.W.A.MacKichen	FW190 destroyed	6m NW Rheine	1200
182 Sqn Typh	2TAF		S/L G.J.Gray	FW190 destroyed	4m E St Vith	1525±
			Lt J.I.A.Watt	- Shared -		
274 Sqn Temp	2TAF		W/O E.Twigg	Bf109 destroyed	7m NE Duren	1105
			S/L E.D.Mackie	Bf109 damaged	Duren	1110
			F/L J.Malloy	Bf109 destroyed	Near Eusenkirchen	1110
411 Sqn Spit	2TAF		F/L R.M.Cook	Bf109 destroyed	Malmedy-St Vith	1110±
			F/O M.G.Graham	Bf109 destroyed	Malmedy area	1110±
			F/L E.G.Ireland	Bf109 destroyed	Malmedy-St Vith	1110±
412 Sqn Spit	2TAF		F/L C.W.Fox	Bf109 destroyed	Rheine A/D	1155±
440 Sqn Typh	2TAF		F/L D.E.Jenvey	Bf109 destroyed	5m SE St Vith	1530
442 Sqn Spit	2TAF		F/O M.A.Perkins	Me262 damaged	Aachen	1055±
486 Sqn Temp	2TAF		F/O B.M.Hall	Bf109 damaged	Near Munster	1250
			F/S S.J.Short	FW190 destroyed	Near Munster	1250
			F/O K.A.Smith	FW190 destroyed	Near Munster	1250
			F/L E.W.Tanner	FW190 destroyed	Near Munster	1250
			F/L E.W.Tanner	FW190 prob.dest	Near Munster	1250
			F/L K.G.Taylor -Cannon	FW190 destroyed	Near Munster	1250

27/28th December 1944

409 Sqn Mosq	2TAF	F/O R.I.E.Britten	Ju88G destroyed	Maeseyck	2235
		F/O R.I.E.Britten	Ju88G destroyed	Kaldenkirchen	2325
410 Sqn Mosq	2TAF	F/L W.G.Dinsdale	Ju88 destroyed	Hechteren area	2200

On 29th December the FW190D-9s of Stab and III./JG 54 were savaged by the Norwegian Spitfire pilots of 331 Squadron in two engagements. Hauptmann Robert 'Bazi' Weiss, credited with 121 victories (left), was shot down and killed, believed by Flight Sergeant K.F.Haanes (centre). Right: An FW190 'Dora-9'.

29th December 1944

3 Sqn	Temp	2TAF	F/L K.A.Thiele	Bf109 destroyed	E Rheine	1130
56 Sqn	Temp	2TAF	F/O W.R.MacLaran	FW190 damaged	10m S Dummer Lake	1535
			F/O J.J.Payton	FW190 destroyed	10m S Dummer Lake	1535
			F/O J.J.Payton	FW190 destroyed	10m S Dummer Lake	1535
			W/O D.C.H.Rex	FW190 damaged	10m S Dummer Lake	1535
			W/O D.C.H.Rex	Bf109 damaged	10m S Dummer Lake	1535
			F/O V.L.Turner	FW190 destroyed	10m S Dummer Lake	1535
168 Sqn	Typh	2TAF	F/L W.G.Huddart	FW190 destroyed	SW Steinfurt	1050
			F/L J.M.Key	- Shared -		
			F/L P.M.Stevens	- Shared -		
			F/L J.D.Stubbs	- Shared -		
			F/O W.G.Huddart	FW190 damaged	12m S Rheine	1050
			F/L J.M.Key	- Shared -		
331 Sqn	Spit	2TAF	2/Lt C.J.Stousland	FW190 destroyed	Just N Rheine	1100
			F/S K.F.Haanes	FW190 destroyed	SW Osnabruck	1100
			F/S K.F.Haanes	FW190 destroyed	SW Osnabruck	1100
			Maj M.Y.Gran	FW190 destroyed	SW Osnabruck	1100
			Maj M.Y.Gran	Bf109 destroyed	SW Enschede	1450
			Maj M.Y.Gran	Bf109 destroyed	SW Enschede	1450
			Maj M.Y.Gran	Bf109 damaged	SW Enschede	1450
			Capt H.G.E.Grundt -Spang	Bf109 destroyed	Enschede area	1450
			Capt H.G.E.Grundt -Spang	Bf109 destroyed	Enschede area	1450
			Capt H.G.E.Grundt -Spang	Bf109 destroyed	Enschede area	1450

331 Sqn	Spit	2TAF	Lt R.A.Watvedt	Bf109 destroyed	Enschede area	1450
			2/Lt O.G.Aanjesen	Bf109 destroyed	S Enschede	1455
			2/Lt J.P.Ditlev -Simonsen	Bf109 destroyed	Enschede area	1455
			Lt R.Dogger	Bf109 destroyed	S Enschede	1455
			Lt R.Dogger	Bf109 destroyed	S Enschede	1455
			2/Lt O.Tidemand -Johansen	Bf109 destroyed	S Enschede	1455
			2/Lt O.Tidemand -Johansen	Bf109 damaged	S Enschede	1455
			Lt T.Woxen	Bf109 destroyed	Enschede area	1455
401 Sqn	Spit	2TAF	F/O G.D.A.T.Cameron	FW190 destroyed	E Enschede	1240±
			P/O D.M.Horsburgh	FW190 damaged	Munster-Rheine	1240±
			F/O A.R.W.MacKay	Bf109 damaged	Munster-Rheine	1240±
			F/O F.T.Murray	FW190 destroyed	Munster-Rheine	1240±
402 Sqn	Spit	2TAF	F/O J.A.W.Lalonde	FW190 damaged	Hengelo-Enschede	1510±
			S/L J.B.Lawrence	FW190 damaged	Hengelo-Enschede	1510±
411 Sqn	Spit	2TAF	F/O R.A.Gilberstad	FW190 destroyed	Bocholt-Borken	1040±
			F/O R.A.Gilberstad	FW190 damaged	Bocholt-Borken	1040±
			F/L R.J.Audet	FW190 destroyed	10m NW Osnabruck	1335±
			F/L R.J.Audet	FW190 destroyed	10m NW Osnabruck	1335±
			F/L R.J.Audet	FW190 destroyed	10m NW Osnabruck	1335±
			F/L R.J.Audet	Bf109 destroyed	10m NW Osnabruck	1335±
			F/L R.J.Audet	Bf109 destroyed	10m NW Osnabruck	1335±
			F/L R.M.Cook	FW190 destroyed	Rheine AD	1335±
			F/L E.G.Ireland	FW190 destroyed	Rheine	1335±
			F/O R.C.McCracken	FW190 destroyed	5m NE Osnabruck	1335±
412 Sqn	Spit	2TAF	F/L C.W.Fox	Ju88 damaged	Rheine AD	0945
439 Sqn	Typh	2TAF	F/O R.H.Lawrence	FW190D destroyed	Near Ahaus	1050
			F/O R.H.Lawrence	Bf109 destroyed	Near Ahaus	1050

30/31st December 1944

85 Sqn	Mosq	BC	S/L F.S.Gonsalves	Ju88 destroyed	5033N 0803E	2035
409 Sqn	Mosq	2TAF	F/O D.M.Mackenzie	Ju88G destroyed	E Harbeck	1946
			S/L R.F.Hatton	Ju88 destroyed	Schoonhoven	0557
410 Sqn	Mosq	2TAF	F/O F.K.Collins	Ju188 damaged	Heinsberg-Sittard	1946
604 Sqn	Mosq	2TAF	Capt O.Kristiansen	Ju88 destroyed	N Venlo	0500

Another successful Norwegian ace on the 29th was Helner Grundt-Spang (left) whose three kills brought his tally to nine (Knut Larsen via Bjorn Bjornstad/Cato Guhnfeld). Bob Lawrence of 439 Squadron (centre) destroyed two fighters on 29th and got a third on 1st January - a very creditable score for a Typhoon pilot. The star of the day however was Dick Audet of 411 (right). He was credited with five kills in a matter of minutes, becoming an 'ace in a day'. He would add five more before falling to Flak on 3rd March 1945.

31st December 1944

137 Sqn	Typh	2TAF	P/O R.A.Egley	FW190 destroyed	NW Osnabrück	1450±
247 Sqn	Typh	2TAF	F/O T.R.Jackson	FW190 destroyed	Petershagen	1208
411 Sqn	Spit	2TAF	F/L J.J.Boyle	Ju88 destroyed	4m SE Rheine	1145±
			F/O M.G.Graham	FW190D destroyed	5m SE Rheine	1145±
416 Sqn	Spit	2TAF	F/O R.W.Tapley	FW190 destroyed	4m SE Metelen	1530
442 Sqn	Spit	2TAF	F/O G.J.Doyle	Bf109 destroyed	SE Munster-Ruhr	1210±
			F/O M.A.Perkins F/L D.M.Pieri	Bf109 destroyed - Shared -	SE Munster-Ruhr	1210±
			F/L R.C.Smith	Bf109 destroyed	SE Munster-Ruhr	1210±
			F/O G.H.Watkin	Bf109 destroyed	SE Munster-Ruhr	1210±

31st December 1944/1st January 1945

85 Sqn	Mosq	BC	F/L A.P.Mellows	He219 destroyed	Unknown	1900±
			F/L P.Endersby	He219 destroyed	Unknown	1945±
219 Sqn	Mosq	2TAF	S/L J.P.Meadows	Ju188 destroyed	N Venlo	0345
			S/L J.P.Meadows	Ju188 destroyed	Venlo	0357
515 Sqn	Mosq	BC	S/L C.V.Bennett	Ju88 destroyed	Lovns Bredning	0115

Chapter Seven

Into Germany

The Allied advances had stalled as winter approached and, to the surprise of the American and British ground commanders, the Germans had unleashed a ferocious armoured assault in December with the intention of splitting the British and American forces and capturing Antwerp. In truth, this was but a bloody and expensive sideshow that robbed the Germans of much of their armour and achieved, in the end, nothing. Now it was the turn of the *Luftwaffe*. At dawn on 1st January 1945 a series of massive airfield strikes took place, taking the RAF and USAAF by surprise and destroying many aircraft. The Germans did not seem to appreciate that aircraft could be - and indeed were - replaced very quickly. Their own losses in aircraft were harder to replace and their losses in trained and experienced fighter pilots and leaders would never be replaced. Very many of these irreplaceable men were among the two hundred or so pilots that did not return that day. The Third Reich was now very firmly on the path to destruction.

1st January 1945

2 Sqn	Spit	2TAF	F/L L.J.Packwood	Bf109 destroyed	W.Amersfoort	0905
137 Sqn	Typh	2TAF	F/L G.Cubley	He111 damaged	10m W Hamelin	0940
			F/O D.E.G.Martyn	- Shared -		
168 Sqn	Typh	2TAF	F/L H.P.Gibbons	FW190 destroyed	Eindhoven	0925
			F/L J.D.Stubbs	Bf109 damaged	Euskirchen	1000
			F/L F.B.Lawless	FW190 destroyed	Euskirchen	1015
268 Sqn	Spit	2TAF	F/L J.B.Lyke	Ju188 destroyed	Nr Zeist	0915
			F/L A.D.Mercer	- Shared -		
			F/L J.B.Lyke	FW190 damaged	Utrecht area	0945

Left: Major Heinz Bär, without doubt one of the greatest fighter pilots in history, led the fighters of JG 3 to strafe Eindhoven airfield on 1st January. They caught several Typhoons on take-off and Bar accounted for two of them. Right: Aftermath. An airfield burns.

Combat Report - 1st January 1945

I was flying Red 2. The Squadron had been on an Armed Recce to Munster and were returning to base after attacking several locomotives. By R/T conversation we learned that 486 Sqdn. were in combat with Huns in an area near base. We opened up and returned to this area in a gradual dive. At 3,000 feet to the East of Volkel we could not see any Huns so I dived down to zero feet and sighted two Tempests chasing a 109G S.E. of Base. The E/A broke starboard and the Tempests broke  away from it and headed towards base. I was about a mile away from the Hun and opening up I overtook him slowly. Chasing him almost due South, N.E. of Helmond I had closed to 500 yards astern of the 109. I fired a short burst aiming ahead of the E/A, endeavoring to make him turn. He still kept straight and level, as I closed to 300 yards I fired another short burst, with no visible results. Closing to 200 yds a short burst produced strikes on the fuselage. Black smoke was emitted from the engine and the 109's speed decreased. I continued firing from line astern, closing rapidly, but the smoke prevented me from observing results, and oil covered my windscreen. I broke Starboard and upwards at 50 yards range, intending to attack again but as I broke to Starboard the E/A turned towards me so I was forced to complete an "S" turn to get onto his tail. As I was positioning myself another Tempest attacked the Hun from line astern, range about 100/150 yards. I saw his strikes and the E/A's engine stopped and the Hun glided straight into a field, belly landed, skidded to Port and hit some trees, in an area due east of Helmond & South of Venrai. As I orbited the scene of the crash intense friendly ack-ack opened up necessitating a hurried retreat from the scene.

I claim one Me. 109G destroyed shared with P/O Shaw.

D.E.Ness, Flying Officer. 56 Squadron

3 Sqn	Temp	2TAF	F/O D.J.Butcher W/O D.R.Worley	Bf109 destroyed - Shared -	3m N Helmond	0935±
			F/O D.J.Butcher W/O D.R.Worley	FW190 destroyed - Shared -	3m N Helmond	0935±
			F/O D.J.Butcher	FW190 destroyed W/O D.R.Worley	3m N Helmond - Shared -	0935±
			F/S M.J.A.Rose	Bf109 destroyed	3m N Helmond	0935±
56 Sqn	Temp	2TAF	F/O D.E.Ness P/O H.Shaw	Bf109 destroyed - Shared -	Near Helmond	1005
80 Sqn	Temp	2TAF	F/O J.W.Garland	FW190 destroyed	15m N Munster	1130
			F/O J.W.Garland	FW190 destroyed	15m N Munster	1130
308 Sqn	Spit	2TAF	Sgt S.Breyner	FW190 destroyed	Near Lockeren	0925±
			F/S Z.Soszynski	FW190 destroyed	Near Lockeren	0925±
			Sgt S.Breyner	FW190 destroyed	Near Lockeren	0925±
			F/L W.Chojnacki	FW190 destroyed	B.61 A/D	0925±

308 Sqn Spit	2TAF	Sgt J.Glowczewski AA unit	FW190 destroyed - Shared -	N Ghent	0925±
		P/O A.Dromlewicz	FW190 destroyed	E Ghent	1000±
		F/L B.Mach	FW190 damaged	B.61 A/D	1000±
		F/L B.Mach	FW190 destroyed	W Terneuzen	1000±
		F/L B.Mach	FW190 destroyed	In river nr Termonde	1000±
		F/L I.Olszewski	FW190 destroyed	E Ghent	1000±
		F/S J.Stanowski	FW190 destroyed	W Ghent	1000±
		F/S J.Stanowski	FW190 destroyed	Ghent	1000±
		W/O S.Bednarczyk	FW190 destroyed	W Terneuzen	1000±
		F/O T.K.Szlenkier	FW190 destroyed	E Ghent	1000±
317 Sqn Spit	2TAF	S/L M.Chelmecki	FW190 destroyed	B.61 A/D	0935±
		F/L R.Hrycak	FW190 prob.dest	B.61 A/D	0935±
		Sgt K.Hubert	FW190 destroyed	Ghent	0935±
		Sgt K.Hubert	FW190 damaged	Near Ghent	0935±
		F/S S.Iwanowski	FW190 damaged	Near Ghent	0935±
		F/L C.Mroczyk	FW190 destroyed	B.61 A/D	0935±
		W/O S.Piesik	FW190 destroyed	Near Ghent	0935±
		W/O S.Piesik	FW190 damaged	Near Ghent	0935±
		W/O Z.Wrowczynski	FW190 destroyed	NE Ghent	0935±
		F/L Z.Zmigrodski	FW190 destroyed	B.61 A/D	0935±
		F/L Z.Zmigrodski	FW190 damaged	B.61 A/D	0935±
401 Sqn Spit	2TAF	F/O G.D.A.T.Cameron	Bf109 destroyed	2-3m radius of base	0925±
		F/O G.D.A.T.Cameron	Bf109 destroyed	2-3m radius of base	0925±
		F/O G.D.A.T.Cameron	Bf109 destroyed	2-3m radius of base	0925±
		F/L W.E.Foster	FW190 damaged	NE Nijmegen	0955±
		F/L J.McKay	FW190 destroyed	Reichwald area	0955±
		F/L J.McKay	Bf109G destroyed	Grave to Nijmegen road	0955±
		F/L J.McKay	FW190 destroyed	NE Grave A/D	0955±
		F/O D.F.Church	Bf109 destroyed	Rheine A/D	1525±
		F/O D.F.Church	FW190 damaged	Rheine A/D	1525±
		P/O D.M.Horsburgh	Bf109 destroyed	Rheine A/D	1525±
		F/L J.C.Lee	Bf109 destroyed	Rheine A/D	1525±
		F/L J.C.Lee	Bf109 prob.dest	Rheine A/D	1525±
		F/L J.McKay F/S A.K.Woodill	Me262 damaged - Shared -	NE Rheine	1525±

Bodenplatte

Top left: Gregory 'Cam' Cameron of 401 Squadron scrambled alone and downed three Bf109s near his base. right: Spitfire IXs of 317 Squadron at Grimbergen, winter 1944. Lower left to right: Flying Officer T.K.Szlenkier of 308 Squadron inspects his kill; Feldwebel Paul Drutschmann of 9./JG 54 baled out of his FW190D-9 following an attack by Pilot Officer A.Dromlewicz of 308 Squadron. Far right, Don Butcher of 3 Squadron joined forces with Doug Worley to bring down two FW190s and a Bf109.

403 Sqn Spit	2TAF	P/O S.Butte	FW190 destroyed	B.56-Evere	0945±
		P/O S.Butte	Bf109 destroyed	B.56-Evere	0945±
		P/O S.Butte	Bf109 destroyed	B.56-Evere	0945±
		F/S G.K.Lindsay	FW190 destroyed	B.56-Evere	0945±
		F/S G.K.Lindsay	FW190 damaged	B.56-Evere	0945±
		P/O M.Reeves	FW190 destroyed	B.56-Evere	0945±
		P/O M.Reeves	FW190 destroyed	B.56-Evere	0945±
411 Sqn Spit	2TAF	F/L R.J.Audet	FW190 destroyed	12m SW Enschede	0940±
		F/L R.J.Audet	FW190 destroyed	12m SW Enschede	0940±
412 Sqn Spit	2TAF	S/L D.H.Dover F/O E.D.Kelly	FW190 destroyed - Shared -	NE Helmond	0950±
		F/L J.B.Doak	FW190 destroyed	NE Helmond	0950±
		F/L B.E.MacPherson	FW190 destroyed	10m NW Venlo	0950±
		F/O V.Smith	FW190 destroyed	NE Venlo	0950±
		F/L W.J.Banks	Ju88 destroyed	Dortmund	1250±
		S/L D.H.Dover	Bf109 destroyed	6m W Guterslohe	1555±
		F/L J.A.Swan	Bf109 destroyed	E Dortmund	1555±
414 Sqn Spit	2TAF	S/L G.Wonnacott	Bf109 destroyed	NE Helmond	0930
		S/L G.Wonnacott	Bf109 destroyed	NE Helmond	0930
		S/L G.Wonnacott	FW190 damaged	NE Helmond	0930
		F/O L.Woloschuk	FW190 destroyed	Near Roermond	1000
		F/O L.Woloschuk	Bf109 damaged	Near Roermond	1000

439 Sqn Typh	2TAF	F/O A.H.Fraser	FW190A destroyed	Near Eindhoven	0945
		F/O A.H.Fraser	FW190D destroyed	Near Eindhoven	0945
		F/O R.H.Lawrence	FW190 destroyed	Near Helmond	0950
		F/O R.H.Lawrence	FW190 prob.dest	Near Helmond	0950
442 Sqn Spit	2TAF	F/L J.P.Lumsden	FW190 damaged	W Venlo	0930
		F/O J.A.T.E.Cousineau - Shared -			
		F/L D.C.Gordon	FW190 destroyed	3m S base	0930±
		F/L D.C.Gordon	FW190 destroyed	3m S base	0930±
		F/L N.A.Keene	FW190 destroyed	NW Venlo	0930±
		F/L J.P.Lumsden	Me262 damaged	S Reichswald Forest	0930±
		F/L D.M.Pieri	FW190 destroyed	W Venlo	0930±
		F/L D.M.Pieri	FW190 destroyed	W Venlo	0930±
		F/L D.M.Pieri	FW190 damaged	W Venlo	0930±
		F/L D.M.Pieri	FW190 damaged	W Venlo	0930±
486 Sqn Temp	2TAF	P/O G.J.Hooper	FW190 destroyed	Venlo	0950±
		P/O G.J.Hooper	Bf109 damaged	Venlo	0950±
		P/O C.J.Sheddon	FW190 destroyed	N Venlo	0950±
		P/O J.Steedman	FW190 damaged	Near Eindhoven	0950±
		F/O W.A.L.Trott	FW190 destroyed	Venlo	0950±
		F/O W.A.L.Trott	Bf109 damaged	Venlo	0950±
		S/L E.A.Umbers	FW190 destroyed	Helmond	0950±
		S/L E.A.Umbers	Bf109 destroyed	Helmond	0950±
610 Sqn Spit	2TAF	F/L F.A.O.Gaze	FW190 destroyed	Malmedy area?	0925±

1/2nd January 1945

23 Sqn	Mosq	BC	S/L J.Tweedale	Ju88 destroyed	nr Ahlhorn	1930
85 Sqn	Mosq	BC	F/L R.T.Goucher	Ju188 destroyed	10m N Münster	1921
			F/L R.T.Goucher	Ju88G destroyed	10m E Dortmund	1936
157 Sqn	Mosq	BC	F/L J.O.Matthews	Ju88 destroyed	S Crailsheim	1940
219 Sqn	Mosq	2TAF	F/L F.F.Reynolds	Bf110 destroyed	20m SE Aachen	2202
406 Sqn	Mosq	FC	F/L R.A.McKay	Ju188 prob.dest	Handorf A/D	2040
			F/L P.E.Etienne	Bf110 destroyed	10m SW Bonninghardt	2115
			F/L R.J.Foster	Ju88 destroyed	A.59	2019
			F/L R.J.Foster	Ju88 destroyed	E.9931	2040
			F/L R.J.Foster	Ju88 destroyed	E.65	2109
604 Sqn	Mosq	2TAF	S/L D.C.Furse	He219 destroyed	F.1580	2109

Bodenplatte - continued

Left: Geoff Wonnacott, a Tac/R Spitfire pilot got two destroyed and one damaged. Centre: Don Pieri of 442 Squadron got two confirmed and two damaged. One victim of Bodenplatte fell to an unlikely cause when the 10./JG 54 'Dora-9' of Leutnant Theo Nibel took a direct hit from a partridge that smashed his radiator. He belly-landed and was captured.

2/3rd January 1945

85 Sqn	Mosq	BC	S/L E.N.Woodman	Ju188 destroyed	Nr Frankfurt	1915
			S/L B.A.Burbridge	Ju88 destroyed	15m SW Ludwigshaven	1925
157 Sqn	Mosq	BC	F/L J.O.Mathews	Ju88 destroyed	10m SW Crailsheim	1940

4th January 1945

3 Sqn	Temp	2TAF	F/L D.C.Fairbanks	FW190 destroyed	13m NE Hengelo	1405
			F/O D,E.Ness	Bf109 destroyed	5m S Osnabruck	1445
			F/L J.H.Ryan	Bf109 destroyed	5m S Osnabruck	1445
80 Sqn	Temp	2TAF	F/O G.A.Bush	FW190 destroyed	12m NE Rheine	1430
			F/S L.B.Crook	FW190 destroyed	12m NE Rheine	1430
			W/O G.W.Dopson	FW190 damaged	12m NE Rheine	1430
			F/O N.J.Rankin	FW190 destroyed	12m NE Rheine	1430
411 Sqn	Spit	2TAF	F/L J.J.Boyle F/L R.J.Audet	FW190 destroyed - Shared -	NE Hengelo A/D	1350±
			F/L R.J.Audet	FW190 destroyed	NW Hengelo AD	1350±
			F/L J.J.Boyle	FW190 destroyed	NE Hengelo AD	1350±

411 Sqn Spit	2TAF	F/L H.D.Carr	FW190 destroyed	Twente AD	1350±
		F/O M.G.Graham	FW190 destroyed	Hengelo	1350±
		F/O M.G.Graham	FW190 destroyed	Hengelo	1350±
442 Sqn Spit	2TAF	F/L M.Johnston	Bf109 prob.dest	10m N Hengelo	1415±
		F/L R.C.Smith	FW190 damaged	10m NE Hengelo	1415±

4/5th January 1945

604 Sqn Mosq	2TAF	F/O P.W.Nicholas	Ju88 destroyed	W Horstmar	0235

5th January 1945

129 Sqn Must	FC	P/O T.Hetherington	Bf109 destroyed	Ludwigshaven	1515
		F/L D.C.Parker	Bf109 destroyed	Ludwigshaven	1515

5/6th January 1945

68 Sqn	Mosq	FC	W/O A.R.Brooking	He111 destroyed	40m E Southwold	2130±
85 Sqn	Mosq	BC	Capt S.Heglund	Bf110 destroyed	N Osnabrück	2230
157 Sqn	Mosq	BC	S/L J.G.Benson	He219 destroyed	18m ENE Hanover	2000
406 Sqn	Mosq	FC	W/C R.Bannock	He111 destroyed	Josum A/D	2025
			W/C R.Bannock	He111 damaged	Josum A/D	2025
515 Sqn	Mosq	BC	F/L A.S.Briggs	Ju88 destroyed	Jagel AD	2026

12/13th January 1945

604 Sqn Mosq	2TAF	W/C F.D.Hughes	Ju188 destroyed	3m S Rotterdam	0200

14th January 1945

3 Sqn	Temp	2TAF	F/L D.C.Fairbanks	Bf109 destroyed	6m SW Paderborn	1105
			F/L D.C.Fairbanks	FW190 destroyed	2m SW Guterslohe	1110
16 Sqn	Spit	2TAF	F/O W.F.Barker	Me163 destroyed	7m SE Dusseldorf	1320
56 Sqn	Temp	2TAF	F/L J.H.Ryan P/O J.E.Hughes	FW190 destroyed - Shared -	SW Guterslohe	1330
			F/O J.J.Payton	FW190 destroyed	SW Guterslohe	1330
64 Sqn	Must	FC	F/L D.A.Drew Sgt A.F.M.Wijting	Ju188 destroyed - Shared -	30m NW Frankfurt	1540
			F/L D.A.Drew Sgt A.F.M.Wijting	FW190 destroyed - Shared -	Frankfurt	1540
			F/S V.B.Cannon	Bf109 destroyed	Frankfurt-Limburg	1540

(Left) Squadron Leader David 'Foob' Fairbanks of 274 Squadron claimed his fourth kill on 4th January, added two more on 14th and, by the time he was taken prisoner on 28th February, had amassed twelve, eleven with the Tempest as the Tempest top-scorer of WW2. 'Spike' Umbers of 486 Squadron (centre) claimed two German fighters destroyed during Bodenplatte (ww2images.com). On 4th January 411 Squadron pilots shot down Leutnant Wilhelm Mayer, commander of 8./JG 26 (right), credited with 27 victories. He did not survive.

64 Sqn	Must	FC	F/O G.Cowpar	FW190 destroyed	Frankfurt	1540
			F/L D.A.Drew	FW190 prob.dest	Frankfurt	1540
			Sgt A.F.M.Wijting	- Shared -		
			F/S L.E.Orton	FW190 destroyed	Frankfurt	1540
			F/O D.A.B.Smiley	FW190 destroyed	Frankfurt	1540
			F/O D.A.B.Smiley	Bf109 destroyed	Frankfurt	1540
			Sgt J.B.Van Mesdag	FW190 destroyed	Frankfurt	1540
184 Sqn	Typh	2TAF	W/O A.J.Cosgrave	Bf109 destroyed	SW Munster	1155±
			W/O J.S.Marshall	Bf109 damaged	SW Munster	1155±
274 Sqn	Temp	2TAF	F/L H.A.Crafts	He219 destroyed	4m E Hamm	0925
331 Sqn	Spit	2TAF	2/Lt J.P.Ditlev-Simonsen	FW190 destroyed	10m W Osnabrück	1530
			Maj M.Y.Gran	Bf109 destroyed	10m W Osnabrück	1530
			Cpt H.G.E.Grundt-Spang	FW190 destroyed	10m W Osnabrück	1530
			Cpt H.G.E.Grundt-Spang	FW190 damaged	10m W Osnabrück	1530
			2/Lt O.K.Roald	Bf109 destroyed	10m W Osnabrück	1530
332 Sqn	Spit	2TAF	Capt K.Bolsted	Me262 destroyed	A/D SW Rheine	1520
			Capt O.G.Aanjesen	FW190 damaged	5m W Osnabruck	1530
			2/Lt O.Wagtskjold	FW190 destroyed	5m W Osnabruck	1530

401 Sqn Spit	2TAF	F/O D.B.Dack	FW190 destroyed	Enschede A/D	1035±
		F/O J.MacKay	FW190 destroyed	Twente A/D	1035±
		F/O J.MacKay	FW190 destroyed	Twente A/D	1035±
		F/O J.MacKay	FW190 destroyed	Twente A/D	1035±
		F/L F.T.Murray	FW190 destroyed	Twente A/D	1035±
411 Sqn Spit	2TAF	F/L R.J.Audet	FW190 destroyed	Enschede	1020±
		F/L J.J.Boyle	FW190 destroyed	4m E Enschede	1020±
		F/O J.A.Doran	FW190 destroyed	2m NE Losser	1020±
442 Sqn Spit	2TAF	F/L J.N.G.Dick	FW190 destroyed	10m SE Enschede	1020±
		F/L J.E.Reade	FW190 destroyed	10m SE Enschede	1020±
		F/O A.J.Urquhart	FW190 destroyed	10m SE Enschede	1020±
486 Sqn Temp	2TAF	W/O C.J.McDonald	Bf109 destroyed	3m N Munster	1155
		W/O J.E.Wood	Bf109 destroyed	E Munster	1210

14/15th January 1945

85 Sqn Mosq	BC	F/L K.D.Vaughan	Ju188 destroyed	5030N 1000E	2143
141 Sqn Mosq	BC	F/L R.Brearley	E/A destroyed	Jüterbog	2135
157 Sqn Mosq	FC	F/S J.Leigh	Bf110 destroyed	5030N 1020E	2330

16/17th January 1945

23 Sqn Mosq	BC	F/L T.Smith	Bf109 destroyed	Fassberg	2135
85 Sqn Mosq	BC	F/L K.D.Vaughan	He219 destroyed	5100N 0900E	2200±
141 Sqn Mosq	BC	F/L D.H.Young	Bf110 destroyed	Magdeburg area	2235
		F/O R.C.Brady	Bf110 destroyed	25m SW Magdeburg	2310
157 Sqn Mosq	BC	F/L A.MacKinnon	Ju188 destroyed	5m E Guterslohe	2310

17th January 1945

3 Sqn Temp	2TAF	F/L D.J.V.Butcher	Bf109 damaged	5m NE Rheine	1600±
401 Sqn Spit	2TAF	F/L L.W.Woods	Bf109 destroyed	Near Arnhem	1450±

17/18th January 1945

219 Sqn Mosq	2TAF	F/L P.G.K.Williamson	Ju88 destroyed	10m E Aachen	0205

22nd January 1945

56 Sqn Temp	2TAF	W/O D.Hutchinson	Bf109 damaged	Near Neede	1215

On 14th January the Norwegian pilots engaged fighters of JG 54, during which Obertleutnant Heinz Seiffert of 11 Staffel was killed. His victor was either John Detlev-Simonsen (centre) or Helner Grundt-Spang, both of 331 Squadron. Detlev-Simonsen chased his opponent into the ground but crashed before he could pull up. It was his first victory. John MacKay of 401 Squadron was more fortunate, credited with shooting down three FW190s of I./JG 1 over Twente airfield, for his fourth to sixth kills. He would end the war with eleven, to which he added a MiG-15 over Korea in 1953 while flying with the USAAF.

56 Sqn	Temp	2TAF	F/O W.R.MacLaren	Bf109 destroyed	Near Neede	1215
168 Sqn	Typh	2TAF	F/L E.C.H.Vernon -Jarvis	Bf109 destroyed	4m E Dulmen	1615
421 Sqn	Spit	2TAF	F/O F.W.Evans	FW190 destroyed	20m E Rheine	1100
			F/L E.S.Smith	FW190D destroyed	E Rheine	1100
			F/L G.E.Stephenson	FW190 destroyed	20m E Rheine	1100
			F/L M.J.Gordon	FW190 destroyed	E Rheine	1100
			F/L T.J.Hoare	FW190 destroyed	E Rheine	1130

22/23rd January 1945

219 Sqn	Mosq	2TAF	F/L G.R.I.Parker	Ju87 destroyed	K.7358	1828
			F/L G.R.I.Parker	Ju87 destroyed	K.7258	1850

23rd January 1945

3 Sqn	Temp	2TAF	F/O H.W.Longley	FW190 destroyed	10m W Guterslohe	1045
			F/O B.Vassiliades	FW190 destroyed	10m W Guterslohe	1045
			F/O B.Vassiliades	FW190 destroyed	10m W Guterslohe	1045
			F/O B.Vassiliades	FW190 damaged	10m W Guterslohe	1045
			F/L J.S.B.Wright	FW190 destroyed	10m W Guterslohe	1045
			F/L J.S.B.Wright	FW190 damaged	10m W Guterslohe	1045
			F/L D.C.Fairbanks W/O J.L.R.Torpey	Ju52 destroyed - Shared -	on t/oGuterslohe	1150
41 Sqn	Spit	2TAF	S/L D.I.Benham	FW190D destroyed	Munster-Wadrop	0930

Peter Williamson of 219 Squadron (far left) claimed his ninth and last victim on the night of 17th March. He had earlier achieved great success in the Middle East. Harold Longley, a Tempest pilot from 3 Squadron, recorded his first kill on 23rd January. Frank 'Casanova' McLeod also drew his first blood on 23rd, when he joined Flying Officer R.V.Dennis in destroying an Me262. - Combat Report opposite.

41 Sqn	Spit	2TAF	S/L D.I.Benham	FW190D destroyed	Munster-Wadrop	0930
			F/O F.M.Hegarty	FW190D destroyed	Munster-Wadrop	0930
			F/L D.J.V.Henry	FW190D damaged	Munster-Wadrop	0930
			F/L W.N.Stowe	FW190D damaged	Munster-Wadrop	0930
56 Sqn	Temp	2TAF	F/O R.V.Dennis F/L F.L.McLeod	Me262 destroyed - Shared -	Achmer	1100
			F/O J.J.Payton	FW190 destroyed	10m NW Rheine	1635
			F/O W.R.MacLaren	FW190 destroyed	10m NW Rheine	1635
			F/O V.L.Turner	Bf109 destroyed	10m NW Rheine	1635
80 Sqn	Temp	2TAF	F/L L.R.G.Smith	Bf109 destroyed	1m NE Lengerich	0920
			F/S L.B.Crook	Bf109 destroyed	SW Guterslohe	0928
			F/L A.Seager	FW190 destroyed	SW Guterslohe	0928
			F/L A.Seager	FW190 prob.dest	SW Guterslohe	0928
			F/S L.B.Crook	FW190 destroyed	E Bohmte	0928
			S/L E.D.Mackie	Bf109 destroyed	1m E Hesepe	1315
			F/L R.J.Holland F/O R.H.Anders	Bf109 destroyed - Shared -	10m NE Achmer	1320
			P/O F.A.Lang F/L D.Price	Bf109 destroyed - Shared -	Bramsche	1320
168 Sqn	Typh	2TAF	F/O J.B.C.Catterns S/L L.H.Lambert F/O P.B.Noble	Ju188 destroyed - Shared - - Shared -	Twente	1710
274 Sqn	Temp	2TAF	F/L R.B.Cole	FW190 damaged	Near Guterslohe	0940
			W/O N.A.Lush	FW190 damaged	Near Guterslohe	0940
			F/L G.Mann	Bf109 destroyed	Near Guterslohe	0940
			F/L G.Mann	Bf109 destroyed	Near Guterslohe	0940
			F/O C.G.Scriven	FW190 destroyed	Near Guterslohe	0940
			F/L L.A.Wood	FW190 destroyed	Near Guterslohe	0940
401 Sqn	Spit	2TAF	F/O D.F.Church	Ar234 destroyed	Bramsche A/D	1030±
			F/L W.C.Connell P/O M.Thomas	Ar234 destroyed - Shared -	Bramsche A/D	1030±

401 Sqn Spit	2TAF	F/O G.A.Hardy	Ar234 destroyed	1½m E Bramsche AD	1030±
		F/L F.T.Murray	Ar234 damaged	Bramsche AD	1030±
		F/L F.T.Murray	Ar234 damaged	Bramsche AD	1030±
		F/O F.E.Thayer	Ar234 damaged	Bransche AD	1030±
		S/L W.T.Klersy	Ar234 damaged	NW Osnabruck	1040±
		F/L W.R.Tew	Ar234 prob.dest	NW Osnabruck	1040±
411 Sqn Spit	2TAF	F/L R.M.Cook	FW190 destroyed	10m NE Munster	1000±
421 Sqn Spit	2TAF	S/L J.D.Browne	FW190 destroyed	Near Lippstadt	1310
		F/O F.W.Evans F/L M.J.Gordon	FW190 destroyed - Shared -	Near Lippstadt	1310
442 Sqn Spit	2TAF	P/O J.P.W.Francis	FW190 damaged	Near Rheine	1355±
486 Sqn Temp	2TAF	F/O R.D.Bremner	FW190 damaged	Near Minden	1330
		F/O R.J.Danzey	FW190 prob.dest	Near Minden	1330
		F/L L.W.Miller	FW190 damaged	Near Minden	1330
		F/O J.H.Stafford W/O A.H.Bailey	Bf109 destroyed - Shared -	Rheine AD	1605
		W/O W.J.Campbell	Bf109 damaged	Rheine AD	1605
		S/L A.E.Umbers	Bf109 destroyed	Rheine AD	1605
411 Sqn Spit	2TAF	F/L R.J.Audet	Me262 destroyed	A/D 6m NE Rheine	1220±

Combat Report - 23rd January 1945

I was flying Yellow 3 on an armed recce to the Hanover area. Whilst orbiting the vicinity of Achmer A/D we saw Spitfires attacking some Me.262's. I saw an E/A flying E. at zero feet across the A/D & broke down onto it with my No. 2 . As we straightened out at zero feet, the a/c was about 3 miles away & slightly to port. The speed gained in the dive helped us to maintain a speed of approx. 400 m.p.h. when we straightened out. Continuing the chase in an easterly direction, we kept slightly below the Hun, the E/A was jinking slightly & we took advantage of this to close the range. After approx. 10 mins. flying the range was closed to 1000 yds. & the E/A was identified as an Me.262. The latter made a gentle turn to port, giving us an immediate advantage, by cutting across the turn we closed to 150 yds. I fired a short burst angle off approx. 30° to port with no apparent effect. My speed was then about 300 I.A.S. Still turning slightly with the 262 I increased deflection to about 40° & fired, observing strikes immediately, I held my fire for about 3 secs. My strikes were on the centre of the fuselage & tail unit; I saw flames & ceased firing. I broke away & next observed the E/A attempting to make a forced landing with the fuselage & starboard jet on fire. He overshot the field which it appeared he was going to land; after his tail unit had hit the ground the a/c lifted & nosed into the next field & exploded. It crashed about 6 miles due south of Nienburg. Cine camera used

I claim 1 Me.262 destroyed, shared with FO R.V. Dennis.

F.L.McLeod, Flying Officer. 56 Squadron

On 23rd January 401 Squadron came upon a group of Ar234 twin-jet bombers circling the airfield at Bramsche. They claimed three destroyed, one 'probable' and four damaged, one of the claimants being Frederick Murray (right) who had claimed his fifth and last confirmed kill on 14th January.

23/24th January 1945

409 Sqn	Mosq	2TAF	F/O M.G.Kent	Ju88G destroyed	Mouth of Schelde	1914
			W/C J.D.Somerville	Ju188 destroyed	3m W Diest	1915

24th January 1945

80 Sqn	Temp	2TAF	F/L R.J.Holland	Bf109 destroyed	2m S Rheine	0845
			F/L D.L.Price	Bf109 destroyed	2m S Rheine	0845
411 Sqn	Spit	2TAF	F/L R.J.Audet	Me262 damaged	Munster	0930±

28/29th January 1945

406 Sqn	Mosq	FC	F/O A.T.Sherrett	Ju188 destroyed	Fanoy	2050

31st January/1st February 1945

85 Sqn	Mosq	BC	F/L A.P.Mellows	He219 destroyed	Near Köln	1824
406 Sqn	Mosq	FC	F/O W.G.Kirkwood	Ju88 destroyed	Ahlhorn A/D	1930
410 Sqn	Mosq	2TAF	S/L R.M.G.Currie	Ju188 destroyed	NW Liege	2320
			F/L W.A.Dexter	Ju88G destroyed	Near Peer	0123
			F/L W.J.Whittaker	Ju88 damaged	Rees	0230
604 Sqn	Mosq	2TAF	F/L C.J.Cross	Ju87 destroyed	Near Sittard	0250
			F/L C.J.Cross	Ju87 destroyed	Near Sittard	0303

1st February 1945

274 Sqn	Temp	2TAF	F/L W.J.Hibbert	FW190 destroyed	Near Rheine	1715

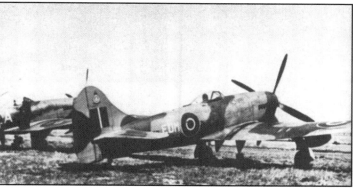

Evan Mackie became one of the top Wing Leaders in 1945. He claimed his seventeenth opponent destroyed on 23rd January while leading 274 Squadron and became Wing Leader 122 Wing in April. He ended the war with a score of twenty, plus three shares. His 122 Wing Tempest is shown right.

1/2 February 1945

25 Sqn	Mosq	FC	F/L J.Lomas	He219 destroyed	NW Germany	2000±
85 Sqn	Mosq	BC	F/L A.P.Mellows	Bf110 destroyed	Stuttgart	1910
219 Sqn	Mosq	2TAF	W/C W.P.Green	Ju88 destroyed	2m SW Rheydt	1910
239 Sqn	Mosq	BC	W/C W.F.Gibb	Bf110 destroyed	Mannheim	2125±
406 Sqn	Mosq	FC	P/O D.MacDonald	Ju188 destroyed	Saarguemines	1945

2nd February 1945

3 Sqn	Temp	2TAF	F/L J.S.B.Wright	Bf109 destroyed	Soltau	1030
			F/L J.S.B.Wright	Bf109 damaged	Soltau	1030
			F/L J.S.B.Wright	Bf109 damaged	Soltau	1030
486 Sqn	Temp	2TAF	F/O R.D.Bremner	Do217 destroyed	AD S Paderborn	1225
			P/O C.J.Sheddan	- Shared -		
			F/O J.H.Stafford	- Shared -		

2/3rd February 1945

85 Sqn	Mosq	BC	W/C W.K.Davison	Ju88 destroyed	4915N 0835E	2315
515 Sqn	Mosq	BC	W/C H.C.Kelsey	Ju88 destroyed	Vechta	2135

3/4th February 1945

409 Sqn	Mosq	2TAF	F/O M.G.Kent	Ju88 destroyed	Nievenheim	2100
410 Sqn	Mosq	2TAF	F/L B.E.Plumer	He219 destroyed	Garzweiler area	2200

7/8th February 1945

29 Sqn	Mosq	FC	F/L J.E.Martin	E/A destroyed		Guterslohe	0015±
239 Sqn	Mosq	BC	F/L D.A.D.Cather	Bf110 destroyed		NE Koln	0215±
			F/L A.J.Holderness	Bf110 destroyed		Ruhr	2330±

8th February 1945

80 Sqn	Temp	2TAF	P/O R.S.E.Verran	FW190 destroyed		20m SE Bremen	0950
274 Sqn	Temp	2TAF	F/L W.J.Hibbert	Bf109 damaged		Near Rheine	0910
			F/O W.F.Mossing	Bf109 destroyed		Rheine	0910
			F/O W.S.J.Stark	Bf109 destroyed		NW Rheine	0910
			F/O T.R.Sutherland	Bf109 destroyed		NW Rheine	0910
402 Sqn	Spit	2TAF	F/L K.S.Sleep	Ju88 destroyed		Coesfeld	0835±
442 Sqn	Spit	2TAF	F/L D.C.Gordon	Ju87 destroyed		SE Wesel	0840±
			F/L D.C.Gordon	Ju87 destroyed		SE Wesel	0840±
			F/L D.C.Gordon F/L G.J.Doyle	Ju87 destroyed - Shared -		Near Wesel, N Ruhr	0840±
			F/L R.B.Barker	Ju87 destroyed		Near Wesel, N Ruhr	0840±
			F/L G.J.Doyle	Ju87 destroyed		Near Wesel, N Ruhr	0840±

9th February 1945

65 Sqn	Must	FC	F/O W.L.Black	FW190 destroyed		Haugesund	1600±
			F/O J.Butler	FW190 destroyed		Haugesund	1600±
			F/L J.W.Foster	FW190 damaged		Haugesund	1600±
			F/L G.Watt	FW190 damaged		Haugesund	1600±
234 Sqn	Must	FC	Maj W.Christie	Ar96 destroyed		Treuchtlingen	1615±
			F/S S.T.Farmiloe	Ar96 destroyed		Treuchtlingen	1615±
			F/S F.G.Stewart	Ar96 destroyed		Treuchtlingen	1615±
326 Sqn	Spit	1TAF	Capt C.J.G.Gauthier Capt R.Motte	Bf109 destroyed - Shared -		Fribourg	1650±

10th February 1945

2 Sqn	Must	2TAF	F/O E.W.A.Jeffries	Bf109G damaged		Lochem	1640
			F/L J.R.MacElwain	Bf109G destroyed		Lochem	1640

11th February 1945

274 Sqn	Temp	2TAF	S/L D.C.Fairbanks	Me262 destroyed		Rheine AD	1105

On 8th February, Flight Lieutenant Ken Sleep of 402 Squadron (above left) caught and destroyed a Ju88 near Coesfeld. It was from NJG 2, flown by Major Paul Semrau, the Kommodore. He was killed. On the same day 442 Squadron pilots found a group of Ju87 Stukas near Wesel and massacred them. Don Gordon (above right) claimed two plus one shared. He would end the war with nine confirmed. The Norwegian pilots - and indeed the RAF - suffered a loss when Rolf Arne Berg, commanding 132 Wing, (right) was killed by Flak during an airfield strafe on 3rd February.

13th February 1945

412 Sqn	Spit	2TAF	F/O E.Gray	Bf110 destroyed	S Lippstadt	1210
			F/L R.P.Harding	- Shared -		
			F/O P.M.Hegarty	- Shared -		

13/14th February 1945

BSDU	Mosq	BC	F/L D.R.Howard	Bf110 destroyed	Near Frankfurt	2033
			F/L D.R.Howard	Bf110 destroyed	Near Frankfurt	2040

14th February 1945

41 Sqn	Spit	2TAF	F/O E.Gray	Me262 damaged	Rheine AD	0815
			F/S C.M.Moyle	FW190D destroyed	Rheine AD	0815
			W/O V.J.Rossow	Me262 damaged	Rheine AD	0815
			W/O L.T.Stevenson	FW190D prob.dest	Rheine AD	0815
			W/O L.T.Stevenson	FW190D damaged	Rheine AD	0815
			F/L F.G.Woolley	FW190D damaged	Rheine AD	0815
80 Sqn	Temp	2TAF	F/O N.J.Rankin	Bf109 destroyed	10m E Celle	1500
184 Sqn	Typh	2TAF	Capt A.F.M.Green	Me262 damaged	N Emmerich	0840
193 Sqn	Typh	2TAF	F/O W.G.Austin	Bf109 destroyed	NE Grave	1333
			W/O K.R.Goodhew	- Shared -		
			F/L J.H.Hilton	- Shared -		

274 Sqn Temp	2TAF	S/L D.C.Fairbanks	Me262 damaged	Rheine - Plantlunne	1700
439 Sqn Typh	2TAF	F/O A.H.Fraser	Me262 destroyed	20m N Coesfeld	0815
		F/O L.C.Shaver	Me262 destroyed	20m N Coesfeld	0815
610 Sqn Spit	2TAF	F/L F.A.O.Gaze	Me262 destroyed	S Emmerich	1710

14/15th February 1945

85 Sqn Mosq	BC	F/L F.D.Win	Ju88 destroyed	Schwabisch Hall AD	0009
406 Sqn Mosq	FC	F/L R.S.Croome	He219 destroyed	SE Gottingen	2230

16th February 1945

65 Sqn Must	FC	W/O J.S.Abbott F/L J.W.Foster	Bf109 destroyed - Shared -	25m SW Aalesund	1430±
		F/L F.H.Bradford	Bf109 destroyed	25m SW Aalesund	1430±
		F/L H.E.Matthews	Bf109 prob.dest	25m SW Aalesund	1430±
		F/L G.S.Pearson	Bf109 destroyed	25m SW Aalesund	1430±
274 Sqn Temp	2TAF	S/L D.C.Fairbanks	Bf109 destroyed	NE Hildesheim	1730
		S/L D.C.Fairbanks	Bf109 destroyed	NE Hildesheim	1730
		F/L W.F.Mossing	Bf109 destroyed	NE Hildesheim	1730
		F/L W.F.Mossing	Bf109 damaged	NE Hildesheim	1730
FEF Mosq	FC	F/L P.S. Compton	FW190 destroyed	Bad Aibling	1700
		F/L P.S. Compton	Bf109 destroyed	Bad Aibling	1727
		F/O K.V.Panter	Bf109 destroyed*	Landau	1727
		F/O K.V.Panter	Bf109 destroyed*	Landau	1727
		F/O K.V.Panter	Bf109 destroyed*	Landau	1727

Note: Panter FTR - PoW. Claims were confirmed post-war.

21st February 1945

268 Sqn Must	2TAF	F/L S.J.Perkins	Me262 damaged	10m S Emmerich	1715
274 Sqn Temp	2TAF	F/L W.J.Hibbert	Ju88 destroyed	S Steinhuder Lake	1700
306 Sqn Must	FC	F/L S.Tronczynski	Do217 destroyed	S Salzwedel	1630
		S/L J.Zulikowski	FW190 destroyed	S Salzwedel	1630
309 Sqn Must	FC	W/O A.Murkowski	FW190 Ddestroyed	25m E Utrecht	1840
313 Sqn Spit	FC	P/O S.W.McCracken	FW190 damaged	E Enschede	1600
315 Sqn Must	FC	S/L T.Andersz	FW190 prob.dest	N Osnabruck	1720
		F/L S.Blok	FW190 destroyed	N Osnabruck	1720
		F/L S.Blok	FW190 damaged	N Osnabruck	1720

On 14th February three pilots from KG(J)51 did not go home. Lyall Shaver - seen here examining a piece of Me262 retrieved from his radiator - and Hugh Fraser (centre) both of 439 Squadron, and Tony Gaze of 610, all destroyed Me262s. Two confirmed kills can be seen below Fraser's cockpit rim, souveniers of 'Operation Bodenplatte' on 1st January. Shaver was later killed in action by Flak .

315 Sqn Must	FC	F/S M.Cempel	FW190 destroyed	N Osnabruck	1720
		W/O B.Czerwinski	FW190 destroyed	N Osnabruck	1720
		F/O T.Haczkiewicz	FW190 destroyed	N Osnabruck	1720
		P/O E.G.Scott	FW190 damaged	N Osnabruck	1720
350 Sqn Spit	2TAF	F/S C.Brahy	Bf109 damaged	Near Rheine	1730
		P/O L.Lambrechts	Bf109 prob.dest	Near Rheine	1730
		P/O L.Lambrechts	Bf109 damaged	Near Rheine	1730
		F/L J.Lavigne	Bf109 destroyed	Rheine-Hopsten area	1730
		F/O A.Van Wersch	Bf109 destroyed	Near Rheine	1730
412 Sqn Spit	2TAF	F/L L.A.Stewart	Me262 damaged	6m E Emmerich	1700±

21/22nd February 1945

157 Sqn Mosq	BC	S/L T.Ryall	Bf110 prob.dest	25m SW Ober Olm AD	2025
239 Sqn Mosq	BC	W/C W.F.Gibb	FW190 destroyed	15m E Worms	2200±
406 Sqn Mosq	FC	W/O F.E.Hamburgh	E/A damaged	Handorf A/D	1940
		F/L D.A.MacFayden	Bf110 destroyed	2m S by E Stormede A/D	2016
488 Sqn Mosq	2TAF	F/L K.W.Stewart	Ju88G destroyed	Groenlo	2058

22nd February 1945

3 Sqn	Temp	2TAF	P/O J.K.Foster	Bf109 damaged	Near Rheine	1445
56 Sqn	Temp	2TAF	S/L P.R.St Quentin	FW190 destroyed	Near Cloppenburg	1420
182 Sqn	Typh	2TAF	F/O W.J.Boots	Ju88 destroyed	NNE Hamm	1020

182 Sqn Typh	2TAF	F/L T.Entwistle	- Shared -		
		F/O I.Ladely	- Shared -		
		F/L D.Murray	- Shared -		
274 Sqn Temp	2TAF	S/L D.C.Fairbanks	FW190 destroyed	NE Rheine A/D	1740
		S/L D.C.Fairbanks	FW190 destroyed	NE Rheine A/D	1740
486 Sqn Temp	2TAF	F/O A.R.Evans	Bf109 destroyed	15m S Munster	1520
		F/O J.H.Stafford	Bf109 destroyed	15m S Munster	1520
122 Wg Temp	2TAF	W/C R.E.P.Brooker	Bf109 damaged	Near Rheine	1445

23rd February 1945

309 Sqn Must	FC	W/O A.Pietrzak	Me262 damaged	Ruhr area	1552

24th February 1945

137 Sqn Typh	2TAF	F/O J.A.Forrest	Bf109 damaged	A.6350	0850
274 Sqn Temp	2TAF	S/L D.C.Fairbanks	FW190 destroyed	Plantlunne	1030
		F/L R.C.Kennedy	Me262 damaged	Near Plantlunne	1740
		F/L R.C.Kennedy	Ju88 destroyed	5m E Plantlunne	1745
		F/L W.F.Mossing	- Shared -		
332 Sqn Spit	2TAF	F/S B.Storaas	FW190 destroyed	NE Zutphen	1000
442 Sqn Spit	2TAF	F/O J.A.T.E.Cousineau	Bf109 destroyed	Near Rheine	1010±
486 Sqn Temp	2TAF	F/L N.J.Powell	Bf109 destroyed	4m NE Bramsche	1010
		S/L K.G.Taylor -Cannon	Bf109 destroyed	4m NE Bramsche	1010

24/25th February 1945

219 Sqn Mosq	2TAF	W/C W.P.Green	Ju87 destroyed	E Julich	2310±
FEF Mosq	FC	F/O R.E.Lelong	FW190 destroyed	Ludwigslust	2138
		F/O R.E.Lelong	FW190 destroyed	Ludwigslust	2138

25th February 1945

33 Sqn Temp	2TAF	F/L A.W.Bower	Bf109 destroyed	S Rheine	0730
		F/L A.W.Bower	Bf109 damaged	S Rheine	0730
		F/S J.E.Fraser	Bf109 damaged	10m SW Rheine	0730
		F/L L.C.Luckhoff	Bf109 destroyed	10m SW Rheine	0730
		F/L L.C.Luckhoff	Bf109 destroyed	10m SW Rheine	0730
		S/L I.G.S.Matthew	Bf109 destroyed	10m SW Rheine	0730

Already an accomplished V-1 killer, Antoni Murkowski (left) of 309 Squadron claimed his second kill on 21st February. Ludovik Lambrechts (centre) opened his scoring on 21st February when 350 Squadron engaged Bf109s of JG 27 over Rheine airfield. Walter 'Jesse' Hibbert of 274 Squadron (right) claimed his fourth victory on February 21st.

33 Sqn	Temp	2TAF	Lt E.D.Thompson	Bf109 damaged	10m SW Rheine	0730
			Lt E.D.Thompson	Bf109 damaged	10m SW Rheine	0730
41 Sqn	Spit	2TAF	F/L D.J.Reid	FW190D destroyed	Rheine A/D	0815
56 Sqn	Temp	2TAF	F/O R.V.Dennis	Bf109 destroyed	15m W Munster	0810
			F/L F.L.MacLeod	Bf109 destroyed	15m W Munster	0810
402 Sqn	Spit	2TAF	F/L B.E.Innis	Me262 damaged	SW Twente	0845±
			F/L K.S.Sleep	- Shared -		
412 Sqn	Spit	2TAF	F/L H.W.McLeod	Bf109 destroyed	5m E Enschede	0800±
			F/L H.W.McLeod	Bf109 prob.dest	5m E Enschede	0800±
416 Sqn	Spit	2TAF	P/O L.E.Spurr	Me262 damaged	NE Munster	0900
442 Sqn	Spit	2TAF	P/O E.C.Baker	Bf109 destroyed	Near Rheine	1140±
			P/O E.C.Baker	Bf109 destroyed	Near Rheine	1140±
			F/L R.B.Barker	Bf109 destroyed	Near Rheine	1140±
			F/L R.B.Barker	Bf109 destroyed	Near Rheine	1140±
			F/L R.B.Barker	Bf109 damaged	Rheine A/D	1140±
			F/L D.C.Gordon	Bf109 destroyed	Rheine A/D	1140±
			F/L R.K.Trumley	Bf109 destroyed	Near Rheine	1140±
			F/L R.K.Trumley	Bf109 destroyed	Near Rheine	1140±

26/27th February 1945

406 Sqn	Mosq	FC	F/O E.A.Oswald	Ju88 damaged	Neubiberg AD	2120

27th February 1945

326 Sqn	Spit	1TAF	Capt H.Jeandet	Bf109 destroyed	Hamersbach	1500±
			Capt de Corvette P.Sire - Shared -			

326 Sqn Spit	1TAF	Capt C.J.G.Gauthier	Bf109 destroyed	Horb	1500±
		Lt Y.Prunget	- Shared -		
		Capt de Corvette P.Sire	- Shared -		
		Sgt D.Roussel	- Shared -		

28th February 1945

3 Sqn	Temp	2TAF	F/L H.K.Hughes	Bf109 damaged	S Hildesheim	1045
			F/L J.A.McCairns	- Shared -		
			F/L H.K.Hughes	Si204 destroyed	S Hildesheim	1045
			F/L J.A.McCairns	- Shared -		
268 Sqn Mosq	2TAF		F/L S.J.Perkins	FW190 damaged	2m N Krefeld	1246
274 Sqn Temp	2TAF		F/S A.E.Gunn	FW190 damaged	9m NE Osnabruck	0800
			F/S A.E.Gunn	FW190 damaged	9m NE Osnabruck	0800
			F/S A.E.Gunn	FW190 damaged	9m NE Osnabruck	0800
			F/S A.C.Inglis	FW190 damaged	9m NE Osnabruck	0800
			F/L F.W.Mossing	FW190 damaged	9m NE Osnabruck	0800

1st March 1945

245 Sqn Typh	2TAF	F/S J.E.Adam	Bf109 prob.dest	Near Bocholt	0918
		P/O R.N.M.Brown	- Shared -		
401 Sqn Spit	2TAF	S/L W.T.Klersey	Bf109 destroyed	Near Dorsten	0910
		S/L W.T.Klersey	Bf109 destroyed	Near Dorsten	0910
		S/L W.T.Klersey	FW190 destroyed	Near Dorsten	0910
		F/L J.MacKay	FW190 destroyed	Near Dorsten	0910
		F/L J.MacKay	FW190 damaged	Near Dorsten	0910
		F/L J.MacKay	Bf109 damaged	Near Dorsten	0910
		F/O A.E.Sawyer	Bf109 prob.dest	Near Dorsten	0910

2nd March 1945

3 Sqn	Temp	2TAF	S/L R.B.Cole	FW190 destroyed	Near Rheine	u/k
41 Sqn	Spit	2TAF	F/L D.J.Reid	Ar234 destroyed	Near Enschede	0750
80 Sqn	Temp	2TAF	F/L R.J.Holland	Bf109 damaged	N Rheine	0850
130 Sqn Spit	2TAF		W/O J.A.Boulton	FW190 destroyed	NE Rheine	0800
			F/S P.H.T.Clay	FW190 destroyed	NE Rheine	0800
			F/L G.G.Earp	FW190 destroyed	NE Rheine	0800
			F/L C.J.Samouelle	FW190 destroyed	NE Rheine	0800
			F/L C.J.Samouelle	FW190 damaged	NE Rheine	0800
			W/O J.W.Turnbull	FW190 prob.dest	NE Rheine	0800
			W/O J.W.Turnbull	FW190 damaged	NE Rheine	0800
137 Sqn Typh	2TAF		W/O J.A.Cunningham	Bf109 damaged	Dulmen	1725

It was not always success for the RAF. On 28th February 274 Squadron Tempest pilots flew a sweep to Rheine, meeting FW190s near Osnabruck. Both Squadron Leader David Fairbanks (left) and Flying Officer John Spence (right) were shot down, by Oberleutnant Theobald Kraus and Unteroffizier Karl-Georg Genth of 10./JG 26.

182 Sqn Typh	2TAF	F/O P.J.Spellman	Bf109 damaged	W Dulmen	1725
222 Sqn Temp	2TAF	F/L V.W.Berg	Bf109 destroyed	5m E Lingen	0800±
		F/L G.W.Varley	Ar234 damaged	Near Rheine	0800±
		P/O R.A.Carson	- Shared -		
		W/O T.B.Hannam	Ar234 damaged	5m E Lingen	0800±
		F/L L.McAuliffe	Bf109 destroyed	5m E Lingen	0800±
		F/O H.E.Turney	Bf109 destroyed	5m E Lingen	0800±
		F/L G.W.Varley	Bf109 destroyed	5m E Lingen	0800±
		F/L G.W.Varley	Ar234 destroyed	5m E Lingen	0800±
350 Sqn Spit	2TAF	F/S J.Groensteen	Bf109 destroyed	NE Rheine	0800
		F/L R.Hoornaert	Bf109 destroyed	NE Rheine	0800
		P/O L.Lambrechts	Bf109 destroyed	NE Rheine	0800
		F/S E.Pauwels	Bf109 damaged	NE Rheine	0800
125 Wg Spit	2TAF	W/C G.Keefer	Bf109 destroyed	NE Rheine	0745

3/4th March 1945

68 Sqn Mosq	FC	F/L D.B.Wills	Ju188 destroyed	40m E Cromer	0230±
		F/L R.B.Miles	Ju188 destroyed	Off East Anglia	0245±
125 Sqn Mosq	FC	W/O D.P.Griffiths	Ju188 destroyed	North Sea	0215
307 Sqn Mosq	FC	F/L C.Tarkowski	Ju188 destroyed	15m WNW Bonn	2256
406 Sqn Mosq	FC	F/L H.G.MacKenzie	Ju88 destroyed	Rheine	2048

4/5th March 1945

456 Sqn Mosq	FC	F/O R.D.Hodgen	Ju188 damaged	30m E Spurn Head	2135

5th March 1945

274 Sqn Temp	2TAF	F/L P.H.Closterman	Bf109 destroyed	Near Hengelo	1715

On 5/6th March Walter Gibb of 239 Squadron claimed his third and fourth kills. One of these was a Ju88G-6 flown by Major Borchers, Kommodore of NJG 5, credited with 43 victories (right). He did not survive.

5/6th March 1945

239 Sqn	Mosq	BC	W/C W.F.Gibb	Ju88 destroyed	30m SW Leipzig	2255±
			W/C W.F.Gibb	Ju88 destroyed	40m N Chennitz	2315±
406 Sqn	Mosq	FC	F/L D.A.MacFayden	Ju88G destroyed	Gerolzhofen	2320

7th March 1945

3 Sqn	Temp	2TAF	F/O B.M.Vassiliades	FW190 destroyed	Near Rheine	1540
56 Sqn	Temp	2TAF	F/O J.J.Payton	FW190 destroyed	Twente-Rheine	1545
			F/O V.L.Turner	Bf109 destroyed	Twente-Rheine	1545
80 Sqn	Temp	2TAF	S/L E.D.Mackie	FW190 destroyed	N Rheine	1545

7/8th March 1945

23 Sqn	Mosq	BC	F/O E.L.Heath	FW190 destroyed	Stendal	2330
406 Sqn	Mosq	FC	F/O A.T.Sherrett	Ju88 damaged	Grove	2040±

8/9th March 1945

85 Sqn	Mosq	BC	F/L J.A.Dobie	Ju188 destroyed	Hagen	2204

9th March 1945

414 Sqn	Spit	2TAF	F/L R.J.Cutting	FW190 destroyed	Near Coesfeld	1505
			F/L R.J.Cutting	FW190 damaged	Near Coesfeld	1505

12 March 1945

19 Sqn	Must	FC	F/L J.Butler	Bf109 prob.dest	90m SW Kristiansand	1600±

Peter Hearne, CO of 19 Squadron (left) claimed his third kill on 12th March and Harry Walmsley of 130 Squadron got his fourth on the 13th. He would go on to command 350 Squadron and ended the war with eleven confirmed kills.

19 Sqn	Must	FC	S/L P.J.Hearne	Bf109 destroyed	90m SW Kristiansand	1600±
401 Sqn	Spit	2TAF	F/L L.N.Watt	Me262 destroyed	SW Wesel	1700±

12/13th March 1945

604 Sqn	Mosq	2TAF	F/L J.W.E.Welford	Ju88 prob.dest	Off Den Haag	0210

13th March 1945

130 Sqn	Spit	2TAF	F/L I.R.Ponsford	FW190 destroyed	5m N Hamm	1655
			F/L I.R.Ponsford	FW190 damaged	5m N Hamm	1655
			F/L H.Walmsley	FW190 destroyed	5m N Hamm	1655
			F/S P.H.T.Clay	FW190 destroyed	5m N Hamm	1655
340 Sqn	Spit	2TAF	Sgt/Ch D.Boudard	Bf109 damaged	Near Bocholt	1250
			Lt J.Carre	Bf109 damaged	Near Bocholt	1250
			Sgt/Ch De Reynal	Bf109 prob.dest	Near Bocholt	1250
			Capt O.Massart	Bf109 damaged	Near Bocholt	1250
350 Sqn	Spit	2TAF	S/L F.Woolley	FW190 destroyed	10m NE Hamm	1425
402 Sqn	Spit	2TAF	F/O H.C.Nicholson	Me262 destroyed	E Munster	1655
145 Wg	Spit	2TAF	W/C R.W.F.Sampson	Bf109 destroyed	Near Bocholt	1250

14th March 1945

222 Sqn	Temp	2TAF	F/L L.McAuliffe	Ar234 destroyed	N Quakenbruck	1715±
			F/O D.G.C.McLeland	- Shared -		

14/15th March 1945

141 Sqn Mosq	BC	F.O. R.D.S.Gregory	E/A destroyed	Lachen	2220±
157 Sqn Mosq	BC	S/L R.D.Doleman	Ju88G destroyed	Lutzkendorf	2157

15th March 1945

80 Sqn	Temp	2TAF	F/O F.A.Lang	Ar234 damaged	5m N Rheine	1200

15/16th March 1945

85 Sqn	Mosq	BC	Capt E.P.Fossum	Ju88 destroyed	Near Hannover	2144

16/17 March 1945

157 Sqn Mosq	BC	F/L J.O.Mathews	Ju88 destroyed	20m S Wurzburg	2111
239 Sqn Mosq	BC	S/L D.L.Hughes	Ju188 destroyed	Nuremburg	2245±
406 Sqn Mosq	FC	F/O A.T.Sherrett	E/A damaged	Crailsheim	2240
		S/L S.E.Murray	Bf110 damaged	Kitzingen	2325

17th March 1945

412 Sqn Spit	2TAF	S/L M.D.Boyd	FW190 destroyed	5m SW Coesfeld	1705±
		F/O V.Smith	- Shared -		
		P/O H.W.Grant	FW190 destroyed	5m SW Coesfeld	1705±

18th March 1945

326 Sqn Spit	1TAF	S/Lt P.Boillot	Bf109 destroyed	Freudenstadt	1650

18/19th March 1945

157 Sqn Mosq	BC	W/O D.A.Taylor	Ju88 destroyed	Hanau	0435
239 Sqn Mosq	BC	W/C W.F.Gibb	He219 destroyed	Witten	0550±

19th March 1945

130 Sqn Spit	2TAF	F/O W.H.Carter	Bf109 damaged	Rheine AD	0930
		F/S P.T.H.Clay	Bf109 damaged	Rheine AD	0930
		F/S G.W.Hudson	Bf109 destroyed	Rheine AD	0930
		F/S G.W.Hudson	Bf109 damaged	Rheine AD	0930
		F/O G.Lord	Bf109 destroyed	Rheine AD	0930

Frank Woolley of 350 Squadron (left) claimed his first victory on 13th March, moving to lead 130 Squadron in April and adding three further kills before the surrender. Olivier Massart of 340 Squadron had two confirmed victories before making a claim for a 'damaged' on 13th March. He was shot down immediately afterwards, baling out to become a 'short-term' prisoner.

130 Sqn	Spit	2TAF	F/O G.Lord	Bf109 damaged	Rheine AD	0930
			W/O A.D.Miller	Bf109 damaged	Rheine AD	0930
326 Sqn	Spit	1TAF	Lt Y.Prunget	FW190 destroyed	Kronau	1735
			Capt de Corvette P.Sire - Shared -			
125 Wg	Spit	2TAF	W/C G.C.Keefer	Bf109 destroyed	Rheine AD	0930

19/20th March 1945

85 Sqn	Mosq	BC	F/L F.D.Win	Bf110 destroyed	Kitzingen	0521

20/21st March 1945

85 Sqn	Mosq	BC	F/L G.C.Chapman	He219 destroyed	30m NW Kassel	0408
			F/L G.C.Chapman	Bf110 destroyed	4900N 0940E	2210
125 Sqn	Mosq	FC	F/L K.Kennedy	Ju188 destroyed	10m E Cromer	2135
406 Sqn	Mosq	FC	F/O D.J.M.McConnell	Ju88 damaged	Marx	0510

21/22nd March 1945

406 Sqn	Mosq	FC	S/L D.B.Freeman	Ju87 destroyed	Kralupy	2345
			S/L D.B.Freeman	Ju87 destroyed	Kralupy	2350
409 Sqn	Mosq	2TAF	F/L R.I.E.Britten	Bf110 destroyed	SE Remscheid	0359
488 Sqn	Mosq	2TAF	F/O K.Fleming	Bf110 destroyed	Near Dortmund	0522

Mustang pilots were kept busy on 23rd March, flying long-range escorts and Rangers. Michael Giddings of 118 Squadron claimed an Me262 damaged near Bremen. He would rise to high post-war rank in the RAF. Mustangs of 309 Squadron (right) out 'looking for trouble' over Germany.

22nd March 1945

56 Sqn	Temp	2TAF	Sgt P.C.Brown	FW190 destroyed	Hesepe	1612
			F/L J.T.Hodges	FW190 destroyed	Hesepe	1612
			F/L G.B.Milne	FW190 destroyed	Hesepe	1612
			F/O V.L.Turner	FW190 destroyed	Hesepe	1612
80 Sqn	Temp	2TAF	F/O G.A.Bush	FW190 destroyed	Hesepe	1612
			F/L R.C.Cooper	FW190 destroyed	Hesepe	1612
			F/O N.J.Rankin	FW190 damaged	Hesepe	1612
			F/L A.Seager	FW190 damaged	Hesepe	1612

Combat Report - 19th March 1945

I was Blue 1 and was with the Squadron on a sweep to the Rheine-Osnabruck area. When Huns were reported at about 0930 I dropped my tank and went down and saw a number of e/a circling the aerdrome at Rheine at about 1,000 ft. I went in behind one ME 109 and closed very fast. The e/a took no evasive action and I opened fire with all guns from dead astern from about 200 yards closing to 50 yards. I saw strikes behind the cockpit. I overshot this e/a and I saw him crash land on the aerodrome. I claim this e/a damaged.

After this I pulled round and saw another 109 but as I closed in I overshot him. The e/a was trying to turn so I pulled round on to him a second time and got behind him. The e/a was trying to do a tight turn. I turned inside him and fired from 200 yards. I saw strikes behind the cockpit and the machine blew up in the air. The pilot was able to bale out and I saw the parachute go down and finish up in a tree about a quarter mile to the east of the aerodrome.

I claim this E/A destroyed.

W/Cdr Keefer reports that after his combat he saw a parachute going down over the east end of the aerodrome.

G Lord, Flying Officer. 130 Squadron

23rd March 1945

118 Sqn Must	FC	F/O J.L.Evans	Me262 damaged	12m SSW Bremen	1005
		F/L K.C.M.Giddings	Me262 damaged	Near Bremen	1005
		F/L W.Harbison	Me262 damaged	Near Bremen	1005
126 Sqn Must	FC	F/O A.D.Yeardley	Me262 destroyed	Harpstedt	1015
129 Sqn Must	FC	F/L G.H.Davis	Me262 damaged	SW Bremen	1020
309 Sqn Must	FC	W/O A.Pietrzak	Me262 damaged	10m S Dummer Lake	1552

23/24th March 1945

219 Sqn Mosq	2TAF	F/L J.C.E.Atkins	FW189 destroyed	Huckingen, nr Duisburg	2115

Chapter Eight

The Reich Collapses

On 23rd March the British Second and American Ninth Armies prepared to cross the Rhine into Germany. This was codenamed *'Operation Plunder'* while an airborne assault became *'Operation Varsity'*. The area of Wesel was prepared by a huge artillery strafe, supported by widespread RAF fighter-bomber missions and, under cover of darkness, the amphibious assault commenced. At dawn on 24th, the airborne attack commenced, despite desperate counter-attacks. Within two days a huge bridgehead had been established and the battle for Germany commenced in earnest. Prime task of the 21st Army Group was to reach the Elbe River and, moving north, to take the great ports of Bremen, Kiel and Hamburg. The task of the 2nd TAF was to destroy the rail and road transport systems, provide close air support to the troops and, above all, to hunt down and destroy the *Luftwaffe*. One important facet of this latter task was the battle against German jets, known as 'rat-catching'. This involved a pair of Tempest pilots on readiness to fly to the airfields around Rheine and attack Me262s on their landing approaches. As the campaign continued, this was expanded to include large-scale airfield strafes. Such was the ferocity of the *Flak* defences that this was a highly dangerous business.

24/25th March 1945

410 Sqn	Mosq	2TAF	F/L G.R.Leask	Bf110 destroyed	Near Greffelkamp	2200
			S/L I.E.McTavish	Ju88G destroyed	Near Etten	0235
604 Sqn	Mosq	2TAF	F/L L.J.Leppard	Bf109 destroyed	Haltern area	2035

25th March 1945

65 Sqn	Must	FC	F/L F.H.Bradford	FW190 destroyed	S Bremanger	1600±
			F/L F.H.Bradford	FW190 damaged	S Bremanger	1600±
			F/O D.W.Davis	FW190 destroyed	S Bremanger	1600±
			W/O J.D.Howells	FW190 destroyed	S Bremanger	1600±
80 Sqn	Temp	2TAF	F/O W.R.Sheaf	Bf109 destroyed	Rees, NE Wesel	0641
127 Sqn	Spit	2TAF	P/O E.A.W.Smith	Bf109 destroyed	SW Bocholt	0725
			F/L A.T.Willis	- Shared -		
222 Sqn	Temp	2TAF	F/L R.P.Dashwood	Bf109 destroyed	Beckum	0705±
			F/O G.W.Marshall	Bf109 destroyed	4m E Beckum	0705±
			F/L W.G.Mart	Bf109 destroyed	Beckum	0705±
			F/O R.H.Reid	- Shared -		
			F/L H.E.Turney	- Shared -		
			F/L H.E.Turney	Bf109 destroyed	3m E Beckum	0705±
			F/L G.W.Varley	FW190 destroyed	SW Quakenbruck	1350±

222 Sqn	Temp	2TAF	F/O W.Donald	FW190 destroyed	SW Quakenbruck	1350±
			F/L G.F.J.Jongbloed	FW190 destroyed	2m NE Haselunne	1350±
412 Sqn	Spit	2TAF	S/L M.D.Boyd	Bf109 destroyed	5m S Winterwijk	1810±
			F/L D.M.Pieri	Bf109 destroyed	5m S Winterwijk	1810±
			F/O V.Smith	Bf109 destroyed	5m S Winterwijk	1810±
PH Wg	Must	FC	W/C P.R.W.Wickham	FW190 damaged	S Bremanger	1600±

25/26th March 1945

219 Sqn	Mosq	2TAF	F/L W.L.Ruffley	Bf110 destroyed	SW Munster	2115
264 Sqn	Mosq	2TAF	S/L C.M.Ramsay	Ju88 destroyed	25m NNE Wesel	2235
			F/L A.Recina	Ju88 damaged	N Nijmegen	2055
409 Sqn	Mosq	2TAF	F/L R.I.E.Britten	Ju88 destroyed	Near Dortmund	2245

26th March 1945

33 Sqn	Temp	2TAF	S/L A.W.Bower F/S C.P.Nisbett	FW190 destroyed - Shared -	10m SE Munster	1520
			F/O R.H.Brown	FW190 destroyed	10m SE Munster	1520
			F/O R.H.Brown	FW190 damaged	10m SE Munster	1520

Combat Report -25th March 1945:

I was flying Blue 3 at approx 9000 feet in the CLOPPENBURG area when aircraft were reported at 12 o'clock above. A few seconds later I sighted 4 FW190's (short nose) at approx 7,000 feet crossing from our starboard to port, diving in NW direction. Blue 1 (F/L Varley) turned to port after the first enemy aircraft and I pulled up over his starboard side to cover his tail against another FW190 which I observed to be following him. This enemy aircraft however then pulled up behind me and we started doing tight turns, gradually losing height. The advantage was at first, slightly with the FW190, which advantage he gradually lost through flicking near the ground which compelled him to slacken his rate of turn. We were now approx 500 feet from the ground. I pulled up and, diving down again gave a one second burst from approx 300 yards with 1½ rings deflection, observing strikes on the tail. I gave two more bursts head on, strikes being observed during the second burst. The FW190 flew past me and, flicking over, one and a half rolls, dived straight into the ground at a position which I pin-point at V 8656. The combat was witnessed by Red 4 (F/O Donald) and by Blue 4 (F/O Roberts).

G.F.J.Jongbloed, Flight Lieutenant. 222 Squadron)

Wing Commander Peter Wickham (left) at the head of the Peterhead Wing, had his last successful combat of the war on 25th March when he damaged a Bf109 near Bremanger. His total stood at ten confirmed. On the night of 26th March Flight Lieutenant Ken Stewart of 488 Squadron claimed his fourth confirmed kill and would end the war with five.

26/27th March 1945

219 Sqn	Mosq	2TAF	F/O G.F.J.Reed	Ju188 destroyed	Zwolle	2325
410 Sqn	Mosq	2TAF	F/L B.E.Plumer	Bf110 destroyed	SW Walsum, E Wesel	2230
488 Sqn	Mosq	2TAF	F/L J.A.S.Hall	Ju88 destroyed	20m N Emmerich	2300
			F/L K.W.Stewart	Bf110 destroyed	8m NW Bocholt	0005
			F/L K.W.Stewart	He111 damaged	Haltern	0030
604 Sqn	Mosq	2TAF	F/O T.R.Wood	Ju88 destroyed	4m SE Wesel	0210

27th March 1945

154 Sqn	Must	FC	W/O V.A.Bunting	FW190 prob.dest	S Lubeck	1535
			F/L N.Lee P/O R.Todd	FW190 damaged - Shared -	S Lubeck	1535
Hun Wg	Must	FC	Lt Col W.Christie	FW190 destroyed	S Lubeck	1535
			Lt Col W.Christie	FW190 destroyed	S Lubeck	1535
			Lt Col W.Christie	FW190 damaged	S Lubeck	1535

27/28th March 1945

219 Sqn	Mosq	2TAF	F/O G.F.J.Reed	He177 destroyed	5m SE Nijmegen	2220

28 March 1945

41 Sqn	Spit	2TAF	F/L T.E.Lawrence	FW190 damaged	Rheine A/D	1310
80 Sqn	Temp	2TAF	F/L A.Seager	Bf109 prob.dest	Osnabruck	1550
			P/O G.W.Dopson	Bf109 prob.dest	Osnabruck	1610
			P/O H.F.Ross	Bf109 damaged	Osnabruck	1610
130 Sqn	Spit	2TAF	W/O J.A.Boulton	FW190 destroyed	S Warendorf	1645
			W/O J.A.Boulton	FW190 prob.dest	S Warendorf	1645

130 Sqn	Spit	2TAF	F/S P.H.T.Clay	FW190 destroyed	S Warendorf	1645
			F/S P.H.T.Clay	FW190 damaged	S Warendorf	1645
			F/O D.A.Stott	FW190 destroyed	S Warendorf	1645
			W/O R.E.Coverdale	- Shared -		
			F/L P.E.Sibeth	FW190 destroyed	S Warendorf	1645
			F/L H.Walmsley	FW190 destroyed	S Warendorf	1645
			F/L H.Walmsley	FW190 destroyed	S Warendorf	1645
			Sgt G.D.Warren	FW190 destroyed	S Warendorf	1645
			F/S B.W.Woodman	FW190 destroyed	S Warendorf	1645
			F/S B.W.Woodman	FW190 damaged	S Warendorf	1645
401 Sqn	Spit	2TAF	F/L J.MacKay	Bf109 destroyed	Dulmen-Coesfeld	1615±
			F/L J.MacKay	Bf109 destroyed	Dulmen-Coesfeld	1615±
416 Sqn	Spit	2TAF	F/L J.W.E.Harten	FW190 destroyed	NE Emmerich	1550
			F/L J.W.E.Harten	FW190 destroyed	NE Emmerich	1550
443 Sqn	Spit	2TAF	F/O W.B.Dalton	Bf109 damaged	S Borken	1600

30th March 1945

402 Sqn	Spit	2TAF	F/L H.J.Cowan	FW190 destroyed	SW Oldenburg	1600±

30/31st March 1945

604 Sqn	Mosq	2TAF	W/C E.S.Smith	Bf109 destroyed	12m NW Dulmen	2024

31st March 1945

80 Sqn	Temp	2TAF	F/O K.Burton	Ju188 destroyed	5m W Dummer See	1800
			F/O G.A.Bush	- Shared -		
			F/L R.C.Cooper	- Shared -		
			P/O G.W.Dopson	- Shared -		
126 Sqn	Must	FC	F/O A.D.Yeardley	Me262 damaged	Bremen-Hamburg	0845
402 Sqn	Spit	2TAF	F/L B.E.Innes	FW190 destroyed	8m W Oldenburg	0700±
			F/O R.W.Lawson	FW190 destroyed	8m W Oldenburg	0700±
			F/O R.W.Lawson	FW190 destroyed	8m W Oldenburg	0700±
421 Sqn	Spit	2TAF	P/O O.H.Levere	FW190 destroyed	12m E Nordhorn A/D	0640

1/2nd April 1945

151 Sqn	Mosq	FC	F/O A.Hollingsworth	Me410 destroyed	15m NW Augsburg	0144

Sigismond Neulinger (left) and Robert Muls (right) of 350 Squadron joined forces on 5th April to destroy an FW190, probably that flown by Unteroffizier Kurt Soder of 15./JG 26.
    (via Serge Bonge).

2nd April 1945

56 Sqn	Temp	2TAF	F/L P.H.Clostermann	FW190 destroyed	Ahlhorn A/D	1910

2/3 April 1945

406 Sqn	Mosq	FC	W/O F.E.Hamburgh	Ju188 destroyed	Schleswig	2350

3 April 1945

126 Sqn	Must	FC	P/O D.Kingsbury	Bf109 destroyed	SW Nordhausen	1700±

3/4th April 1945

239 Sqn	Mosq	BC	F/L D.L.Hughes	Ju188 destroyed	Location unknown	0115±

4/5th April 1945

85 Sqn	Mosq	BC	F/L C.W.Turner	Ju188 destroyed	Near Magdeburg	2244
406 Sqn	Mosq	FC	W/C R.Bannock	FW190 damaged	Demenhorst A/D	2130
			W/C R.Bannock	E/A destroyed	Demenhorst A/D	2325

5th April 1945

56 Sqn	Temp	2TAF	F/L P.H.Clostermann	FW190D damaged	Osnabruck - Hamelin	1215
			F/L P.H.Clostermann	FW190D damaged	Osnabruck - Hamelin	1215
65 Sqn	Must	FC	F/O W.L.Black	Bf109 destroyed	Vaagso	1600±
			S/L J.W.Foster	Bf109 destroyed	Vaagso	1600±
			F/L C.O.E.Hamilton -Williams	Bf109 destroyed	Vaagso	1600±
			F/L J.M.W.Lloyd	Bf109 prob.dest	Vaagso	1600±
			F/L G.S.Pearson	Bf109 destroyed	Vaagso	1600±
			F/L G.S.Pearson	Bf109 prob.dest	Vaagso	1600±

243

350 Sqn	Spit	2TAF	P/O R.Muls	FW190 destroyed	NE Meppen	1055
			F/S S.H.Neulinger	- Shared -		
402 Sqn	Spit	2TAF	F/L E.R.Burrows	FW190 damaged	Lingen area	1220±
			F/L H.Cowan	FW190 prob.dest	Lingen	1220±
			F/L H.Cowan	FW190 damaged	Lingen	1220±
			F/L W.F.Peck	FW190 destroyed	NE Lingen	1220±
			F/L W.F.Peck	Bf109 damaged	NE Lingen	1220±
			F/L W.F.Peck	Bf109 damaged	NE Lingen	1220±
			F/O A.G.Ratcliffe	Bf109 destroyed	Lingen	1220±

6th April 1945

56 Sqn	Temp	2TAF	S/L R.W.A.MacKichan	FW190 destroyed	Near Stolzenau	1505
			S/L R.W.A.MacKichan	FW190 destroyed	Near Stolzenau	1505
			F/O J.J.Payton	FW190 destroyed	Near Stolzenau	1505
80 Sqn	Temp	2TAF	F/L R.C.Cooper	FW190 destroyed	Hoya	1730
			F/O L.Smith	FW190 destroyed	Hoya	1730
486 Sqn	Temp	2TAF	F/O C.J.Sheddan	Ju87 destroyed	Stolzenau	2000
			F/O C.J.Sheddan	Ju87 destroyed	Stolzenau	2000

7th April 1945

56 Sqn	Temp	2TAF	Sgt G.J.Swindells	Bf109 damaged	10m E Dummersee	2035
65 Sqn	Must	FC	F/O W.L.Black	FW190 damaged	Sogne Fjord	1615±
			F/L G.S.Pearson	FW190 destroyed	Sogne Fjord	1615±
			F/L G.S.Pearson	FW190 destroyed	Sogne Fjord	1615±

7/8th April 1945

157 Sqn	Mosq	BC	W/C K.Davison	FW190 destroyed	N Molbis	2340
406 Sqn	Mosq	FC	F/L D.A.Gillis	He111 destroyed	Mensdorf, NE Leipzig	0005
488 Sqn	Mosq	2TAF	F/L K.W.Stewart	Bf110 destroyed	20m SE Osnabruck	2320

8/9th April 1945

85 Sqn	Mosq	BC	F/L H.B.Thomas	Ju88 destroyed	20m W Lutzkendorf	1905

On 6th April Jimmy Sheddan of 486 Squadron (left) claimed a brace of Stukas at Stolzenau, while Jim 'Joe' Payton of 56 Squadron (2nd left) got an FW190. On 9th April, Flight Lieutenants J.Mencel and M.Gorzula, Mustang pilots from 309 Squadron, each got an Me262 near Hamburg.

9th April 1945

64 Sqn	Must	FC	F/O A.D.Woodcock	Me262 damaged	SW Hamburg	1800±
80 Sqn	Temp	2TAF	S/L E.D.Mackie	Ar 96 destroyed	Fassberg	1935
			S/L E.D.Mackie	Ar 96 destroyed	Fassberg	1935
			F/O W.R.Sheaf	Ar 96 destroyed	Fassberg	1935
126 Sqn	Must	FC	F/O A.D.Yeardley	Me262 destroyed	Hamburg area	1800±
306 Sqn	Must	FC	S/L J.Zulikowski	Me262 destroyed	15m W Hamburg	1755
309 Sqn	Must	FC	F/L M.Gorzula	Me262 destroyed	15m W Hamburg	1755
			F/L J.Mencel	Me262 destroyed	15m W Hamburg	1755
			W/O A.Murkowski	Me262 destroyed	15m W Hamburg	1755
			W/O A.Murkowski	Me262 damaged	15m W Hamburg	1755

9/10th April 1945

219 Sqn	Mosq	2TAF	P/O R.L.Young	He177 destroyed	Hirschberg area	0345
406 Sqn	Mosq	FC	F/L D.A.McFayden	Ju88G destroyed	Lubeck/Blankensee	2350
			F/L D.A.McFayden	Ju88G destroyed	Lubeck/Blankensee	0010
515 Sqn	Mosq	BC	W/C H.C.Kelsey	Ju88 damaged	Lubeck AD	2245
			W/C H.C.Kelsey	Ju188 destroyed	SE Hamburg	2300

10th April 1945

130 Sqn	Spit	2TAF	S/L M.R.D.Hume	Ju188 destroyed	Landing Stade AD	1935
165 Sqn	Must	FC	F/O J.N.Haslope	Me163 destroyed	Manstorf AD	1805
486 Sqn	Temp	2TAF	F/L W.E.Schrader	FW190 destroyed	Nienburg	2015

10/11th April 1945

239 Sqn	Mosq	BC	P/O P.O.Falconer	He111 destroyed	AD nr Berlin	2300±
406 Sqn	Mosq	FC	F/L P.E.Etienne	He111 destroyed	Schonefeld	2345
			F/L P.E.Etienne	Ju88 destroyed	Finsterwalde	0003
			F/O D.J.M.McConnell	E/A damaged	Bel Jocksdorf	2342
410 Sqn	Mosq	2TAF	F/L R.D.Schultz	Ju188 destroyed	10m N Osnabruck	2237

11th April 1945

19 Sqn	Must	FC	S/L P.J.Hearne	Bf109 destroyed	Lister	1530±
41 Sqn	Spit	2TAF	F/L F.A.O.Gaze	Ju52 destroyed	Ottersburg	1000
65 Sqn	Must	FC	W/O J.D.Howells	Bf109 damaged	S Norway	1730±
			F/L R.L.Sims	Bf109 damaged	S Norway	1730±
222 Sqn	Temp	2TAF	W/O T.B.Hannam F/L J.L.Lawson S/L E.B.Lyons F/O P.H.Reid P/O G.Sharrett 135 Wing	Jet destroyed - Shared - - Shared - - Shared - - Shared – - Shared –	T/o Fassberg AD	1930±
135 Wg	Temp	2TAF	W/C H.M.Mason 222 Squadron	Jet destroyed - Shared -	T/o Fassberg AD	1930±

11/12th April 1945

406 Sqn	Mosq	FC	Lt S.W.Filkosky (US)	E/A damaged	Prague/Ruzyne A/D	0340
FIDS	Mosq	FC	F/L F.R.L.Mellersh	Ju88 destroyed	Berlin	2309

12th April 1945

33 Sqn	Temp	2TAF	F/O D.J.Ter Beek	Bf109 destroyed	W Ulzen	1350
			F/O D.J.Ter Beek	Bf109 damaged	W Ulzen	1350
			F/O D.J.Ter Beek	Bf109 damaged	W Ulzen	1350
			Capt E.D.Thompson	Bf109 destroyed	W Ulzen	1350
			F/S P.W.C.Watton	Bf109 destroyed	W Ulzen	1350
			F/S P.W.C.Watton	Bf109 damaged	W Ulzen	1350
41 Sqn	Spit	2TAF	F/L F.A.O.Gaze F/L M.V.Rake	Ar234 destroyed - Shared -	W Bremen	1700
56 Sqn	Temp	2TAF	F/O D.E.Ness	FW190 destroyed	5m E Fassberg	1930
274 Sqn	Temp	2TAF	F/L J.D.Morrison F/L D.M.Nicholls	Ju88 destroyed - Shared -	5m NE Fassberg	0920
486 Sqn	Temp	2TAF	F/L J.H.Stafford	FW190 destroyed	E Ludwigslust	1935

On 14th April Squadron Leader J.B.Shepherd of 41 Squadron (left) found an Me163 Komet being towed by a Bf110 and shot both down in short order. That night Flight Lieutenant Philippe Etienne of 406 Squadron (right) claimed his fourth confirmed success over Berlin.

13/14th April 1945

85 Sqn	Mosq	BC	F/L K.D.Vaughan	He219 destroyed	5350N 1000E	0031
600 Sqn	Mosq	FC	S/L G.Hammond	FW190 destroyed	M.3448	2037
			S/L G.Hammond	FW190 damaged	M.3448	2037

14th April 1945

19 Sqn	Must	FC	S/L P.J.Hearne	Bf109 destroyed	Lister	1530±
41 Sqn	Spit	2TAF	S/L J.B.Shepherd	Bf110 destroyed	Nordholz A/D	1900
			S/L J.B.Shepherd	Me163 destroyed	Nordholz A/D	1900
326 Sqn	Spit	1TAF	Capt H.Jeandet LV R.L.Dejean	FW190 destroyed - Shared -	Herrenberg	1810±
			Sgt R.Habert	FW190 destroyed	Habert	1810±
			LV M.Gleize Sgt/Ch A.Girard	FW190 destroyed - Shared -	Herrenberg	1810±
			Capt C.J.G.Gauthier Lt G.Amarger Asp E.Criqui Sgt D.Roussel Sgt A.Plataret	Bf109 destroyed - Shared - - Shared - - Shared - - Shared -	Erbach	1810±
486 Sqn	Temp	2TAF	F/O C.J.Sheddan	FW190 destroyed	Near Ludwigslust	1650
			W/O W.J.Shaw	FW190 destroyed	Perleberg -Ludwigslust	1930
			F/O S.J.Short	Bf109 damaged	Perleberg -Ludwigslust	1930

14/15th April 1945

157 Dqn	Mosq	BC	F/L R.J.V.Smyth	Ju88 damaged	20m E Munich	2240±
239 Sqn	Mosq	BC	S/L D.J.Raby	Ju88 destroyed	Potsdam	0030±
406 Sqn	Mosq	FC	F/L P.E.Etienne	Ju88 destroyed	Berlin/Tutow A/D	0023
			S/L S.E.Murray	E/A damaged	Berlin/Tutow A/D	0122
FIDS	Mosq	ADGB	F/O C.A.Bailey	Ju88 destroyed	20m NW Berlin	2320

15th April 1945

56 Sqn	Temp	2TAF	F/L N.D.Cox	Ar234 destroyed*	Kaltenkirchen A/D	1015
			F/L J.A.McCairns	- Shared –		
80 Sqn	Temp	2TAF	S/L E.D.Mackie	FW190 destroyed	10m SE Ulzen	0915
			Sgt W.F.Turner	- Shared -		
			486 Squadron	- Shared -		
			F/L A.Seager	FW190 destroyed	8m NW Celle	1825
421 Sqn	Spit	2TAF	F/O J.V.Marsden	FW190 damaged	10m NE Rethem	2045
			2TAF	F/O A.G.Scott	- Shared -	
430 Sqn	Spit	2TAF	F/L W.M.Middleton	FW190 destroyed	Near Ulzen	0930
486 Sqn	Temp	2TAF	W/O R.J.Atkinson	FW190 destroyed	10m SE Ulzen	0915
			F/O A.R.Evans	FW190 destroyed	10m SE Ulzen	0915
			W/O G.Maddaford	FW190 destroyed	10m SE Ulzen	0915
			F/S R.A.Melles	FW190 destroyed	10m SE Ulzen	0915
			F/O B.J.O'Connor	FW190 destroyed	10m SE Ulzen	0915
			F/O B.J.O'Connor	FW190 destroyed	10m SE Ulzen	0915
			80 Squadron	- Shared -		
			F/O A.I.Ross	FW190 destroyed	10m SE Ulzen	0915
			F/L W.E.Schrader	FW190 destroyed	10m SE Ulzen	0915
			F/L W.E.Schrader	FW190 destroyed	10m SE Ulzen	0915

15/16th April 1945

515 Sqn	Mosq	BC	P/O L.G.Holland	Ju52 destroyed	Near Schleissheim	2145

16th April 1945

41 Sqn	Spit	2TAF	S/L J.B.Shepherd	FW190 destroyed	Hagenow	2020
			F/O J.F.Wilkinson	FW190 destroyed	Near Hagenow	2020
56 Sqn	Temp	2TAF	F/L F.L.McLeod	He111 damaged	Neustadt A/D	1345
			F/O W.M.Wallis	- Shared -		

On 16th April. Richard 'Boy' Brooker, the 122 Wing CO (left), was jumped by Bf109s of IV./JG 27 and was shot down and killed. On the same day Mike Kilburn of 80 Squadron (centre), got his sixth and last victory. On the right is shown a crash-landed FW190, from which the lucky pilot walked away.

80 Sqn	Temp	2TAF	F/L M.P.Kilburn	FW190 destroyed	Nr Pritzwalk	1835
			F/L R.B.Prickett	FW190 destroyed	Near Pritzwalk	1835
411 Sqn	Spit	2TAF	F/O C.D.W.Wilson	He111 destroyed	Near Grabow	1400±
			F/O D.J.Bazett	FW190 destroyed	5m SW Parchim	1755±
			F/L D.C.Gordon	Ju88 destroyed	5m SW Parchim	1755±
442 Sqn	Must	FC	F/O R.J.Robillard	FW190 destroyed*	NE Berlin	1750
			F/O L.H.Wilson	- Shared –		

Note: Provenence doubtful

			F/L W.V.Shenk	FW190 prob.dest	Finow AD, NE Berlin	1750
486 Sqn	Temp	2TAF	W/O W.J.Shaw	FW190 destroyed	Neustadt A/D	0905
			F/O C.J.Sheddan	-Shared -		
			F/O J.W.Reid	FW190 destroyed	Ludwigslust A/D	1900
			F/L W.E.Schrader	FW190 destroyed	Ludwigslust A/D	1900
611 Sqn	Must	FC	F/O G.A.Jones	FW190 destroyed	Eberswald, nr Berlin	1730
			F/O G.A.Jones	FW190 destroyed	Eberswald, nr Berlin	1730
			W/O K.Mack	FW190 destroyed	Eberswald, nr Berlin	1730
			F/L B.Partridge	FW190 destroyed	Eberswald, nr Berlin	1730
			F/L B.Partridge	FW190 damaged	Eberswald, nr Berlin	1730
			P/O I.G.Walker	FW190 prob.dest	Eberswald, nr Berlin	1730
			P/O T.Ward	FW190 prob.dest	Eberswald, nr Berlin	1730
Hun Wg	Must	FC	Lt Col W.Christie	FW190 destroyed	Eberswald, nr Berlin	1730
125 Wg	Spit	2TAF	W/C G.C.Keefer	FW190 damaged	Near Hagenow	2020

17th April 1945

41 Sqn	Spit	2TAF	F/O F.M.Hegarty	Ju88 destroyed	Lubeck A/D	0630
80 Sqn	Temp	2TAF	F/L W.B.Galloway	FW190 damaged	Near Lubeck	1145

Desmond Watkins, Marcel Doncq and Andre Kicq of 250 Squadron all destroyed FW190s on 20th April. (via Serge Bonge)

80 Sqn	Temp	2TAF	Capt R.A.Henwick	FW190 destroyed	Grevesmuhlen	1145
			Capt R.A.Henwick	FW190 damaged	Grevesmuhlen	1145
			P/O R.S.E.Verran	FW190 destroyed	4m S Lubeck	1145
			P/O R.S.E.Verran	FW190 damaged	4m S Lubeck	1145
130 Sqn	Spit	2TAF	F/L H.Walmsley	Ju252 destroyed	Vechlin	1400
274 Sqn	Temp	2TAF	F/L R.C.Stockburn Sgt J.Wilson	Ju88 destroyed - Shared -	20m SW Hamburg	0735
350 Sqn	Spit	2TAF	F/S A.Kicq	FW190 destroyed	SW Hamburg	1405
401 Sqn	Spit	2TAF	F/O J.P.W.Francis	Bf109 destroyed	Ludwigslust A/D	1100±
403 Sqn	Spit	2TAF	F/L J.D.Lindsay	FW190 damaged	20m S Hamburg	1720±

17/18th April 1945

85 Sqn	Mosq	BC	W/C W.K.Davison	Ju88 destroyed	Near Munich	0410±

18th April 1945

56 Sqn	Temp	2TAF	F/O W.M.Wallis	Ju88 damaged	Ludwigslust circuit	1900

19th April 1945

130 Sqn	Spit	2TAF	W/O P.T.H.Clay	FW190 destroyed	Hagenow	1850
			F/L I.R.Ponsford	FW190 destroyed	Wismar	1855
401 Sqn	Spit	2TAF	S/L W.T.Klersy	FW190 destroyed	Hagenow AD	1545±
402 Sqn	Spit	2TAF	F/O H.R.Robertson	FW190 damaged	Hagenow AD	1015±
			F/O H.C.Dutton	FW190 destroyed	Near Hagenow AD	1015±
			F/O H.C.Dutton	FW190 damaged	Near Hagenow AD	1015±

Pierre Clostermann of 3 Squadron claimed a pair of FW190D-9s on 20th April. He is shown flying his Tempest JF-E 'Le Grand Charles' - 'Big Charlie' along the Dortmund-Ems canal. A controversial figure, he was nevertheless a great fighter pilot and will always be respected by fighter enthusiasts.

402 Sqn	Spit	2TAF	F/O D.B.Riddell	FW190 damaged	Hagenow AD	1015±
			F/O C.B.MacConnell	Ju88 destroyed	Schwerin Lake	1410±
412 Sqn	Spit	2TAF	F/L D.J.Dewan	FW190 destroyed	Hagenow	1005±
			F/O G.M.Horter	FW190 destroyed	Hagenow	1005±
			F/L D.M.Pieri	FW190 destroyed	Hagenow	1005±
			F/L D.M.Pieri F/L L.A.Stewart	FW190 destroyed - Shared -	Hagenow	1005±
222 Sqn	Spit	2TAF	F/O G.Walkington	E/A destroyed	Husum	1200

19/20th April 1945

151 Sqn	Mosq	FC	F/L T.Lindsay	He219 damaged	30m SW Westerland	2320
BSDU	Mosq	BC	F/L D.R.Howard	Ju88 destroyed	S Denmark	2328

20 April 1945

3 Sqn	Temp	2TAF	F/L P.H.Clostermann	FW190 destroyed	10m SW Hamburg	2030
			F/L P.H.Clostermann	FW190 destroyed	10m SW Hamburg	2030
41 Sqn	Spit	2TAF	P/O P.T.Coleman	FW190 destroyed	N Neuruppin A/D	1505
			S/L J.B.Shepherd	FW190 destroyed	Kremmen Forest, N Oranienburg	1930
			S/L J.B.Shepherd	FW190 destroyed	Kremmen Forest, N Oranienburg	1930
			F/L J.F.Wilkinson	- Shared -		

41 Sqn	Spit	2TAF	F/O E.Gray	FW190 destroyed	Teschendorf		1930
			Sgt P.F.Scott F/L J.F.Wilkinson	FW190 destroyed - Shared -	Kremmen Forest		1930
			W/O L.T.Stevenson	FW190 destroyed	Teschendorf Wood		1930
			W/O V.J.Rossow	Me262 prob.dest	SE Neuruppin A/D		2005
130 Sqn	Spit	2TAF	F/L H.Walmsley	FW190 destroyed	Near Oranienburg		1510
			F/L I.R.Ponsford	FW190 destroyed	Near Oranienburg		1510
			F/L I.R.Ponsford	FW190 prob.dest	Near Oranienburg		1510
			F/L I.R.Ponsford	FW190 damaged	Near Oranienburg		1510
			F/L C.J.Samouelle	Bf109 destroyed	Near Wittstock		1930
350 Sqn	Spit	2TAF	F/O M.Doncq	FW190 destroyed	Near Neuruppin		1940
			F/L D.R.Howarth	FW190 destroyed	NW Berlin		1940
			F/S A.Kicq	FW190 destroyed	NW Berlin		1940
			F/S A.Kicq	FW190 damaged	NW Berlin		1940
			F/L R.Muls	FW190 damaged	NW Berlin		1940
			P/O D.J.Watkins	FW190 destroyed	Near Neuruppin		1940
401 Sqn	Spit	2TAF	F/O J.H.Ashton	Bf109 destroyed	SW Schwerin		1600
			F/O J.A.Ballantine	Bf109 destroyed	SW Schwerin		1600
			F/O J.A.Ballantine	Bf109 destroyed	SW Schwerin		1600
			F/L R.H.Cull	Bf109 destroyed	SW Schwerin		1600
			F/O D.W.Davis	Bf109 damaged	SW Schwerin		1600
			F/O J.P.W.Francis	Bf109 destroyed	SW Schwerin		1600
			F/O J.P.W.Francis	Bf109 damaged	SW Schwerin		1600
			F/O R.C.Gudgeon	Bf109 damaged	SW Schwerin		1600
			S/L W.T.Klersey	Bf109 destroyed	SW Schwerin		1600
			S/L W.T.Klersey F/L L.W.Woods	Bf109 destroyed - Shared -	SW Schwerin		1600
			F/L J.MacKay	Bf109 destroyed	SW Schwerin		1600
			F/L W.R.Tew	Bf109 destroyed	SW Schwerin		1600
			F/L L.W.Woods	Bf109 destroyed	SW Schwerin		1600
			F/L W.R.Tew	Bf109 destroyed	SW Schwerin		1600
			F/O J.P.W.Francis	FW190 destroyed	Hagenow A		1940
			F/O J.P.W.Francis	FW190 damaged	Hagenow A		1940
			F/L R.H.Cull	FW190 destroyed	Hagenow AD		1940
			F/O D.B.Dack	FW190 destroyed	Hagenow AD		1940
			F/O G.D.A.T.Cameron	FW190 destroyed	Hagenow A/D		1940
			F/O G.D.A.T.Cameron	FW190 damaged	Hagenow AD		1940

  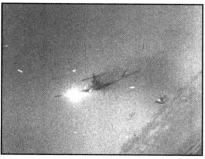

Bill Klersey of 401 Squadron (left) got a Bf109 and a 'shared' on the afternoon of the 20th, then got two FW190s in the evening, bringing his final score to fourteen. Next day Warren 'Smokey' Schrader of 486 Squadron got his seventh (of eleven). Both would survive the war. The frame from a combat film (right) shows a Bf109 being 'radically redesigned' over Germany.

401 Sqn	Spit	2TAF	F/L L.N.Watt	FW190 destroyed	Hagenow A/D	1940
			F/L L.N.Watt	FW190 damaged	Hagenow A/D	1940
			S/L W.T.Klersy	FW190 destroyed	Hagenow AD	1940
			S/L W.T.Klersy	FW190 destroyed	HagenowAD	1940
402 Sqn	Spit	2TAF	F/O T.B.Lee	FW190 destroyed	10m NW Hagenow	1935±
			F/L R.J.Taggart	FW190 destroyed	10m NW Hagenow	1935±
125 Wg	Spit	2TAF	W/C G.C.Keefer	Bf109 destroyed	Wittstock	1940

20/21st April 1945

| 264 Sqn | Mosq | 2TAF | F/O P.N.Lee | Ju88 destroyed | 20m W Berlin | 2145 |

21st April 1945

402 Sqn	Spit	2TAF	F/L E.R.Burrows	Bf109 destroyed	NE Ulzen	1600±
			F/O H.C.Dutton	Bf109 damaged	10m S Hitzacker	1600±
			F/L W.O.Young	Bf109 damaged	Near Hitzacker	1600±
			F/O D.Leslie	Bf109 destroyed	Schnackenburg	1630
			S/L H.P.M.Zary	Bf109 destroyed	Schnackenburg	1630
411 Sqn	Spit	2TAF	F/L S.M.McLarty	Bf109 destroyed	W Parchim	1815±
486 Sqn	Temp	2TAF	F/O A.R.Evans	FW190 destroyed	E Wismar	1820
			F/L W.E.Schrader	Bf109 destroyed	Schwerin AD	1820

21/22nd April 1945

23 Sqn	Mosq	BC	W/O P.L.East	Ju188 destroyed	10m NW Lister	2345±
264 Sqn	Mosq	2TAF	S/L C.M.Ramsay	Ju88 prob.dest	35m NW Berlin	2120
			W/O A.S.Davis	Ju188 destroyed	5m SW Nauen	2130
			F/O J.Daber	Ju290 destroyed	35m W Berlin	0425
			F/O J.Daber	Ju290 destroyed	35m NW Berlin	0435
410 Sqn	Mosq	2TAF	F/L R.D.Schultz	Ju88 destroyed	Ferrbellen, nr Berlin	2230
			F/L R.D.Schultz	Ju88 destroyed	Ferrbellen, nr Berlin	2300
488 Sqn	Mosq	2TAF	F/O W.A.Craig	He111 damaged	Butzer area, nr Magdeburg	0525
			P/O G.S.Patrick	Ju52 destroyed	Rhinow, nr Magdeburg	0530

22nd April 1945

411 Sqn	Spit	2TAF	F/O M.F.Doyle	FW190 destroyed	Near River Elbe	1740
			F/L E.T.Gardner	- Shared -		

22/23rd April 1945

264 Sqn	Mosq	2TAF	S/L C.M.Ramsay	Ju88G destroyed	2m S Havelberg	0333
456 Sqn	Mosq	FC	W/O W.H.McWhinney	E/A damaged	Bad Aibling	0235±

23rd April 1945

130 Sqn	Spit	2TAF	F/L H.Walmsley	Bf108	Parchim	1830
			F/L H.Walmsley	Bf108	Parchim	1830
274 Sqn	Temp	2TAF	F/S A.C.Inglis	FW190 destroyed	Eggebeck AD	1215
			F/S A.C.Inglis	FW190 destroyed	Eggebeck AD	1215
			F/S A.C.Inglis	Ju188 destroyed	Eggebeck AD	1215
403 Sqn	Spit	2TAF	F/L W.N.Dove	FW190D destroyed	Near Zeven	0615
			F/L H.R.Finley	FW190D destroyed	Near Zeven	0615

23/24th April 1945

219 Sqn	Mosq	2TAF	F/O J.C.E.Atkins	Ju88 destroyed	30m E Stendal	0205
264 Sqn	Mosq	2TAF	F/O W.H.Foster	He111 destroyed	40m NW Berlin	2140
406 Sqn	Mosq	FC	P/O W.Anaka	E/A damaged	Lärz	0205
			P/O W.Anaka	Ju88 destroyed	SE Wittstock	0227
			W/C R.Bannock	Ju88 destroyed	4m SE Wittstock	0320

409 Sqn	Mosq	2TAF	F/O E.E.Hermanson	He111 destroyed	Ludwigslust area		2215
			F/O E.E.Hermanson	Ju87 destroyed	Ludwigslust area		2245
			F/O E.E.Hermanson	Ju87 destroyed	Wittenberge		2303
			P/O J.Leslie	Ju52 destroyed	Near Karow, Wittenburge		0325
409 Sqn	Mosq	2TAF	F/O J.H.Skelly	Ju52 destroyed	Near Wittenberge		2235
			F/O J.H.Skelly	Ju52 destroyed	Near Wittenberge		2255

24th April 1945

130 Sqn	Spit	2TAF	F/L W.Bruce	FW190 destroyed	Neustadt	0650
			F/L G.M.Corbett	FW190 damaged	Neustadt	0650
			F/L C.J.Samouelle	FW190 destroyed	Neustadt	0650
			F/L C.J.Samouelle	FW190 damaged	Neustadt	0650
			F/S W.B.Woodman	FW190 destroyed	Neustadt	0650
			F/L W.Bruce F/L W.N.Stowe	Bf109 destroyed - Shared -	NW Neuruppin	0925
			S/L F.G.Woolley	Bf108 destroyed	W Wismar	0715
			W/O R.E.Coverdale	FW190 destroyed	W Hagenau	0735
			F/L P.E.Sibeth	Bf109 damaged	Rechlin	1920
			F/L P.E.Sibeth	FW190 destroyed	Rechlin	1920
			F/O C.E.Mertens	FW190 damaged	Rechlin	1925
			F/L W.N.Stowe	FW190 destroyed	Rechlin	1935
327 Sqn	Spit	1TAF	S/Lt Brognois	Bf109 damaged	Thaunhausen, SE Augsburg	0720
			Sgt Morou	- Shared -		
			S/Lt Suisse	Bf109 destroyed	Thaunhausen, SE Augsburg	0720
350 Sqn	Spit	2TAF	P/O A.Van Eeckhoudt P/O D.J.Watkins	He111 destroyed - Shared –	N Pritzwalk	1700
350 Sqn	Spit	2TAF	F/L G.R.J.De Patoul S/L H.E.Walmsley	FW190 prob.dest FW190 destroyed	Kleinen A/D Kleinen A/D	1930 1930

24/25th April 1945

264 Sqn	Mosq	2TAF	F/L S.J.Moss	FW190 destroyed	40m NW Berlin	2110
406 Sqn	Mosq	FC	F/O J.H.Wyman	FW189 destroyed	Neubrandenburg	2305
			F/O J.H.Wyman	Ju290 damaged	Copenhagen	0245
409 Sqn	Mosq	2TAF	P/O L.E.Fitchett	Ju52 destroyed	S Wittstock	0045
			W/C R.F.Hatton	Ju290 destroyed	Plau, E Parchim	0408

George Keefer, leading 125 Wing (left), claimed his twelfth and last kill and Emile Pauwels of 350 Squadron his only two confirmed successes on 25th April. (via T Spencer)

488 Sqn	Mosq	2TAF	F/L R.D.Bergemann	Ju88 damaged	Near Bremen		0220
			S/L F.W.Davison	Ju52 destroyed	N Brandenburg		2258
515 Sqn	Mosq	BC	W/C H.C.Kelsey	Do217 destroyed	6m N Prague		2220

25th April 1945

41 Sqn	Spit	2TAF	F/L P.Cowell	Me262 prob.dest	Lubeck		0900
			F/L P.Cowell	Me262 damaged	Lubeck		0900
			W/O J.A.Chalmers P/O P.T.Coleman	Ju188 destroyed - Shared -	10m W Plauer Lake		1415
130 Sqn	Spit	2TAF	W/O J.A.Boulton	Ju87 prob.dest	Schwerin		0810
			F/L I.R.Ponsford	FW190 damaged	Muritz See		0825
			F/L I.R.Ponsford	Bf109 destroyed	Rechlin AD		0825
			F/L G.M.Corbett	Bf109 damaged	Rechlin AD		0830
130 Sqn	Spit	2TAF	W/O M.Ockenden	FW190 damaged	Near Lubeck AD		0845
			F/L W.N.Stowe W/O M.Ockenden	Me262 prob.dest - Shared -	Landing Lubeck AD		0845
			P/O F.E.F.Edwards	FW190 destroyed	AD near Pritzwalk		1230
			P/O E.Pauwels	FW190 destroyed	Rechlin A/D		1250
			P/O E.Pauwels	FW190 destroyed	Rechlin A/D		1250
			S/L H.E.Walmsley	FW190	Near Rechlin A/D		1255
			F/O P.Delorme	FW190 damaged	Near Rechlin A/D		1255
			S/L F.G.Woolley	Si204 destroyed	AD near Pritzwalk		1400

On 26th Guy Gigot of 350 Squadron (left - via Serge Bonge) claimed his first confirmed victory and Pilot Officer J.W.Shellard of 182 Squadron joined two other Typhoon pilots in destroying an Me262. (ww2images.com)

403 Sqn	Spit	2TAF	F/O R.C.Shannon	FW190 destroyed	Hagenow A/D	1045
486 Sqn	Temp	2TAF	F/O K.A.Smith	Me262 destroyed	Lubeck/Blankensee	0840
125 Wg	Spit	2TAF	W/C G.C.Keefer	FW190 destroyed	AD near Pritzwalk	1230

25/26th April 1945

| 264 Sqn | Mosq | 2TAF | P/O J.Hutton | FW190 destroyed | W Berlin | 2150 |
| 488 Sqn | Mosq | 2TAF | P/O J.W.Marshall | FW189 destroyed | N Wittenburg | 0435 |

26th April 1945

263 Sqn	Typh	2TAF	W/O H.Barrie	Me262 destroyed	2m NE Niebull	1005
			F/L W.J.Fowler	- Shared -		
			P/O J.W.Shellard	- Shared -		
350 Sqn	Spit	2TAF	F/O M.Doncq	FW190 destroyed	W Plauer Lake	1310
			F/S G.Gigot	- Shared -		
			F/O P.Leva	- Shared -		
350 Sqn	Spit	2TAF	S/L H.E.Walmsley	- Shared -		
			F/S G.Gigot	FW190 destroyed	W Plauer Lake	1310

26/27th April 1945

| 488 Sqn | Mosq | FC | P/O J.W.Marshall | FW189 destroyed | N Wittenberg | 0435 |

27th April 1945

| 130 Sqn | Spit | 2TAF | W/O A.D.Miller | Ju188 damaged | Near Wismar | 0820 |

28th April 1945

41 Sqn	Spit	2TAF	W/O J.A.Chambers	He111 destroyed	Near Niendorf	1745
			F/O P.T.Coleman	- Shared -		
			F/L P.H.Hale	- Shared -		
			F/S C.M.Moyle	- Shared -		
			F/L F.A.O.Gaze	FW190 destroyed	Schwerin A/D	2010±
			F/L J.F.Wilkinson	- Shared -		
			F/L J.F.Wilkinson	FW190 destroyed	Schwerin A/D	2010±
403 Sqn	Spit	2TAF	F/L L.Foster	Do217 destroyed*	S Tostedt	1655

Note: Believed to have been a Si204.

486 Sqn	Temp	2TAF	F/O O.D.Eagleson	Ju52 destroyed	W Plauen	1850
			F/L J.W.Reid	- Shared -		

29th April 1945

412 Sqn	Spit	2TAF	F/O A.T.Gibb	FW190 destroyed	Near Winsen	1250±
			F/O A.T.Gibb	FW190 destroyed	Near Winsen	1250±
			F/L R.L.Hazel	FW190 destroyed	Near Winsen	1250±
			F/O J.H.MacLean	FW190 destroyed	Near Winsen	1250±
			F/O C.D.W.Wilson	FW190 damaged	Near Lauenburg	1445±
486 Sqn	Temp	2TAF	S/L W.E.Schrader	Bf109 destroyed	Near Lauenburg	1330
			S/L W.E.Schrader	FW190 destroyed	Near Lauenburg	1330
			F/O O.D.Eagleston	FW190 destroyed	Near Lauenburg	1340
			F/O O.D.Eagleston	FW190 damaged	Near Lauenburg	1340
			F/O A.R.Evans	FW190 prob.dest	Near Lauenburg	1340
			S/L W.E.Schrader	Bf109 destroyed	Near Lauenburg	1340
			W/O N.D.Howard	- Shared –		
			W/O N.D.Howard	Bf109 damaged	Near Lauenburg	1340
			F/O C.S.Kennedy	FW190 destroyed	Near Lauenburg	1340
			S/L W.E.Schrader	Bf109 destroyed	Near Lauenburg	1350
486 Sqn	Temp	2TAF	F/O C.J.McDonald	FW190 destroyed	S Ratzeberg	1645
			W/O J.R.Duncan	FW190 destroyed	S Ratzeberg	1645
			F/L J.W.Reid	FW190 destroyed	S Ratzeberg	1645
			F/O A.R.Evans	FW190 destroyed	2m S Bergerdorf	2045

30th April 1945

3 Sqn	Temp	2TAF	F/O J.T.Adams	FW190 destroyed	SW Lauenburg	0945
			S/L R.B.Cole	Bf109 prob.dest	SW Lauenburg	0945
			P/O A.Jones	FW190 damaged	SW Lauenburg	0945

41 Sqn	Spit	2TAF	F/L F.A.O.Gaze	FW190 destroyed	N Lauenberg	2020
			S/L J.B.Shepherd	FW190 destroyed	Lauenberg	2020
			S/L J.B.Shepherd	Bf109 destroyed	Lauenberg	2030
56 Sqn	Temp	2TAF	F/S M.L.Kennaugh Sgt N.Willis	Ju352 destroyed - Shared -	5m W Wismar	1445
130 Sqn	Spit	2TAF	F/O G.Lord	FW190 destroyed	Banzkow	0845
			F/L W.N.Stowe	FW190 destroyed	Banzkow	0845
			F/L W.N.Stowe F/O T.L.Trevorrow	FW190 destroyed - Shared -	Banzkow	0845
			P/O F.E.F.Edwards F/L I.R.Ponsford	FW190 destroyed - Shared -	Schwerin Lake	1125
			P/O F.E.F.Edwards	FW190 destroyed	Schwerin Lake	1130
			F/L I.R.Ponsford	FW190 destroyed	Schwerin Lake	1130
			F/L I.R.Ponsford P/O F.E.F.Edwards F/L I.R.Ponsford	FW190 destroyed FW190 destroyed - Shared -	Schwerin Lake Near Schweiner	1130 1135
130 Sqn	Spit	2TAF	S/L F.G.Woolley	FW190 destroyed	Winsen	1350
			F/S B.W.Woodman	Si204 destroyed	Schwerin Lake	1730
350 Sqn	Spit	2TAF	F/L P.M.Bangerter	FW190 destroyed	Near Schwerin Lake	1045
			F/L P.M.Bangerter	FW190 destroyed	Near Schwerin Lake	1045
			F/L P.M.Bangerter P/O D.J.Watkins F/S G.Gigot	FW190 destroyed - Shared – - Shared -	Near Schwerin Lake	1045
			F/S G.Gigot	FW190 destroyed	Near Schwerin Lake	1045
			P/O D.J.Watkins	FW190 destroyed	Near Schwerin Lake	1045
			P/O D.J.Watkins	FW190 destroyed	Near Schwerin Lake	1045
402 Sqn	Spit	2TAF	F/L D.R.Drummond	FW190 destroyed	6m S Schwerin lake	1130±
			F/L F.E.W.Hanton	FW19 destroyed	5m SE Schwerin lake	1130±
			F/L F.E.W.Hanton	FW190 damaged	5m SE Schwerin lake	1130±
			F/L S.M.Knight	FW190 destroyed	Schwerin	1130±
			F/L S.M.Knight	Ju188 destroyed	E Schwerin lake	1130±
			F/L W.O.Young	FW190 destroyed	Schwerin lake	1130±
			F/L W.O.Young	FW190 damaged	Schwerin lake	1130±
			F/L E.R.Burrows F/L S.M.Knight	Ju88 destroyed - Shared -	Kalkhorst	1525
403 Sqn	Spit	2TAF	F/L A.E.Fleming	Bf109 destroyed 8	Kirch/Grabow	1715
411 Sqn	Spit	2TAF	F/O M.F.Doyle	FW190 destroyed	Near Lauenburg	2000±
412 Sqn	Spit	2TAF	F/L D.M.Pieri	FW190 destroyed	15m E Hamburg	1930±
			F/L R.B.Barker	Bf109 destroyed	E Lauenburg	1940±

412 Sqn	Spit	2TAF	F/L R.B.Barker	Bf109 damaged	E Lauenburg		1940±
			S/L M.D.Boyd	Bf109 destroyed	4m NE Lauenburg		1940±
			S/L M.D.Boyd	Bf109 destroyed	4m NE Lauenburg		1940±
			S/L M.D.Boyd	Bf109 damaged	4m NE Lauenburg		1940±
			F/L L.A.Stewart	FW190 destroyed	4m NE Lauenburg		1940±
486 Sqn	Temp	2TAF	W/O G.Maddaford	Bf109 damaged	Ludwigslust A/D		1350

1st May 1945

3 Sqn	Temp	2TAF	F/L H.W.Longley	Ju88 destroyed	20m NE Hamburg		2100
41 Sqn	Spit	2TAF	F/S P.F.Scott	FW190 damaged	Schwerin Lake		1300
			F/S P.F.Scott	FW190 damaged	Schwerin Lake		1300
			2/Lt C.S.Bodtker	FW190	S Schwerin Lake		1300
			F/L P.Cowell	FW190 destroyed	Schwerin Lake		1300
			F/L P.Cowell	FW190 destroyed	Schwerin Lake		1300
			W/O I.T.Stevenson	FW190	SE Wittenberg		1925
			P/O P.T.Coleman	FW190	SE Wittenberg		1940±
			P/O P.T.Coleman	FW190	Schwerin Lake		1940±
			P/O P.T.Coleman	FW190	Schwerin Lake		1940±
			F/O E.Gray	FW190	5m SE Schwerin Lake		2030±
			S/L J.B.Shepherd	- Shared -			
56 Sqn	Temp	2TAF	F/S M.L.Kennaugh	He111 destroyed	Schwerin		1535
			Sgt N.Willis	- Shared -			
130 Sqn	Spit	2TAF	F/O G.Lord	Bf109 destroyed	SW Holzendorf		1615
			F/S B.W.Woodman	He111 damaged	Lubeck		1900
350 Sqn	Spit	2TAF	P/O P.Leva	FW190 destroyed	Near Schwerin Lake		1750
			F/S H.Boels	FW190 destroyed	Near Schwerin Lake		1755
			F/S H.Boels	FW190 destroyed	Near Schwerin Lake		1755
			F/S R.Muls	FW190 destroyed	Near Schwerin Lake		1755
401 Sqn	Spit	2TAF	S/L W.T.Klersey	FW190 damaged	Lubeck/Blankensee		2015±
403 Sqn	Spit	2TAF	P/O D.Leslie	FW190 damaged	Near Burgdorf		1040
			W/O R.C.Neitz	FW190 destroyed	Burgdorf		1040
			W/O R.C.Neitz	FW190 damaged	Near Burgdorf		1040
			W/O R.C.Neitz	FW190 damaged	Near Burgdorf		1040
			F/L C.L.Rispler	FW190 damaged	Near Burgdorf		1040
			F/L C.L.Rispler	FW190 damaged	Near Burgdorf		1040
			F/O R.C.Shannon	FW190 prob.dest	Near Burgdorf		1040

On 1st May 1945 Peter Cowell of 41 Squadron and 121-victory Experte Heinz Marquardt of IV./JG 51 met over Schwerin Lake. The cannon of the Spitfire XIV blew the FW190D-9 apart and Marquardt was fortunate to survive. Many years later they met - and became firm friends. No hatred, just professionalism. As it should be. (both via P.Cowell).

412 Sqn	Spit	2TAF	F/O R.C.Shannon	FW190 damaged	Near Burgdorf	1040
			F/O R.C.Shannon	FW190 damaged	Near Burgdorf	1040
			F/O R.C.Shannon	FW190 damaged	Near Burgdorf	1040
			F/L R.Young	FW190	Near Burgdorf	1040
421 Sqn	Spit	2TAF	F/L K.M.Langmuir	FW190 destroyed	N Schwerin	2030
			F/O E.H.Mann	- Shared -		
			W/O P.S.Murphy	- Shared -		
486 Sqn	Temp	2TAF	S/L W.E.Schrader	Bf109 destroyed	Bad Segeberg	1315
126 Wg	Spit	2TAF	W/C G.W.Northcott	FW190D damaged	Schwerin	1600±

2nd May 1945

3 Sqn	Temp	2TAF	P/O J.T.Adams	Me262 damaged	E Kiel	2050
			F/L N.W.Walker	JuW34 destroyed	NW Elmshorn	1800
			W/O E.Wright	- Shared -		
41 Sqn	Spit	2TAF	W/O J.A.Chalmers	Fi156 destroyed	Near Schwerin Lake	0700±
			W/O J.A.Chalmers	Fi156 destroyed	Near Schwerin Lake	0700±
			F/O R.D.A.Smith	Fi156 destroyed	Schwerin	0700±
56 Sqn	Temp	2TAF	F/L R.V.Garton	FW190 destroyed	NE Eutin	1310
			F/L R.V.Garton	Fi156 destroyed	NE Eutin	1310
			F/L F.L.McLeod	FW190 destroyed	NE Eutin	1310
			Sgt N.Willis	- Shared -		
			F/L J.Sowerbutts	FW190 destroyed	NE Eutin	1310
			F/S P.Tullie	Ju52W destroyed	N Neustadt	1815
			F/S P.Tullie	Ju52W damaged	N Neustadt	1815
			W/O A.J.Brocklehurst	BV138 destroyed	Near Eutin	2025
			Sgt N.Willis	- Shared -		
			Sgt G.J.Swindells	Fi156 destroyed	5m W Gruber	2028

130 Sqn	Spit	2TAF	F/O G.Lord	Bu131 destroyed	Near Schwerin Lake	0615
			F/S B.W.Woodman	Bu131 destroyed	Near Schwerin Lake	0615
			F/O G.Lord	Bu131 destroyed	Near Schwerin Lake	0615
			F/O G.Lord F/S B.W.Woodman	Bu131 destroyed - Shared -	Near Schwerin Lake	0615
			P/O F.E.F.Edwards F/O C.E.Mertens	Bf109 destroyed - Shared -	Schwerin A/D	0850
			W/O R.E.Coverdale	Fi156 damaged	N Schwerin Lake	1250
181 Sqn	Typh	2TAF	Sgt C.J.Boon F/L B.N.E.Ford-Coats	Ju188 destroyed - Shared -	Near Eutin	0715±
182 Sqn	Typh	2TAF	S/L J.Derry	Ju188 destroyed	T/o Lubeck	0550±
			S/L J.Derry	He111 damaged	Ldg Lubeck	0550±
184 Sqn	Typh	2TAF	F/O J.H.Whaley	S/E E/A destroyed	N Selmsdorf	1630
			Sgt A.A.V.Maxwell	He111 damaged	Travemunde	1640±
350 Sqn	Spit	2TAF	F/L P.M.Bangerter F/S A.Kicq F/O A.Van Eckhoudt P/O D.J.Watkins	Ar234 destroyed - Shared - - Shared - - Shared –	Hohn A/D	1710
403 Sqn	Spit	2TAF	F/O F.W.Town	He111 destroyed	3m W Lubeck	1645
411 Sqn	Spit	2TAF	F/O G.N.Smith	Me262 damaged	5m SW Lubeck	1130±
			F/O C.D.W.Wilson	Bf109 destroyed	Near Lubeck	1130±
414 Sqn	Spit	2TAF	F/L D.I.Hall	FW190 destroyed	Nr Neustadt-Glewe	1300±
			F/L D.I.Hall	FW190 destroyed	Nr Neustadt-Glewe	1300±
			F/L D.I.Hall	FW190 destroyed	Nr Neustadt-Glewe	1300±
			F/L D.I.Hall	FW190 damaged	Nr Neustadt-Glewe	1300±
			F/L D.I.Hall	Bf108 destroyed	Nr Neustadt-Glewe	1300±
			F/L D.I.Hall	Bf108 damaged	Nr Neustadt-Glewe	1300±
			S/L J.B.Prendergast	FW190 destroyed	Wismar harbour	1350
			S/L J.B.Prendergast	FW190 destroyed	Wismar harbour	1350
439 Sqn	Typh	2TAF	F/L J.H.Cook	FW44 destroyed	Near Schonberg	1145
			F/L J.O.Gray	Fi156 destroyed	Near Schonberg	1145
443 Sqn	Spit	2TAF	F/O M.J.Clow F/L H.R.Finley	Ju88 destroyed - Shared -	Bad Segeberg	1610
486 Sqn	Temp	2TAF	F/O O.D.Eagleston	FW44 destroyed	7m S Schwerin	0620
			W/O N.D.Howard P/O W.J.Shaw	FW190 destroyed - Shared -	S Neumunster	1330

| 486 Sqn | Temp | 2TAF | W/O N.D.Howard
P/O W.J.Shaw | Fi156 destroyed
- Shared - | Near Plon | 1330 |
| | | | S/L C.J.Sheddan
F/O D.J.Thompson | Flg boat destroyed
- Shared - | Heiligenhaven | 2030 |

3rd May 1945

3 Sqn	Temp	2TAF	F/L H.K.Hughes	Fi156 destroyed	Plauen	0830
			F/L H.W.Longley W/O D.G.Saunders	Fi156 destroyed - Shared -	Plauen	0830
			F/L H.K.Hughes	FW44 destroyed	Itzehoe area	2015
41 Sqn	Spit	2TAF	F/L D.F.V.Rake	Ju188 destroyed	Norderstapel-Husum	0800
56 Sqn	Temp	2TAF	W/O A.J.Brocklehurst	FW190 destroyed	12m NE Lubeck	1430
130 Sqn	Spit	2TAF	P/O F.E.F.Edwards F/O T.L.Trevarrow	Ju188 destroyed - Shared -	Near Grossenbrode	0800
274 Sqn	Temp	2TAF	F/L J.A.Houlton	Do217 destroyed	40m SW Kiel	1320
402 Sqn	Spit	2TAF	S/L D.G.Gordon	Fi156 destroyed	Near Husum	1040±
416 Sqn	Spit	2TAF	P/O L.E.Spurr F/O R.W.Tapley	Do217 destroyed - Shared -	W Schwarzenbeck	1845
443 Sqn	Spit	2TAF	S/L T.J.DeCourcey F/O W.A.Marshall F/L R.G.Sinn	Ju88 destroyed - Shared - - Shared -	W Kappeln	1805
486 Sqn	Temp	2TAF	W/O J.R.Duncan	Ju88 destroyed	NE Jagel	1745
			F/L C.J.McDonald	Ju88 destroyed	NE Jagel	1745

4th May 1945

| 411 Sqn | Spit | 2TAF | F/L D.F.Campbell
F/O T.L.O'Brien | He111 destroyed
- Shared - | NW Flensburg | 0640± |

5th May 1945

| 130 Sqn | Spit | 2TAF | F/L D.G.Gibbins
F/S V.J.Seymour | Si204 destroyed
- Shared - | W Hamburg | 0630 |

Epilogue

And so the great struggle came to an end. The fighter pilots of the Royal Air Force, including those from the Commonwealth countries, Poland, Czechoslovakia, France, Belgium, Holland, Norway and indeed the United States, had finally prevailed, but at great cost. The epic stand known today as the Battle of Britain had begun the journey but the mid-war years, when the RAF fighters had largely been outclassed by German technology and the *Luftwaffe* fighter pilots had fought over their occupied lands, times had been hard.

The improvements in aircraft performance had belatedly achieved parity, but it must be said that the *Luftwaffe* fighter pilots were worthy opponents: skilful, well-equipped and confident, they fought hard and well. Once the massive numerical superiority afforded by the United States Army 8th and 9th Air Forces came into the equation the issue was never really in doubt - provided that the correct strategic decisions were made. This proved to be the case for the invasion of France. The Allied air forces had quite literally pushed the *Luftwaffe* back into Germany to defend the *Reich* and thus total air supremacy went to the RAF and the USAAF over the invasion area. From that point onwards, it was merely a matter of time. The defeat of the *Luftwaffe* was inevitable, but it is to the credit of the German aircrews that it took almost another year before victory was complete. The final months saw the Allied fighter pilots ranging across Germany destroying the *Luftwaffe* in the air and on the ground in huge numbers.

Thus the fighter pilots and aircrews of the Royal Air Force wrote a chapter into the history of air warfare that can never possibly be repeated and it is by their courage and sacrifice that this series of volumes has been written.

I salute them all.

John Foreman
Radlett
2012